Rethinking American Emancipation
Legacies of Slavery and the Quest for Black Freedom

On January 1, 1863, Abraham Lincoln announced the Emancipation Proclamation, an event that soon became a bold statement of presidential power, a dramatic shift in the rationale for fighting the Civil War, and a promise of future freedom for four million enslaved Americans. But the document marked only a beginning; freedom's future was anything but certain. Thereafter, the significance both of the Proclamation and of emancipation assumed new and diverse meanings, as African Americans explored freedom and the nation attempted to rebuild itself. Despite the sweeping power of Lincoln's Proclamation, struggle, rather than freedom, defined emancipation's broader legacy. The nine essays in this volume unpack the long history and varied meanings of the emancipation of American slaves. Together, the contributions argue that 1863 did not mark an end point or a mission accomplished in black freedom; rather, it initiated the beginning of an ongoing, contested process.

William A. Link is Richard J. Milbauer Professor of History at the University of Florida. His books include *Roots of Secession: Slavery and Politics in Antebellum Virginia*; *Righteous Warrior: Jesse Helms and the Rise of Modern Conservatism*; *Atlanta, Cradle of the New South: Race and Remembering in the Civil War's Aftermath*; and *Southern Crucible: The Making of an American Region*.

James J. Broomall is Director of the George Tyler Moore Center for the Study of the Civil War and Assistant Professor in the History Department at Shepherd University. A contributor to *Creating Citizenship in the Nineteenth-Century South*, Broomall's writings have also appeared in *A Companion to the U.S. Civil War*, in the *Journal of the Civil War Era*, and in *Civil War History*.

Cambridge Studies on the American South

Series Editors

Mark M. Smith, *University of South Carolina, Columbia*
David Moltke-Hansen, *Center for the Study of the American South, University of North Carolina at Chapel Hill*

Interdisciplinary in its scope and intent, this series builds upon and extends Cambridge University Press's long-standing commitment to studies on the American South. The series will not only offer the best new work on the South's distinctive institutional, social, economic, and cultural history but will also feature works in a national, comparative, and transnational perspective.

Titles in the Series

Robert E. Bonner, *Mastering America: Southern Slaveholders and the Crisis of American Nationhood*

Ras Michael Brown, *African-Atlantic Cultures and the South Carolina Lowcountry*

Christopher Michael Curtis, *Jefferson's Freeholders and the Politics of Ownership in the Old Dominion*

Louis A. Ferleger and John D. Metz, *Cultivating Success in the South: Farm Households in Postbellum Georgia*

Craig Friend and Lorri Glover, *Death and the American South*

Luke E. Harlow, *Religion, Race, and the Making of Confederate Kentucky, 1830–1880*

Ari Helo, *Thomas Jefferson's Ethics and the Politics of Human Progress: The Morality of a Slaveholder*

Susanna Michele Lee, *Claiming the Union: Citizenship in the Post–Civil War South*

William A. Link and James J. Broomall, editors, *Rethinking American Emancipation: Legacies of Slavery and the Quest for Black Freedom*

Scott P. Marler, *The Merchants' Capital: New Orleans and the Political Economy of the Nineteenth-Century South*

Peter McCandless, *Slavery, Disease, and Suffering in the Southern Lowcountry*

James Van Horn Melton, *Religion, Community, and Slavery on the Colonial Southern Frontier*

Barton A. Myers, *Rebels against the Confederacy: North Carolina's Unionists*

Damian Alan Pargas, *Slavery and Forced Migration in the Antebellum South*

Johanna Nicol Shields, *Freedom in a Slave Society: Stories from the Antebellum South*

Brian Steele, *Thomas Jefferson and American Nationhood*

Jonathan Daniel Wells, *Women Writers and Journalists in the Nineteenth-Century South*

Rethinking American Emancipation

Legacies of Slavery and the Quest for Black Freedom

Edited by

WILLIAM A. LINK

University of Florida

JAMES J. BROOMALL

Shepherd University

CAMBRIDGE
UNIVERSITY PRESS

CAMBRIDGE
UNIVERSITY PRESS

32 Avenue of the Americas, New York, NY 10013-2473, USA

Cambridge University Press is part of the University of Cambridge.

It furthers the University's mission by disseminating knowledge in the pursuit of education, learning, and research at the highest international levels of excellence.

www.cambridge.org
Information on this title: www.cambridge.org/9781107421349

First published 2016

Printed in the United States of America

A catalog record for this publication is available from the British Library.

Library of Congress Cataloging in Publication Data
Rethinking American emancipation : legacies of slavery and the quest for Black freedom / William A. Link, University of Florida, James J. Broomall, Shepherd University.
pages   cm. – (Cambridge studies on the American South)
ISBN 978-1-107-42134-9
1. Slaves – Emancipation – United States.   2. African Americans – History – 19th century.   3. United States – Race relations – History – 19th century.   4. African Americans – Social conditions – 19th century.   5. Southern States – Social conditions – 19th century.   I. Link, William A., editor, author.   II. Broomall, James J., editor, author.
E453.R44   2015
2015026743
305.896′073–dc23

ISBN 978-1-107-07303-6 Hardback
ISBN 978-1-107-42134-9 Paperback

Contents

Contents

Figures

Notes on the Editors and Contributors

Justin Behrend, Associate Professor, Department of History, SUNY Geneseo. Behrend's first book, *Reconstructing Democracy: Grassroots Black Politics in the Deep South after the Civil War*, appeared in 2015. His notable articles include "Facts and Memories: John R. Lynch and the Revising of Reconstruction History in the Era of Jim Crow" in the *Journal of African American History* (Fall 2012) and "Rebellious Talk and Conspiratorial Plots: The Making of a Slave Insurrection in Civil War Natchez" in the *Journal of Southern History* (February 2011).

William A. Blair, Liberal Arts Professor of American History and Director of the George and Ann Richards Civil War Era Center, Penn State University. A scholar of the Civil War era, Blair has amassed an extensive publication record, including *Virginia's Private War: Feeding Body and Soul in the Confederacy, 1861–1865* (1998); *Cities of the Dead: Contesting the Memory of the Civil War in the South, 1865–1914* (2004); and *With Malice toward Some: Treason and Loyalty in the Civil War Era* (2014).

James J. Broomall, Assistant Professor, Department of History, Shepherd University and Director of the George Tyler Moore Center for the Study of the Civil War. A scholar of the nineteenth-century South, he is currently writing a manuscript-length study of masculinity and emotions in the Civil War–era South. Publications include "Personal Reconstructions: Southern Men as Soldiers and Citizens in the Post–Civil War South" in *Creating Citizenship in the Nineteenth-Century South* (2013) and "'We

Are a Band of Brothers:' Manhood and Community in Confederate Camps and Beyond," in *Civil War History* (2014).

Gregory P. Downs, Associate Professor, University of California, Davis. Downs studies the political and cultural history of the United States in the nineteenth and early twentieth centuries. His *Declarations of Dependence: The Long Reconstruction of Popular Politics in the South, 1861–1908* (2011) was a *Choice* Outstanding Academic Title. His most recent book is *After Appomattox: Military Occupation and the Ends of War* (2015).

Laura F. Edwards, Peabody Family Professor, Department of History, Duke University. Edwards is a scholar of women, gender, and the law in the nineteenth-century South. She has published *Gendered Strife and Confusion: The Political Culture of Reconstruction* (1997), *Scarlett Doesn't Live Here Anymore: Southern Women in the Civil War Era* (2000), *The People and Their Peace: Legal Culture and the Transformation of Inequality in the Post-Revolutionary South* (2009), and *A Legal History of the Civil War and Reconstruction: A Nation of Rights* (Cambridge, 2015).

Carole Emberton, Associate Professor, Department of History, University at Buffalo. A historian of the Civil War era and Reconstruction, Emberton has published *Beyond Redemption: Race, Violence and the American South after the Civil War* (2013). Emberton also recently published the award-winning essay, "Only Murder Makes Men: Reconsidering the Black Military Experience" in the *Journal of the Civil War Era* (September 2012).

Allison Fredette, Adjunct Professor, Department of History, Appalachian State University. Awarded her PhD from the University of Florida in 2014, Fredette's work has been published in *West Virginia History: A Journal of Regional Studies*. She is currently revising her dissertation into a book manuscript on the relationship between gender roles and regional identity in the mid-nineteenth-century border South.

William A. Link, Richard J. Milbauer Professor, Department of History, University of Florida. Link has published extensively on a variety topics ranging across three centuries. His major works include *The Paradox of Southern Progressivism, 1880–1930* (1992), *Roots of Secession: Slavery and Politics in Antebellum Virginia* (2003), and, most recently, *Atlanta, Cradle of the New South: Race and Remembering in the Civil War's Aftermath* (2013).

Paul Ortiz, Associate Professor and Director of the Samuel Proctor Oral History Program, University of Florida. Ortiz's first book, *Emancipation Betrayed: The Hidden History of Black Organizing and White Violence in Florida from Reconstruction to the Bloody Election of 1920* (2005), received the Harry T. and Harriette V. Moore Book Prize from the Florida Historical Society and the Florida Institute of Technology. He also co-edited and conducted oral history interviews for *Remembering Jim Crow: African Americans Tell about Life in the Jim Crow South* (2001).

John Stauffer, Professor of English and of African and African American Studies, Harvard University. A specialist in the fields of nineteenth-century American literature and culture, Stauffer examines slavery, abolitionism, and religion. His books include *Giants: The Parallel Lives of Frederick Douglass and Abraham Lincoln* (2008) and *The Black Hearts of Men: Radical Abolitionists and the Transformation of Race* (2002). Stauffer has also published more than fifty articles.

Yael A. Sternhell, Assistant Professor of History and American Studies, Department of English and American Studies, Tel Aviv University. Her *Routes of War: The World of Movement in the Confederate South* (2012) won the Francis B. Simkins Award from the Southern Historical Association and was a finalist for the Lincoln Prize. Her "Revisionism Reinvented? The Antiwar Turn in Civil War Scholarship" appeared in the June 2013 issue of the *Journal of the Civil War Era.*

Acknowledgments

Any writing endeavor is collaborative, but none more so than an edited collection. As such, in the course of assembling this volume, we incurred a number of debts. We appreciate the backing of the University of Florida, which provided funds to support an extraordinary conference in February 2013, held on the 150th anniversary of the Emancipation Proclamation. Entitled "The Shadow of Slavery: Emancipation, Memory, and the Meaning of Freedom," the conference drew scholars from around the country to think about new ways of reconsidering the understanding and impact of the destruction of slavery. A team of graduate students in the Richard J. Milbauer Program in Southern History helped to plan, organize, and realize the conference. We appreciate the efforts of this team, which included Angela Diaz, Allison Fredette, Chris Ruehlen, and Clay Cooper, all of whom have now finished their degrees and are beginning careers with bright futures. Ultimately, the conference created a forum that fostered the exchange of new ideas, insights, and perspectives on emancipation and its legacy, and first sparked our interest in crafting an essay collection.

A group of remarkable scholars underpin this volume. Each contributor generously devoted himself or herself to realizing the collection, often drafting and redrafting their work. We thank them for their dedication and collegiality, their participation and enthusiasm, all of which exemplifies what is best about our profession. It's not always the case that an edited volume moves forward – and coheres intellectually – and we appreciate the privilege of working with all the authors. It was, in sum, an extremely gratifying and rewarding experience to work with such talented people.

We are especially indebted to Debbie Gershenowitz of Cambridge University Press, who, from the beginning, embraced this project enthusiastically. Debbie has been instrumental in the evolution of this volume into a book, and we have relied on her advice and support. The editors of the *Cambridge Studies on the American South* series, David Moltke-Hansen and Mark Smith, have been great supporters and useful critics, and we appreciate their help. The project also greatly benefited from Cambridge's anonymous readers and their trenchant comments and astute reading; we are very grateful for their extraordinary efforts.

Collaborating with new colleagues and working with old friends has made this project worthwhile. But its conclusion causes pause for reflection. Throughout the course of this work we have relied heavily on the intellectual and emotional support of Susannah and Tish, whose examples inspire us. In them we find meaning and through them we find worth.

William A. Link
James J. Broomall

Introduction

William A. Link and James J. Broomall

It is American iconography. On January 1, 1863, Abraham Lincoln issued the Emancipation Proclamation, a bold presidential war measure indicating a dramatic shift in the rationale for fighting the Civil War and a promise of future freedom for 4 million enslaved Americans. Yet the document marked just a beginning. Only after the spring of 1865, when the North's military victory toppled the South's powerful slaveholding class, were the enslaved guaranteed liberation. Freedom's future was far from certain, however. Long after January 1863, the significance of both the Proclamation and emancipation assumed new meanings. During the ensuing generations, African Americans explored freedom, even while the nation hoped to rebuild itself and the government attempted to reconstruct the South. Events would ultimately demonstrate that, despite the sweeping power of Lincoln's Proclamation, the struggle over freedom and the problem of coercion defined emancipation's wider legacy. Ultimately, as historian Laura F. Edwards observes in her Epilogue to this volume, freedom's journey "was a long one, because slavery's influence was so pervasive."

Rethinking American Emancipation: Legacies of Slavery and the Quest for Black Freedom contains nine essays that reconsider the origins, impact, and meaning of the end of slavery. It relies on several generations of rich scholarship about emancipation that has documented how the Civil War became a violent struggle to end the world's largest and most powerful system of slavery.[1] The destruction of slavery has become a central element in our understanding of how the cataclysmic Civil War helped to remake American society. During the war years, both Abraham Lincoln and Frederick Douglass framed slavery's death as the catalyst for a national "rebirth." "This revolutionary – *regenerative* – conception of the war," writes historian David Blight, "launched black freedom and future equality on its marvelous, but always endangered, career in American history and memory."[2]

Collectively, the essays in this volume constitute a complex portrait of emancipation and its aftermath, thereby demonstrating new ways of considering the sources of slavery's demise. Was emancipation accomplished by political and military policies from above, or by self-emancipation from below? How important were slaves' actions versus those of Congress, the president, and military authorities? Even after slavery formally ended in 1865 with the Thirteenth Amendment, freedom's boundaries remained fluid and contested. Slavery's destruction engendered fierce struggles over how emancipation unfolded and what its implications were for the United States. In fundamental ways emancipation was a turning point that Americans have had to "confront or deflect" since 1863.[3]

The book's central focus is on the former slaveholding states, but it also considers the implications of freedom beyond their borders. Reconstruction-era policies reshaped the American West, and those policies were connected to what occurred in the South. *Rethinking American Emancipation* is defined temporally in the Civil War era, though the volume's final section on memory brings the narrative into the twentieth century. It is our contention that only with a wide lens do national patterns in realizing emancipation become visible, whereas only through case studies can we witness the ways in which people and local communities directed definitions of freedom to meet specific demands. The essays herein, though diverse in subject, ultimately offer a broad but not exhaustive survey of emancipation's meanings and an examination of the challenges of and the contests over the realization of freedom.

The year 1863 neither began nor ended the fight over black freedom: rather, Lincoln's presidential order constituted but one voice in an era of revolutions that shaped the nineteenth century. As historian Thomas C. Holt observes, "actual emancipation exposed the difficulty of applying" anti-slavery ideology "to radical transformations in the social relations of culturally different populations."[4] With emancipation, he continues, came the rise of an "explicitly racist ideology that gained a hitherto unprecedented intellectual and social legitimacy," which undermined universal freedom.[5] Emancipation, however remarkable, left many questions unanswered and did not assure permanent change. Rather, the next half-century became a period in which the contours of freedom were defined and redefined, as black and white Americans struggled over emancipation's meanings and consequences.

This contested narrative has largely been lost among public audiences and in popular culture. Few commemorations and little discussion of slavery's legacy marked the sesquicentennial of the Emancipation Proclamation.[6] Triumph, not tumult, Edward L. Ayers argues, continues to shape a national storyline that reconciles "the great anomaly of slavery with an overarching story of a people devoted to liberty."[7] The tenor of Ayers's 1998 observation still rings true. As the essays collectively suggest, the persistence of "unfreedoms" and the lingering legacy of slavery followed the Thirteenth Amendment. Much of emancipation's aftermath involved a struggle over its meaning, as competing narratives became constructed around memories of slavery, freedom, and Civil War. The popular American narrative that posits 1865 as the end of slavery and the beginning of freedom has obscured lingering "unfreedoms" such as convict leasing, persisting racial violence, and peonage in the postbellum American South. The assumption that slavery ended and freedom began at the Civil War's end also obscures how later global emancipation movements inform our own national narrative. Further, the continuation of racial, ethnic, sectarian violence and oppression across the globe demonstrates there is little justification for a narrative of inevitable moral progress beginning with nineteenth-century emancipation movements.[8]

Part of the popular misunderstanding of emancipation's legacy is rooted in the binary between freedom and slavery. Indeed, freedom's very definition is rooted in its antithesis, slavery.[9] This dichotomous formula sets clearly defined boundaries for freedom and slavery but also disallows for the ambiguities of the lived experience, the persistence of "unfreedoms," and the uncertainty of citizenship in unequal societies. Indeed, as Frederick Cooper, Thomas C. Holt, and Rebecca J. Scott point out, freedom is a "social construct, a collectively shared set of values reinforced by ritual, philosophy, literary, and everyday discourse."[10] Thus, time and place shape freedom and further highlight its malleability. In the postbellum American South, as historians have widely recognized, unfettered freedom did not follow political emancipation for African Americans. Instead, many African Americans struggled against violence, feared reenslavement, endured painful memories of slavery, and clashed with white supremacists over the rights of citizenship. At the same time, African Americans also celebrated their freedom by constructing social movements and organizations that promoted emancipation. For a time at least, countervailing forces determined post–Civil War freedoms. These struggles are quite familiar to historians who have been, David Brion Davis once contended, "less content with theories of progressive currents washing away the dregs of an evil past."[11]

Historians have long challenged a celebratory view of American freedom. Invaluable studies by David Brion Davis, James M. McPherson, Eric Foner, and Ira Berlin, among others, emphasized the problem of freedom, which defined many of the scholarly debates from the 1960s into the early twenty-first century.[12] "Freedom has always been a terrain of conflict," Foner writes, "subject to multiple and competing interpretations, its meaning constantly created and recreated."[13] A host of scholars, seeking to understand the lived experience of emancipation, have discarded the binary of slavery versus freedom, focusing instead on conflicts over freedom. These studies revealed, Rebecca Scott notes, the "complex interactions among former slaves, former masters, and the state."[14]

New scholarship, encouraged by the work of the University of Maryland's Freedmen and Southern Society Project, systematically documented slavery's destruction and ensuing debates over freedom.[15] Scholarly contributions that consider the problem of freedom continue to offer important perspectives demanding that we recognize emancipation's limitations. For example, the recently published edited collection, *Slavery's Ghost*, asserts that scholars must consider "how ideas about racial authority circulating in the mid-1800s shaped the material and conceptual limits to African American autonomy and indicate just how narrow and precarious the passageways out of slavery proved to be for enslaved workers in the rural South."[16]

Recently, historians such as Thavolia Glymph, Susan Eva O'Donovan, Jim Downs, and Hannah Rosen have demonstrated that emancipation introduced not only freedom but also danger and tragedy, thereby creating a historiographical shift deemed by some "new revisionism."[17] This scholarship has emphasized a darker story of emancipation, often highlighting victimhood and suffering.[18] Jim Downs, a prominent voice from this camp, recently called for new research "to more rigorously interrogate the forces of racism in shaping the African American experience, examine the suffering and challenges former slaves confronted, and fearlessly admit that some slaves made problematic decisions that need to be contextualized, not used to prop up racist assumptions made a century ago."[19] Although this scholarship continues to examine broadly the problem of freedom, these historians re-center the discussion by giving readers a grim view of how emancipation unfolded on the ground. There are limits to what new revisionists can explain, however. This perspective has, at points, neglected how struggles coexisted with successes. Yael Sternhell has recently urged historians to approach the Civil War with uncertainty and realism while also simultaneously appreciating the liberation of 4 million Americans as a "tremendously positive outcome of the war."[20]

Rethinking American Emancipation demonstrates that triumph and tragedy, along with success and sadness, co-existed as African Americans considered the meaning and legacy of emancipation. By focusing not on single events but rather the challenges associated with freedom, the authors portray emancipation as a contradictory, uncertain process that included diverse manifestations ranging from slaves' wartime acts of resistance and sabotage, to African Americans' invocation of emancipatory internationalism to advance labor causes in the early twentieth century. On the one hand, this volume builds on scholarship that has envisioned emancipation within the context of a long freedom movement that began under slavery, flowered during the American Civil War, and concluded during the civil rights movement of the 1960s. Emancipation, as Martha S. Jones maintains, should be seen as a process in which Lincoln's Emancipation Proclamation "becomes but one moment in an elaborate scene that included Congress, the military, and enslaved people."[21] This intellectual tradition has gained renewed strength with the call for a "long civil rights movement."[22]

On the other hand, *Rethinking American Emancipation* also emphasizes how competing movements, moments, and memories reshaped the narrative of a long emancipation. Many black Americans, for example, interpreted the Emancipation Proclamation and the Thirteenth Amendment as just part of a larger global struggle against slavery that began in the eighteenth century. Recognizing that the destruction of slavery defined the Civil War, African Americans insistently articulated this view through memorializations, speeches, and public events. Conversely, the psychological devastation of slavery continued to evoke strong memories as some African Americans feared reenslavement.

Freedom remains central to emancipation's story, but what does that concept mean and to whom? As Laura F. Edwards observes in her Epilogue, "individual conceptions of emancipation and the state's policies led in unpredictable directions." Freedom involved unprecedented interaction between African Americans and the federal government on the ground, as freedpeople pressed military officers with complaints ranging from labor disputes to marriage contracts. The essays in this collection, working from varied perspectives, help us to understand the subject's complexity. The authors explore *which* emancipation moments gained

the most importance to *different* historical actors, and how these emancipations were eventually assigned new meaning through memory.

Rethinking American Emancipation also seeks to broaden our understanding of the political dimensions of emancipation. While the state had
been an important actor throughout the first half of the nineteenth century, Civil War and emancipation marked turning points in the state's
role. The Union military provided the most important example of the
state's new reach. During the war, military intervention in congressional
elections directed the outcome of key political races. After the war's end,
the federal military was the single most important force promoting
African Americans' citizenship. But the military was also large and
diverse, with mixed motives and different effects. Several authors in this
volume reveal the complicated lived experiences of, and interactions
among, African Americans, Union soldiers, and white citizens. Each
group shaped and understood differently life without slavery and, collectively, they gave final meaning to emancipation. Non-state actors, such as
freedpeople and women, influenced the political language and style of
men. Their claims on liberty, in other words, directed political actions. On
the other hand, several scholars in the volume stress the state's importance
in shaping freedom. As Steven Hahn recently observes, the Civil War and
emancipation created a "political force with its own imperial dimensions:
a new American nation-state."[23] A number of our authors take seriously
how the state's expanded power pushed the freedom struggle during the
Civil War but also contributed to a burgeoning cultural imperialism in the
postbellum era, evident in military policies in the American West.

The long memory of slavery continued to shape postwar freedoms.
Indeed, the continued construction of memories of emancipation brings
discussions of freedom deep into the twentieth century. These more
contemporary concerns demonstrate the struggles over who defines
the past and for what uses. Narratives of slavery and freedom powerfully defined how individuals remembered and ultimately used emancipation to shape their lives. Memories shifted over time but slavery
continued to cast a long shadow over the lives of blacks and whites.

Rethinking American Emancipation is organized into three categories: "Claiming Emancipation," "Contesting Emancipation," and
"Remembering Emancipation." Part I, "Claiming Emancipation," considers initial demands for freedom. Rather than a culminating moment
in time, emancipation requires a broader view. As Yael A. Sternhell
notes in Chapter 1, during the war years hundreds of thousands of
African Americans pursued acts of self-liberation by striking out on

Southern roadways and creating their own liberation movement. Although emancipation is often imagined "as an event of mythic proportions," she contends it was "first and foremost a complex lived experience, a daily reality that took multiple, shifting, and often contradictory forms." Acts of self-liberation explicitly demonstrate the personal dimensions to the transition between slavery and freedom. But that is only one dimension to emancipation. Interactions between the US Army and African Americans in the war's immediate aftermath suggest how a developing political partnership helped to chart the murky waters of the post–Civil War South. For those slaves who remained on Southern plantations, Gregory P. Downs notes in Chapter 2, freedom came gradually in the months after Appomattox as the Army spread across the countryside. For Downs, then, freedom became a claim about status, an acknowledgment of "acquired rights," and a promise of future action.

Downs's attention to a statist vision of freedom prefaces William A. Blair's explanation of military interference in local elections during the Civil War.[24] Politically, although the Proclamation was a decisive act of wartime presidential power, it hardly marked an end to struggle. The political efforts that eventually yielded the Thirteenth Amendment, Blair explains, rested, in part, on military intervention in local elections and hard-nosed political tactics. Remarkably, these episodes have been almost entirely neglected in the scholarship, yet provide important context for the political dimensions of the freedom struggle.

Part II, "Contesting Emancipation," considers clashes over emancipation's definition. After the Civil War, the entirely new social landscape disquieted white Southerners. Allison Fredette, in Chapter 4, takes us to the contested terrain of Kentucky and Virginia to examine marriage patterns. Within the white household, black freedom threatened male mastery and undermined female authority. As Fredette contends, homes became contested spaces in which whites struggled to redefine their prewar position or maintain an antebellum social order. Her border-state case studies illuminate contrasting reactions to the transition from slave to free households. Beyond the household, violence became a regular, if tragic, feature across the South and into the western territories. Justin Behrend examines a little known electoral contest in Concordia Parish, Louisiana, in 1876. African American men and women seized wartime opportunities and made powerful claims on citizenship, demanding legal protection and exercising new rights. Yet the long memory of slavery continued shaping postwar freedoms. Behrend maintains that fears were so great among black voters that many claimed a Democratic victory would literally mean their reenslavement, and intensified the stakes in the election. Freedpeople considered the ballot to be a key bulwark in keeping slavery in the shadows.

Carole Emberton, in Chapter 5, shifts the conversation away from the problem of freedom to the problem of coercion. By examining the complex reactions to the Modoc War and the Colfax Massacre, Emberton gauges "popular understandings of the implications of emancipation and Southern Reconstruction for the nation's advancing imperial endeavors." As she points out, the Civil War and Reconstruction were "part of a longer, and in some minds, darker history of territorial expansion and conquest."

"Remembering Emancipation" composes Part III. Memory, historian Bruce Baker explains, "is the organic, continuous connection of a people with their past."[25] Each of the contributors in the volume's final section engages this organic connection by considering how narratives of slavery and freedom powerfully defined how individuals remembered and ultimately used emancipation to shape their lives. In Chapter 7, "African Americans and the Long Emancipation in New South Atlanta," William A. Link takes us to Atlanta, Georgia, which represented the archetypal New South city. Link posits a counter-narrative to Grady's Atlanta founded upon a New South future and an Old South past by weaving together a complex array of African American institutions and voices that emphasized black equality and advancement that came with emancipation but also pointed out slavery's legacy of continued racism. Complex claims on emancipation's meaning played out across the American South, the Caribbean, and Central America, as Paul Ortiz contends in Chapter 8. Between the 1820s and 1920s African Americans observed not one, but many different emancipation celebrations. In the antebellum era, free black communities celebrated Haitian Independence, British West Indian Emancipation, as well as key battles in the Latin American Independence Wars, which eventually led to the abolition of slavery in South America. This essay further unveils the rich traditions of Black Internationalism in the commemoration of emancipations, as well as the opposition of black working-class communities to the growing shadow of American imperialism in the late nineteenth and early twentieth centuries.

John Stauffer shares Ortiz's long view of emancipation and its competing claims. In Chapter 9, "Remembering the Abolitionists and the Meanings of Freedom," Stauffer observes that in the twentieth-century abolitionists (black and white radicals whose most passionate desire was the end of slavery) and emancipationists (liberals whose most passionate desire was the preservation of the Union) have been uncoupled to promote sectional reconciliation. By so doing, popular audiences, filmmakers, and scholars have deemphasized social change as a process stemming from a continuous interaction between people at the margins and those in the seats of power. By conjoining abolitionists and emancipationists, Stauffer posits emancipation as a social revolution but also an ongoing process.

Laura F. Edwards, in her Epilogue, explores some further implications of freedom and unfreedom. Why should historians assume, she points out, that a straight line existed "between *individual* efforts to end slavery or to achieve freedom and the *legal* abolition of slavery?" Slavery could not end until the legal and constitutional structure supporting it changed radically. Enslaved people forced the matter, insisting, through their actions, that the political structure confront the "depth and breadth of the legal issues involved and difficulties of eradicating slavery" from the law. Yet even the adoption of the Thirteenth Amendment, though ending slavery, brought only a half-freedom for slaves. The continued force of the past institutionalization of slavery was difficult to eradicate.

The recent release of the motion picture *Lincoln*, focusing on the political fight to pass the Thirteenth Amendment, gripped popular audiences and thrust the struggle to end slavery into the public conversation. Historians offered mixed reaction. Some praised the film, taking note of historical authenticity, while others were disturbed by an oversimplification of the role of black abolitionists or charged the writers with an overreliance on outdated scholarship.[26] The struggle over freedom continues to incite debate and elicit contrasting reactions.

Rethinking American Emancipation focuses attention on an array of historical actors and their competing claims on freedom. Moving chronologically forward, the essays suggest emancipation as a dynamic process, though this is not a progress-driven story. Strides toward freedom did not always mean success, as political setbacks and racial violence, especially, contested the entitlements of universal citizenship. This emphasis on process places our work in an evolving historiographical discussion that looks to an array of factors, contingencies, and individual efforts that ultimately produced emancipation. It is a story that is both heartening and disturbing, as Americans continued to struggle over their future without slavery.

NOTES

1. See especially James M. McPherson, *The Struggle for Equality: Abolitionists and the Negro in the Civil War and Reconstruction* (Princeton, N.J.: Princeton University Press, 1964); Joel Williamson, *After Slavery: The Negro in South Carolina during Reconstruction, 1861–1877* (Chapel Hill: University of North Carolina Press, 1965); Leon Litwack, *Been in the Storm So Long: The Aftermath of Slavery* (New York: Vintage, 1979); Ira Berlin et al., eds., *The Destruction of Slavery*, in *Freedom, A Documentary History of Emancipation, 1861–1867*, ser. 1, vol. I (New York: Cambridge University Press, 1985); Eric Foner, *Nothing but Freedom: Emancipation and Its Legacy* (Baton Rouge: Louisiana State University Press, 1983); Ira Berlin et al., *Slaves No More: Three Essays on Emancipation and the Civil War* (New York: Cambridge University Press, 1992). Steven Hahn, *A Nation under Our Feet: Black Political Struggles in the Rural South from Slavery to the Great Migration* (Cambridge, Mass.: Harvard University Press, 2004); Thavolia Glymph, *Out of the House of Bondage: The Transformation of the Plantation Household* (New York: Cambridge University Press, 2008); Stephanie McCurry, *Confederate Reckoning: Power and Politics in the Civil War South* (Cambridge, Mass.: Harvard University Press, 2010); and Bruce Levine, *The Fall of the House of Dixie: The Civil War and the Social Revolution That Transformed the South* (New York: Random House, 2013).
2. David Blight, *Race and Reunion: The Civil War in American Memory* (Cambridge, Mass.: Belknap Press of Harvard University Press, 2001), 18.
3. Blight, *Race and Reunion*, 18.
4. Thomas C. Holt, "'An Empire over the Mind': Emancipation, Race, and Ideology in the British West Indies and the American South," in J. Morgan Kousser and James M. McPherson, eds., *Region, Race, and Reconstruction: Essays in Honor of C. Vann Woodward* (New York: Oxford University Press, 1982): 283–331 (quotation on 283).
5. Holt, "An Empire over the Mind," 284.
6. On this subdued mood, see Steven Hahn, "The Emancipationist Century: American Slavery, American Freedom, and the Distance between Them," *The New Republic* (26 May 2014), www.newrepublic.com/article/117620/pr oblem-slavery-age-emancipation-reviewed (accessed July 21, 2015).
7. Edward L. Ayers, "Worrying about the Civil War," in Karen Halttunen and Lewis Perry eds. *Moral Problems in American Life*, (Ithaca: Cornell University Press, 1998), 145–166: esp. 156.
8. David Brion Davis, *The Problem of Slavery in the Age of Emancipation* (New York: Knopf, 2014), 336. Also see Peter Kolchin, "Reexamining Southern Emancipation in Comparative Perspective," *Journal of Southern History* 81, no. 1 (February 2015): 7–40.
9. *Oxford English Dictionary*, s.v., "Freedom." David Brion Davis pushes the point further, positing: "Because slavery has long epitomized the most extreme form of domination and oppression, it has served as a metaphor for rejecting almost every deprivation of freedom (including 'enslavement' to sex, greed,

drugs, ignorance, and even ambition)." Davis, *The Problem of Slavery in the Age of Emancipation*, 335.

10. Frederick Cooper, Thomas C. Holt, and Rebecca J. Scott, *Beyond Slavery: Explorations of Race, Labor, and Citizenship in Postemancipation Societies* (Chapel Hill: University of North Carolina Press, 2000), 9.

11. David Brion Davis, *The Problem of Slavery in Western Culture* (1966; New York: Oxford University Press, 1988), 27.

12. See especially Davis, *The Problem of Slavery in Western Culture*; McPherson, *The Struggle for Equality*; Foner, *Nothing but Freedom*; Berlin et al., *Slaves No More*.

13. Foner, *The Story of American Freedom*, xv.

14. Rebecca Scott, "Comparing Emancipations: A Review Essay," *Journal of Social History*, vol. 20, issue 3 (Spring 1987): 565–583 (quotation on 565).

15. Concurrently, pioneering works by Seymour Drescher, Thomas C. Holt, Rebecca Scott, and Sidney W. Mintz (though several of the aforementioned scholars – such as David Brion Davis and Eric Foner – also worked comparatively) explicitly examined an age of revolution and emancipation through a comparative lens. This rich intellectual tradition has stimulated an array of provocative conversations. Recently, for example, Steven Hahn examined emancipation in the American South in conjunction with the slave rebellion at Saint Domingue. Hahn reframes African Americans' actions during the Civil War as a great slave rebellion that "was even more far-reaching" than events in Haiti. Steven Hahn, *The Political Worlds of Slavery and Freedom* (Cambridge, Mass.: Harvard University Press, 2009), 96.

16. Richard Follett, Eric Foner, and Walter Johnson, *Slavery's Ghost: The Problem of Freedom in the Age of Emancipation* (Baltimore: Johns Hopkins University Press, 2011), 2.

17. Susan Eva O'Donovan, *Becoming Free in the Cotton South* (Cambridge, Mass.: Harvard University Press, 2007); Glymph, *Out of the House of Bondage*; Hannah Rosen, *Terror in the Heart of Freedom: Citizenship, Sexual Violence, and the Meaning of Race in the Postemancipation South* (Chapel Hill: University of North Carolina Press, 2009); and Jim Downs, *Sick from Freedom: African-American Illness and Suffering during the Civil War and Reconstruction* (New York: Oxford University Press, 2012).

18. On this historiographical trend, see Yael A. Sternhell, "Revisionism Reinvented?: The Antiwar Turn in Civil War Scholarship," *The Journal of the Civil War Era*, 3, no. 2 (June 2013): 239–256.

19. Jim Downs, "Sectional Economies," Forum Discussion, "The Future of Civil War Era Studies," *The Journal of the Civil War Era*, 2, no. 1 (March 2012): 10.

20. Sternhell, "Revisionism Reinvented?," 252.

21. Martha S. Jones, "History and Commemoration: The Emancipation Proclamation at 150," *The Journal of the Civil War Era* 3, no. 4 (December 2013): 452–457 (quotation on 454).

22. Jacquelyn Dowd Hall, "The Long Civil Rights Movement and the Political Uses of the Past," *The Journal of American History* 91, no. 4 (March 2005): 1233–1263.

23. Hahn, "The Emancipationist Century," 43.
24. See Chapter 3.
25. Bruce E. Baker, *What Reconstruction Meant: Historical Memory in the American South* (Charlottesville: University of Virginia Press, 2007), 5.
26. For a relatively positive review, see Allen Guelzo, "A Civil War Professor Reviews 'Lincoln,'" *The Daily Beast*, 27 November 2012, www.thedaily beast.com/articles/2012/11/27/a-civil-war-professor-reviews-lincoln.html (accessed September 16, 2014). For some of the issues with the film, see Patrick Rael, H-slavery Discussion Board, 7 January 2013, http://h-net.msu.edu/cgi-bin/logbrowse.pl?trx=vx&list=h-slavery&month=1301&week=a&msg=IcErysudzvOAANxS31HoLA&user=&pw= (accessed September 16, 2014).

PART ONE

CLAIMING EMANCIPATION

Bodies in Motion and the Making of Emancipation

Yael A. Sternhell

Emancipation figures in our imagination as an event of mythic proportions, a sea change splitting American history into two. Yet for enslaved
Southerners, emancipation was first and foremost a complex lived experience, a daily reality that took multiple, shifting, and often contradictory
forms. Slavery, a system encompassing millions of people, fell apart in
thousands of different ways.

Over the last few decades, historians have been able to reconstruct the
general contours of the emancipatory process. We now know that the
destruction of slavery was slow and uneven, generally following the path
of the Union Army's haphazard progress in conquering the South. We
know that some slaves leaped at the sight of the first Union soldier, while
others exercised extreme caution and stayed on the plantation for months
or years after freedom became a fact. We know that certain bondspeople
found new opportunities for work, education, and family life soon after
ridding themselves of their masters, while others suffered, sickened, and
died trying to build new lives.

Perhaps most acutely, we are now aware of the many different ways in
which slaves actively took part in bringing about their own liberation. On
the plantation, enslaved men and women used the circumstances of wartime to reshape discipline even while their legal status remained the same.
They worked less, stole more, pushed back against physical punishment
and stood up to masters and mistresses who no longer seemed omnipotent. Slaves whose owners had fled in the face of the enemy burned down
the Big House or emptied it of valuables, while others enthusiastically
served as informers, spies, and scouts for the Union Army. The destruction
of slavery did not happen on a particular day or as a result of a particular

act. It materialized across time and space, through countless manifestations of resistance and sabotage, some invisible, some in full view.[1]

Within their arsenal of weapons, flight from bondage was the most potent means for slaves to fundamentally transform their own condition as human chattel while at the same time undermine the slave society as a whole. Emancipation happened first and foremost on Southern roads, where hundreds of thousands of African Americans undertook acts of individual self-liberation through the independent movement of their bounded limbs. Large-scale flight instigated freedom in three different yet interrelated ways: it liberated those who succeeded in getting to a place of safety; it subverted slavery in the farms and plantations from which the runaways had fled; and it forced the Union Army to confront African Americans not as an abstraction, a "peculiar and powerful interest," in Abraham Lincoln's words, but as three-dimensional, fully volitional human beings resolved to decide their own fate.[2]

Yet at the same time, the movement of enslaved men and women away from their masters was also part of a larger phenomenon typical of societies buckling under the pressures of war. Runaway slaves were not the only fugitives occupying the roads of the South during the four-year conflict. They were joined by untold thousands of deserters, stragglers, and skulkers trying to get away from military service; by an estimated quarter-million white refugees fleeing enemy occupation; and by thousands of Northern prisoners of war escaping incarceration in camps. The Confederacy was a world of departures and captures, where hundreds of thousands of people were running away from coercive authority. Thus even as they were carrying out the greatest revolution in American history, fugitive slaves were also just one element in a larger and multifaceted universe of flight. The second part of this essay examines emancipation as a form of human mobility in times of war, inextricably tied to other currents of movement sweeping through the Confederate South. Looking at emancipation as motion allows us to ground the process in a wider context, to understand its meaning and its nature not only as an episode in the generations-long black freedom struggle, but also as part of the South's rapid transformation from an unyielding slavocracy into a feverish society at war.

***

The single most important factor instigating the movement of slaves was the advance of the Union Army. By May 12, 1861, as navy ships were making their way down the Virginia coast, slaves were already reported to be disappearing from plantations on Gwynn Island in the Chesapeake Bay.[3] On May 23, three slaves who belonged to a Confederate colonel arrived at the Union base of Fortress Monroe and told the soldiers that their master was planning to remove them to South Carolina, where they would be put to work for the Rebel Army. The Federal commander, General Benjamin Butler, agreed to take them in. The following morning, when requested to return the fugitives, he refused, explaining that the slaves were considered enemy property and could therefore be confiscated as contraband of war. Almost inadvertently, a crucial precedent had been set.[4]

Despite great variations in geography, topography, and the nature of warfare in different parts of the South, the same pattern repeated itself time and again. Wherever Union soldiers arrived, neighborhood slaves immediately began flocking into their lines. In November 1861 the Union navy landed on the Sea Islands of South Carolina. Approximately 7,000 enslaved men and women resisted their masters' attempts to remove them and remained. By the summer of 1862 they were joined by 3,000 more, and at the end of the war, the number of fugitive slaves on the islands reached 30,000.[5] "Everywhere the blacks hurry in droves to our lines," wrote a Northerner from Hilton Head Island, South Carolina, in late 1861. "They crowd in small boats around our ships; they swarm upon our decks; they hurry to our officers, from the cotton houses of their masters, in an hour or two after our guns are fired."[6] In March 1862 Federal forces occupied New Bern, North Carolina, and were immediately confronted with masses of fleeing slaves from the countryside. The commanding general reported to his superiors that "the city is being overrun with fugitives from surrounding towns and plantations ... it would be utterly impossible if we were disposed to keep them outside of our lines as they find their way to us through woods & swamps from every side."[7]

In northern and central Virginia, where the Union Army was never too far, flight was particularly rampant. According to one estimate, 30,000 enslaved Virginians had escaped by 1863.[8] "As soon as the Yankees got hyar the slaves begun to run away from their mistresses and masters," described a free African American living in Fredericksburg. "They went by hundreds. You'd see 'em gittin' out of hyar same as a rabbit chased by a dog. Some carried little bundles tied up, but they could n't tote much. Often the women would walk along carrying a child wrapped up in a blanket. Fifteen miles from hyar they got to the Potomac, and the Yankee gunboats would take 'em right to Washington. Then they'd pile in wherever they could git. They never come back this way."[9]

The arrival of Union forces in the lower Mississippi Valley upended slavery in the Mississippi Valley, where 700,000 slaves toiled in some of the largest plantations in the South. In the fall of 1864, Sherman's March to the Sea brought emancipation to locales where slavery had remained largely intact. Between 20,000 and 25,000 slaves joined the march as it made its way through Georgia and the Carolinas, increasing the overall number of fugitive slaves in the region to 95,000.[10]

Who were the runaways? At first, fugitives reaching Union lines were mostly young men, who enjoyed the twin advantages of peak physical strength and greater geographical literacy. As time went by, however, women, children, and the elderly also started leaving, often in droves. The numbers speak for themselves: In early 1863, the population of two fugitive slave camps near Memphis contained 52 percent children, 25 percent adult females, and 23 percent adult males.[11] A few months later, a medical inspector visiting a contraband camp near Vicksburg, Mississippi, found more than 10,000 women and children congregating around a Union base.[12] Census returns from 1863 show a gender breakdown of 54 percent men and 46 percent women among fugitive slaves in five Virginia counties occupied by the North.[13]

The rise in the rates of female flight is also evident in runaways' testimonies. Husbands who had succeeded in getting to Union camps went back for their wives, despite the very real threat of getting caught. When Samuel Ballton returned to his place of bondage after having escaped, he ran into whites whom he had to persuade that he had been taken prisoner by Union soldiers and was now happily going back to his master. Interviewed in 1910, he remembered the moment he could tell his wife, "Rebecca, I'm going to take you to freedom with me," as the proudest of his life.[14] Yet women were also initiating their own liberation. Mothers, normally the most cautious and immobile of slaves, also began taking extreme risks, fleeing with young children in the middle of the night and walking for days until reaching a Union post.[15] Others were so desperate to leave they abandoned their children in the most precarious circumstances. A Virginian recalled her older sister, who "had a baby boy that she left behind with a daughter who had been used so bad it made her crazy. While her mother was gone the baby died."[16]

Runaways included every subset within the enslaved population, from field workers to domestic laborers, from the most troublesome to the most obedient. Owners were often shocked to learn that those whom they trusted most were the first to leave. William Patterson Smith was a wealthy planter and businessman from Gloucester County, Virginia. In

August 1862 he reported on the "elopement of a large portion of the most valuable negroes belonging to me, numbering to this date, as many as 55 – of these 26 were men and boys, 17 women and girls and 12 children. Two of the men were almost as old as myself and what their expectations were by a change of life and country, it is impossible to conjecture." Though none had come back, Smith was certain that his escaped slaves were already regretting their decision to leave. "Very many of them have no doubt found it all a delusion and have wished themselves situated in their quiet and peaceful homes, where I predict they enjoyed themselves more than they can or ever will do again." Smith was not sorry to hear rumors that some had paid with their lives: "several of the boys since running away, I learn, have died at York and one of the men sick ever since he reached there." Despite these dire predictions, in January 1863 another two of his female slaves, along with their children, fled the plantation. Smith's son, receiving the news, was surprised "that some more of the servants had gone off they behaved so well when the Yankees were there that I thought they thoroughly disgusted with them and no more of them would go then I suppose however they were induced to go by husbands." Whites found any number of ways to explain the departures of their seemingly content and pampered slaves. The result, however, was one and the same. In areas where the Union Army had penetrated, the institution of slavery was withering away.[17]

News about the situation near the frontlines trickled back into slave communities that had remained stable and had a palpable effect on the slave-master relationship and on the daily lives of the enslaved. Even when most or all bondspeople in a particular household remained and continued to work, whites reported insolence, laziness, and general "demoralization," a euphemism for all manner of slave disobedience.[18] As early as January 1862 planters were complaining about their slaves being in a "high state of insubordination" and bidding "open defiance" to the authority of overseers.[19] In June, a female slaveholder described life in the beleaguered town of Winchester, Virginia, which constantly changed hands between Union and Confederate forces: "there has been another stampede amongst the servants lately ... we are all being led by paths we know not of; I am sure Billy will go; Sarah is sick in her room, nearly all the time, and Emily devotes most of her time to her baby."[20] The possibility of escape, even when unrealized, shook the master-slave relationship to its core.

The arrival of runaway slaves into Union lines also had a formative effect on the Northern approach to slavery. The great majority of Union soldiers who served in the South had never seen a slave, never mind had a meaningful interaction with one. Steeped in the virulent racism of their time, they abused the fugitives in every conceivable way. Women were raped, children died of hunger, and men worked without pay. Soldiers often offered ready assistance to slaveowners trying to locate their missing property, while generals barred the entrance of fugitives into Union lines altogether. Life in contraband camps, as historians have shown, was no less cruel and often more deadly than any form of enslavement.[21]

Yet at the same time, face-to-face encounters and the invaluable services former slaves provided soldiers also laid the ground for new sentiments and unexpected alliances. Northern soldiers grew used to the presence of Southern blacks and came to appreciate their value as servants, cooks, laundresses, informants, teamsters, and nurses. Already in December 1861, Major E. Waring Jr., an officer serving in Missouri, wrote in protest of an order to exclude fugitive slaves from the camp and return those who had already entered to their owners. "These people are mainly our servants, and we can get no others," he wrote. "They have been employed in this capacity for some time – long enough for us to like them as servants, to find them useful and trustworthy, and to feel an interest in their welfare." A Maryland slaveholder who attempted to recover his human chattel from Camp Fenton reported that he was followed by a large crowd of soldiers throwing volleys of stones and "crying shoot him, bayonet him, kill him, pitch him out, the nigger stealer the nigger driver." When six superintendents of contraband camps in the Department of Tennessee were asked to evaluate the "intelligence" of the men and women under their charge, four answered along the lines of "far more intelligent than I supposed," and one claimed it was "as good as that of men, women, & children anywhere, of any color, who cannot read." Wartime freedom, however fragile, gained a foothold through these initial exchanges between Union authorities and runaway slaves.[22]

Even more critically, the mass arrival of bondspeople into Union lines forced the Federal government to confront the institution of slavery head on. Some historians have emphasized the magnitude of the Republican attack on slavery in the early years of the war, including its banning in the western territories and in Washington, DC, the suppression of slavery on the high seas, and the de-facto annulment of the fugitive slave clause of the Constitution. Yet these new policies, momentous as they were, often conflicted with the prevalent notion that secession was merely a hysterical response by a minority of fanatical slaveowners to the Republican victory in the elections of 1860. Most Southerners, it seemed, were fundamentally loyal to the United States and would abandon the Confederacy if only convinced that the Federal government was truly committed to protecting their rights. Moreover, ensuring the security of slavery under the Union was seen as an absolute prerequisite for holding on to Maryland, Delaware, Kentucky, and Missouri, the four slave states that did not secede.[23]

In this uncertain political climate, the masses of black men and women streaming into Union lines, offering their labor in the service of the United States, had a crucial impact on Congressional action and on Northern public opinion. This became evident as early as August 1861, with the passage of the First Confiscation Act, which allowed the Army to confiscate property, including slaves, used in aid of the rebellion. The Second Confiscation Act, passed in July 1862, went much further, declaring "forever free of their servitude" all slaves owned by Confederate supporters or slaves living within Confederate lines.[24] While both acts were driven by repeated losses on the battlefield and a growing recognition of the South's military might, the idea of slaves as a vital element in the war did not originate in Congress. It emerged from the daily realities of war in the field, where enslaved Americans physically came forth and presented themselves to the occupying Army as an indispensable tool. During the Peninsula Campaign in the summer of 1862, as Glenn David Brasher has shown, the manifold contributions of the area's slaves to the Union effort effectively shaped the course of the campaign and "played a pivotal role in helping to convince a broad range of Northerners that emancipation was a military necessity."[25] Thus, even as the arrival of the Union Army in the South gave slaves their initial opportunity to act, their physical movement away from the plantations and into Union lines instigated a revolutionary change in the attitudes of Northerners, opening hitherto inconceivable possibilities for ending slavery through political action.

According to the Union Army's figures, by the end of the Civil War 500,000 black Southerners had ended up behind its lines. This estimate, highly questionable to begin with, tells us little about what had actually happened during the war. It includes many who did not actively reach Union posts but became free when the Army occupied their neighborhoods.[26] Even more critically, it does not reveal the untold number of attempts to escape that ended in failure but had a highly destabilizing effect on slavery nonetheless. Historians have often analyzed slave flight in the Civil War in one of two ways. Some have emphasized quick disintegration, the emptying out of plantations in a matter of days; others have stressed the resilience of slavery and the fact that most slaves remained in place until the spring of 1865.[27] What has often gotten lost is the vast middle ground between these ends, a history of unsuccessful ventures that kept slaves in the fields but intensified the violence and laid bare the tensions resting at the heart of the relationship between master and slave. Ex-slaves remembered these efforts, even though they often came to naught. "My uncle Ed Miles run away to the North and joined with Yankees during the War," recounted Mattie Logan, who was enslaved in Mississippi. "He was lucky to get away, for lots of them who tried it was ketched up the patrollers. I seen some of them once. They had chains fastened around their legs, fastened short, too, just long enough to take a short step. No more running away with them chains anchoring the feets!"[28]

Owners' wartime records also chronicled a daily struggle against their slaves' determination to become free. Some laconically mentioned a "great stampede among the negroes. Great many stopped."[29] Others proudly shared the details, as if their successes in foiling escapes were feats of heroism and ingenuity rather than the naked exercise of brute force. In August 1862 William Elliott of South Carolina reported to his son on the events of the previous week, when the white family was awoken in the middle of the night to learn that "all the prime hands at Oak lawn had gone off to the Yankees!" Elliott immediately left for the nearest Confederate post, woke up the general and asked him for a "body of horses." The officer complied, and the family received on loan a "lieutenant's guard," which they used to ride between the neighborhood plantations until they "had the good fortune to get ahead of the absconding negroes, and put an end to their purpose." The runaways, realizing that their plan had been discovered, "returned privately to the plantation while it was yet night – thinking to prevent exposure." The next day, after learning the facts of the attempt from a slave who was caught and interrogated, Elliott "proceeded to punish them by whips and handcuffing. Sam and Thomas Ralph has sent to the Work House in Charleston to be sold. The rest are being watched and chained at night until the police of the river can be secured as to leave us at liberty to release them."[30]

Indeed, the scope and significance of slave flight are evident in the efforts the white South made to stop it despite the turmoil of war. While most men who used to staff slave patrols were now away from home, owners and overseers who stayed behind collaborated with state authorities in finding new ways to police the movement of blacks. Neighborhoods recruited every available male, including the very young and very old. Along with Confederate pickets, guerilla forces, provost guard units, and regular infantry they managed to terrorize the enslaved into staying put.[31] Those who were captured fleeing were shot on the spot, run over by the patrol's horses, or dragged on the ground to the nearest jailhouse.[32] Prince Bee recalled what happened to his brother after he was caught trying to escape: "The old Master whipped him 'til the blood spurted all over his body, the bull whip cutting in deeper all the time. He finish up the whipping with a wet coarse towel and the end got my brother in the eye. He was blinded in the one eye but the other eye is good enough he can see they ain't no use trying to run away no more."[33] While in the antebellum period slaves were rarely executed for attempting to escape, runaways in wartime were frequently put to death. A former slave from Georgia who escaped into Union lines during the battle of Chattanooga remembered how "every black man that the Confederates ketched goin' toward the Yankee lines they killed anyhow. They'd leave no life in him, and if they ketched a slave woman they'd treat her the same."[34] When six fugitive slaves were caught in Henry Middleton's South Carolina neighborhood by the local patrol, three were returned to their masters and three were hanged. "The blacks were encouraged to be present," Middleton reported. "The effect will not be soon forgotten."[35]

Yet regardless of the hardships, the dangers, and the profound uncertainty facing the men and women who took to the roads, escapes from the plantations continued unabated until the end of the war. Running away was a deeply personal decision, and its chances for success were determined by highly local conditions, from the lay of the land to the position of the Union Army on a particular night. Yet taken together, the hundreds of thousands of escapes attempted by Southern slaves amounted to a tidal wave of motion with a ripple effect that reached far and wide across the land. As tall tales about runaways circulated among both masters and slaves, all realized that the institution of bondage was undergoing an irreversible change. The spurious stability of peacetime, the illusion that black people could perennially be kept in check, could not be sustained once flight became a viable option, even if just for a minority of slaves. Mass flight was not an organized rebellion crippling slavery in one decisive blow. Yet in many ways it was the engine behind emancipation, a collective effort of resistance through movement, with the human body as its weapon of choice.

***

As with slave runaways, the actual number of deserters from the Confederate Army is extremely difficult to gauge. The official figure stands at 103,400, yet other contemporary evidence suggests that numbers may have been considerably higher.[36] In November 1863 Secretary of War James A. Seddon assessed that absentees from the Army comprised over one third of its overall numbers. By the end of the war, half of all enlisted soldiers – 200,000 men – were recorded as absent from duty.[37]

Unsurprisingly, historians strongly disagree on how to interpret these contradictory facts. Mark A. Weitz argues that the lower figure is unreliable and "seems inconsistent with evidence from letters, diaries, reports, and newspapers that indicates desertion was much more frequent."[38] Weitz's own work on Georgia troops, as well as studies of North Carolina units support this claim, portraying desertion as a pervasive phenomenon with a crucial impact on the course of the war.[39]

Alternately, Gary W. Gallagher offers a radically different interpretation of the higher estimates, suggesting that among those listed as absent late in the war were "men detailed for duty elsewhere, under arrest in camp, sick in field hospitals ... prisoners of war, men on furlough, and those in general hospitals due to illness or battlefield wounds." Most absentees, in short, were away for good reason and were anything but defectors from the Confederate cause.[40] In his study of Virginia soldiers, Aaron Sheehan-Dean suggests that absences from the Army peaked in 1862 but declined afterwards as men adjusted to the service and came to see desertion as a "shameful crime against the state and the nation." The total number of Virginians who deserted the Army over the course of the war, according to Sheehan-Dean's calculations, was just 15,000.[41]

Yet as is the case with runaway slaves, official numbers on white fugitives do not actually tell us very much about what happened on the ground. Desertion, according to Weitz, is "a voluntary, illegal departure from service with the intent never to return."[42] But in the Confederate Army, unauthorized movement took many different forms and had many different purposes. While some soldiers absconded since they had lost faith in the cause and did not plan to return, many others were driven by very different considerations. There were those who left the ranks only for a day or two, to get some rest, visit nearby relatives or search for food. Others withdrew for several weeks and went home to make a crop, take care of sick wives, see their children, or rebuild houses destroyed by Union troops. Orders concerning missing soldiers often acknowledged the variety of transgressions common in the Army by grouping together absentees of different sorts. One issued by General Pierre T. Beauregard in November 1863 offered a lucrative award to "any person who arrested and delivered to any enrolled officer of a district a deserter, skulker, or any other person or soldier absent without leave."[43] The decision by a soldier to violate movement regulations, in short, was not necessarily permanent, nor was it meant as a political statement.[44] This is why it was never confined to a particular subset of the Confederate Army. Its different forms and configurations appeared among rich and poor, young and old, privates and officers, conscripts and volunteers, in the western Confederacy and in the east. Whether they were defined as deserters or skulkers, stragglers or absentees, Confederate soldiers constantly used their legs to express their discontent with the hardships of the service or to fulfill their commitment toward those who needed them at home. Thousands of men who did not mean to desert altogether still broke ranks and left the Army when faced with the overpowering exigencies of war.

Yet the prevalence of unauthorized movement did not result merely from the difficulties of life during wartime, but also from the soldiers' deeply rooted sense of self. In the antebellum period, mobility was an essential right of white men. Along with voting, owning property, and bearing arms, it demarcated their status as a privileged caste and set them apart from slaves and white women who were denied the freedom to move at will. Making soldiers out of the region's undisputed masters meant forcing them to give up this essential right and adhere to the strictures of military discipline. This proved to be a largely unattainable goal. Throughout the war, movement functioned simultaneously as a form of resistance, a strategy of survival, and a means of self-assertion for white men determined to retain some measure of the independence that defined who they were before the war.

Soldiers began leaving the Army as soon as the initial enthusiasm of secession wore off. By the fall of 1862, the situation had reached the point of crisis. When the Confederate Army invaded Maryland in September, only 37,000 of the Army's 55,000 enlisted men actually made it to the battle of Antietam.[45] Four days later, an exasperated Robert E. Lee wrote to Jefferson Davis that "a great many men belonging to the Army never entered Maryland at all; many returned after getting there, while others who crossed the river kept aloof. The stream has not lessened since crossing the Potomac."[46] The soldiers who dropped out were not necessarily deserters, and most returned to the ranks at some point. But the ease with which they abandoned the service at a particularly crucial moment reveals both their determination to exert control over their own bodies and their officers' failure to stop them from doing so. Both would continue to plague Confederate military operations until the end of the war.

Over the next two and a half years, absenteeism ebbed and flowed, usually in direct correlation to the Army's accomplishments on the battlefield and the overall prospects of the Confederate cause. During the spring of 1863, when the South marched from one victory to the next, desertion was kept at bay. Yet that summer, following the dual defeats at Gettysburg and Vicksburg, movement away from the Army resumed. Virginians retreating from Pennsylvania took unauthorized leaves to visit home, while others gave up altogether. "It is nothing strange to see from 8 to 10 in gangs going on making for different parts of Virginia and North Carolina," wrote Mary Davis from southern Virginia on August 9, 1863.[47]

Even as the Army was able to keep its units together and continue fighting, the deteriorating situation on the homefront posed a constant challenge to men's motivation to remain in the ranks. "They say the yankees ar runing a way by rigament and our Army isant mutch beter thay ar runing a way by company and ar talking about runing away by the rigament," reported Michael Freeze on the state of affairs in his unit. Wives writing from North Carolina "say that they ar starving and cant hold out more then too month longer and I hard a heap of men sware that if their families would sufer that they would stack armes and go hoom."[48] In their applications for leave of absence, soldiers recounted time and again the hardships that had befallen their families and emphasized their responsibilities as men. One told of a letter from an "aged mother" asking her son to come home for the funerals of his wife and father and to help care for his four little children who were now left with "no male assistance." Another spoke of three children, "very ill with diphtheria" and "no male person close, to render my family any assistance."[49]

At other times, however, circumstances prompting soldiers to request a leave of absence were somewhat less than catastrophic. Soldiers routinely expected leaves to be granted in order to take care of "important business," like the Virginia soldier who requested a five-day furlough on March 20, 1864, "for the purpose of attending to my private affairs and to visit the city for the purpose of forwarding some $8,000 which must be attended to before the 25 inst." A particularly bold request came from Private William L. Cheatham, who in April 1864 applied for leave in order to continue his work as the county surveyor of Appomattox County. His initial application had been denied, yet that did not stop Cheatham from trying again. "I enlisted in the army early in the present struggle while enjoying the benefits of to me a fairly lucrative position constituting the support of my family." At the time, he was "under the impression that I would be able to retain my office for the benefit of those I love and who are dependent upon me and that I might, at times, secure the privilege of attending to its duties."[50]

Cheatham's special request was approved and he was allowed to go home for thirty days. Yet even when an application was denied, many soldiers simply took the road. On January 4, 1865, after having spent another Christmas in camp, Grant Taylor confided to his wife that he intended "to come home next April if I do not get a furlough before and they do not pay me off."[51] Some soldiers did not even bother keeping their plans secret. During the same winter, the men of Hood's Texas Brigade wrote President Jefferson Davis an unequivocal letter, threatening to desert unless granted some time off: "We stated in it that we want to be on an equality withe the rest of the troops, that they were getting furloughs and our Brigade was getting non," recounted one of the petitioners to his niece back home. "We also stated to the president that we had him in the service four years and faught as hard as any troops ever did, and all that we asked of him was to put us on an equality with the rest of the troops and if he did not we would put ourselves on an equality and that was as good as to sa that we would go home any hour."[52] These Texan soldiers were some of the Confederacy's hardest fighters. Over the course of the previous three years, they had proven themselves in battle time and again. Yet the habits of social domination were simply too ingrained in their minds. Taking an unauthorized leave of absence epitomized soldiers' refusal to accept the idea that a white man serving in the military had relinquished agency over his own limbs.

While military authorities showed considerable patience for soldiers' needs and desires as free white men, toleration eventually ran its course. Starting in the spring of 1862, the government took decisive action to stop the Army from falling apart. The provost-guard was expanded to the division and corps level, all non-medical furloughs were revoked, and conscription was enacted by Congress in Richmond. By the fall of 1862, provost forces were monitoring every road and railway where armies were camped and train conductors were instructed to ensure that every soldier was carrying a valid passport. In 1864 the writ of habeas corpus was suspended for all desertion cases, and Congress passed a law that made helping deserters an offense punishable by a fine of up to $1,000 or by a prison sentence of up to two years.[53] Infantry units were pulled from combat duty on a regular basis to look for missing soldiers in forests, hills, and caves. Men serving in one regiment in the Army of Northern Virginia grew so used to the task of searching for missing comrades they

reported on it in their diaries as a routine activity, in entries like "David
Barnum with the squad who went to hunt deserters returned today. They
caught 8 or 10, & had a right pleasant time."[54]

    Thus as the war expanded and intensified, the roads of the South
teemed with runaways of both races, who had previously stood on opposite sides of a strict racial divide but were now facing analogous threats
and obstacles on their way to freedom. Like the black flight from plantations, white flight from the Army evolved from an individual enterprise
into a group activity. A conscription officer in South Carolina reported to
his superior that "it is not uncommon for squads of ten or fifteen to come
in from the Army, having made their way across the country on foot, and
generally bringing their arms."[55] Fleeing the Army also forced deserters
away from the roads, the domain of masters, and into the woods, the
traditional habitus of runaway slaves.[56] "A good many men were so
afraid of being conscripted that they spent their time loafing and bumming
in the woods," remembered a Virginia woman.[57] Years later, an ex-slave
from Texas offered a shrewd summary of what had happened to the white
men in his neighborhood: "I 'member how some 'r' march off in her
uniforms, lookin' so gran' 'n' den how some 'r' dem hide out in de
wood' to keep from lookin' so gran'."[58]

    Confederate soldiers were sent on assignments that combined the
duties of the slave patrol and the provost guard by looking for both
runaway slaves and free white men avoiding military service. In South
Carolina, the provost marshal of Charleston ordered his guards in July
1862 to "examine carefully every vehicle capable of concealing a person
and to arrest every one not having the proper passport," as it was
reported that "soldiers without passports and negroes" were sneaking
past the sentries on the bridges. A runaway slave trying to cross the
Ashley River winding through town confirmed that Confederate pickets
were indeed stationed every half-mile, and each one "stopped the waggon, read the pass, and had the right to search the waggon." The
following spring, an entire regiment was ordered to enter Williamsburg
and "arrest all persons liable to conscription," as well as "all the runaway negroes to be found."[59]

    The rich experience the white South had accumulated in dealing
with runaway slaves was also evident in the punishment meted out to
deserters. Lighter penalties included head shaving and solitary con-
finement. Harsher policies were peculiarly similar to punishments
dispensed to runaway slaves. Men were branded, sent to hard labor
with a ball and chain, or were sentenced to bucking and gagging.

Some were subjected to whipping, the most emblematic punishment of slavery. Offenders were tied to a tree, their backs bare, and often received thirty-nine lashes, a number habitually used in the South to discipline slaves.[60] Confederates were clearly uncomfortable with the use of the whip against deserters, which created a dangerous symmetry between masters and slaves. In April 1863 Congress in Richmond outlawed the practice but records indicate that it remained in use for the duration of the war.[61]

Like the public executions of runaway slaves, the shooting of deserters also became a mass spectacle, as entire units were hauled out to watch and learn. On one occasion, a mortified soldier described the ritual of execution in his brigade. The soldiers "were drawn up, on three sides around the place of execution. By and by, two ambulances, with a file of soldiers on each side and a guard in front and rear might be seen, making a slow approach up to the spot. Then a band went in front and played the 'dead march.'" In this case, the message seems to have come through. "I felt the moment after the volley was fired, an indescribable & mixed sensation of sickness & horror at the sight."[62]

Despite the use of these and other harsh and unusual means, all in all, the techniques developed during peacetime failed to meet the test of war. In theaters of military action, the determination of slaves to free themselves and the overwhelming might of the Union Army hindered even the most rigorous efforts by slave patrols and home guard units. Elsewhere, soldiers' sense of personal freedom, compounded by the mobile nature of the war, stood in the way of the manifold forces acting as military police. Yet desertion and emancipation were not merely similar phenomena. The profusion of runaways on the roads of the Confederacy embodied two dramatic changes that gradually materialized as the conflict raged on: the ascent of black freedom and the descent, if only temporary, of white freedom. The pathways of the South served as a point of convergence for these parallel but inverted processes. While African Americans were winning their freedom through movement away from the plantations, white men who joined the Army were forced to relinquish their right to move at will. While slave patrols were losing their effectiveness, a growing police operation for capturing soldiers was taking hold. The simultaneous manhunts that took place across the Confederacy were an intersection between the slaves' new ability to act, resist, and fight for their liberation through movement, and soldiers' new subjugation to Army discipline and its coercive powers. Though they had emerged from two diametrically opposed points of departure, the circumstances

of war threw blacks and whites into conflicts over freedom of motion, an
essential right which no free person could do without.

***

Emancipation coincided and intermingled with another form of wartime
flight, the exodus of white civilians from their homes. In both cases, the
arrival of the Union Army was the decisive factor spurring people to act.
The first white refugees of the war left their homes in Northern Virginia as
soon as Union soldiers appeared in the summer of 1861. As the war grew
in ferocity and scope, so did the movement of white civilians away from
their homes. Early in the war, displaced persons could be seen on the roads
of the Shenandoah Valley, the Peninsula, Kentucky, Tennessee, and New
Orleans. The capture of the Mississippi Valley in 1863 brought a second
wave of refugees, and the third wave was propelled by Sherman's march
through Georgia and the Carolinas.[63] In countless locales, news of the
Union Army's imminent arrival set off a universal panic, like the one
evident on the streets of Nashville in February 1862: "Men and women
were to be seen running to and fro in every portion of the city, and large
numbers were hastening with their valuables to the several railroad
depots, or escaping in private conveyances to some place of fancied
security in the country," recounted an eyewitness. "Every available vehicle was chartered, and even drays were called into requisition, to remove
people and their plunder, either to the country or to the depots, and the
trains went off crowded to their utmost capacity, even the tops of the cars
being literally covered with human beings."[64]

   While the population of refugees included white Southerners from all
walks of life, the majority of families who fled their homes belonged to
the region's upper classes.[65] As early as August 1862 Edmund Ruffin
remarked that the only families left in his section of Virginia were those
"too poor to move." In May 1863 a British traveler observed "signs of
preparations for immediate skedaddling" in most of the prosperous
plantations along the shores of the Mississippi River.[66] Large slaveholders were particularly prone to fleeing in the face of an advancing
Union Army, as this was the only means to salvage their way of life.
While these privileged families made up for a relatively small exodus in
terms of the number of people involved, the hurried, frightened flight of
the Southern elite in the face of its mortal enemies was an important
event in the history of the region. Even if just for an instant, an
entrenched and confident ruling class was stripped of both material
comforts and control of its own fate.

Two examples will suffice. A member of a Louisiana sugar-planting family which left its home when the Union Army took New Orleans described the plight of the rich and comfortable, now cramped aboard a steamboat, traveling along the Mississippi River, seeking a place of rest:

We who had lived on the plantation, with the greatest abundance of food and supplies of all kinds, have not felt the effects of the war, but now that we are refugees and in a part of the country that has been drained of much that it produced, and the white laboring man has joined the Army, leaving the fields but scantily cultivated, we begin to feel the want of food. Our party consists of seven in the family and eighteen servants, and the officers and crew of the steamboat, making many mouths to feed; frequently we are not allowed to land if there are few provisions in the place, and are met at the wharf by men with shotguns, who not politely, but very forcibly, request us to move on, and it is not an unusual thing for us to have nothing but sweet potatoes and corn bread to eat for days at a time.[67]

Decades later, the son of a well-off Atlanta family still had a clear recollection of an aristocracy struggling to save the precious belongings that were the hallmark of its privileged life. "Of course, we couldn't carry everything, but we took along most of our best carpets and rugs, some feather beds, our piano, and our set of china. We left our sewing-machine – and at that time sewing-machines weren't very plentiful."[68] The same abundant resources that enabled wealthy families to seek new homes encumbered their departures and embodied the vulnerability of a ruling class thrown on the road.

As the United States grew increasingly committed to emancipation, the arrival of the Union Army also invoked the specter of a new racial order. Some slaveholders were not embarrassed to admit they were fleeing in fear of a slave insurrection. "Everybody and everything trying to get on the cars . . . all fleeing the Yankees, or worse still, the Negroes," reported Kate Stone, another member of the Louisiana planter class. Her own family decided to abandon its fine home and move to Texas after a neighboring plantation was ransacked and its owners threatened with murder by their slaves and Union soldiers. They left at night, in perfect silence, fearing that any noise "would bring the Negroes down on us."[69]

Blacks who witnessed the flight of their masters were fully aware of the profound irony inherent in the situation. A popular wartime song named *Kingdom Comin'* put this sentiment into verse:

> Say, darkies, hab you see de massa
> Wid de muffstash on his face,
> Go along de road some time dis mornin'
> Like he gwine to leab de place?
> He seen a smoke way up de ribber

Whar de Linkum gunboats lay.
He took his hat, an' lef' berry sudden,
An' I spec' he run away!
CHORUS
De massa run! ha, ha!
De darkey stay! ho, ho!
It mus' be now de kingdom comin'
An' de year ob Jubilo![70]

In her study of the plantation household, where black and white women coexisted on the most unequal terms, Thavolia Glymph argues that the war "brought down with it – at least for a time – the quite substantial divisions between southern women by race and class, freedom and unfreedom, citizenship and statelessness."[71] This was perhaps most clearly evident on Southern roads. For both black and white women, the experience of wartime flight was a sharp departure from traditional norms. In the antebellum period, mistresses and female slaves were both restricted in their movements compared to the men with whom they shared their lives. While white women were nominally free, their ability to move at will was severely limited by cultural mores that confined them to their homes. Within the boundaries of slavery, females were substantially less mobile than their male counterparts and their geographical literacy was narrower. Black women did not serve as drivers or teamsters and were less likely than men to receive tasks that required movement beyond the farm or plantation where they were held in bondage. Men were also the ones who traveled to visit their families when couples were enslaved by different owners.[72]

As black and white refugee convoys made their way across the Southern landscape, the confluence of circumstances was, at certain moments, on vivid display. While wealthy white households moved through the South with pianos, carpets, and feather beds, black fugitives also attempted to salvage their precious belongings. A Northerner watching a crowd of five thousand former slaves travel into Union-held territory described the sights: "They came in all sorts of vehicles and all sorts of animals, remnants of massa's property," he wrote. "The vehicles were loaded with the odds + ends of their household duds, which were a motley mess, + on which were piled the little ones – all these duds were what could be put on the wagons in the hurry of departure."[73]

Yet the similar circumstances also bespoke crucial disparities. Once again, the roads of the Confederacy provided the setting for an intersection between the rising tide of black freedom and the declining fortunes of the white South. While black women were practicing a new freedom of motion, white women were experiencing the hardships of involuntary relocation; while black women were abandoning places of bondage where they were degraded and dehumanized, white women were leaving cherished homes where they had usually enjoyed a measure of comfort and stability. For black women, movement away from the plantations signaled the beginning of a new life, while for whites it was the end of an era. The motion of refugees in the Confederate South was the essence of the simultaneous yet antithetical processes of change that the war had touched off. On the road, black and white women shared similar experiences of flight and displacement; at the same time, the larger meaning of their movement was worlds apart.

***

Elsewhere in this volume, Gregory P. Downs takes issue with historians' inclination to frame emancipation in spatial and temporal terms, a "sweet land of liberty" or "freedom-time," two metaphors that fail to capture the highly complex and uncertain transition from slavery to freedom. Emancipation, Downs argues, could only be realized through the power of the state to defend freedpeople's legal claims.[74] The end of slavery came months or years after Appomattox, as Union soldiers made their way through the countryside, pressing freedom on recalcitrant owners and granting ex-slaves the protection of armed force.

This important argument contributes to our understanding of emancipation as a gradual and highly contested process that was far from guaranteed by military defeat. Yet it comes at the risk of marginalizing the experience of the Confederacy as a wartime society, riven by the mass dislocations and profound disruptions inherent to a long and hard war. While freedom as an irrefutable fact was by no means a fait accompli when Lee surrendered, the breakdown of slavery commenced during the war and as a result of the circumstances created by war. Downs is right that the emancipatory process in the American South did not end in 1865. But it did begin in 1861.

Furthermore, while historians might have gone too far in deploying the metaphor of space in their interpretations of complex political processes, the "spatial turn" in Civil War scholarship, as Stephen Berry has recently defined it, actually takes a highly material approach to the study of space and movement.[75] The *Visualizing Emancipation* project at the University of Richmond's Digital Scholarship Lab and the articles it has spawned by Scott Nesbit and Edward L. Ayers provide a spatial view of emancipation as a gradual, shifting, and highly contingent process, transpiring simultaneously on local, regional, and national scales. Borrowing from historical geography, William G. Thomas and Kaci Nash have identified a new type of Civil War locale, the "funnel point," an interstitial zone distinct from both the battlefield and home front, through which the Union Army channeled vast quantities of men, animals, bacteria, and materiel. Lorien Foote has uncovered a wave of escapes from prisoner-of-war camps in South Carolina during the last months of the war, arguing that their movement and the efforts to stem it contributed directly to the collapse of Confederate authority across the state.[76] This scholarly vein also relates to a growing interest in the environmental history of the war, evident in recent work by Lisa Brady, Megan Kate Nelson, and Kathryn Shively Meier, who all place the geographical spaces within which war happens at the center of their stories and examine how humans fighting wars remake these spaces while being remade by them.[77]

FIGURE 1: "Cumberland Landing, Va. Group of 'contrabands' at Foller's house." *Source: James F. Gibson, May 14, 1862. Courtesy of the Library of Congress, Prints and Photographs Division, LC-B811-383.*

My own interpretation of how space functioned in the Civil War, both in this essay and the book on which it draws, posits that in areas of the Confederacy where the war was actually fought, spatial mobility was an essential experience for Southerners of all stripes and a formative power in shaping the political, social, and cultural processes that defined the four-year history of the Confederate States.[78] The Southern road in the Civil War was neither metaphorical nor idealized, but a multifaceted terrain of struggle, a site where liberation and subjugation interlocked and overlapped. As multitudes of Southerners made their way through the Confederacy's war-torn landscapes, emancipation, desertion, and flight from enemy occupation combined to fundamentally undermine the social and political order of the Confederate South. This was a convoluted, protracted process, and some of its outcomes would eventually be reversed. Yet during four years of upheaval, it had a transformative effect.

FIGURE 2: "Stampede of slaves from Hampton to Fortress Monroe." *Source: Artist unknown, Courtesy of the Library of Congress, Prints and Photographs Division, LC-USZ62-105557.*

NOTES

1. Important studies of slave resistance during the Civil War include Joel
    Williamson, *After Slavery: The Negro in South Carolina during
    Reconstruction, 1861–1877* (Chapel Hill: University of North Carolina
    Press, 1965); Leon Litwack, *Been in the Storm So Long: The Aftermath of
    Slavery* (New York: Vintage, 1979); Ira Berlin et al., eds., *The Destruction of
    Slavery*, in *Freedom, A Documentary History of Emancipation, 1861–1867*,
    ser. 1, vol. I (Cambridge, UK: Cambridge University Press, 1985); Steven
    Hahn, *A Nation under Our Feet: Black Political Struggles in the Rural
    South from Slavery to the Great Migration* (Cambridge, Mass.: Harvard
    University Press, 2004); Thavolia Glymph, *Out of the House of Bondage:
    The Transformation of the Plantation Household* (New York: Cambridge
    University Press, 2008); Stephanie McCurry, *Confederate Reckoning: Power
    and Politics in the Civil War South* (Cambridge, Mass.: Harvard University
    Press, 2010); and Bruce Levine, *The Fall of the House of Dixie: The Civil War
    and the Social Revolution That Transformed the South* (New York: Random
    House, 2013).
2. Abraham Lincoln, Second Inaugural Address, March 4, 1865.
3. Mary T. Hunley Diary, May 12, 1861, p. 1, in the Mary T. Hunley Diary,
    1861–1864, #330-z, Southern Historical Collection, Louis Round Wilson
    Special Collections Library, University of North Carolina at Chapel Hill,
    hereafter cited as SHC.
4. Robert Francis Engs, *Freedom's First Generation: Black Hampton, Virginia,
    1861–1890* (Philadelphia: University of Pennsylvania Press, 1979), 18–22;
    Louis S. Gerteis, *From Contraband to Freedman: Federal Policy toward
    Southern Blacks, 1861–1865* (Westport, Conn.: Greenwood Press, 1973),
    11–18; Adam Goodheart, *1861: The Civil War Reawakening* (New York:
    Knopf, 2011), 293–347; Levine, *Fall of the House of Dixie*, 97.
5. Williamson, *After Slavery*, 4–5; Julie Saville, *The Work of Reconstruction:
    From Slave to Wage Laborer in South Carolina, 1860–1870* (Cambridge, UK:
    Cambridge University Press, 1994), 37.
6. John W. Blassingame, *Slave Testimony: Two Centuries of Letters, Speeches,
    Interviews, and Autobiographies* (Baton Rouge: Louisiana State University
    Press, 1977), 359.
7. Berlin et al., *The Destruction of Slavery*, 81.
8. William Alan Blair, *Virginia's Private War: Feeding Body and Soul in the
    Confederacy, 1861–1865* (New York: Oxford University Press, 1998), 122.
9. Clifton Johnson, ed. *Battleground Adventures: The Stories of Dwellers on the
    Scenes of Conflict in Some of the Most Notable Battles of the Civil War*
    (Boston: Houghton Mifflin, 1915), 143.
10. Edmund L. Drago, "How Sherman's March through Georgia Affected the
    Slaves," *Georgia Historical Quarterly* 57 (1973): 361–375; Leslie A.
    Schwalm, *A Hard Fight for We: Women's Transition from Slavery to
    Freedom in South Carolina* (Urbana: University of Illinois Press, 1997), 125.
11. John Cimprich, "Slave Behavior during the Federal Occupation of Tennessee
    1862–1865," *Historian* 44, no. 3 (1982), 335–346; Stephanie M.H. Camp,

Closer to Freedom: Enslaved Women and Everyday Resistance in the Plantation South (Chapel Hill: University of North Carolina Press, 2004) 125–126.

12. James Downs, *Sick from Freedom: African-American Illness and Suffering during the Civil War and Reconstruction* (New York: Oxford University Press, 2012), 27.

13. Berlin et al., *The Destruction of Slavery*, 91.

14. Blassingame, *Slave Testimony*, 546.

15. Ibid., 456.

16. Johnson, *Battleground Adventures*, 155.

17. William Patterson Smith to Christopher, August 12, 1862, Box 10; William Thomas to Father, January 19, 1863, Box 11, William Patterson Smith Papers, Duke Library.

18. Clarence L. Mohr, *On the Threshold of Freedom: Masters and Slaves in Civil War Georgia* (Athens: University of Georgia Press, 1986), 113; Gregg L. Michel, "From Slavery to Freedom: Hickory Hill, 1850–80," in Edward L. Ayers and John C. Willis, eds., *The Edge of the South: Life in Nineteenth-Century Virginia* (Charlottesville: University Press of Virginia, 1991), 109–133, x, 256.

19. William L. Furlow, Request for Leave of Absence, Box 150, Edward S. Willis Papers, Brock Collection, The Huntington Library, San Marino, Calif., hereafter cited as HL; Kate Stone and John Q. Anderson, *Brokenburn: The Journal of Kate Stone, 1861–1868* (Baton Rouge: Louisiana State University Press, 1995), 35.

20. Mrs. Hugh Lee Diary 1862–1865, June 26, 1862, p. 155, Mary Greenhow Lee Papers, Stewart Bell, Jr. Archives Room, Handley Regional Library, Winchester, Virginia, hereafter cited as SBJ.

21. Wilma A. Dunaway, *The African-American Family in Slavery and Emancipation* (Cambridge, UK: Cambridge University Press, 2003); Downs, *Sick from Freedom*; Thavolia Glymph, "This Species of Property: Female Slave Contrabands in the Civil War" in Edward D. C. Campbell, ed., *A Woman's War: Southern Women, Civil War, and the Confederate Legacy* (Richmond: Museum of the Confederacy, 1996). On William T. Sherman and Henry H. Halleck's orders to bar fugitives or return them to their masters, see Berlin et al., *The Destruction of Slavery*, 278–279, 417.

22. Berlin et al., *Destruction of Slavery*, 422, 361; Ira Berlin et al., eds., *The Wartime Genesis of Free Labor: The Lower South* in *Freedom, A Documentary History of Emancipation, 1861–1867*, ser. 1, v. III (New York: Cambridge University Press, 1990), 684–697.

23. For different positions in the debate, see James Oakes, *Freedom National: The Destruction of Slavery in the United States, 1861–1865* (New York: Norton, 2013); Eric Foner, *The Fiery Trial: Abraham Lincoln and American Slavery* (New York: Norton, 2010); James M. McPherson, *Abraham Lincoln and the Second American Revolution* (Oxford: Oxford University Press, 1991).

24. On the confiscation acts, see Silvana Siddali, *From Property to Person: Slavery and the Confiscation Acts, 1861–1862* (Baton Rouge: Louisiana State University Press, 2005).

25. Glenn David Brasher, *The Peninsula Campaign and the Necessity of Emancipation* (Chapel Hill: University of North Carolina Press, 2012), 228. Brasher's nuanced study also reveals the paradoxical and surprising ways in which Southern slaves figured in this process. It was also their centrality to the Confederate war effort, both real and imagined, which impressed upon Northerners the necessity of enacting emancipationist measures.

26. David Blight has suggested that the number of slaves who reached Union lines by early 1865 was between 600,000 and 700,000. David W. Blight, *A Slave No More: Two Men Who Escaped to Freedom: Including Their Own Narratives of Emancipation* (Orlando: Harcourt, 2007), 160. Earlier estimates are in W. E. B. Du Bois, *Black Reconstruction: An Essay toward a History of the Part Which Black Folk Played in the Attempt to Reconstruct Democracy in America, 1860–1880* (New York: Russell & Russell, 1935), 66; Williamson, *After Slavery*, 3; Eugene D. Genovese, *Roll, Jordan, Roll: The World the Slaves Made* (New York: Pantheon Books, 1974), 90.

27. For two widely disparate interpretations of emancipation, see Susan E. O'Donovan, *Becoming Free in the Cotton South* (Cambridge: Harvard University Press, 2007) and Armstead L. Robinson, *Bitter Fruits of Bondage: The Demise of Slavery and the Collapse of the Confederacy, 1861–1865* (Charlottesville: University of Virginia Press, 2005).

28. George P. Rawick, *The American Slave: A Composite Autobiography*, 19 vols. (Westport, Conn.: Greenwood Press, 1972), vol. VII, Oklahoma and Miss. narr., pt. 1, 189.

29. Sally Lyon Taliaferro, Diary, 1859–1864, July 5, 1862, Library of Virginia, Richmond, Virginia.

30. William to Dear William, August 25, 1862, Elliott and Gonzales Family Papers, Documenting the American South. University Library, The University of North Carolina at Chapel Hill, docsouth.unc.edu/imls/gon zales/gonzales.html.

31. Schwalm, *Hard Fight for We*, 106–107; Stephen V. Ash, *When the Yankees Came: Conflict and Chaos in the Occupied South, 1861–1865* (Chapel Hill: University of North Carolina Press, 1995), 162–165.

32. James L. Roark, *Masters without Slaves: Southern Planters in the Civil War and Reconstruction* (New York: Norton, 1977), 74; Litwack, *Been in the Storm So Long*, 57; Berlin et al., *Destruction of Slavery*, 794; Ash, *When the Yankees Came*, 163; Mohr, *On the Threshold of Freedom*, 214–220.

33. Rawick, *American Slave*, vol. VII, Oklahoma and Miss. narr., pt. 1, 16.

34. Johnson, *Battleground Adventures*, 257–258.

35. Quoted in Roark, *Masters without Slaves*, 74.

36. Mark A. Weitz, *More Damning than Slaughter: Desertion in the Confederate Army* (Lincoln: University of Nebraska Press, 2005), ix.

37. *The War of the Rebellion: The Official Records of the Union and Confederate Armies*, 128 vols. (Washington, 1881–1901), ser. IV, vol. II, 995, hereafter cited as *OR*; Weitz, *More Damning than Slaughter*, 269; Ella Lonn, *Desertion during the Civil War* (New York: The Century Co., 1928), 27–30; Brian Holden Reid and John White, "'A Mob of Stragglers and Cowards':

Desertion from Union and Confederate Armies, 1861–1865," *Journal of Strategic Studies* 8, no. 1 (1985): 64–77.

38. Weitz, *More Damning than Slaughter*, ix.
39. Mark A. Weitz, *A Higher Duty: Desertion among Georgia Troops during the Civil War* (Lincoln: University of Nebraska Press, 2000); Richard Bardolph, "Confederate Dilemma: North Carolina Troops and the Deserter Problem, Part I," *North Carolina Historical Review* 66 (1989): 61–86; Bardolph, "Inconstant Rebels: Desertion of North Carolina Troops in the Civil War," *North Carolina Historical Review* 41, no. 2 (1964): 163–189; Rand Dotson, "The Grave and Scandalous Evil Infected to Your People: The Erosion of Confederate Loyalty in Floyd County, Virginia," *Virginia Magazine of History and Biography* 108, no. 4 (2000): 393–434.
40. Gary W. Gallagher, "Disaffection, Persistence, and Nation: Some Directions in Recent Scholarship on the Confederacy," *Civil War History* 55, no. 3 (2009): 329–353 (quotation on 350).
41. Aaron Sheehan-Dean, *Why Confederates Fought: Family & Nation in Civil War Virginia* (Chapel Hill: University of North Carolina Press, 2007), 92–93, 145, 227, n17.
42. Weitz, *A Higher Duty*, 35.
43. Special Orders 233, Headquarters Department of South Carolina, Georgia, and Alabama, November 8, 1863, Box 70, James William Eldridge Collection, HL.
44. For a similar point, see Aaron W. Marrs, "Desertion and Loyalty in the South Carolina Infantry," *Civil War History* 50, no. 1 (2004): 47–65.
45. Ezra A. Carman, *The Maryland Campaign of September 1862*, ed. by Joseph Pierro (New York: Routledge, 2008), 465. Gallagher offers a slightly higher estimate of "fewer than 40,000" in "The Autumn of 1862: A Season of Opportunity," in Gary W. Gallagher, ed., *Antietam: Essays on the 1862 Maryland Campaign* (Kent, Oh.: Kent State University Press, 1989), 1–13.
46. *OR* ser. 1, vol. 19, p. 143.
47. Mary P. Davis to Cousin Ben, August 9, 1863, Mary P. Davis Papers, David M. Rubenstein Rare Books & Manuscript Library, Duke Library, hereafter cited as DMR.
48. Michael Freeze to wife, April 13, 1863, Michael Freeze Letters, SBJ.
49. Francis McCelanaham to Captain Pearce, Nov. 13, 1863, Box 72, James Eldridge Collection; Nathan M. Proffitt, August 28, 1863, Box 70, James William Eldridge Collection.
50. (?) to Captain Pearce, March 20, 1864, Box 74, James Eldridge Collection; William L. Cheatham to Capt. Pearce, April 4, 1864, Box 72, James William Eldridge Collection.
51. Ann K. Blomquist and Robert A. Taylor, eds., *This Cruel War: The Civil War Letters of Grant and Malinda Taylor, 1862–1865*. (Macon, Ga.: Mercer University Press, 2000), 321.
52. Robert T. Wilson to niece, December 17, 1864, Robert Wilson Papers, Historical Research Center, Texas Heritage Museum, Hill College, Hillsboro, Texas.

53. Lonn, *Desertion during the Civil War*, 78–83; Blair, *Virginia's Private War*, 67–68; Kenneth Radley, *Rebel Watchdog: The Confederate States Army Provost Guard* (Baton Rouge: Louisiana State University Press, 1989), 94–95, 153; Weitz, *More Damning than Slaughter*, 101, 239; Bardolph, "Confederate Dilemma, Part I," 182; Bessie Martin, *Desertion of Alabama Troops from the Confederate Army* (New York: Columbia University Press, 1932), 197–205.

54. G. Ward Hubbs, ed., *Voices from Company D: Diaries by the Greensboro Guards, Fifth Alabama Infantry Regiment, Army of Northern Virginia* (Athens: University of Georgia Press, 2003), 195. See also 194, 345.

55. *OR*, ser. IV, vol. II, 769.

56. On the South's rival geographies, see Camp, *Closer to Freedom*, 135–137; John Michael Vlach, *Back of the Big House: The Architecture of Plantation Slavery* (Chapel Hill: University of North Carolina Press, 1993), 12–17.

57. Johnson, *Battleground Adventures*, 340.

58. Rawick, *American Slave,* supp. ser. II, vol. IX, pt. 8, Texas narr., 3484.

59. Alexander Haskell Brown Record Book 1862, July 25, 1862, 00091-z, SHC; Blassingame, *Slave Testimony*, 700. John Robert Bagby to Betty, April 16, 1863, section 4, Bagby Family Papers, Virginia Historical Society, Richmond, Va.

60. Lonn, *Desertion during the Civil War* 58; Bardolph, "Confederate Dilemma, Part I," 198; Peter S. Carmichael, "So Far from God and So Close to Stonewall Jackson: The Executions of Three Shenandoah Valley Soldiers," *Virginia Magazine of History and Biography* 111, no. 1 (2003): 33–66; Drew Gilpin Faust, "Christian Soldiers: The Meaning of Revivalism in the Confederate Army," *Journal of Southern History* 53, no. 1 (1987): 63–90.

61. *OR*, ser. IV, vol. II, 49; Samuel Walkup Diary, June 23, 1863, DMR; Eldred J. Simkins to Eliza Simkins, September 2, 1864, file 180, Simkins Family Papers, HL. Charles E. Brooks has found staunch resistance of soldiers to punishment reminiscent of slavery. Brooks, "The Social and Cultural Dynamics of Soldiering in Hood's Texas Brigade," 558–559.

62. Hubb, *Voices from Company D*, 254.

63. George C. Rable, *Civil Wars: Women and the Crisis of Southern Nationalism* (Urbana: University of Illinois Press, 1989), 182–183.

64. *The Great Panic: Being Incidents Connected with Two Weeks of the War in Tennessee, By an Eye Witness* (Nashville: Johnson & Whiting, 1862), 9–11.

65. Joan E. Cashin, "Into the Trackless Wilderness: The Refugee Experience in the Civil War," in Edward D. C. Campbell et al.eds. *A Woman's War: Southern Women, Civil War, and the Confederate Legacy,* (Richmond: Museum of the Confederacy), 36; Mary Elizabeth Massey, *Refugee Life in the Confederacy* (Baton Rouge: Louisiana State University Press, 1964); Ash, *When the Yankees Came*, 18–19; Rable, *Civil Wars*, 184–185.

66. Edmund Ruffin and William Kauffman Scarborough, *The Diary of Edmund Ruffin*, 3 vols. (Baton Rouge: Louisiana State University Press, 1972) vol. II, 410; Arthur James Lyon Fremantle, *The Fremantle Diary: Being the Journal of Lieutenant Colonel James Arthur Lyon Fremantle, Coldstream Guards, on His Three Months in the Southern States* (Boston: Little, Brown, 1954), 72.

67. Frances Hewitt Fearn and Rosalie Urquhart, *Diary of a Refugee* (New York: Moffat, 1910), 16.
68. Johnson, *Battleground Adventures*, 267.
69. Stone and Anderson, *Brokenburn*, 191, 199.
70. Quoted in Litwack, *Been in the Storm So Long*, 112. For other versions, see Rawick, *American Slave*, vol. II, S.C. narr. Part 2, 197; Newman Ivey White, *American Negro Folk-Songs* (Cambridge, Mass: Harvard University Press, 1928), 171. On the origins of this song, see Kate Masur, "'A Rare Phenomenon of Philological Vegetation': The Word 'Contraband' and the Meanings of Emancipation in the United States," *Journal of American History* 93, no. 4 (2007): 42–43.
71. Bruce Collins, *White Society in the Antebellum South* (London: Longman, 1985), 70, 76; Camp, *Closer to Freedom*, 28, 36–37; Michael P. Johnson, "Runaway Slaves and the Slave Communities in South Carolina, 1799 to 1830," *William and Mary Quarterly* 38 (1981): 418–441; John Hope Franklin and Loren Schweninger, *Runaway Slaves: Rebels on the Plantation* (New York: Oxford University Press, 1999), 210–212.
72. Glymph, *Out of the House of Bondage*, 133.
73. Diary of Isaac Shoemaker, March 3, 1864, DMR.
74. See Chapter 2.
75. Clayton Butler, "The Strength of Civil War History: An Interview with Historian Stephen Berry," *Civil War Trust* website: www.civilwar.org/education/history/civil-war-history-and-scholarship/stephen-berry-interview.html (accessed July 21, 2015).
76. Edward L. Ayers and Scott Nesbit, "Seeing Emancipation: Scale and Freedom in the American South," *Journal of the Civil War Era*, 1, no. 1 (March 2011): 3–24; Scott Nesbit, "Scales Intimate and Sprawling: Slavery, Emancipation, and the Geography of Marriage in Virginia," *Southern Spaces*, July 19, 2011. www.southernspaces.org/2011/scales-intimate-and-sprawling-slavery-emancipation-and-geography-marriage-virginia (accessed July 21, 2015); William G. Thomas and Kaci Nash, "Places of Exchange: An Analysis of Human and Material Flows in Civil War Alexandria, Virginia," *Civil War History* (forthcoming); Lorien Foote, "'They Cover the Land Like the Locusts in Egypt:' Fugitive Federal Prisoners of War and the Collapse of the Confederacy," *Journal of the Civil War Era* (forthcoming).
77. Lisa Brady, *War upon the Land: Military Strategy and the Transformation of Southern Landscapes during the American Civil War* (Athens: University of Georgia Press, 2012); Lisa Brady, "From Battlefield to Fertile Ground: The Development of Civil War Environmental History," *Civil War History* 58, no. 3 (September 2012), 305–321; Megan Kate Nelson, *Ruin Nation: Destruction and the American Civil War* (Athens: University of Georgia Press, 2012); Kathryn Shively Meier, *Nature's Civil War: Common Soldiers and the Environment in 1862 Virginia* (Chapel Hill: University of North Carolina Press, 2014).
78. Yael A. Sternhell, *Routes of War: The World of Movement in the Confederate South* (Cambridge, Mass.: Harvard University Press, 2012).

2

Force, Freedom, and the Making of Emancipation

Gregory P. Downs

Historians have long struggled to describe the kind of freedom slaves were emancipated into. Because freedom is so famously difficult to define, and because purely legalistic definitions of freedom as "not slavery" don't leave much analytic room to maneuver, scholars often turn to metaphorical language. While the particular meaning of emancipation in the 1860s South took many different forms, one set of languages that emerged in the 1840s and 1850s provided a particularly useful, but also at times limiting, way of thinking about freedom as a space to move into. This essay investigates the development of spatial and other metaphors of freedom in antebellum America and their limits in explaining the particular freedom that emerged at the end of the Civil War.

The primary obstacle to understanding freedom lies in its notoriously slippery definitions. Historians of U.S. slavery often follow the language of escaped slaves themselves by stating not what freedom was, but where it was. Henry Bibb, one of the sharpest autobiographers of the antebellum era, captured the power and elusiveness of slavery in evocative passages where he stood on the bluffs over the Ohio River, "looking over on a free State, as far north as my eyes could see, I have eagerly gazed upon the blue sky of a free North." For Bibb, the Ohio River's marking line between slavery and freedom gestured toward the even brighter division between Canada, "a land of liberty," and the United States. "Oh! Canada, sweet land of rest – Oh! When shall I get there? Oh, that I had the wings of a dove, that I might soar away to where there is no slavery."[1] Thinking about freedom as a place made particular sense to Bibb, who eventually lived in the North, and farther north in Canada. In the regionally fragmented antebellum United States, the notion of a sweet land of liberty (a

42

phrase immortalized in a song written in 1831) seemed unavoidable. As the movement for gradual emancipation ground to a halt at the Mason-Dixon line, Americans of all colors confronted an increasingly divided country, where not just laws but broader ways of conceiving slavery, race, and freedom seemed to be geographically determined.

Since patrols denied slaves freedom of movement, the association between a journey and liberty seemed self-evident; escape was claiming the freedom to be able to move toward freedom. Many memoirs drew upon this metaphor, from the Crafts' *Running a Thousand Miles to Freedom*, to William Troy's *Hair-Breadth Escapes from Slavery to Freedom*, to – embedded within longer titles – Frederick Douglass's *Escape from Bondage*, to Louis Hughes's *From Bondage to Freedom*. In a period saturated with biblical references, the idea of freedom as a place one moved to resonated as well with the story in Exodus of a flight "out from Egypt" and the "house of bondage" (a phrase repeated twenty-two times in the King James Version of the Bible) and with the line in Psalms that "I walk at liberty."[2] It would have been hard to write about freedom in the 1840s or 1850s without tying it to real or imagined geographies.[3]

Buttressed by its biblical allusions and a national obsession with freedom talk, this association between space, movement, and freedom long outlived the antebellum sectional crisis. Martin Luther King Jr. not only spoke of the mountain top and the Promised Land, but titled his memoir of the Montgomery Bus Boycott *Stride toward Freedom*, and Nelson Mandela famously named his memoir *Long Walk to Freedom*. Given these resonances, historians often treat freedom both as a place and the act of moving toward it. Just to pull from some prominent titles in U.S. history, we have *Closer to Freedom*, *Crossroads of Freedom*, *Freedom's Port*, *Terror in the Heart of Freedom*, *Freedom Bound*, *Freedom's Shore*, *South of Freedom*, *Along Freedom Road*, *Bound for Freedom*, *Between Freedom and Bondage*, *Frontiers of Freedom*, *Freedom Just around the Corner*, and of course the iconic *From Slavery to Freedom*. Although this titling is common in U.S. history, it is not unique to it. We also have *Bitter Road to Freedom* about post-World War II Europe and Michael Collins's posthumous essays in *Path to Freedom*, among many others.

Drawing upon the rupture of emancipation and abolition between 1863 and 1865, other works break up a historical moment between slavery-time and freedom-time (*Sick from Freedom*, *Political Worlds of Slavery and Freedom*) or use quantitative languages, invoking an ideal measure of freedom against which reality is found wanting (*More Than Freedom*, *Freedom Is Not Enough*, *Fragile Freedom*, *Shades of Freedom*,

Degrees of Freedom). In these, freedom is a place and time apart, a nirvana that the world can never match. Against those stable, if vague, invocations, Eric Foner's fluid conception of freedom as an "essentially contested concept" or keyword eliminates the teleology but at the expense of clarity. Freedom in these terms can mean anything people said it meant even if they seem to be clearly referring to problems that we might more fruitfully group under terms like equality, belonging, citizenship, access, or personal liberation.[4]

More worrisome than the titles themselves is the way that metaphors of freedom as space or time burrow into our analysis. While it was inevitable for writers in a period of sectional crisis to emphasize the spatial nature of freedom, as it was commonsensical for others writing after emancipation to treat freedom as a break in time, this language obscures what is most central about freedom. What made the metaphors so powerful for King or Mandela or Collins is exactly what makes them so flimsy for historians: their teleology. Social movements rely upon teleologies of future progress to keep people hopeful; scholars, however, depend upon shedding those teleologies. Casting, even metaphorically, freedom as the place we are moving toward either by our steps or through the pull of the river of time makes freedom an end state, not a category of analysis. (In some ways, the category of freedom as an ideal measure inverts this problem by reversing the teleology, making freedom a shore we have never and will never reach.) The march of freedom draws us toward a thin, individualized, decontextualized understanding of the ideal, rather than practical meaning, of freedom. While scholars creatively create elbow room for nuance within the strictures of language, and Yael Sternhell in this volume persuasively argues that the spatial turn within Civil War studies has maintained an eye on material conditions, the problem nevertheless remains. Subtle, even brilliant, attention to nuance may not be enough to rescue the many uses of freedom from definitional confusion. In fact, an emphasis upon complexity rather than clarity may be one of the problems we face. Sternhell herself struggles to define freedom satisfactorily, at times treating it as the act of movement, at times as an inner state of liberation, at times as the arrival at a place where a slave's freedom was recognized.[5]

Although there are several problems with seeing freedom as a place or endpoint, two create the most confusion. First, the vision of freedom as a place fed a now-stale debate about who freed the slaves that continues to make freedom overly individualized and decontextualized. Second, this vision of freedom as a place obscures what many nineteenth-century observers knew to be true about freedom: that it existed in its most meaningful form only within the arms of a powerful state. By inclination and training, historians typically turn away from words like "only." The disciplinary impulse to embrace complexity, and the fear of being exposed by counter-examples, all nudge us – usually helpfully – to soften our statements. But here, an impulse toward self-protection should take a backseat to conceptual clarity. Undoubtedly freedom was, as Sternhell writes, a "complex lived experience, a daily reality that took multiple, shifting, and often contradictory forms." And, certainly, slavery "fell apart in thousands of different ways," and "slaves actively took part in bringing about their own liberation" and the transformation of U.S. society more broadly. But confusing the extraordinary complexity of the process with the meaning of freedom and conflating the causes of freedom with the state of freedom obscures both what the process was and what freedom is.[6]

While it is important to analyze the feelings that inspire flights to freedom, conflating inner feelings with the status of freedom makes it impossible to define what freedom actually is. Even more fraught is the association of freedom with liberation from all constraint, which leads Sternhell to the confusing claim that the Civil War led to "the descent, if only temporary, of white freedom" because Confederate policies to pre-vent desertion limited "freedom of motion, an essential right which no free person could do without." If Confederate soldiers were themselves not free, or if – as Sternhell recognizes – white women are not free because their mobility was widely constrained, then Sternhell is defining unfree-dom as an extraordinarily common human condition, not just then but now. Almost all people operate under either legal or social constraints that limit their mobility or choices. Although it might be useful to adhere to such a stringent definition of unfreedom, Sternhell in fact does not stick to it. Instead she defines freedom entirely differently for ex-slaves, who were, in most ways, far more constrained in their mobility than Confederate soldiers or white women, even after they reached U.S. lines.[7] Freedom then serves simultaneously to mark a utopian promised land of the absence of constraint and a widely available internal state of liberation, making it a condition that is at once impossible and omnipresent.

The confusions around freedom are not particular to any writer; they are part of a broader scholarly usage that emerges, I believe, from both the linguistic messiness of the term and the particular cultural moment in which historians took up the freedom paradigm that shapes emancipation studies. By emphasizing personal liberation, historians drew upon a powerful, and admirable, interest in personal agency that, while

sometimes appearing to be radical, was profoundly liberal in its vision of
the relationship of individuals to society. At the same time, and drawing
from some common wellsprings, the story of personal liberation was
also – with great nuance – a piece of a general cultural turn against the
state in the 1960s and 1970s, a curling in of leftist and rightist anti-statism
upon each other.[8] Finding freedom in individual actions or in collective
political organizing, works within this paradigm made actual government
policy less relevant than its ideological or cultural origins. By making
personal freedom an internal state, and unfreedom a series of external
constraints, historians came close to constructing a situation in which,
almost by definition, the state could only restrain freedom. A liberation
story became a libertarian one.

An incipient anti-statism makes it impossible to understand the fall of
slavery or to separate slavery from other forms of coercion. If we cannot
clearly separate slaves' brave actions and internal states from their external status, then we will inevitably fall into confusions, where slaves gain
their freedom by their feelings and actions but, through a mysterious
definitional shift, lose their freedom to external coercion. Clarity instead
demands that we separate the quest for freedom from the status of freedom. That status had concrete meaning in relation to other structures of
society; it required defense. Since ex-slaves – like all human beings –
lacked the ability to constantly defend themselves against all infringement,
they – like us – needed the intervention of forceful external agents, generally the state, to make their freedom meaningful. Absent the potential
for such forceful interventions, no one's freedom is defensible, no matter
how powerfully they may desire it.[9]

Maintaining our focus upon such coercions, however, is difficult. It
casts the emancipation story – and freedom itself – in a grim light to
emphasize new forms of coercion rather than liberation. More broadly,
it runs up against a paradox of being governed; a successfully functioning
state generally conceals its coercive powers when it can. Inevitably, some
white Northerners, like some contemporaries, lost track of their own
dependence upon forceful coercion for their freedom. Some in fact imagined that their freedom did not rely upon coercion at all but was a natural
state, a piece of property, something they consumed. This helped them
blur the line between freedom and feelings of personal liberation, as it
helps us too forget the way our freedom depends not just upon our actions
but also upon the potentially forceful, even deadly, intervention of the
state against people who might try to squash it. But ex-slaves and some of
their allies understood all too well that without coercion freedom would

become an empty term. Only by restricting the actions of white Southerners could black Southerners finally become free. While such force might come from quasi-state organizations – like self-defense leagues – in practice, in the face of the power of planters and white Southerners, it required the intervention of external agents in the shape of the state.

Understanding the centrality of state recognition to the status of freedom helps us grapple with a key intervention ex-slaves and their allies made over the war, as some defined freedom in explicitly statist terms. Defining freedom posed different problems in 1865 than it had in the 1840s and 1850s. Then, geographical metaphors sufficed; people left slavery for the land of freedom. But in 1865, the nearly 3 million slaves still held in bondage at war's end experienced the dawn of freedom in the same places where they had lived as slaves. This at-home freedom in the face of violent efforts to maintain slavery prompted freedpeople to press an extraordinary range of complaints upon federal officers in the South in the months after Appomattox; in turn, these complaints and evidence of slaveowners' violence and disloyalty prodded officers and Bureau agents toward what they called "practical freedom." This statist vision of freedom depended not on geography – for most people were in roughly the same place where they had been enslaved – or upon magical chronological transformation – for proclamations did not stop slaveowners' violent efforts to restrain them – but instead upon recognition. During the 1860s, freedom was not a place or a historical break in time; it was a claim, an acknowledgement of "acquired rights," and a pledge of future action, all in one. Thus, as William A. Blair writes in Chapter 3 of this volume, freedom was inherently "contested and dynamic." As Laura F. Edwards argues in the Epilogue, attention to the "terrain on which individuals worked – terrain defined by the power of the state" helps us capture the central role of the "backing of law and the willingness of government to enforce it." It depended upon both the assertions of freedpeople and the presence of agents of the state, in this case officers, soldiers, and Bureau agents. By thinking of freedom as being embedded within the government, as belonging to and with government, rather than as liberation from government, we can see freedom as the beginning of a process of status claims, not as an endpoint. This meant that freedom was inherently a place of contest and of coercion, a way of asking for particular forms of forceful aid to overcome restraints. But this human dependence upon external intervention also made freedom fragile, as Justin Behrend argues in Chapter 6. If freedom were an internal state, then the fears of reenslavement he studies would be absurd. But they carried weight precisely because ex-slaves recognized the retreat of the government that they had called upon repeatedly in the 1860s and 1870s to defend their freedom. Ex-slaves' engagement with the centrality of government action does not undermine their impact upon the nation's history. Instead, it captures the breadth of their influence. For it was precisely their understanding that individual actions or feelings were not enough that led them to seek the massive changes in law and policy – including coercive policies that permitted the national government to declare martial law – that in turn remade the nation's constitutional and legal order.[10]

Capturing this mid-century appraisal of state force and personal freedom requires looking at multiple levels. To show this intertwined transformation, in this essay I examine the treatment of force and freedom at three different planes. First, I show the way that one individual ex-slave described the centrality of coercion to the breakdown of slavery and to personal emancipation. Second, I examine the transformation in high political discussions of force and freedom that ex-slaves helped push onto the nation's agenda and that in turn helped shape the Freedmen's Bureau and Thirteenth Amendment in the crucial winter of 1864–1865. Finally, I sketch out the kinds of policies the government turned to after surrender in 1865 as slaves convinced some officers and politicians that coercion would be required to end slavery and construct what they called practical freedom. Although each topic demands more thorough investigation than I can provide here, examining them briefly in combination gives a sketch of the vast reconfiguration of the meaning of freedom and governance taking place as the war continued.

The complex interplay between individual action and state coercion in fashioning freedom becomes clearest when seen through an individual case. Even – and perhaps especially – the most heroic ex-slaves recognized the need for external support to defend their claim of freedom. One of the most exquisite post-war efforts to balance slave agency and federal authority in shaping emancipation came from the pen of Louis Hughes, who was a slave in Mississippi and Alabama during the war. Hughes had tried to escape four times, but still found himself enslaved a month after Joseph B. Johnston's surrender to William T. Sherman. Well into June, he waited and "tried to be content" as U.S. soldiers were "still raiding all through that section. Every day some town would be taken, and the slaves would secretly rejoice." The wait was lengthy, however. While U.S. soldiers had a large presence 100 miles away in Memphis, they were just beginning to exert control over the section of northern Mississippi around

Panola County through a detachment in Senatobia. Although the U.S. Army had occupied and burned Oxford – thirty miles distant – during the war, it did not report a post-surrender detachment there until July 1865.[11]

Rather than collapsing after surrender, slavery constricted. "We were held with a tighter rein than ever. We were not allowed to go outside of the premises." Hughes's owners enforced control over the region more rigorously than ever, and continued to stop neighbors' slaves on the highway to inspect their passes. "Just think of the outrage upon those poor creatures in forcibly retaining them in slavery long after the proclamation making them free had gone into effect beyond all question!" Hughes wrote. This consistent enforcement led him to question the idea that the war's end would naturally bring emancipation. "If we listen to them we shall be here until Christmas comes again," Hughes told a fellow slave named George Washington. Although Hughes's wife feared that he would be killed if he escaped, he and Washington "talked considerably about the Yankees, and how we might get away. We knew it was our right to be free, for the proclamation had long been issued – yet still they held us . . . We knew that Memphis was headquarters for the Union troops, but how to reach it was the great question." One day in late June 1865, he and Washington left. "The parting was heart-rending, for we knew the dangers were great, and the chances were almost even that we should not meet again." They reached Memphis a day later and waited in a long line of black people to speak with the officer in charge of freedpeople. "We want protection to go back to Mississippi after our wives, who are still held as slaves," they told him. To this, the officer replied that they needed no permission as "you are both free men to go and come as you please." But the officer's conception of freedom did not capture their reality. "Why Colonel," Hughes replied, "if we go back to Mississippi they will shoot the gizzards out of us." The officer was sympathetic but unable to help because he could not spare any soldiers. As they walked back into Mississippi, Hughes and Washington met two soldiers who sketched out the range of responses that slaves met from United States troops. The captain at nearby Senatobia, they warned Hughes, was not trustworthy because he had "been sweetened by the rebel farmers." Instead they directed Hughes to ask two sympathetic soldiers in the "last tent on the line in the camp."[12]

In exchange for ten dollars and a promise of ten more, those Senatobia soldiers slipped away and rode to the master's house with them. There they told a servant named Frank, "Go in and tell your master . . . to come out, we want to see him." Here, the soldiers told a crucial and revealing lie. They said they would need feed for seventy-five horses. In this falsehood, the soldiers revealed that force, not just vague authority, shaped their understanding of their power. They did not rely upon their uniforms but upon the lie that there was an entire troop of cavalry coming behind them. Hughes wondered at the soldiers' courage. Victory, he knew, had not sheathed them in invincibility in a "country of which they knew nothing except that every white man living in it was their enemy." Had their master "thought that there were but two soldiers, it is certain that they would have endeavored to prevent us getting away again, and one or more of us would undoubtedly have been killed." While Hughes's and Washington's wives loaded belongings into the wagon, the master's son threatened to kill them. Meanwhile, the master and the parish minister stood guard by the road "to keep the slaves from running away to the Yankees." The soldiers confronted them, asking, "Why have you not told these two men, Louis and George, that are free men – that they can go and come as they like?" With nine other slaves following, Hughes and Washington headed toward Senatobia, where they paid the soldiers, and the men "cheered us, and seemed glad that they had rendered us service." They arrived in Memphis, "the city of refuge," around the 4th of July with "thousands of others, in search of the freedom of which they had so long dreamed." There was a reason why people fled to Memphis. "Everywhere you looked you could see soldiers." Reflecting on the incident three decades later, Hughes understood that "it is true that we should have been free, sooner or later," but the soldiers' intervention had kept Hughes's and Washington's families together. Later in the summer when freedom came more broadly to northern Mississippi, many families were separated, some forever.[13]

In Hughes's story, we see the enormously complex nature of post-surrender emancipation. Even after surrender, owners patrolled, checked passes, and asserted power over their slaves. Hughes's story therefore illuminates the deep interconnection between force and eman-cipation. Running away was for him necessary but not sufficient; he ran not to escape but to find people who could recognize and defend his family's freedom. To do this, Hughes needed not just the two soldiers but also their ruse of a whole troop behind them in order to escape with his family. What they needed was not just a proclamation but the power to enforce it. The soldiers' response also suggests the critical role of individual sympathy in driving the military reaction to enslavement. Not all soldiers were sympathetic; the captain at Senatobia favored the rebels. Even those soldiers who were sympathetic, like the officer in Memphis, often could not help. But sympathetic soldiers were crucial to Hughes's escape with his family, even if financial motivations also drove them. Finally, the story directs us toward the allure of cities and *Spatial?* towns with Army outposts. While Hughes did not stay in Memphis, he went there not just because it was a city but because it was a city full of soldiers. His freedom had emerged through his personal bravery but also in the presence of soldiers, and it would be defended both by his own actions and their power.

While contemporary discussions of freedom, and its close cousin, liberty, typically set the concept in opposition to a coercive state, the war and the stubborn power of slavery after surrender taught both white officers and black freedpeople to accept the role of state violence in making freedom possible and sustainable. Rather than freedom from coercion, emancipation was by necessity freedom through continuing coercion of slaveowners. Slavery could not end with dramatic laws or proclamations. As Hughes and many officers and freedpeople recognized, pronouncements were never self-enforcing. Ending slavery would require consistent enforcement that could only be provided by the Army with the assistance of the much-smaller number of Bureau agents.

Far from Pontotoc, Mississippi, the dilemmas that Louis Hughes faced were reshaping political debate and policy about the government's role in freedom. The war brought a revolution in the way politicians faced the government's role in fashioning freedom. The heroic efforts and careful pleas of hundreds of thousands of slaves like Louis Hughes helped to transform policy debates first among federal officers in the Southern states and then in Washington, D.C. For some politicians, the nature of the conflict and the dawning awareness of the challenges in the South over-threw antebellum presumption that freedom was a place or a moment in time. Prior to the war, mid-nineteenth-century politicians and thinkers from Karl Marx to Democrat Stephen Douglas to abolitionist Frederick Douglass understood the seemingly inextricable relationship between slavery and the state. Without government, chattel slavery could not survive, because slaves would run away and slaveowners would be unable to count on selling them at a high price. By casting slavery as the product of a powerful government, some anti-slavery thinkers made abolition into a form of government retreat, the removal of state supports for the institution. Withdraw support from slavery, this idea ran, and it would collapse. In its place, individual liberty and participatory democracy would rebuild the South. Prior to the war, anti-slavery politicians and activists simultaneously aggrandized and reduced slavery's impact upon society. Drawing upon a rhetorical critique of the Slave Power to attract a broader public audience, anti-slavery politicians made slaveowners both omnipotent and peculiarly easy to displace. Slavery was everywhere and controlled almost everything; removing slavery, however, could be quick and immediately effective. While naïve in retrospect, this double vision placed the movement within still-powerful Jacksonian distrust of big government and also injected hope in oppositional politics.[14] If anti-slavery politicians made slavery seem too powerful, they could end up accidentally convincing their audience that there was nothing to be done about it. Against the possibility of resignation, they constructed a slavery whose tentacles were long but also slippery. This formulation, however, left little room for positive government action to undo the impact of slavery; it left little room for government at all.

Even as late as January 1865, John A.J. Creswell, a Republican congressman from Maryland, described slavery in this doubled way. Slavery in Maryland had been the very definition of tyranny. "The master was *absolute lord*; the slave and the slave's posterity were *abject bondmen*." In politics, "slavery was omnipotent in Maryland, when it brooded over our legislative assemblies and courts of justice like death." With the fall of slavery, however, everything changed. "The deliverer came, and at the sound of her voice every shackle fell and the slave was transformed quickly into a freeman a soldier." Although there would inevitably be some suffering during wartime, the path to freedom was clear. "Say to the negro, hereafter you shall work for hire, and shall receive and appropriate your own wages; and as sure as it is the law of God for the white man that truth is better than error, and freedom better than slavery, so will experience vindicate the same great principles for the black man."[15] In a similarly minded poem celebrating slavery's demise, anti-slavery writer and editor William Cullen Bryant denounced slavery's "scourge," its "stony eye," and its "guilty power." For all slaveholders' authority, however, their power was transitory. Nationally, those politicians who once "quailed" and "Obeyed thy mandate," now "scoff at the pale, powerless thing thou art." For individual slaves, at "the appointed hour," the shackles fell, "and he whose limbs they galled/Stands in his native manhood, disenthralled." The idea of being "disenthralled" captures the sharp but fleeting power of slavery. To be enthralled was to be either enslaved or held spellbound; disenthralling a person meant simply breaking the spell of slavery.[16]

During the war, other politicians, intellectuals, and military officers struggled toward the idea slavery would not dissolve but would have to be destroyed. Some long-time anti-slavery advocates and some – like

Edwin Stanton and Ulysses S. Grant – who had stayed distant from anti-slavery developed a structural critique of the institution that led them toward a structural vision of emancipation and abolition as positive government projects. Slavery would not die; slavery would have to be killed. Government was both the root of and threat to freedom. Slavery was both the product of government action and an institution that government could not easily unmake.[17]

Although the structural anti-slavery position surfaced as early as the war's first days, it took on new resonance after the Emancipation Proclamation and military victories in the West. The vast emancipations in the Mississippi Valley in 1863–1864 more directly shaped congress-men's understandings of the challenge they faced. In the Mississippi Valley, loyalist or optimistic planters in Louisiana and Mississippi largely stayed put. This was the problem the American Freedmen's Inquiry Commission studied as they journeyed through the South in 1863 and 1864. In a supplemental report to Secretary of War Edwin Stanton tell-ingly titled "The Mastership and Its Fruits," commission member James McKaye described the challenges of eradicating slavery in a region where masters and ex-slaves were "still face to face in the presence of the great revolution." "The difficulty is not with the emancipated slave; but with the old master, still enthralled by his old infatuation." Masters' enduring social power and continued commitment to slavery threatened to make freedom "little else than danger, ill usage, deprivation, sickness, and bereavement." While planters admitted that slavery was "for the present, broken up," they bided their time until they could once again use the "civil power of the State ... for the maintenance of what, to them, doubtless appears the paramount object of all civil authority, of the State itself, some form of slave system."[18]

Masters' determination to preserve slavery presented new problems to Northerners. War forced anti-slavery thinkers to new ideas; "only in the terrible glare ... did the true nature of the mastership, and the order of slavery founded upon it, begin to reveal itself to the popular understanding." Bitter experience taught the North that abolition and emancipation would require "not only the release of the slave popula-tion from their bonds and the degradation thereby imposed upon them; but the deliverance of the master population also, wholly and forever, from their mastership." To do this, the government would have to go beyond nullifying the laws of slavery and instead guarantee black civil and voting rights, break up large plantations, and establish "some uniform system of supervision and guardianship for the emancipated

population in the interim of their transition from slavery to freedom."
Most broadly, McKaye argued, the war revealed the essential, if often
forgotten relationship between human beings and their governments.
What the Army faced in Mississippi was not particular to freedpeople;
all people, not just black people, had needed government "supervision
and assistance" in the transition to free labor.[19]

As these reports from the field worked their way to Washington,
Congress continued to wrestle with the problem of ending slavery. In
the regular 1864 congressional session, opponents blocked both the
Thirteenth Amendment and Freedmen's Bureau Bill from becoming law.
Over the fall, however, electoral and military victories helped inspire
Congress to act. After the fall of Atlanta in September 1864, the question
of what would follow surrender suddenly seemed more pressing and more
concrete. Empowered by a resounding Republican victory in the
November election, Republicans returned in December for the lame-
duck Congress with the intention of passing the bills.[20]

Congressional debates over the Bureau and the Thirteenth
Amendment revealed the ways that war had unsettled old habits of
thinking. As slaves ran to U.S. lines, the American Freedmen's Inquiry
Commission delivered its reports, and Confederates fought hard to
sustain slavery, many anti-slavery politicians themselves were disenthralled. Where once they hoped slavery might slip suddenly from the
shoulders of both slaves and the nation, now they reckoned with the
tenacity of its power. Slavery "had an infernal strength greater than any
of us supposed," Maine Republican Congressman Frederick Pike said.
Senator Charles Sumner, a guiding force behind the Bureau bill, argued
that "even emancipation is not enough. You must see to it that it is not
evaded or nullified, and you must see to it especially that the new-made
freedmen are protected in those rights which are now assured to them . . .
Call it protection; call it what you will. The power of the Government
must be to them like a shield." Rather than limiting the government's
role to emancipation, Sumner used the end of slavery to illuminate the
state's role in everyone's life. "Are we not all under the general super-
intendence of the police, to which we may appeal for protection in case
of need?" Government shaped the freedom not just of freedpeople but of
all people. The following day, Sumner argued that freedmen "may now
justly look to the national Government as their guardian. It is that
Government which has given to them the great boon of freedom. It is
for us to go further, and see that freedom is something more than a

barren letter. We must see that it is a living word, of which they can avail themselves always."[21]

Other anti-slavery politicians kept slavery separate from broader issues of governance by making the new Bureau a wartime exception. Instead of revealing all people's constant dependence upon government, the Bureau should set wartime as an unusual and temporary state that disrupted normal life. In this view, peace would be restored not at the end of battles but in the moment that the Bureau became unnecessary. "We all see that the time must come, in a few years, when the operations of this Department must cease," Republican Congressman Thomas Dawes Eliot said. But "it will not do to end our care of freedmen when the war ends." Republican Senator Samuel Pomeroy voted for the bill despite its "look of permanency." "For twenty-five years I have maintained in this country everywhere that the negroes could take care of themselves."[22] In a compromise, this Bureau bill extended the agency's life for a year after hostilities closed.

It is alluring to paint objections to the Bureau's permanency as moderate defections from a Radical program, but the divisions were more complicated. Against those congressmen who imagined constant positive government intervention in everyday life, some turned to Jacksonian and Jeffersonian views that society regulated itself through individual liberty and participatory democracy. Instead of more government, freedom in peacetime emerged through personal privacy and broad enfranchisement. Senator William Sprague believed, like his father-in-law Chief Justice Salmon Chase, that extending the vote to black men would make other state actions unnecessary. In this vision – which would become increasingly alluring to some Radicals – democracy made governance irrelevant. "When a man can vote, he needs no special legislation in his behalf ... Do this, and no Freedmen's Bureau is necessary." Republican Senator Henry Lane supported some versions of the Bureau bill but worried over its statist implications. "I would make them free under the law; I would protect them in the courts of justice; if necessary, I would give them the right of suffrage ... but I wish to see no system of guardianship and pupilage and overseership ... We make them free upon the theory that they deserve freedom."[23] While the lines were never crudely drawn, the anti-slavery movement would struggle with these competing lessons of emancipation. Did a complete emancipation demand positive government or voting rights?

As some anti-slavery politicians developed their positive views of government, their opponents quickly turned old anti-slavery arguments against the Bureau. By prying at the anti-statist roots of abolitionism, they tried to tie the Bureau's defenders in knots. Why, they asked, did freed-people need government help if they were indeed equal to whites? "If you make him a freeman, and he is worthy of being a free man, allow him to go forth and attend to his own interests," Democratic Senator Lazarus Powell of Kentucky said. Instead, Republicans wished to put "masters over them to manage them." Unionist Senator John B. Henderson of Missouri claimed the Bureau undermined the entire anti-slavery theory. "What was the old argument in favor of the institution of slavery? ... It was that the African race is not competent to self-government, that the negro is not able to take care of himself, that he needs a guardian ... I believe to-day that if you turn loose the negroes of the southern States and tell them to take care of themselves they will do it." To capture the immediacy of emancipation, Henderson urged his colleagues to stop call-ing an ex-slave a "freedman." "I do not like the term; let the 'd' be dropped from it." Instead of being in the process of becoming freed, they were immediately free. Republican Senator John P. Hale said con-gressmen "virtually give the lie to the whole teaching of the anti-slavery men and women of the country so far as I have known anything of them for the last twenty years. You now say that the colored race are not competent to take care of themselves, that they want guardians and officers to protect them."[24]

In response, the Bureau's defenders developed structural critiques of slavery and government. Rather than a spell that could be disenthralled, slavery was an institution that had long-lasting effects upon self, state, and society. Republican Senator Lot Morrill sympathized "very thor-oughly" with the idea that slaves should be automatically ready for freedom but found himself baffled as previously pro-slavery politicians now cast themselves as the champions of black equality. Those who once argued that slaves were "not fit for freedom; that his only condition was that of servitude; that he must have a master and he must be a slave," now claimed that ex-slaves could achieve freedom spontaneously. Morrill changed his position in the other direction because of the "great facts" they all had to confront as they reckoned with emancipa-tion. "They come upon the surface of society unprotected, uncared for, unprovided for. Are they to exist in this unorganized, unprovided con-dition, or is it the Government which is responsible for it, the Government which has freed them, to step in and take the direction and care of these freedmen? ... We are committed, according to my understanding of the case, to some provident care and supervision over this helpless, dependent class of persons." Morrill mocked the notion that slavery could be shed so simply in wartime. "In the infinite disorder that now reigns in those States . . . there is no personal security and there is no personal protection for the rights of these men . . . We are committed to the policy that it is the duty of the Government in some way to intervene with its authority, its protecting care, over these persons." Against those who claimed the Bureau grew from paternalistic racism, Republican Senator John Conness reminded congressmen that the bill supported white refugees, too; not just black people but all people relied upon government. "I am very much inclined to believe that both white and black persons in this country who are in good health and of certain ages are abundantly able to take care of themselves," he said. "While that proposition may be true, it is also true, I apprehend, that in the sudden change from slavery to freedom there must be a great many black people who require assistance from us."[25]

Within this argument about slavery and emancipation was another set of disputes about the reach and power of government. Against both the Thirteenth Amendment's enforcement clause and the Bureau bill, Democrats critiqued what they saw as a revolutionary reach of the federal state into the counties and towns of the nation. Emancipation and abolition were revolutionary not just because they extended rights to blacks but because they created entirely new forms of rights by building new ways of accessing the federal government. Congressman Robert Mallory complained that the amendment created an "imperium in imperio in every State in the Union where slaves are free . . . It is not only a step toward the conversion of the Government from a federative to a consolidated one, but it will be the accomplishment of that purpose." Congressman Samuel Cox claimed the Thirteenth Amendment would "annul the municipal control of each State over domestic matters. Is your proposition simply to abolish slavery? Or is it a measure to invest the Federal Government with authority to enslave the local white citizen, hold him in vassalage to a central power, and assume the right to dictate to the States what their home policy shall be on home affairs?"[26]

The most-elaborate denunciation of this newly intrusive government was New York Democrat James Brooks's long oration against "homogeneity." What the Thirteenth Amendment aimed to do was to create a new uniformity in the nation. "Homogeneity, we are told, must exist through this hitherto thirty-four States of this Union. The Union cannot exist unless we are a homogeneous people." This theory failed, Brooks argued, not just because of its racial egalitarianism but also because of its vision of government. Drawing broadly upon contemporary and historical comparisons, Brooks claimed that empires survived when they governed diverse peoples with a light hand. Recounting his own walks across England, Brooks described the range of language and custom among the Gaels, the Welsh, and the English. "No effort has ever been made in England by any edict of the British Parliament at any time, or on any occasion, to have a homogeneous people. There is no centralization, no consolidation there." Reaching to the past, he claimed that "homogeneity never existed throughout the vast Roman empire ... autonomy, or self-independence, was the principle on which the great Roman empire was reared and maintained ... It was not possible for Rome; it was not possible for Athens; it will not be possible for the Government at Washington, with all the telescopes which they may mount upon the highest pinnacles in this city, to look over the vast territory from Passamaquoddy to the Rio Grande and Oregon, and to regulate the local rights and privileges of the millions and millions of people ... The vastness of the territory to be subjugated is its great defense." Centralization created not conformity but civil wars.[27] Brooks defined governments by their inherent limits. Whether or not states should impose themselves on their peripheries was not the issue; for good or ill, they could not do so. Even great empires could not extract much from their people.

Some Republicans frankly acknowledged a reformulation of rights and government power. Congressman Amos Myers mocked "that great question of 'homogeneity.'" The 1864 election showed that "we want 'homogeneity' as a nation ... We want the homogeneity of patriotism, and not of treason; of Unionism, and not of disseveration; that of geographical and social attachment, and not of physical disintegration and governmental antagonism." Radical leader Thaddeus Stevens responded by separating culture from law. While empires always embraced other races, language groups, and customs, "the question of homogeneity has nothing to do with the abolition of slavery. If the gentleman had shown that confederations could have no uniform laws operating over all their members, he would have argued to the point. This is a question of the *uniformity* of national laws operating over the whole republic."[28]

On the ground in the ex-Confederacy, and especially near the end of battles, converging redefinitions of freedom impelled new policies to ensure it. Empowered by the war's end and by the Thirteenth Amendment, commanders in hundreds of Army posts in the summer of 1865 formed the machinery of the newly ambitious and accessible federal government. Just as runaway slaves had played crucial roles in shifting

Northern politicians' understanding of slavery, the freedpeople who approached officers in the field transformed those soldiers' views of freedom. As slaveowners' resistance in the Mississippi Valley inspired Congressional action, so, too, did planters' increasingly violent efforts to remake slavery teach officers to use government against them. Imagining that slaves could make their own freedom makes slavery too weak, government too obscure, freedom too vague.

The great problem that soldiers and slaves faced at the end of the fighting in the Civil War was that slavery continued. Even months after Appomattox, Army officers, Bureau agents, and ex-slaves reported that the institution survived in regions that U.S. soldiers had not reached. Of the nearly 4 million slaves in the United States in 1860, the vast majority – perhaps 2.75 million – were still held in bondage as the Confederate armies surrendered. Of course the terms of that slavery had changed. With the wartime breakdown of plantation discipline, some planters shifted to wages or sharecropping, and some slaves stopped working or refused to plant cash crops. Appomattox did inspire some planters to announce the end of slavery and make new arrangements with the freedpeople, and some slaves responded to the news by claiming freedom for themselves, but in many places it was the presence of soldiers who finally signaled the end of the institution.[29]

Over the spring and summer of 1865, officers and Bureau agents reported finding "slavery everywhere." In some regions, planters simply hid the existence of the war's end. In others they retained control of the roads in ways that kept slaves from running. Other planters believed that the restoration of their states would bring peace that ended the power of the Emancipation Proclamation and a defeat of the Thirteenth Amendment. With that, they would be able to sue for their property in court. As they faced the stubborn survival of slavery, officers and Bureau agents wrestled with the limits of legal pronouncements. Freedom could not emerge simply from a proclamation but would have to be weeded out place by place, and by force. Officers and agents learned from ex-slaves like Louis Hughes to see that freedom was a statist project, one that could only be fulfilled by proximity and power.[30]

Soldiers' struggles against slavery explain the ongoing occupation of the South. In the immediate weeks after the largest Rebel armies surrendered, U.S. troops spread out across the South, occupying more than 400 county seats and market towns in the ex-Confederacy as they disestablished or re-established local governments. Having either engaged with magistrates or appointed police, these Army outposts might have shrunk back into capital cities in summertime, but instead they maintained their reach over the South, holding on to more than 400 outposts into the Fall of 1865. In some states with aggressive commanders, the Army pulsed outward to ninety posts in Georgia in the Fall of 1865, and thirty-seven in Florida; others stayed stable or declined slightly. The Army held its grip on the Southern countryside in order to pry slavery's hands from power. While many slaves ran to liberty, most defined their final freedom through announcements after Appomattox. This was particularly true for women, children, and older slaves who could not or would not leave their families to run to U.S. lines but worked to keep communities intact and alive at home. This does not mean slaves were passive recipients of freedom; it means they worked to understand and acquire freedom as they also recognized the importance of government recognition to their own efforts.[31] Slaves recognized this; they ran to soldiers not just because they had guns but also because they could provide the recognition that freedom demanded. However our own actions support our freedom, freedom properly defined does not exist internally; it exists when recognized by the other. The reason for this is obvious; freedom alone does not bring any guarantees of its endurance. A freedom without fear of infringement has never existed, and will never exist. To be meaningful, freedom requires recognition because true freedom carries the promise that violations will be met with force, even if smoothly functioning societies obscure this central fact. Slaves needed soldiers not because they were afraid at the moment of emancipation but because they needed to know where they should turn when their freedom was attacked, as they knew it would be.

In the thrill and agony of emancipation, slaves and soldiers revealed the central role of the state in shaping both slavery and freedom in ways that echoed Hughes's experience. While most ex-slave autobiographies were not as nuanced and descriptive as Hughes's, many of those published after the war described the crucial role of U.S. soldiers and agents in ending slavery. In his description of the end of slavery in his landmark *Up from Slavery,* Booker T. Washington acknowledged that slaves had been talking about freedom for a long time but also that the moment a soldier or agent read the Emancipation Proclamation was a powerful one. Slaves did not need the federal government to tell them they wanted or deserved freedom, but they did need government to convey the authority that freedom depended upon.[32]

In interviews conducted seventy years later, many elderly former slaves remembered soldiers' participation in a ritual of emancipation that simultaneously proclaimed freedom and undermined the masters' power. While scholars sometimes dismiss their stories because they were relayed decades later by people who were children at emancipation and were frequently talking to white Southern interviewers, the records offer access to women and barely literate men whose stories are not recounted in memoirs. Mary Anderson, a slave in Franklinton, North Carolina, captured the many layers of knowledge that slaves possessed of freedom. During the war, the "news went from plantation to plantation," and slaves "prayed for freedom." One day, they heard loud booming sounds, and their master told them, "Men, women and children, you are free. You are no longer my slaves. The Yankees will be here." For an hour, everyone waited until they saw a long line of United States soldiers marching from Louisburg. "They called the slaves, saying, 'Your are free.'" While Anderson did not mention the response to the master's statement, the soldiers' announcement unleashed a deep excitement. "Slaves were whooping and laughing and acting like they were crazy. Yankee soldiers were shaking hands with the Negroes and calling them Sam, Dinah, Sarah, and asking them questions."[33] When soldiers did not arrive, freedpeople often sought out freedom rituals by traveling to neighboring towns in search of provost marshals, post commanders, or the newly arriving Freedmen's Bureau agents.

Depending upon soldiers to ratify freedom made the end of slavery piecemeal and disjointed. On Mattie Logan's plantation in Mississippi, a Northerner came to the plantation and told the slaves in the field that they were free, but "he didn't know about the cabin we lived in and didn't tell my folks nothing about it." A while later the master called her parents in and told them they were free.[34] Ambrose Douglass, held a slave in North Carolina, captured the perils of tying emancipation to soldiers' presence. "I guess we musta celebrated 'mancipation about twelve time ... Every time a bunch of No'thern sojers would come through they would tell us we was free and we'd begin celebratin'. Before we would get through somebody else would tell us to go back to work, and we would go."[35] Other planters tried to keep ex-slaves working on the land by announcing their freedom before soldiers arrived.

Although wage labor and marriage shaped part of the definition of freedom, other aspects of freedom also mattered. Drawing upon the expansive local governments of the increasingly wage-labor North, the persistent power of Whig ideological support for a strong central state, and the exigencies of war, many Republicans developed a broad vision that freedom depended upon attachment to a state that restrained everyone. As Northern officers and agents moved southward, their experience with slavery gave weight to the belief that a strong government was necessary to restrain disorder and chaos. To them, freedom and unrestrained liberty therefore seemed increasingly like opposites, not just because Northern soldiers feared black people wandering around as vagrants, but also because they came to believe freedom existed only through government coercion. With their eye upon the state, they made freedom and order not contradictory but complementary. But when freedpeople drew upon other old American (and generally rural) traditions of tying freedom to land ownership, this found less headway with soldiers and agents.

As they struggled to define the freedom that would signal peacetime, provost marshals, post commanders, and Bureau agents tried to determine what infringements demanded a response. Could free people be whipped by their employer? Was a right to testify integral to freedom? Did freedom demand a general sense of fair play? Were people subject to intensifying campaigns of violence truly free? If not, then who could guarantee freedom and by what means? Over and over again, freedpeople brought these questions to Bureau agents and Army outposts, asking whether their condition constituted freedom. While the question of property ownership would be settled later in the summer by the president, many other policies were worked out on the ground in the interactions between officers and freedpeople.

Across the South, Army officers and Freedmen's Bureau agents created a notion of freedom as defensible rights through the complaints they received from freedpeople. In Army posts or in standalone Bureau offices, agents responded to complaints about the treatment of freedpeople by expanding the meaning of freedom and developing a newly concrete notion of defensible rights. After Bureau agents worked through the continued existence of slavery and distributed contracts, they began to wrestle with the persistence of "plantation discipline" through whipping or other forms of ritual punishment.[36] Turning from actual enslavement to the feel of freedom, agents and officers warned that unchecked planter power "would render the position of the negro more grievous than before."[37] Military officials in turn used war powers to ban whipping, dispatched troops into the countryside to respond to complaints of bad treatment, overruled discriminatory laws, and arrested violent planters. These rights supported not just legal but practical freedom. This posed a problem, however. If practical freedom depended upon the proximity of the Army, what would happen when the Army went home? This was one of the dismaying questions that hung over emancipation – and the very definition of freedom – in the months after the end of fighting. If practical freedom truly depended upon the proximity of a federal government's coercive power, then what would happen when that coercive power went home? Although freedpeople constructed self-defense organizations, Republican congressmen fashioned federal court remedies, and reconstructed state governments tried to make defensible state laws to protect freedom, the relationship between freedom and proximate force was a troubling one.

While there would be no permanent wartime, for the years after Appomattox, the Army's posts in the South shaped the timing and meaning of emancipation. The need to sustain freedom meant ongoing occupation at outposts where the soldiers changed both freedpeople's organizing strategies and their sense of the power of the national government. Freedpeople taught soldiers to define occupation through the defense of rights. In turn, access to officers gave leading freedpeople a rare practical good they could deliver to their potential constituents. Relying upon coercion created its own dilemmas. On the one hand, the Army in some places – especially Charleston and Savannah and for a time in Richmond – treated freedpeople cruelly. There was certainly no shortage of racist soldiers. On the other hand, the Army moved units and even commanders who mistreated freedpeople, and many racist soldiers seemed to hate Confederates much more than freedpeople as they witnessed violent attacks on freedpeople, white Northerners, and even soldiers.[38] Through it all freedpeople were "always fleeing to the nearest Military post and seeking protection of the law."[39] In Mississippi, freedpeople stayed on plantations in the river belts that had been occupied during the war, but fled from other regions where there was "no civil or military law" to get "to the nearest military post with all their children and effects."[40] Although almost all United States soldiers attracted freedpeople's attention, black soldiers particularly captured ex-slaves' imagination. The image of the former in uniform signaled the revolutionary impact of the war, and buttressed their hopes for future equality. Black soldiers also hosted schools and churches in the barracks.

One traveler through Georgia captured the complexity of depending upon soldiers' presence to define freedom. He had no illusions that soldiers would use their power wisely; he knew of terrible stories of "outrages" by cavalry in Savannah. Still, he saw that freedpeople flocked to the outposts, viewing soldiers as imperfect but available vessels for justice. As he pondered the centrality of troops, he wondered what would follow their departure. The Army opened up a new vision for him of rights making that reached into every precinct and crevice "with power in the national executive, to enforce it in behalf of every American citizen. We are establishing an American nationality; let us at the same time establish an American citizenship." To be meaningful it would have to be both enforceable and present. "Let it not be subject to the prejudices and caprices of sections but give it the right to assert itself everywhere." He could see only one hope for the future, the extension of war powers into peacetime. "The protection we have now only under the abnormal war powers of the President . . . should become part of the fundamental law of the nation."[41]

This permanent extension of wartime into peace was, of course, not to be. Even the most active Radicals did not wish a long-term occupation of the South but hoped that federal laws, amendments, and enfranchisement would create defensible rights. In some ways, of course, they were prescient; the framework of federal protection of freedom established between 1866 and 1875 became the prototype for the 1950s and 1960s establishment of civil rights. While scholars sometimes blame the Supreme Court for thinning those rights in the nineteenth century, in fact the primary challenge was not the lack of abstract rights but of recognition.

Without a contemporary Justice Department (the Attorney General employed two clerks in 1865), there was no mechanism for enforcement, and the Enforcement Acts against the Ku Klux Klan were quickly shorn away by hostile congressional Democrats. If practical freedom meant acquired rights that would be defended by proximate allies, parts of that freedom evaporated in the 1870s through 1900s not because the rights did not exist or because freedpeople did not assert them, but because they lacked proximate allies to enforce them.

By thinking about the relationship between freedom and force, we can shed the alluring tug that metaphors of a land of freedom or time of freedom exert, sometimes unconsciously, over our analysis. Instead of freedom as an endpoint toward which we are inexorably drawn or an ideal we can never match, we might capture the particular definition of freedom on the ground at war's end, the interactive nature of freedpeople's engagement with soldiers, and the challenge of sustaining a freedom built upon access to defenders who would not remain. Despite American attachment to constitutionalism on both the left and the right, freedom was a disappointment not because of imperfectly crafted amendments but because of what John Hope Franklin defined a half-century ago as a basic lack of force. Thinking about the limitations of freedom through the lens of enforcement may help construct new storylines of emancipation and Reconstruction, and to once again wrest Reconstruction from the pull of the civil rights–movement narrative and to permit us to see it on its own terms, with its peculiar problems of governance and state building. At the same time, this emphasis on enforcement may also be a useful prod to a civil rights–movement literature that at times emphasizes grassroots mobilizing and high legal pronouncements over the 101st Airborne (and the nationalized Arkansas National Guard) that cleared the streets and opened the doors in Little Rock. While it is understandable that we might wish to elide the role of force in making rights, and to see the limitations of the past in ideological or cultural terms, I do not believe that we will be able to make sense of the gains and limits of emancipation and Reconstruction until we wrestle with the painful, contradictory, but compelling interrelationship between freedom and coercion.   ⤲

NOTES

1. Henry Bibb, *Narrative of the Life and Adventures of Henry Bibb: An American Slave,* written by himself (New York: The Author, 1849), 28–30.
2. *Psalms* 119:45, from King James Bible.
3. Along with the broader works on the spatial turn cited by Sternhell, important work on slaves' imaginative reconfiguration of their geographic space includes Stephanie M.H. Camp, "'I Could Not Stay There': Enslaved Women, Truancy and the Geography of Everyday Forms of Resistance in the Antebellum South," *Slavery & Abolition* 23, no. 3 (2002): 1–20; Stephanie M. H. Camp, *Closer to Freedom: Enslaved Women and Everyday Resistance in the Plantation South* (Chapel Hill: University of North Carolina Press, 2004); Anthony E. Kaye, "Neighborhoods and Nat Turner: The Making of a Slave Rebel and the Unmaking of a Slave Rebellion," *Journal of the Early Republic* 27, no. 4 (2007): 705–720; Kaye, "Neighbourhoods and Solidarity in the Natchez District of Mississippi: Rethinking the Antebellum Slave Community," *Slavery & Abolition* 23, no. 1 (2002): 1–24; Kaye, *Joining Places: Slave Neighborhoods in the Old South* (Chapel Hill: University of North Carolina Press, 2007).
4. "No idea is more fundamental to Americans' sense of themselves as individuals and as a nation than freedom," Foner wrote. Eric Foner, *The Story of American Freedom* (New York: Norton, 1999), xiii, xv. Orlando Patterson historicizes conflicts over freedom without losing sight of the word's ultimate meanings in Patterson, *Freedom in the Making of Western Culture* (New York: Basic Books, 1991).
5. Sternhell, Chapter 1 of this volume.
6. Sternhell, Chapter 1.
7. Sternhell, Chapter 1.
8. The freedom paradigm arose in the 1960s and 1970s as both leftist and rightist critiques of the state shifted toward a broad anti-statism. By the 1990s, Foucault's critique of a nebulous power and his association of liberal state

coercion and mid-twentieth-century totalitarianism reinforced a tendency to
see state action as the instigating event for declension narratives on both the
left and right.

Foner's nuance saved Reconstruction from some of the excesses of other
fields, but the trend toward portraying atomized individuals beset by an
intrusive state does play out in Reconstruction historiography. With more
distance from both 1960s anti-statism and 1990s critiques of power, it is now
time for a reading of Reconstruction that treats freedom, once again, as
embedded in the state, not just in opposition to it. On the broader question
of anti-statism on both left and right since the 1960s, see Michael B. Katz,
"Was Government the Solution or the Problem?: The Role of the State in the
History of American Social Policy," *Theory and Society* 39, no. 3–4 (2010):
487–502; Katz, "The Existential Problem of Urban Studies," *Dissent* 57, no.
4 (2010): 65–68; Daniel T. Rodgers, *Age of Fracture* (Cambridge, Mass:
Harvard University Press, 2011).

9. For an effort to redefine mid-nineteenth-century history upon the struggle to
define new boundaries for coercion, see Steven Hahn, "Slave Emancipation,
Indian Peoples, and the Projects of the New American Nation-State," *Journal
of the Civil War Era* 3, no. 3 (2013): 307–330.

10. See in this volume William A. Blair, Chapter 3; Justin Behrend, Chapter 6; and
Laura Edwards, Epilogue.

11. Louis Hughes, *Thirty Years a Slave: From Bondage to Freedom, the
Institution of Slavery as Seen on the Plantation and in the Home of the
Planter* (Milwaukee: South Side Printing Co., 1897), 172–187.

12. Hughes, *Thirty Years a Slave*, 172–187.

13. Ibid.

14. On the Slave Power rhetoric, see Leonard L. Richards, *The Slave Power: The
Free North and Southern Domination, 1780–1860* (Baton Rouge: Louisiana
State University Press, 2000); David Brion Davis, *The Slave Power
Conspiracy and the Paranoid Style* (Baton Rouge: Louisiana State
University Press, 1970); Eric Foner, *Free Soil, Free Labor, Free Men: The
Ideology of the Republican Party Before the Civil War* (New York: Oxford
University Press, 1970), 73–102. On the Democratic roots of anti-slavery
politics, see Jonathan H. Earle, *Jacksonian Antislavery and the Politics of Free
Soil, 1824–1854* (Chapel Hill: University of North Carolina Press, 2004).

15. *Congressional Globe,* 38th Cong., 2nd Sess., 120–122.

16. *Atlantic Monthly,* July 1866, 120–122.

17. Scholars still struggle to reconcile slavery's strengths and weaknesses. No
recent historian except David Goldfield has argued that slavery was on a
natural path to extinction, and most writers understand planters' economic
strength and their power over statewide and national politics. This portrayal
of slavery's vitality still sits uneasily with plantation-focused studies that
emphasize the thinness of planter control. Over the past decade, Nell
Painter's effort to capture slavery's impact upon slaves has led scholars
increasingly to investigate the impact of violence and other forms of surveil-
lance upon slave life. Recent work by Walter Johnson and Edward Baptist
pushes toward synthesizing a view of slavery's national and internal power in

ways that undermine earlier emphasis upon slave agency. David R. Goldfield, *America Aflame: How the Civil War Created a Nation* (New York: Bloomsbury, 2012); Nell Irvin Painter, "Soul Murder and Slavery: Toward a Fully Loaded Cost Accounting" in Painter, *Southern History across the Color Line* (Chapel Hill: University of North Carolina Press, 2002): 15–39; Walter Johnson, *River of Dark Dreams: Slavery and Empire in the Cotton Kingdom* (Cambridge, Mass.: Harvard University Press, 2013); Edward E. Baptist, *The Half Has Never Been Told: Slavery and the Making of American Capitalism* (New York: Basic Books, 2014).

18. James MacKaye, *The Mastership and Its Fruits: The Emancipated Slave Face to Face with His Old Master. A Supplemental Report to Hon. Edwin Stanton, Secretary of War* (New York: Loyal Publication Society, 1864), 4, 21–22, 25, 29–30.

19. Ibid., 33–38.

20. *U.S. Statutes at Large*, vol. 13, 507–509.

21. *Congressional Globe*, 38th Cong., 2nd Sess., 487–488, 961, 989.

22. Ibid., 694, 959–960.

23. Ibid., 960, 985.

24. Ibid., 962–963, 985, 1308.

25. Ibid., 985–986, 988.

26. Ibid., 125, 179–182.

27. Ibid., 38–41.

28. Ibid., 84–86, 124.

29. I develop the argument about occupation, the end of slavery, and construction of defensible rights in Gregory P. Downs, *After Appomattox: Military Occupation and the Ends of War* (Cambridge, Mass.: Harvard University Press, 2015).

30. Charles Bentzoni to Dear Sir, July 7, 1865, RG 107, M 752, Reel 13, Registers and Letters Received by the Commissioner of the Bureau of Refugees, Freedmen, and Abandoned Lands, 1865–1872: Letters Received, Mar.–Oct. 1865, National Archives, Washington D.C.; Leon F. Litwack, *Been in the Storm So Long: The Aftermath of Slavery* (New York: Knopf, 1979), esp. 113–118.

31. For data on the occupation, see Gregory P. Downs and Scott Nesbit, "Mapping Occupation: Force, Freedom, and the Army in Reconstruction," http://mappingoccupation.org.

32. Booker T. Washington, *Up from Slavery: An Autobiography* (Garden City, New York: Doubleday & Co., 1900), 19–23.

33. *Slave Narratives: A Folk History of Slavery in the United States from Interviews with Former Slaves*, (Washington, D.C.: Library of Congress, 1941), North Carolina, vol. XI, Part 1, 23–24.

34. Ibid., Oklahoma, vol. XIII, 190–191.

35. Ibid., Florida, vol. 3, 103.

36. Charles C. Soule to O. O. Howard, June 12, 1865, RG 107, M 752, Reel 17, Registers and Letters Received by the Commissioner of the Bureau of Refugees, Freedmen, and Abandoned Lands, 1865–1872: Letters Received, Mar.–Oct. 1865, National Archives, Washington, D.C.; Thomas W. Conway

to Howard, May 26, 1865, RG 107, M 752, Reel 14, Registers and Letters Received by the Commissioner of the Bureau of Refugees, Freedmen, and Abandoned Lands, 1865–1872: Letters Received, Mar.–Oct. 1865, National Archives, Washington, D.C.

37. T. W. Conway to Howard, July 21, 1865, RG 107, M 752, Reel 14, Registers and Letters Received by the Commissioner of the Bureau of Refugees, Freedmen, and Abandoned Lands, 1865–1872: Letters Received, Mar.–Oct. 1865, National Archives, Washington, D.C.

38. After decades of skepticism about Army officers' commitment to anti-slavery, recent work has emphasized the role of the war in turning previously moderate or even conservative officers into committed emancipators by 1863 and 1864. See, especially, Chandra Manning, *What This Cruel War Was Over: Soldiers, Slavery, and the Civil War* (New York: Knopf, 2007).

39. C.H. Van Wyck to Major Burger, Sept. 1, 1865, enclosed in George Meade to Secretary of War, Sept. 20, 1865, A 1370, RG 94, M 619, National Archives, Washington, D.C.

40. Samuel Thomas to O.O. Howard, Oct. 12, 1865, RG 107, M 752, Reel 22, Registers and Letters Received by the Commissioner of the Bureau of Refugees, Freedmen, and Abandoned Lands, 1865–1872: Letters Received, Oct. 1865–Feb. 1866, National Archives, Washington, D.C.

41. *Army and Navy Journal*, Oct. 21, 1865, 130–131.

3

Military Interference in Elections as an Influence on Abolition

William A. Blair

The abolition of slavery required more than a presidential proclamation; it also involved a tough legislative battle – one that benefited from having sympathetic lawmakers come to Washington because of elections that Union soldiers screened. Consequently, there is an additional story of emancipation that remains under-appreciated – how the political process unfolded during wartime through questionable military intervention that contributed to the Thirteenth Amendment. Viewing the coercive measures that aided emancipation underscores, like the other essays in this volume, that the process was contested and dynamic. And, as Gregory P. Downs affirms in Chapter 2, the arms of a powerful state added muscle to the freedom struggle. Military officers on the ground, both during and after the war, could set the tone and tempo for freedom's coming. But while his story includes the interaction of freedpeople with soldiers, this one demonstrates how officials in Washington supported the deployment of the military in a way that ostensibly contradicted the principles of a democracy. These were actions taken against supposedly loyal people, not a defeated enemy. The Thirteenth Amendment owes part of its birth to hard-nosed tactics that included soldiers screening elections, which the practitioners at the time rationalized as preventing domestic traitors from disturbing free elections.

Abraham Lincoln allowed soldiers to prevent traitors from exercising the franchise – a fact that has not escaped historians. In the 1920s, E. Merton Coulter's work on Kentucky noticed the military's interference in elections in the border states and decried the practice. Without necessarily referring to troops stationed at the ballot box, more recent historians have shown the president as embracing a tough brand of politics, but doing so selectively in order to achieve high ideals. In this view he was a nationalist, conscious of reining in executive powers at the proper time. However, the military's role in emancipation remains present primarily in state studies or discrete monographs: general histories and biographical treatments of Lincoln in particular have overlooked the fact that, under the chief executive's watch, the military's interference in elections allowed for pro-administration men to gain public office in time to further the cause of emancipation.[1]

Political scientist Richard Franklin Bensel, in contrast, offers the intriguing hypothesis that the intrusion of federal arms into the democratic process may have, in fact, made the difference in the outcome of the war by easing the way for the right men at the right moment to assist the administration's goals. Throughout the war, but especially during 1863, the Union military supervised elections, primarily in the border states, where public officials feared divided loyalties might disrupt elections. In this region, where slavery remained protected from the Proclamation, soldiers guarded polling places, disqualified candidates, closed precincts, and enforced loyalty oaths aimed at Democratic opponents of Lincoln. The ultimate goal of these men and their superiors may have resided more in preservation of the Union than in changing the equation for freedom in the country. If so, the unintended consequences of their actions still achieved such a purpose. In 1863, a minimum of two congressional seats benefitted, as well as a number of state positions. In addition, the executive branch, which controlled the Army, furloughed right-thinking soldiers both in 1863 and 1864 so they could vote in home districts. Authorities also pressured military officers to resign if they seemed inclined to support Democratic peace candidates.[2]

It may puzzle contemporary sensibilities how contingent the federal process of emancipation was, and why authorities both high and low could sanction interference with elections. Even as late as the summer of 1864, War Democrats – the soldiers and citizens who supported Lincoln's policies even though they were not within his political party – embraced emancipation as a limited means to defeat the rebel traitors, expecting that slaves who were not freed by the military during the war might well remain in bondage. The editor of the Green Bay, Wisconsin, newspaper erupted in outrage in 1864 when he learned that the president dictated emancipation for all slaves as an essential negotiation point for ending the war with the Confederacy. "This puts the whole war question on a new basis," Charles D. Robinson told Lincoln, "and takes us War Democrats clear off our feet, leaving us no ground to stand upon."[3] The nation's precedent for emancipation in wartime was the Revolutionary War, when slaves achieved freedom by fighting for the Patriots. But bondage remained the norm for most of the enslaved. Abolition in the early republic was determined by state governments, not the national legislature. So it was possible – no matter if realistic – for people in some quarters to conceive of a limited emancipation even in the 1860s. Plus, the use of a constitutional amendment to end slavery contradicted beliefs in a "static" Constitution: that changing the fundamental law, in the words of historian Michael Vorenberg, would "stain the national character and render life rudderless" by challenging the work of the founding generation. It took until deep into 1864 before even Republicans came to a consensus on a constitutional amendment as the vehicle for abolition.[4] Full emancipation required a sustained, hard effort on many levels, with the Army instrumental both in enforcing military emancipation in the insurgent states and, as we now see, in helping to enact a general, permanent freedom.

Elections in the border region became worrisome for federal soldiers and civil authorities, who recognized the possibility of secession sympathizers intimidating Unionists. At this point in America's history, it was much easier to influence an election. No secret ballot existed – an innovation that would come later in the nineteenth century, when Americans borrowed the idea from the Australians. In America during the Civil War, prospective voters came to the polls with pre-printed tickets, many of them clipped from newspapers, which they then handed over to election judges, most often through a voting window. From the time that a voter entered the vicinity of a precinct, ample opportunity existed to discern how he was going to vote, giving opponents a chance to interfere. Election Days, hardly solemn occasions, could become boisterous – and sometimes dangerous. Party agents plied voters with whiskey, hired people to intimidate voters from the other side, falsified voter identification, and manipulated returns. Some voters died and others sustained wounds. And this was the political culture typical of *peacetime*.[5] Given the tensions of a Civil War, and the uncertainty over security in the border region, Republicans and Unionists often considered the military's presence at the polls a necessity.

The president understood the political culture in which he operated. In fact, he was a more than capable practitioner. Before the war, while campaigning for the U.S. Senate seat, he worried about the other side using itinerant Irish railroad workers to stuff ballot boxes for Stephen Douglas. To Norman Judd, a Chicago attorney who managed the campaign in northern Illinois, Lincoln made "a bare suggestion." He asked, "When there is a known body of these voters, could not a true man, of the 'detective' class, be introduced among them in disguise, who could, at the nick of time, control their votes?" He added in a classic Lincoln metaphor: "It would be a great thing, when this trick is attempted upon us, to have the saddle come up on the other horse." He mentioned that he "talked, more fully than I can write," to another political crony who would convey additional information to Judd. What those details were that he could not put into writing, and what they actually may have done during the polling, only heaven knows. In his assessment of Lincoln as a politician, David Donald called him a "master wirepuller" who knew how to oversee patronage, platform, and candidates in Illinois.[6]

Lincoln allowed the military to supervise elections, but finding a link between the military's interference at polling precincts and advancing emancipation by whatever means remains speculative. Whether with the intention of influencing the Thirteenth Amendment, or with a desire to protect the ballot from enemies of state, the intrusion of soldiers into elections resulted in anti-slavery legislators and U.S. congressmen coming to power during a crucial moment of the war. And even if motivations cannot be nailed down precisely, the exercise reveals the jaw-dropping nature of "normal" nineteenth-century American politics and an under-appreciated part of the process of emancipation. Historians have duly noted the military's importance for freedom in prompting the flight of slaves in the Confederate States and enforcing the spirit of Lincoln's Proclamation.[7] Less frequently have they considered the military's hard war that was conducted away from the battlefield and in the streets of the communities loyal to the Union. What it took to win the Civil War was often dirty business in which the Constitution became stretched and soldiers committed acts that should raise eyebrows, even as these very same acts figured mightily in the march toward freedom.

At first, the northern public did not mind military interference in elections and the legislative process. They justified such measures as fighting disunion and ferreting out the traitors in their midst. In 1861, even a conservative Union general such as George B. McClellan had no trouble enforcing the arrests of the Maryland legislators because it appeared that secessionists remained embedded in the fabric of northern politics. By 1863, however, political life changed dramatically in the Union, making the military's use in elections more controversial. Democrats in particular began to decry various acts by the administration, such as arrests of newspaper editors and religious figures, as attempts to stifle a political opposition. The mood among a segment of Democrats turned sour against both military arrests and the presence of troops in elections as soldiers interfered with either the campaigning or the balloting in Ohio, Kansas, Kentucky, Missouri, and Maryland.

In 1863 the most controversial event of all was the arrest and trial by military commission of Clement L. Vallandigham for treason against the United States. It exposed a dynamic that was fairly typical, with actions occurring out in the field without necessarily having been initiated from Washington. Major General Ambrose Burnside, who supervised the Department of the Ohio, had issued directives that essentially defined any expression of sympathy for the rebels as a possible capital offense. General Orders No. 38 probably were known by the War Department, and thus sanctioned, but Burnside appears to have acted on his own in directing his soldiers to arrest Vallandigham for making a political speech while running for governor of Ohio. Vallandigham was tried in a military court, convicted, and sentenced to imprisonment for the duration of the war. Lincoln did not want to make the politician a martyr and so changed the punishment to banishment.[8] But the incident created a firestorm that drew greater attention to the military interfering with elections and added momentum to the growing opposition to Lincoln's administration of the war.

Federal intervention in elections took place throughout 1863 in the border states of Delaware, Kentucky, Missouri, and Maryland, with the results generally favoring supporters of Lincoln's policies. On July 31, Burnside issued General Orders No. 120 for his Department of the Ohio – which included portions of the Midwest and Kentucky – that declared martial law for the elections that August. Burnside said the rebels intended to intimidate the loyal voters, "forcing the election of disloyal candidates." He had a point: rebels under Confederate Brigadier General John Hunt Morgan threatened the region. Burnside indicated that civilian election judges would administer the balloting, supported by soldiers who protected the rights of loyal citizens and maintained "the purity of the suffrage." What one said in public mattered, as the military often interpreted criticism of the administration or cheers for the Confederacy as traitorous speech. In western Kentucky, a military commander prohibited from voting persons under arrest or imprisoned "for uttering disloyal language or sentiments."[9]

In Lexington on August 3, 1863, Election Day, described by a woman as "unusually quiet," resulted in a large Unionist victory. The election featured military interference. One officer in particular adopted Draconian measures. Brigadier General Jeremiah T. Boyle, an anti-slavery

Republican, ran for Congress and jailed his opponent. That sounds bad enough, but astonishingly there was more. He then declared that anyone voting for the peace Democrat would be considered a Confederate sympathizer whose property could be seized. A Kentucky woman noted in her diary that she believed that fewer than half of the state participated in the election.[10] Boyle did not win the election, revealing the public's distaste for his aggression, but the Union Democrats more compatible with Lincoln's policies gained majorities in both branches of state government, as well as the governor's office.

This instance was repeated elsewhere in Kentucky. Pro-administration candidate Thomas E. Bramlette was elected governor over Charles A. Wickliffe, a congressman and outspoken critic. After the election, the Democratic Party in the state produced a pamphlet in which it outlined the irregularities by soldiers which likely affected the outcome. The authors alleged that the names of Democratic candidates were stricken from poll books, among other indiscretions.[11] Still, Kentucky was a hard nut to crack. Bramlette, too, eventually turned against Lincoln and the federal government's recruitment of African Americans as soldiers. The state voted against Lincoln in 1864 and did not ratify the Thirteenth Amendment until a very late, primarily symbolic, gesture in 1976.

Maryland and Delaware provided more interesting stories demonstrating how interference in elections contained a bonus for the process of emancipation. In Maryland, the government clearly affected at least one congressional race as well as lesser political offices, with anti-slavery men winning a majority of the seats. The military commander of the region, Brigadier General Robert Schenck, issued General Orders No. 53, which called on provost marshals to arrest disloyal persons who approached polling places, to support judges of elections in requiring an oath of loyalty to the United States, and to report election supervisors who did not require an oath. When called on to explain his actions by Lincoln, Schenck made a beeline for Washington. As he told Stanton, "If it [Order. No. 53] is revoked, we lose this State."[12] Lincoln listened and probably became convinced that Schenck did not exaggerate the possibility of violence at the polls. He also noted that the state had no loyalty oath as a requirement for voting, which meant there was no screening process at the state level for qualifying loyal voters. Under the circumstances, federal intervention made some sense, although not to the governor of the state, who strenuously objected. However, Lincoln modified the order, rewording the first paragraph to eliminate the phrase that encouraged the military to arrest disloyal people at the ballot box. Instead, his editing instructed the military to maintain the peace, omitting the mandate to arrest reputedly ~~disloyal voters. But he let the~~ overall policy stand, allowing Schenck to post his troops at precincts on Election Day.[13]

The most egregious interference in Maryland occurred in the First District, on the southern tip of the eastern shore of the Chesapeake Bay. In the election for Congress, John A.J. Creswell, Unconditional Unionist (translation: pro-emancipationist), defeated John W. Crisfield, Union candidate (translation: Union without emancipation). In 1862, Crisfield in fact had written a scathing rejection of Lincoln's plan for compensated emancipation in the border states, a document signed by twenty-one congressmen, who saw the measure as a "radical change of our social system." A slaveowner himself, Crisfield could hardly be expected to help the cause of abolition.[14] On November 4, 1863, Captain Charles C. Moore presided over the balloting. He shut down the election after exactly one person had voted in a precinct that had traditionally featured more than 300 voters. The person who triggered the cavalry officer to act was the second man to step up to cast his ballot – the congressional candidate's son.

Arthur Crisfield had tried to vote legally, but the military prevented him from submitting a ballot on behalf of his father. The cavalry officer overseeing this district grilled the younger Crisfield on his political beliefs. Was he loyal? Yes. Had he taken arms up against the United States? No. Did he consider the rebellion an unholy war that ought to be put down? Yes. Would he sacrifice his property to put down this rebellion? Yes. Finally, an election judge protested the procedure, claiming that the officer's questioning slowed the balloting so much that it jeopardized finishing within the allotted time. Captain Moore had a ready solution: he ordered his soldiers to arrest the judges of elections and shut down the polling place, leaving on record the one and only vote cast.[15] The elder Crisfield had served as a Whig in the Thirtieth Congress with Lincoln, but he was not on the right side now.

Nonetheless, the president paid Crisfield the courtesy of letting authorities investigate the matter. He endorsed putting Captain Moore on trial before a military commission for exceeding the parameters of General Orders No. 53. The commission, however, quickly exonerated the captain, saying the judges of elections had brought the arrests on themselves by refusing to administer oaths, thus disobeying the order from Schenck. The election stood. And the man more favorable to the administration went to Washington, where he provided support for the Thirteenth Amendment.[16]

An investigation by a Maryland legislative committee in January 1864 recorded additional meddling on the part of soldiers. Election Day had arrived with three different tickets in circulation. The ballots for Unconditional Unionists (supporters of Lincoln) were printed on yellow paper, Conservative Unionists (not total supporters of Lincoln) on white paper, and Democrats (definitely against Lincoln) on ... it does not matter, because they had virtually no presence in this campaign. This election came down to a choice between yellow tickets (good for Lincoln) and white tickets (bad for Lincoln). Quickly, it became clear that the soldiers allowed yellow tickets to be cast – sometimes without requiring an oath of loyalty – while white ballots provoked a challenge, initiated a test oath, or caused voters to be sent home without casting a ballot.[17]

In the neighboring state of Delaware – also under General Schenck's jurisdiction – one of the congressional campaigns took a strange turn because of what had happened in Maryland. The results invariably favored the cause of anti-slavery, even though no supporter of the administration could have anticipated such an outcome. Peace Democrat Charles Brown, referred to by his detractors as the anti-emancipation candidate, opposed Republican N.B. Smithers for Congress in a special election to fill a vacancy created by a death. The Democratic press confidently predicted victory for its champion. To say that the Republican won in a landslide does not quite capture the strangeness of the picture. In more than thirty precincts spanning three entire counties and the city of Wilmington, the Democratic candidate captured a measly thirteen votes to his opponent's nearly 8,000. Only four precincts reported any votes for him at all, meaning that most precincts posted zero, after zero, after zero. Do these figures reveal more tampering by the military?[18]

Not quite. Schenck had put into place the same directives as he had in Maryland; however, the Army had little work to do because of the unique reaction among Democrats. They boycotted the election. A few days before the polling, the Democrats in Delaware learned that Schenck intended to have his soldiers "support" judges of elections in the qualification of voters to ensure the purity of the ballot. It sounded like Maryland all over again, with the promise of intervention by soldiers at the polls. Democrats responded by encouraging voters to stay home to draw attention to how ridiculous the situation had become. Brown withdrew as a candidate just before the balloting and party leaders in New Castle County issued a public statement for voters to stay away from the polls. The party members listened, allowing the Republican sympathetic to emancipation to earn a victory that was virtually unopposed.[19]

Although the military concentrated on the border region, they did at times exert their muscle on elections elsewhere. Burnside, of course, arrested the gubernatorial candidate in Ohio. Additionally, Indiana was an especially sensitive spot containing peace Democrats whom the government watched closely. In 1864, the military made arrests that resulted in a famous postwar ruling by the Supreme Court, *Ex parte Milligan*, which overturned the convictions of four men who had been tried in a military court for disloyalty. In 1863, a Union general banned in the state the organization of Democratic societies patterned after the Republican Union Leagues, which were not harassed. Soldiers also stationed themselves near polling places in Indianapolis. Intimidation there caused a number of Democrats to remain home. During a campaign rally in May 1863, soldiers rushed the speakers' platform of a Democrat. When fighting broke out, soldiers arrested Democrats for their defiance, for carrying concealed weapons, and for uttering disloyal sentiments.[20]

When considering the elections of 1863, it becomes clear that the military's screening of traitors at polling precincts served the cause of an anti-slavery Union. Favorable congressmen for the administration joined the Thirty-eighth Congress from Maryland and Delaware, as well as from Ohio. They supported the anti-slavery stand of the administration and remained stalwarts in Lincoln's corner when it came to voting for the Thirteenth Amendment.[21] One careful analysis of the impact of military intervention at the polls for the Thirty-eighth Congress that sat from 1863 to 1865 indicates that Unconditional Unionists – supporters of the administration from the border states – gave the Republicans a working majority in the House. All of them won office from elections in which the military had intervened. "Without the support of the Unconditional Unionists," Bensel concluded, "the Republicans would have fallen short of a majority by five votes when the Thirty-eighth Congress convened." Four of five pro-emancipation members had come from Maryland as a result of the 1863 election; a fifth had come from Delaware. Bensel added that many loyalists obviously believed that "democratic principles had to be violated in order for the Union to survive."[22]

What was Lincoln's hand in these affairs? Did he view these measures as necessary to protect the administration's policies and encourage momentum for anti-slavery legislation? Or was he convinced that the military needed to monitor the polls for reasons of national security? Or, alternatively, was he focused on the greater concern of winning the war and let subordinate officers have their way? The case can only be built circumstantially. It is clear that he allowed for interference by the military in elections. And it is equally certain that he hoped to gain support for permanent emancipation of slaves by encouraging the election of pro-emancipation politicians in the border states and in the U.S. Congress. Yet it would be disingenuous to say that emancipation represented the only priority, rather than constituting an important piece among a cluster of concerns. He worried about maintaining the Union, about winning battles, about handling a growing political opposition, and about how to protect emancipation as an enduring policy. During election season, he clearly also was consumed, as an avid party man, with how best to maintain the prospects of the Republican Party. Multiple goals would be served by having the right men in state legislatures and the U.S. Congress, although it is perhaps more accurate to say that he would not have wanted these goals jeopardized by rebel sympathizers employing intimidation of their own at the ballot box. He may have thought, with his experience from the 1858 election: better to have the saddle come up on the other horse.

From late July through December 1863, many northern public officials, Radical Republicans among them, thought they had the end of the war in sight and had begun thinking about how to reconstruct the nation. Victories at Gettysburg and Vicksburg had given them this impression. No one at the time knew it would take nearly two more years to conquer the South. Writing a British radical that July, Charles Sumner said, "We are too victorious. I fear more from our victories than our defeats." He was worried that the war could end before slavery was permanently ended.[23] The subject occupied the minds of cabinet officers and became a matter openly advocated by politicians such as Charles Sumner. The president, key advisers, and public commentators alike considered how to put the nation back together again without slavery.[24]

Yet the president remained quiet about the need for an amendment to end slavery in a moment of military triumph. Even during 1864 – between the emergence of the amendment and the Republican convention – Lincoln made no public pronouncements about the process, choosing instead to work privately.[25] He understood the sensitivity of the matter. In 1863, he had the chance to see how passionate the opposition was to general emancipation from the reactions to a controversial letter written by the War Department solicitor that revealed the pulse of the North. And the news was not encouraging.

In late July 1863, William Whiting took a suspended leave from his position to make a trip to Europe, which seems to have been at the instigation of Stanton, Seward, or Chase – perhaps all three. The goals are murky, but that is not what concerns us here. It was the letter that Whiting wrote to the Philadelphia Union League while making his journey that earns attention. It generated a firestorm in the Democratic press. He had declared that the Civil War had grown to a public war between belligerents. For him, this influenced Reconstruction by giving the federal government enormous powers. He foresaw, accurately, that if the defeated rebels could exercise their power in the government once again, they would send to the Congress the same traitors and conspirators who had led the country into war. They would, he predicted, use their state laws and courts to continue opposing the U.S. Constitution. Again, this was an accurate take on the situation. Then he made his most controversial point. Because the conflict had grown to the scale of a public war, he argued, the national government had *carte blanche* in readmitting the rebellious states. Conquerors could do as they pleased with a vanquished foe. The bottom line for Whiting was that there should be no reunion unless loyal people in the states created new constitutions that eliminated slavery, even if those constitutions needed to be forced on the electorate by the federal government.[26] To some, this represented a repudiation of the belief in self-determination as a hallmark of a democracy. And it would not be the last time that forced institution of laws and constitutions would come up. The idea actually became implemented during congressional Reconstruction.

In 1863 the timing was not right for Whiting's ideas: the letter received lukewarm support in moderate Republican journals and dismissal from the Democratic press. A correspondent to the *New York Times* agreed that slavery must end in the country, but disputed Whiting's interpretation that the rebels were belligerents. Democrats considered his letter a reflection of the Republicans in Lincoln's cabinet and speculated that the president supported the policy. One writer observed: "The intimate relations of Mr. Solicitor Whiting with the administration naturally cause his elaborate letter on reconstruction to be scanned with more attention than is due to its intrinsic weight." The same writer believed that such a policy suggested that the administration will continue to press for war without considering an armistice as an option.[27] *The New York Herald* took a more inventive position. Its editorialist rejected the plan as a waste of time. Southern states would find a way around this interposition of federal authority, one that meddled with the constitutional privileges and reserved rights of states. If Louisiana, for example, called a state convention that abolished slavery for admission to the Union, what prevented political leaders there from convening another convention that passed a constitution re-instating slavery? The constitution specified that states established or abolished slavery. "It is a local affair. Mr. Whiting's plan of operations can be rendered effective only by abandoning the federal constitution or by amending it. Otherwise, in 1863, Louisiana may be manipulated into a free State and restored to the benefits of the Union only to be transformed again into a slave State in 1864."[28]

The reception of this letter could not have been comforting to Lincoln. It came during a time when a consensus had not come even among Republicans on the need for an amendment to end slavery. It demonstrated that public support was still a work in progress for how to end slavery, not only in the slaveowning border states, but also in the free states. Lincoln had to be aware of the letter: he apparently considered Whiting a capable person in an important post. Sumner called him a friend and an "admirable lawyer *in the full confidence of the Presdt.*" Secretary of the Navy Gideon Welles was less enchanted with the man, whom he characterized as conceited and inclined to intrigues. However, he also acknowledged Whiting's connections and influence. In July 1863 he remarked, "This Solicitor Whiting has for several months been an important personage here." Seward, Chase, and Lincoln had referred to him as a patriotic volunteer. "My admiration is not as exalted as it should be," he added.[29] It cannot be said that Lincoln authorized a trial balloon for general emancipation through Whiting's letter; it is more likely that he learned from the reactions. Whatever the case, Whiting was back in his job very soon. And Lincoln continued to work behind the scenes to push for a general emancipation.

During 1863 Lincoln and his advisers also were trying to figure out how to restore the disloyal states to the Union that had come under federal control, revealing that the old strategy of handling emancipation at the state level remained in play. Union-occupied Louisiana drew a great deal of attention. Treasury Secretary Chase told a correspondent that the president had read to him a letter addressed to Major General Nathaniel P. Banks, the officer in charge of the military department, in which Lincoln had expressed his preference for a new state constitution recognizing the conditions of his proclamation – meaning to prohibit slavery. In these uncertain times, a change to Louisiana's constitution presented a safer course than trying to push for an amendment to the fundamental law of the land. A new state constitution raised no issues concerning federalism or the abrogation by a central power of a state's rights and privileges. Lincoln's eventual letter sent to Banks was suggestive rather than decisive. He said he would be "glad" if Louisiana enacted a new constitution that adopted the Emancipation Proclamation. Chase told an acquaintance that the letter was cautious and claimed it did not express Lincoln's preferences as strongly as the president felt them.[30]

Attention to the border states made good political sense, for they held the wild cards for emancipation. If they became part of a movement to forge new constitutions without slavery, then all the better. The lobbying for, and ratification of, an amendment to end slavery nationally became easier. Even if a state approach failed, the elections of 1863 might empower politicians at both the state and national levels who believed in anti-slavery or who could support the need for additional manpower and other elements necessary to bring the conflict to an end. A lot remained at stake. Consequently, the political composition of the border states was vital for sustaining the administration's goals, including continuing to take the fight to the rebels as well as to end slavery everywhere. Keeping a close eye on those states – especially to prevent rebel sympathizers from influencing elections – was a priority.

The importance of the 1863 elections for anti-slavery was recognized at the time. Chase wrote an acquaintance in November that he and his comrades "are rejoicing exceedingly over the triumphs in Maryland & Missouri," and that he hoped for an additional triumph in Delaware. In Missouri, the legislature convened in November to select a U.S. senator. Radical B. Gratz Brown joined his colleague John B. Henderson in the Senate. Although Henderson was a Democrat and a member of the Conservatives faction, he ended up being a co-author of the Thirteenth Amendment that was introduced in early 1864. Brown was among the most Radical of men who had criticized Lincoln for proceeding too slowly on ending slavery. Such a person certainly did not hurt the cause of emancipation in the Senate. Thomas J. Durant, the recipient of Chase's letter, could not have agreed more with the assessment of the elections. Durant was in the midst of working on the reconstruction of the federally occupied portions of Louisiana. He fired back a reply rejoicing "in the triumph of the holy cause of human freedom in Delaware, Maryland, Missouri, and hope for equal results in Louisiana."[31] The border states weighed heavily upon the minds of emancipation's supporters.

Yet another military officer who would help the cause of ending slavery joined the Thirty-eighth Congress. Soon after the elections in Maryland, Schenck resigned his commission in order to assume the seat in Congress that he had won in October 1862, adding another pro-administration voice to the lower chamber. He represented Ohio, and had defeated Vallandigham for the seat. Perhaps needless to say, Schenck backed the administration's position on habeas corpus and brought with him to the Congress an anti-slavery sensibility that was an asset to the president. Every last body mattered in maintaining the Republican majority, especially for the passage of an amendment to the Constitution.

As a correspondent for the *New York Tribune* reflected on the impact of the 1863 elections, he seemed to validate that soldiers had interfered in

order to protect the cause of anti-slavery. In this case, the writer was trying
to deflect criticism of soldiers performing this duty in order to influence
abolition. Also, he seemed to protest too much. The writer lauded the
efforts of General Schenck for clearing obstacles to achieve the right
results, "no one now cares to inquire how." The item continued: "The
President would not only not interfere in our matters, but forbade the
exercise of any Federal influence, beyond the moral support, that his own
hostility to Slavery afforded, and Gen. Schenck did nothing that any real
friend of his country could except to. He simply did his duty. He protected
the ballot-box from violence and the pollution of traitors' votes, so far as
his power went."[32] The "purity of the ballot" was the metaphor that
condoned soldiers interfering with the democratic process.

With Kentucky digging in its heels, Maryland and Missouri were
considered especially crucial for building momentum for enacting anti-
slavery constitutions. Missouri took until 1865 to push through such a
measure, but its citizens had foreshadowed a gradual end to slavery in
the summer of 1863. During the fall elections the military was put on
notice to protect the ballot in a state rife with political strife and guerrilla
problems. There, loyalty oaths required by state authorities gave radicalism the ability to push forth freedom for slaves. Even though the
Maryland elections of 1863 sent four out of five pro-emancipation
representatives to the Congress, it was just as vital that anti-slavery
candidates won state positions to call for a convention to create a new
constitution. On February 22, 1864, the Union State Convention met in
Baltimore, selecting as president Creswell – the man who had benefited
from Captain Moore's intervention at the polls. This entity had been
created in May 23, 1861, and had appointed a central committee that
ran the party machinery for the state. It had once favored conservative
unionism but now leaned in the opposite direction. The delegates issued
a statement of support for Lincoln and added, "They also approve the
policy of the present Administration, and declare in favor of an immediate and unconditional Emancipation in Maryland, and the abolition of
Slavery everywhere in the rebellious States as the imperative condition of
the reinstatement of the Union."[33]

Lincoln was more than on board with the emancipation movement in
Maryland: he pressed for it – hard. In March 1864, he wrote Creswell that
he was anxious for emancipation in Maryland "in some substantial
form." The state legislature had enacted a law calling for a vote by the
people in April in order to decide on calling a convention for a new
constitution. Lincoln thought the public misconstrued that he favored a

gradual over immediate emancipation. He had given that impression only because he believed that gradual freedom would produce less destitution and be more "satisfactory," perhaps meaning that more people in the country were inclined to accept such a position. But he did not mind it if the Union preferred the immediate course.[34]

After Maryland voted in favor of calling for a convention to change the constitution, the president journeyed to Baltimore in April 1864 to address the Sanitary Fair. He obviously wanted to reinforce the step Maryland had taken and to lobby for a state constitution that ended slavery. But he did so discreetly, taking an indirect approach to remind his listeners that the war had affected domestic slavery. He employed a lesson on semantics – how liberty meant different things to different people: "With some the word liberty may mean for each man to do as he pleases with himself, and the product of his labor; while with others the same word may mean for some men to do as they please with other men, and the product of other men's labor." He offered the metaphor of a shepherd who drives the wolf from the sheep's throat "for which the sheep thanks the shepherd as a *liberator*, while the wolf denounces him for the same act as the destroyer of liberty, especially as the sheep was a black one." Plainly, the wolf and the sheep did not agree on the definition of liberty. "Recently," he added, "the people of Maryland have been doing something to define liberty; and thanks to them that, in what they have done, the wolf's dictionary, has been repudiated." The anti-slavery constitution eventually passed in October 1864, but only by a very narrow margin – fewer than 400 votes out of 60,000 cast.[35] This total hardly represented a mandate within the state, but it did represent a hard-won victory for emancipation.

There were other ways to influence voting besides screening voters at precincts, showing Lincoln again as using all the items in his political tool kit. The executive branch had quite a resource within its hands in the soldiers who also remained citizens. They had the right to vote. And they were under the control of the executive branch. The administration demonstrated adroitness at shifting the pieces on the chessboard to use this resource to its advantage. Writing nearly fifty years after the war, Charles A. Dana unapologetically recalled that during his stint in the bureaucracy during the 1864 presidential campaign "all the power and influence of the War Department ... was employed to secure the re-election of Mr. Lincoln." He remembered seeing a constant flow of telegrams from all over the country requesting leaves for officers and furloughs for privates who were needed in close districts.[36]

When the war began, only one state allowed soldiers to vote when outside of their election districts. Everyone at the time considered that the Army contained a majority of men who supported the administration's measures for ending the war, which meant losing precious voters unless something could be done. By the 1864 presidential election, largely at the instigation of Republican legislatures, nineteen states adopted absentee balloting for soldiers. But in the meantime, the solution became to furlough the right units and individuals at the right time to return to their home states to cast ballots. Even though Pennsylvania had come on board the absentee ballot train by 1864, Lincoln still had Generals George G. Meade and Philip Sheridan furlough a total of 10,000 Pennsylvania troops to make it look like the home vote in the Keystone State favored him. In advance of the election, Stanton fired clerks from various Bureaus who voted Democratic, generals in the Army cashiered or demoted officers suspected of supporting the peace candidates, and officers denied circulation of Democratic Party materials in camp. The extent of voter intimidation within the military is just coming to light in a book by Jonathan W. White on the soldier vote in the 1864 presidential election.[37]

How do we put into perspective Lincoln, the Army, election interference, and emancipation? First, there is no evidence that Lincoln planned a strategy of military oversight of elections to install the political muscle to push forward general emancipation through a constitutional amendment. The evidence is not clear that he orchestrated these events; however, he likely recognized the utility of letting them unfold – and that the impact on final emancipation became an added benefit from the actions of soldiers at polling places. Military officers were notorious for taking positions that forced Washington to accept them, reject them, or modify them. This happened with Burnside's arrest of Vallandigham. It also happened with Schenck's orders in Maryland, when Lincoln needed convincing about the possibility of disloyal people disrupting the polling. And it happened on other occasions, especially with the emancipation orders of Generals John C. Frémont and David Hunter, which Lincoln reversed.

Yet it is possible to see Lincoln as realizing that soldiers supervising elections in these sensitive areas served multiple goals: electing people who wanted to sustain the conflict as well as aiding in general emancipation. He worked behind the scenes to promote various means for achieving permanent emancipation, especially through encouraging new state constitutions in the border states and Union-occupied Confederate territory. His commitment to emancipation, often challenged by people at the time and historians much later, cannot be denied. He understood the importance of getting pro-administration politicians into state and federal offices, necessary for continuing to prosecute the war, heading off the peace movement by Copperheads, and moving against slavery. He sanctioned, if not ordered, the use of the military at polling precincts, primarily in the border states where one might have expected the most potential violence against Unionists and the most chances of having peace Democrats gain ground. He encouraged the War Department and generals to furlough soldiers who likely would vote Republican or Unionist.

To his credit, Lincoln did not endorse or allow widespread use of the military at elections throughout the Union. Most of the intervention occurred in sensitive areas in which the case could be made that potential traitors threatened the election process, enhancing the possibility of disunion. Moreover, the practice declined for the presidential election in 1864. Major General Lew Wallace, who replaced Schenck in charge of the Middle Department that spanned Maryland and Delaware, ordered the military to stop interfering in elections. Soldiers could respond only if public officials or judges of elections asked for help, and the latter request had to come in writing.[38]

The unfolding of emancipation was a process, with uncertain beginnings and endings. As both Downs and Sternhell show, the process was a contingent one, constantly evolving. Freedom for 4 million enslaved African Americans depended on political change and military force, and the Thirteenth Amendment made black freedom permanent. Although this story exposes a hard side to the coming of emancipation, the use of the military in this fashion should not come as a surprise. The country then was not what it is today. Intelligence agencies and an internal security system were virtually non-existent before the war. There was no Federal Bureau of Investigation; no Central Intelligence Agency; not even a Department of Justice. No equivalent to the Department of Homeland Security came into being. The government then had little idea about how to identify, much less handle, internal threats during a time when treason seemed to be everywhere. Traitors potentially sat in government jobs. Spies betrayed troop positions to the enemy. Nervous generals sent messages to superiors about disloyal people lurking at home who might use violence to dissuade Unionists from voting. Elections were naturally more spirited then, with fraud and intimidation a routine part of the culture. There was a lot to lose, should the wrong people gain public office – especially if it came through violence or other extralegal means. This is not to excuse the more egregious actions by the military, such as preventing Arthur Crisfield from voting for his father. Excessive behavior happened, and it is not clear that military intervention was truly needed to protect the Republican victories. But the military interference of elections provides an often overlooked ingredient in a complicated, multi-faceted story for the advance of freedom in this country. The Army did more than free slaves in the South; it helped win the battles for emancipation on the home front.

FIGURE 3: "Portrait of Maj. Gen. Robert C. Schenck, officer of the Federal Army."
Source: Mathew Brady. Courtesy of the Library of Congress, Prints and Photographs Division, LC-B813-1399.

NOTES

Portions of this essay have appeared in the following book by William A. Blair, *With Malice toward Some: Treason and Loyalty in the Civil War Era* (Chapel Hill: University of North Carolina Press, 2014).

1. Don E. Fehrenbacher, "The Anti-Lincoln Tradition," *Journal of the Abraham Lincoln Association*, 4:1 (1982), http://hdl.handle.net/2027/spo. 2629860.0004.103 (accessed January 8, 2013); E. Merton Coulter, *The Civil War and Readjustment in Kentucky* (1926; reprinted., Gloucester, Mass., Peter Smith, 1966). Works on Maryland have taken note of the military interference with elections in that state. A somewhat critical assessment of the actions can be found in Charles Lewis Wagandt, *The Mighty Revolution: Negro Emancipation in Maryland, 1862–1864* (Baltimore: Johns Hopkins Press University, 1964), 157–184, while Jean H. Baker dismisses the influence as sour grapes by partisan opponents who lost the elections in her *The Politics of Continuity: Maryland Political Parties from 1858 to 1870* (Baltimore: Johns Hopkins University Press, 1973), 88–89. For a more forgiving view of Lincoln's use of arrests and their targeted nature, see Mark E. Neely, Jr., *The Fate of Liberty: Abraham Lincoln and Civil Liberties* (New York: Oxford University Press, 1991). For a more recent treatment of Lincoln, see Eric Foner, *The Fiery Trial: Abraham Lincoln and American Slavery* (New York: Norton, 2010). It should be noted that most of the respected biographies of the president in recent decades have not mentioned the military's interference in elections.

2. Richard Franklin Bensel, *The American Ballot Box in the Mid-Nineteenth Century* (New York: Cambridge University Press, 2004), 261–262. For another study that highlights the military's activity in civilian elections, see Blair, *With Malice toward Some*, esp. ch. 6. For a good study of intimidation in the military during the 1864 election, see Jonathan W. White, *Emancipation, the Union Army, and the Reelection of Abraham Lincoln* (Baton Rouge: Louisiana State University Press, 2014).

3. Charles D. Robinson to Abraham Lincoln, August 7, 1864, Series 1, General Correspondence 1833–1916, Abraham Lincoln Papers, Library of Congress, hereafter cited as ALP.

4. Michael Vorenberg, *Final Freedom: The Civil War, the Abolition of Slavery, and the Thirteenth Amendment* (New York: Cambridge University Press, 2001), 5–6, 9–18 (quotation on p. 15).

5. Bensel, *The American Ballot Box*, 8–25, 293–295.

6. Peter Roy Basler, ed., *The Collected Works of Abraham Lincoln*, 9 vols. (New Brunswick, N.J.: Rutgers University Press, 1953), vol. 3, 329–330; David Herbert Donald, "A. Lincoln, Politician," in *Lincoln Reconsidered: Essays on the Civil War Era* (1947; New York: Vintage, 1956), 66–67.

7. For one of the more recent statements about the military's importance in providing avenues for freedom, see Edward L. Ayers and Scott Nesbit, "Seeing Emancipation: Scale and Freedom in the American South," *The Journal of the Civil War Era*, 1 (March 2011): 3–24.

8. See, for instance, James M. McPherson, *Battle Cry of Freedom: The Civil War Era* (New York: Oxford University Press, 1988), 596–597.

9. U.S. War Department, *The War of the Rebellion: A Compilation of the Official Records of the Union and Confederate Armies*, 127 vols., index, and atlas (Washington, D.C.: GPO, 1880–1901), ser. 1, vol. 23, pt. 1: 728, and ser. 1, vol. 23, pt. 2: 572, hereafter cited as *O.R.*; *The American Annual Cyclopaedia and Register of Important Events of the Year 1863* (New York: D. Appleton & Company, 1864), 568.

10. William Marvel, *Burnside* (Chapel Hill: University of North Carolina Press, 1991), 264–265; Frances Dallam Peter, *A Union Woman in Civil War Kentucky: The Diary of Frances Peter*, eds. John David Smith and William Cooper, Jr. (Lexington: University Press of Kentucky, 2000), 147, 148–149.

11. Coulter, *Civil War and Readjustment in Kentucky*, 178; Richard Smith to Thomas T. Eckert, August 5, 1863, ALP. For charges of election irregularities on the part of soldiers, see William A. Dudley, *Overthrow of the Ballot! A Complete History of the Election in the State of Kentucky*, August 3, 1863, https://archive.org/stream/overthrowofballooodudl#page/no/mode/2up (accessed August 4, 2014).

12. Robert C. Schenck to Edwin M. Stanton, November 1, 1863, ALP; *O.R.*, ser. 3, vol. 3:968.

13. Wagandt, *The Mighty Revolution*, 158–160.

14. Foner, *The Fiery Trial*, 213.

15. *Report of the Committee on Elections, on Contested Elections in Somerset County, Together with the Testimony Taken before that Committee, January Session, 1864* (Annapolis: Bull & Tuttle, 1864), 9–12. For an excellent study of the 1863 elections, see Charles L. Wagandt, "Election by Sword and Ballot: The Emancipationist Victory of 1863," *Maryland Historical Quarterly* 59, no. 2 (June 1964): 143–164.

16. John W. Crisfield to Montgomery Blair, November 14, 1863, ALP.

17. *Report of the Committee on Elections, on Contested Elections in Somerset County*, 9–12, 27–28, 30–31.

18. *Tribune Almanac and Political Register for 1863* (New York: Greeley & McElrath, 1864), 6.

19. *Daily Constitutional Union*, November 20, 1863; *Daily National Intelligencer*, November 18 and 21, 1863; *New York Times*, November 21, 1863.

20. Frank L. Klement, *Dark Lanterns: Secret Political Societies, Conspiracies, and Treason Trials in the Civil War* (Baton Rouge: Louisiana State University Press, 1984), 98–100.

21. *Congressional Globe*, 38th Cong., 1st Sess., 660, 2996; 2nd Sess., 531. The one person difficult to trace is Webster, who appears to have missed the votes on February 15 and June 15, 1864.

22. Bensel, *The American Ballot Box*, 261–262.

23. Beverly Wilson Palmer, ed., *The Selected Letters of Charles Sumner: Volume 2, 1859–1874* (Boston: Northeastern University Press, 1990), 184.

24. Vorenberg, *Final Freedom*, 33.

25. Ibid 126.

26. John Niven, *Gideon Welles: Lincoln's Secretary of the Navy* (New York: Oxford University Press, 1973), 467–468; *The New York Herald*, August 11, 1863; *New York Times*, August 12, 1863.

27. *New York Times*, August 14, 1863; *Portland Daily Advertiser*, August 21, 1863. Also see *Wisconsin Daily Patriot*, August 22, 1863, for a similar assessment that the letter represented the wishes of the administration.

28. *New York Herald*, August 11, 1863.

29. Palmer, ed., *Selected Letters of Charles Sumner*, 184 [emphasis his]; Howard K. Beale, ed., *Diary of Gideon Welles: Secretary of the Navy under Lincoln and Johnson*, 3 vols. (New York: W. W. Norton & Company, Inc., 1960), vol. 1, 381.

30. Basler, *Collected Works*, 6:365; John Niven, ed., *The Salmon P. Chase Papers: Volume 4, Correspondence, April 1863–1864*, (Kent, Oh.: Kent State University Press, 1997), 119–120.

31. Niven, ed., *Chase Papers*, 4:194, 208.

32. *New York Tribune*, February 16, 1864.

33. *Easton Gazette*, February 27, 1864.

34. Basler, ed., *Collected Works*, 7:226–227.

35. Foner, *The Fiery Trial*; Basler, ed., *Collected Works*, 7:301–302.

36. Charles A. Dana, *Recollections of the Civil War: With the Leaders at Washington and in the Field in the Sixties* (New York: D. Appleton, 1913), 260.

37. White, *Emancipation, the Union Army, and the Reelection of Abraham Lincoln*. Also see Blair, *With Malice toward Some*, 174–175, 224–229.

38. Blair, *With Malice toward Some*, 230.

PART TWO

CONTESTING EMANCIPATION

4

"One pillar of the social fabric may still stand firm": Border South Marriages in the Emancipation Era

Allison Fredette

From the moment the first slaves took flight during the Civil War, the process of emancipation profoundly shook the core of traditional white Southern society. Throughout the antebellum slave South, law and custom reinforced a strictly hierarchal social structure, upholding elite white male authority over both social inferiors and household dependents. Many Southerners understood that slavery and gender roles within the household were irrevocably linked and that an attack upon one was an attack upon the other. By the 1860s, secession debates and Confederate rhetoric urged Southerners to defend their households, both black and white, as well as their way of life against northern attackers.[1] Yet, by taking up arms to defend their homes, Southerners unintentionally brought about the end of the slave system and threatened the household itself. With the end of the war, both emancipation and divorce exposed the inherent dissolvability of social relationships, ultimately threatening to reveal white male authority as tenuous and unstable. If ties such as marriage were not obligatory but voluntary, how fixed could other social contracts be?[2]

As slaves left plantations from Texas to Virginia, both slaveholding and non-slaveholding white Southerners reevaluated their gender roles within the home. With emancipation, the Southern household became a newly contested landscape, as white men and women struggled either to redefine their positions or maintain the social order that typified Southern life before the war.[3] As this volume contends, however, black emancipation was a messy and uneven process, making its impact on the South's white population and their attempts to reorder or reclaim the household equally uneven. Analyzing the appellate and chancery divorce cases of one former border state and one former Confederate state in the immediate postwar years contributes to a more complete picture of this varied and complex process and demonstrates the pivotal role of place (specifically, border places) in emancipation's story.[4] This chapter addresses the impact of emancipation on white marriages in Kentucky and Virginia during the first eight years following the Civil War, using this comparative approach to argue that emancipation's effect on Bluegrass gender roles was muted by the state's hybrid border culture and antebellum experiences. More specifically, postbellum Kentuckians' rhetoric and motivations for separation remained consistent with their antebellum cases, reflecting a continued desire for mutuality and individualism in their relationships, while Virginians decried the breakdown of racial mastery, connected it with potential disruptions to their hierarchical households, and demanded obedience and loyalty from both former slaves and spouses.[5]

Black freedom meant disruption and tumult to white Southerners, and many fought back as best they could. Inevitably, many white Southerners clung to the past, refusing to adapt to the changes wrought by emancipation. With the passage of the Black Codes and the initial rejection of the Fourteenth Amendment throughout much of the South, former Confederates made it clear that changes in the racial order would not come easily. Additionally, because of the close connection between a gendered hierarchy and racial mastery, these same white Southerners were in no hurry to reform marriage or marital roles either. Alongside a racial backlash, many white Southerners reinforced their support for a patriarchal household structure based on female dependence and male authority.[6]

Since slaveholding border states such as Kentucky never technically seceded, the process of emancipation in these places differed from that of Confederate states such as Virginia. In addition, a lack of large-scale warfare and its accompanying displacement and destruction meant Kentuckians transitioned more smoothly, in some ways, into the postwar years.[7] Nonetheless, many residents of the Bluegrass State shared their former Confederate neighbors' animosity toward racial progress. As Aaron Astor and Anne Marshall have demonstrated, in the years following emancipation Kentuckians passed some of the harshest racial laws in the South and began to re-imagine and re-assess their wartime allegiance.[8] However, I argue that unlike in many other Southern states, emancipation's impact on white Kentuckians' marital relationships was surprisingly minimal, reflecting the state's history as a flexible borderland long before the war that placed them on the line between two nations. While it is clear that emancipation, in many ways, had a disruptive and profound impact on much of white Southern society, this chapter explores one place and context in which it did not.

In Kentucky, a border state that one scholar famously argued joined the Confederacy *after* the war, the softened impact of black emancipation on white Southern gender roles may also have contributed to white citizens' ability to ignore emancipation and black freedom altogether.[9] Doing so allowed Bluegrass residents to overlook their Union allegiance and join in a Confederate Lost Cause mentality not necessarily reflective of their Civil War experience. In this way, a close study of Bluegrass marriage in the postwar years also sheds light on the early construction of an altered white memory of emancipation.

The connection between black emancipation and white marital roles, so well documented in other regions, proves tenuous at best in Kentucky.[10] In a pattern established before the war, antebellum Kentuckians' attitudes toward household gender roles proved adaptable, allowing greater numbers of divorces under more flexible statutes than their Virginia brethren. Although their acceptance of a philosophy of individualism and mutuality in marriage was not necessarily unique in the South, their letters, diaries, and court cases demonstrate a greater prevalence and depth of this acceptance than in other regions. However, while firmly part of a national trend toward greater equity in marital relationships, Kentuckians did not extend this same enlightened attitude toward their relationships with slaves or free blacks, nor did their use of this philosophy in their marriages lessen their attachment to a racial hierarchy. Two explanations prove useful. First, slavery itself differed in Kentucky from other parts of the South, with a greater percentage of small farms and hired slaves. In Kentucky, slavery already existed alongside a flourishing free labor market and industrial sector.[11] Second, and most crucially, their border mentality of compromise and fusion allowed them to accept multiple philosophies and ideologies without necessarily viewing one as threatening the other.[12] Free labor did not necessarily threaten slavery. Likewise, changes to slavery did not necessarily threaten white families. Because of a culture built on the middle ground between so many different geographical, economic, and political views, Kentuckians disassociated rival philosophies in a way that differed from other white slaveholding Southerners. This meant that black emancipation, while threatening to race relations, was not necessarily so to white households. Additionally, while to most white Southerners restoring a prewar social system meant re-establishing both racial and gender hierarchy, the same was not true of Kentuckians.

In the prewar years, Kentucky's border location had significant ramifications upon its residents' households. Centrally located in an ever-expanding nation, Kentuckians maintained strong social and cultural ties with relatives and friends throughout the greater Midwest, North, and South. Travelers crisscrossed the state, reshaping it with their diverse ideas and philosophies. Economically, the state also lay on a middle ground. While slavery still retained a firm hold upon the state's economy, Kentuckians in cities such as Louisville began to diversify their economy.[13] Slaves in the state still experienced the harsh effects of bondage, but they were more likely to labor on small farms or to be hired out to other owners. In addition, Kentuckians glorified the political moderation of native sons such as Henry Clay, whose compromises averted disaster on multiple occasions. Ultimately, the level of cross-regional contact in Kentucky created a "heterogeneous border culture," one that very much affected residents' understanding of marriage and marital roles.[14]

Records in this study reflect the attitudes and marriages of both slaveholding and non-slaveholding white residents of Kentucky and Virginia. While non-slaveholders certainly did not replicate exactly the attitudes of slaveholders, scholars have shown that slaveholders often set the ideal, in terms of household relations and gender roles.[15] In addition, non-slaveholders still lived within a society founded upon black bondage and its accompanying racial hierarchy, and their relationships could not help but be influenced by this (or not influenced by this) in similar ways to slaveholders. Kentuckians' broad attitudes may have been shaped by the larger share of non-slaveholders in their population, but this influenced a larger social milieu, rather than just specific households.

While antebellum Kentuckians largely supported a strict racial hierarchy and slavery itself, this same attitude about dependence did not necessarily extend to their marriages, some of which featured a high degree of egalitarianism and mutuality.[16] Because of their border culture's proclivity for adaptation, Kentuckians could conceive of households defined by these contradictory attitudes. Therefore, during the postwar years, while emancipation ended slavery's role in the household and social order, it did not, as it did elsewhere in the South, threaten individuals' roles as wives and husbands. A sense of place and its effect on identity and culture is critical to understanding the ways in which the emancipation experience, as well as its impact on white attitudes and lives, differed throughout the South.

Kentuckians' reaction to the loss of their slaves and the slave system as a whole caused a resurgence in white supremacist attitudes, but there was no noticeable shift away from the antebellum pattern of companionate marriage and lenient divorce laws.[17] In the demands they made against partners in divorce cases, Kentuckians continued to express the same antebellum ideals for marriage that typified their complicated prewar border households. Although divorce itself is a disruptive process much like emancipation, the marital separations in Kentucky reflect continuity from the prewar era and an attempt to uphold companionate ideals.[18] The fact that Kentuckians could continue to divorce at the same antebellum rate, despite the fact that divorce threatens social unity, demonstrates that they did not draw the same connections between gender and emancipation as other white Southerners in the postwar period.

Of course, notwithstanding many white Southerners' best efforts to maintain the organic structure of household hierarchy, emancipation and the end of the Civil War brought slow change to the political and social landscape, moving the South toward what some historians have termed a more "mainstream ... American development."[19] For example, while Southerners still trailed Northerners and Westerners in rates of divorce, liberalization in the law occurred. Often through the efforts of Reconstruction governments, constitutions and state codes evolved to allow more divorces.[20] However, unlike other Southern places, Kentuckians still experienced this postbellum, post-emancipation adaptation through the unique lens of their border experience. First, in their case, the change began before the war, not as a result of it.[21] Kentucky's divorce code remained unaltered in the wake of emancipation, and their postwar petitions built upon the companionate ideals rooted in 1850s households. Second, while the number of divorce cases and minor aspects of the law changed in states like Virginia, the core content of divorce petitions and the fundamental nature of the law stayed much the same, reflecting a greater resistance to a contractual and individualistic form of marriage.[22] A brief comparison between the divorce records of Kentucky and Virginia during the years 1865 to 1873 demonstrates the differing pace and quality of change in these two states following emancipation.

Kentucky does not fit into the current narrative regarding emancipation's influence on white families. Some historians argue that the threat of emancipation caused white Southerners to reinforce antebellum gender roles, while others contend that emancipation led to a flood of changes in the household.[23] However, in the case of the Bluegrass State and marriage, the process of emancipation may not have been the disruptive process it was elsewhere, and its ultimate meaning must be evaluated in this light. Studying Kentucky's postwar marriages deepens our understanding of emancipation and its long-term effect on white Southern society. The impact of emancipation on the household and white marriage roles varied throughout the South, depending on geographical and cultural attitudes, wartime experience, the structure of pre-war relationships, and each state's peculiar Reconstruction.

Kentuckians neither sought nor desired emancipation at the beginning of the war, and most reacted angrily to that eventual outcome. Although pro-slavery, Kentuckians hesitated when their fellow Southerners angrily called for secession and war in the early days following Lincoln's election. Following their well-worn path of moderation, many argued that the election's results did not justify secession and adopted a "wait-and-see" policy toward the new president. Others stated that slavery would be better protected within, not outside the United States, pointing out that Kentucky would become the northern border of a new nation, with slaves fleeing across the Ohio at even greater rates. Even after the fall of Fort Sumter and Lincoln's call for troops pushed Virginia, Arkansas, North Carolina, and Tennessee into the arms of the Confederacy, the Bluegrass State's legislature declared, "Kentucky should, during the contest, occupy the position of strict neutrality."[24] So long as neither army invaded, they worked to maintain this position. When the Confederate Army invaded Kentucky in September 1861, however, Kentucky officially became a Union state.

During the first years of the war, Lincoln worked to maintain the vital border state's shaky loyalty by shielding it from the blow of emancipation. Early attempts by Union leaders to encourage emancipation and freedom among the slaves of the border states met with angry resistance from Kentucky's citizens and Lincoln's ultimate disapproval. "I hope to have God on my side, but I must have Kentucky," Lincoln was reported to have said of his birthplace. However, by mid 1862, Lincoln decided the military benefits of emancipation outweighed its drawbacks and announced the preliminary Emancipation Proclamation. The document did not apply to Kentucky's slaves, declaring free only those living in areas under rebellion. Kentucky's slaves refused to wait, however. As early as 1861, many fled to the Union Army, and although Lincoln's initial call for black troops also did not apply to Kentucky, thousands of the state's slaves enlisted elsewhere. By 1864, the Union Army agreed to accept those still remaining in the state. Because of Kentucky's resistance to emancipation, most of the state's male slaves actually obtained their freedom through their military service.[25] Nonetheless, at the end of the war, about a third of the state's slaves remained in bondage.

After the war, Kentucky refused to ratify the Thirteenth Amendment and even tried to reject a March 1865 congressional act that freed all slaves who had served in the Union Army. Many slaves in Kentucky only became free with national ratification of the Thirteenth Amendment on December 18, 1865. (Kentucky itself refused to ratify the amendment and would not do so until the late twentieth century.)[26] Emancipation, however, did not end the debate regarding the status of blacks in the state. In Kentucky, a fierce resistance sprang up, and a wave of racial violence swept the former Union state. Additionally, because many of the state's most virulent opponents of racial equality had actually fought for the Union, few were disenfranchised in the postwar years, allowing a more conservative government to control the fortunes of freedpeople. Blacks, never a majority in the state, could not form the same protective political coalitions as in the Deep South. Eventually the Freedmen's Bureau intervened, despite Kentucky's wartime status, to stop the state from stripping blacks of their rights to a fair trial and other crucial civil liberties.[27]

Emancipation's implications for household relations had long struck a chord of fear in the hearts of white Southern leaders. Antebellum Northerners, many linked to the abolition movement, urged reforms for married women's property rights and began the liberalization of divorce, both of which threatened what Peter Bardaglio calls a Southern "network of households grounded in dependence and inequality."[28] Southerners resisted such reforms in the years leading up to the war, and many feared that Reconstruction governments might impose these changes upon Southern households without Southerners' approval. In fact, they were not wholly wrong. In the wake of Congressional Reconstruction, new legislatures convened and revised state constitutions, many of which included changes to divorce statutes. Although Southern Redeemers repealed many of these provisions when they gained power in the early 1870s, ideas of contractualism in marriage infiltrated the South. Exacerbated by the collapse of the slave system and the growing re-integration of the nation, slow changes occurred within Southern households, especially in the rate of divorce. More Southerners filed for divorce, and divorce laws themselves became less rigid, allowing for separation in a greater number of cases.[29]

Yet the pace and quality of Kentucky's postwar marital evolution and its relationship to emancipation is unique in its own right, as reflected in the state's rate of divorce, charges filed, and language and rhetoric. While the number of divorces increased (to varying extents) throughout the South, Kentucky's slow continued growth built on antebellum changes, not outside disruptions specific to the postbellum period. In addition, the rhetoric used in Kentucky's divorce petitions, including a higher number of references to no-fault divorce and "mutual" needs, as well as less justification for the decision to separate, indicates that the character of those divorces also differed from other Southern locales. For example, in comparison to Virginians, Kentuckians divorced after shorter marriages, waited less time after a marital crisis to petition the chancery courts, and filed using fewer charges. In Kentucky, divorce laws and attitudes toward marriage continued to evolve in favor of ones based on companionate ideals such as reciprocity and individualism. Rather than turn to a patri-archal model of household gender roles, Kentuckians used prewar changes to weather the storm of emancipation.

Comparing the divorce records of two counties, one in Kentucky and one in Virginia, further demonstrates the unique patterns found in Kentucky marriages in the postbellum era. Home to Frankfort (the state's capital), Franklin County, Kentucky, featured many traits typical of its state. Before the war, the county's numerous small farms housed three thousand slaves, nearly a third of its entire population.[30] Although most Franklin County slaveowners owned a smaller number of slaves than those of other Southern states, the racial hierarchy and human bondage upon which society was based influenced residents' social ideals.[31] Nevertheless, many of these men and women embraced a different under-standing of marriage and divorce than one might expect in such a com-munity. Between 1850 and 1861, Franklin County residents filed for divorce on forty-eight occasions, and the chancery court granted their request almost 60 percent of the time.[32] Franklin County petitioners also admitted fault in divorce cases and joined their partner in asking for a separation, defying the legal resistance to marital collusion held through-out the country. They constructed loving relationships based upon mutual affection and economy and sought redress through the legal system when their marriages did not meet these expectations.

Meanwhile, located about sixty miles from the nation's capital, Fauquier County, Virginia, had a different antebellum experience, both with slavery and with divorce. Fauquier County slaves, almost 50 percent of the total population, labored long hours on larger plantations than those of Franklin County, Kentucky.[33] Despite having a far greater popu-lation than Franklin County, Fauquier County residents filed for only eight divorces between 1850 and 1861, and the county's chancery court granted only one of them.[34] In their petitions, Fauquier County citizens employed a language of male authority and mastery accompanied by female submission and obedience. They rarely joined their spouses in requesting divorces and displayed fewer of the tendencies toward mutuality in relationships.

In the postbellum years, specifically 1865 to 1873, Fauquier County residents exhibited only a slightly greater desire for divorce, despite the enormous disruption of soldiers' absences, women's wartime independence, and emancipation itself. During that period, wives and husbands in Fauquier County filed for divorce a dozen times. Meanwhile, sixty-five Franklin County residents sought a divorce from their spouse, many citing adultery, abandonment, or just a loss of love. Statewide, stark differences are also apparent between Kentucky and Virginia's postbellum record. Although both states had roughly the same population (1,321,011 and 1,225,163 respectively), Kentuckians petitioned for over thirty-five hundred divorces, while Virginians requested one-fifth that amount – about seven hundred – from 1867 to 1875.[35]

Postwar divorce had different implications for Kentuckians and Virginians. Kentuckians, living in a border culture that had always drawn its ideals from both slaveholding and non-slaveholding regions, adapted more easily and with less resistance to post-emancipation household upheaval; many Virginians, meanwhile, believed that society itself was under attack. Antebellum Kentuckians embraced mutuality and contractualism in marriage and divorce while still maintaining the slave system. Therefore, postwar Kentuckians could simultaneously urge a return to strict racial hierarchy, without it affecting an ongoing evolution in gender relations and household structure. Virginians struggled more noticeably with the transition because they did not share the same pattern of compromise and fusion as Kentuckians. To them, reconstructing the antebellum social order meant clinging to a patriarchal system in the household and reinforcing the permanence of all relationships. Often, judges stood on the front lines of this battle, stabilizing an unsteady social order.

For example, Virginia state Justice Joseph Christian urged Virginians to refrain from divorce in the postwar years. During one 1867 appellate divorce case, he rejoiced, "Happily for the interests of society, and the sanctity of marital rights and relations, suits of this character are not of frequent occurrence in this State." According to Christian, Virginians rarely filed for divorce because of the "purity of social life and the inviolable sanctity of the marriage bond" in Virginia.[36] Though he and his fellow justices upheld Georgiana Bailey's divorce from her husband, James, they expressed "hope that such cases may be in the future as infrequent as they have been in the past." Gesturing to the recent loss of the war and the slave system, they tellingly prayed that:

> amid the whelming tide of social and political revolutions which threaten to sweep away all the forms of our cherished southern civilization, one pillar at least of the social fabric may still stand firm, and that the time may never come when the sacred bond of matrimony can be lightly broken, or the holy duties and high obligations it imposes, can be disregarded with impunity; but that marriage may be in the future, as it has been in the past, be ever recognized in Virginia as an institution to be cherished by law and sanctified by religion, as one upon which alone the happiness and purity of social and domestic life must ever depend.[37]

With the end of slavery, marriage became the next threatened institution of patriarchal control. White Virginians like Judge Christian felt that society was changing rapidly enough without dangerous "experimentation" with marital law. Throughout the South, many former slaveholders turned inward, relying on their domestic relationships to bolster their shaken masculinity. As a result, they sought to maintain some form of dependency within the home, even without their slaves.[38] Yet, in Kentucky, this "pillar" had begun to collapse even before emancipation began. As a result, it did not become the last vestige of Southern civilization as it was for some, like Judge Christian.

Other Virginians shared this attitude. For example, John Craig, a Fauquier County resident, echoed Judge Christian's sentiments about marriage and divorce in postwar Virginia. In response to his wife's 1870 divorce bill, John Craig wrote that he was "advised that the marriage tie is one of love solemnity & obligation & not dissolvable at the caprice of parties – and that although rapidly advancing in radicalism the state of Virginia is not yet up to Indiana in the cause of free love & general licentiousness."[39] Like Christian, Craig argued that Virginia was radicalizing too fast and fought to maintain the antebellum structure of marriage and divorce in the state. Both focused on the ease of divorce and, more specifically, individuals' *choice* to end their relationships. Divorce, like emancipation, revealed the impermanence of household relationships and hierarchical roles. After all, if a slave did not owe his master obedience and allegiance, did a wife owe her husband the same? Additionally, although neither Craig nor Christian mentioned the role of gender, the fact that both objected when a wife filed for divorce suggests that giving women the ability to end these relationships, especially without cause, was even more dangerous to white Southern social hierarchy.[40]

In their divorce records, however, Kentuckians display far fewer tendencies toward panic than their Virginian counterparts. While Kentuckians disparaged the racial changes occurring upon emancipation, their divorce petitions reflect less resistance to postwar adaptation in the home. Whereas Virginians like Craig and Christian fought to defend marriage as a sacred "obligation" for both parties, Kentucky law allowed residents to end their marriages for a wide range of reasons, including a loss of affection. Kentuckians might even agree to do so, a rare concept at the time. In much of the nineteenth-century United States, a couple's agreement to divorce was known as "collusion" and usually gave the court grounds to deny the divorce. Although no state yet embraced modern no-fault divorce, Kentuckians' use of mutual separation indicates a greater acceptance of contractualism and individualism in the state. In other words, Kentuckians more readily accepted the impermanence of marriage as a contract and the individual's role in both forming and ending that relationship. Both beliefs, taken to their extreme, had profound implications for gender roles and hierarchy in the home.[41]

Beginning in the antebellum period but continuing even after emancipation, Kentucky was one of only two states to allow divorce on the grounds of voluntary separation.[42] Most petitioners still charged their spouses most frequently with abandonment, rather than voluntary separation. Rather than a mutual decision to end a marriage, abandonment meant one person was at fault for a marriage's end, and the court required the wronged spouse to wait merely a year before filing for divorce. Nevertheless, although more infrequently used, voluntary separation became an option for some and a symbol that at least some of Kentucky's legislators, judges, and citizens had come to accept the legal philosophy of contractualism. Additionally, as Kentuckians sought companionate marriages more often, they began to hold their relationships to higher standards. Many argued that a relationship without common interests or emotional love was a failure, even if no cruelty, neglect, or abandonment had occurred. In such cases, courts should allow the two partners to agree to end their marriage, as one would with any contractual relationship.[43]

Kentucky judges upheld this view, allowing colluding couples to get divorces and accepting the contractual nature of marriage itself. Other judges, like Judge Christian of Virginia, sought to defend and keep permanent the hierarchical antebellum notion of family roles.[44] Christian argued that courts needed to "prevent parties who were weary of the bond of matrimony, and impatient of its restraints and obligations, from obtaining the aid of the court through their own collusion and default."[45] In Kentucky, though, an antebellum acceptance of contractualism continued even after the social turmoil of emancipation. Kentucky judges certainly did not welcome divorce and marital dissolution, but they reflected more on the personal tragedy of it than the social ramifications. After listening to one divorce case, Judge Belvard J. Peters ruled that when "neither party is shown to be without fault and the allowance for maintenance is reasonable, a decree of divorce will not be disturbed upon appeal."[46] His unruffled attitude suggests that this concept had gained some acceptance in the state.

Part of a transatlantic shift toward companionate marriages based on love and mutuality, Kentuckians also sought divorce when their relationships no longer reflected these ideals.[47] Both in their desire for more equitable roles for husbands and wives in their relationships, as well as in their desire for divorce when this did not happen, Kentuckians reflected a greater acceptance of contractualism and individualism in the post-emancipation years than Virginians. For example, E. Hensley, a middle-aged man from Franklin County, Kentucky, cited "irreconcilable differences" with his wife when he filed for divorce in September 1867. Divorce for Hensley was not a dramatic occurrence, resulting from unforgivable adultery or some other sin, but a remedy for his failed companionate relationship. The Franklin County Circuit Court upheld this as a viable argument, granting both spouses a divorce.[48] Provided couples met the basic requirements of the law (no cohabitation for five years and no intent to reunite), judges continued to view these charges as valid, despite their implications for the permanence of the marital relationship.

Kentuckian A. P. Carr also sought a companionate marriage based upon mutual interests and affection. She called her marriage "an unfortunate one" in her June 1869 divorce petition. Unfortunately, the couple's "dispositions, education, and temperaments were so different, they did not and could not agree" she complained. Her husband, W. H. Carr, responded to her petition, "unit[ing] in her prayer that they both be divorced."[49] The court quickly divorced the two. Others were less clear about the exact cause of their separation but fully admitted that both partners desired it. John J. Crittenden, a man "of color," married Agnes Jane Wilson in July 1866, but the couple lived together for less than a year before separating in May 1867. In his 1872 petition to the Franklin County Circuit Court, John stated only that the pair separated by "mutual consent." The court called two witnesses to confirm the marriage and separation (a deviation showing the court's suspicion of the legality of some black marriages), before granting John's request.[50]

Kentucky courts granted divorces for mutual separation even before the war, but the implications of this decision became even more radical in the postwar era. Allowing couples to decide collectively to end their relationship recognized the authority of both partners in marriage and in the household. It undercut the type of hierarchy required of many Southern homes. Just as emancipation threw one form of household dependence into question, mutual separation and collusion undermined another. Additionally, divorce itself suggested that certain social and familial ties were dissolvable, a dangerous suggestion in the era of emancipation. In spite of this, though, many Kentuckians chose to end their marriages through divorce, demonstrating the ways in which emancipation's impact differed depending upon the place and culture in which it occurred. Black freedom meant something different to white Kentuckians and white Virginians; while both feared the racial turmoil, emancipation did not threaten white gender roles in Kentucky to the same extent that it did in Virginia.

As Bluegrass courts granted more divorces on the grounds of mutual separation, some Kentucky couples chose to admit their mistakes and join their partner in requesting a divorce. Therefore, even petitions charging adultery, abandonment, or neglect reflected the same attitudes as those citing mutual separation – a growing acceptance of divorce as a legitimate solution to marital grievances. Over half of Franklin County's accused spouses who responded to a divorce petition either filed a cross-bill or acquiesced to the divorce. For example, when B.B. Sayre charged his wife, Catharine, with abandoning their marital home a mere three months after their wedding, she admitted freely that she "left his house with the intention of abandoning him as her husband." She would never live with him again, she vehemently assured the court. As such, she was "satisfied that it will be best for both him and herself" that they obtain a divorce."[51] The Franklin County Circuit Court agreed.

Did those accused spouses who did not respond to their partners object to the divorce? Why did they not also file and agree with their spouses that divorce was necessary? It can be difficult to tell, and less than a fifth of Franklin County spouses responded to their accusers. Many had left the state; others may have thought a silent assent through non-reply was more effective in obtaining the desired divorce than any answer at all.[52] However, another possibility remains. Franklin County residents may have felt little need to defend their reputations and to object to a divorce.

In Fauquier County, Virginia, on the other hand, almost 60 percent of spouses responded to their partner's claims. Some, like John Craig, fought against the divorce, citing the indecency of such an action. Many sought to clear their good names from the shame of divorce and accusations of adultery or abandonment.

In Fauquier County, even spouses who agreed to a partner's divorce strenuously denied all charges filed against them by the petitioning spouse. Joseph Brent, for one, objected strongly to his wife's accusations of abuse and abandonment. Ultimately, he did not want to "throw any obstacle" in the way of a divorce, but he wanted to set the record straight. According to Joseph, his wife, Sarah, had been another man's mistress before the couple's marriage, rather than the "virtuous maiden" he believed her to be.[53] While Virginian Arthur Sullivan also agreed with his wife's request for the couple's divorce, he denied her accusations of neglect and abandonment. He had tried "in every way to promote their [his wife and her children's] welfare by rendering such aid advice and assistence [sic] in all matters that concerned them as he could." He did not choose to leave but was forced to do so by Mary Sullivan's "violent and unreasonable temper."[54]

Both Joseph Brent and Arthur Sullivan agreed to a divorce, a small step toward the mutuality of Kentucky divorces, but neither was willing to take any blame and in fact felt obligated to shift it fully to their spouses. Their decision to do so reflects the harsher social judgment against divorces in their Virginia county than in Franklin County, Kentucky. Both men felt it necessary to protect their images and tarnish that of their wives. The legal system in Fauquier County necessitated a level of fault on one party not required in Franklin County. Divorce cases, after all, were crafted narratives, designed to obtain the goal of separation. While Kentuckians began to forego emotionally fraught language in their antebellum divorce petitions, choosing instead to rely on the letter of the law, Virginians in postwar Fauquier County still felt it necessary to spin a tale of woe for the courts.[55]

Virginia spouses emphasized the moral failings of their partner and, ultimately, their own innocence, knowing that the court would only allow a divorce under such stringent circumstances. Perhaps many petitioners knew that Judge Christian's view was common – that "amid the whelming tide of social and political revolutions which threaten … our cherished southern civilization, one pillar at least of the social fabric may still stand firm."[56] White perceptions of emancipation had profound effects on gender roles in the years following the Civil War. Because many Virginia judges, unlike some in Kentucky, saw emancipation as a threat to white household roles, they resisted other forms of social change such as divorce. As such, litigants in the Old Dominion had to work harder to prove the necessity of their separation.

Virginian Susannah Suddoth, who had been married to William Suddoth since 1841, told the Fauquier County Circuit Court that she preferred "long to suffer in silence and carry with her uncomplainingly through life the burden of her blasted hopes," than to "brin[g] her grief upon the public gaze." Though her husband drank frequently, and abused and neglected her, Susannah forgave him on multiple occasions. She did not file for divorce until he took up housekeeping with another woman.[57] Susannah's statements make it clear that she did not see all offenses as divorceable crimes, and the court probably agreed with her. She had to prove that she chose formal marital dissolution as a last resort, not a frivolous impulse or "caprice," and her length of marriage and moral credentials make that clear.[58]

She, like her fellow Virginians, stayed in her marriage longer than the average divorce petitioner from Franklin County, Kentucky. Half of those Fauquier County residents filing after the war had been married longer than ten years; a quarter had actually been married more than twenty years. On the other hand, three-quarters of Franklin County petitioners had been married less than five years.[59] Kentuckians had more faith in their ability to obtain a divorce quickly and with fewer charges than their Virginia counterparts. Not only did Virginia couples endure longer marriages before divorce, they also waited much longer than Franklin County residents to ask for said divorce. Whereas only 10 percent of Franklin County petitioners waited more than five years after a known marital crisis to file for divorce, more than 40 percent of Fauquier County petitioners did.[60]

Mary Sullivan, for instance, waited well over a decade to petition the Fauquier County Court for her divorce. A widow with children, she married Arthur Sullivan in September 1853. They lived together only five months before he abandoned her home, never to return. Mary waited until after the war to file, though, and insisted that "although maltreated, [she] would not ask for the interposition of a court of equity if she alone were involved in the misfortune."[61] She only did so for her son, she assured the court.

Even in their departing words to their spouses, some Kentuckians – often women – expressed a greater confidence in their ability to end their relationships on their own terms. Lenarca McDonald told her husband, Ambrose, that she was "a free woman" and "would go where she

pleased," when she left their home and marriage in late spring 1866.[62]
Similarly, after William Warren confronted his wife, Cynthia, about her
adulterous ways and the possible paternity of their son, she told him she
was "a free woman and would do as she pleased."[63] She soon abandoned
their home, fleeing with their children to Indiana. Although not definitive,
Lenarca McDonald and Cynthia Warren's use of the rhetoric of freedom
in making unconventional marital choices also suggests a weakening in
the patriarchal structure of the border South household during the post-
emancipation period.[64] Not only were Kentuckians less worried about the
impact of emancipation on white gender roles, many seem inspired by the
possibilities it opened up. As politicians, planters, and other leaders
debated the meaning of emancipation, the rights and roles of freedpeople,
and, ultimately, the definition of freedom itself, this discussion inevitably
influenced the rhetoric of some divorcing couples in the postwar years.

In addition to the length of their marriages and their use of fault-based
language, Virginians resisted post-emancipation legal change in other
ways as well. For example, Virginia petitioners continued to ask for
divorces from bed and board and for women to sue "by their next friends"
(a legal term reflecting their incapacity to act in their own name). Again,
although the number of divorces rose, the quality of the cases stayed much
the same. A third of Fauquier County petitioners asked only for a divorce
a mensa et thoro. Divorce *a mensa et thoro*, or divorce from bed and
board, amounted to little more than a legal separation, granting a couple
the right to live apart but denying either party the right to remarry.[65]

Those requesting divorce *a mensa et thoro* may have objected to a full
divorce upon moral grounds, a reflection of Virginia's postwar social
attitude, or they may have believed the court would not grant them a
full divorce for their charges, a reflection of Virginia's stricter legal code.
Kentucky state statutes, conversely, granted full divorces for numerous
reasons, including abandonment, cruelty, and adultery, while Virginia
law continued to maintain adultery as the sole cause for absolute
divorce.[66] Either way, the comparison with Franklin County is stark.
There, not a single one of the sixty-five petitioners chose to file for a
divorce *a mensa et thoro*, and they still achieved a higher rate of success
with their petitions than residents of Fauquier County.

Furthermore, in Fauquier County, Virginia, married women continued
to sue with their next friend, suggesting that the law still considered them
incompetent to stand alone and independent in their own divorce cases. In
the nineteenth century, women sued with the help of their next friend
because of the legal incapacity as *femes covert*. When women married,

they lost their legal status, becoming one with their husbands. A "next friend" (usually a male friend or on rare occasions a single woman) made it possible for married women, previously incapable of suing in court, to file for divorce. Courts obligated minors, those labeled mentally incapacitated, or others unable to act for themselves to sue with a next friend. Kentucky judges, even at the more conservative appellate level, viewed the concept of a "next friend" as outdated.[67] According to Judge George Robertson, a wife had the "right to sue in her own name for alimony and divorce."[68] Franklin County residents clearly agreed. Not a single woman filing for divorce in the county mentioned a "next friend." In Fauquier County, though, every woman who filed for divorce did so with a "next friend." Virginia's retention of the "next friend" standard reflects a general unwillingness to believe that women could be legal actors on their own, or, further, rational, decision-making partners in marriage. As previously stated, women's growing independence could be especially threatening in the postwar years, when white men needed some level of patriarchal control despite emancipation.[69]

Virginia courts required greater justification for divorce, but at the same time, marriages themselves may also have become more volatile in this uncertain postwar world. Ultimately, emancipation shook the very core of white male identity and made Southern men feel "marginalized." According to Laura Edwards, "not only did the borders of their households shrink but the very basis of [white men's] mastery was called into question."[70] It is not unreasonable to assume that some men took out this frustration on the dependents who remained – their wives. For example, though John and Virginia Walden had been married since the 1850s, their relationship grew increasingly acrimonious in the postwar years. In the months approaching their 1867 separation, John cursed his wife and told her he "wished she was dead." Once, he repeatedly punched her in the head, and another time he "tried to throw her over the barristers of the stairway saying he would bread her d-d neck." She sued for divorce after he drove her from their home with a carriage whip. John Walden defended his actions as necessary because his wife had been "insubordinate."[71]

Of the Fauquier County wives who charged their husbands with abandonment during the postwar years, two-thirds added additional charges – including cruelty, neglect, and adultery. In Franklin County, on the other hand, nearly 60 percent of those wives who charged their husbands with abandonment relied on that charge alone. Either Virginians' relationships grew more contentious in the postbellum period, a reflection of emancipation's larger social tensions, or the law's demands forced them to combine numerous charges to justify the socially risky decision to divorce.

Either way, Kentuckians, like Catherine Bailey and Mary Mack, exhibited a greater tendency toward legal simplicity in the postwar years, knowing that both society and the courts were more receptive of divorce in their state. Born Catherine and Mary Ridley, the two sisters from Franklin County married within a week of each other in early February 1866. The pair shared more than the timing of their nuptials, however. In August 1866, George Bailey abandoned Catherine, and by September, Horace Mack abandoned Mary as well. As the sisters experienced so much together, it is perhaps fitting that they filed for divorce in the Franklin County Circuit Court on the same day – June 11, 1868. Displaying a rare bureaucratic desire for efficiency, the court allowed their mother's testimony to be used in both cases, the only witness for either sister. Within weeks of her deposition, the court gave both sisters divorces and full rights as unmarried women.[72] Their simple and effective cases reflect the spirit of contractualism and legal continuity found in post-emancipation Kentucky cases.

In March 1864, Benjamin Mourning, a sixty-year-old widower from Franklin County, Kentucky, married Laura Alley, a widow and the mother of several young children. Although Lincoln's 1863 Emancipation Proclamation did not apply to Bluegrass slaveholders such as Benjamin, he, like other Kentuckians, nonetheless felt the effects. Worried that he would lose his remaining slaves, Benjamin feared the impact on his household. Before his marriage, he told friends that Laura seemed to be an "intelligent business woman and good housekeeper," and that he sought her hand in marriage to "keep his house" if emancipation occurred. Ironically, this marriage, created out of fear of emancipation, crumbled at the same moment that such a future seemed certain. By the end of May 1865, Benjamin threw Laura out of his house, an event that led to her successful 1866 divorce petition.[73]

Benjamin and Laura's tumultuous relationship symbolizes the domestic ripples caused by black emancipation in the South during the immediate postwar years. As shown in this volume, emancipation was a contested process with a variety of meanings for both black and white Southerners. However, analyzing the impact of emancipation in a border state like Kentucky demonstrates the ways in which this process differed not only based on one's color and class, but also based on one's region. As it did throughout the South, emancipation in Kentucky threatened both public and private racial hierarchies, leading to a backlash within the state toward its newly freed population. In the years following the war, Kentuckians would implement harsh economic and political measures against blacks, as well as participate in the wave of racial violence that swept the South. However, as Kentuckians' divorce records indicate, black emancipation did not have the same disruptive impact on white gender roles within the household as it did in other regions.

FIGURE 4: "Unidentified soldier in Confederate uniform and his wife, Sarah A. Dasher."
Source: Unidentified photographer. Courtesy of the Library of Congress, Prints and Photographs Division, LC-DIG-ppmsca-33440.

Ultimately, the process of emancipation in the border South must be filtered through its unique antebellum experience. Because of their prewar hybrid border culture, Kentuckians exhibited a high level of adaptability within their households. In the 1850s, many residents embraced the companionate ideal, as well as liberalized divorce laws, while still maintaining a strong slave system in their state and in their homes. By the time emancipation did occur, the ties between gender and racial hierarchy in the state had grown weak, allowing citizens to experience seemingly contradictory views toward changes in the household. As historians continue to debate the impact of emancipation and its long-term meaning for white and black Southerners, it is worth remembering the ways in which the process of emancipation could be fractured by the complex, divided culture of a Southern borderland.

NOTES

1. Painting the Confederate cause as one of familial protection drew the sympathy and support of Southerners from all walks of life and created fiery support among the women of the South. Stephanie McCurry, *Masters of Small Worlds: Yeoman Households, Gender Relations, and the Political Culture of the Antebellum South Carolina Low Country* (New York: Oxford University Press, 1995), 293.
2. Peter W. Bardaglio, *Reconstructing the Household: Families, Sex, and the Law in the Nineteenth-Century South* (Chapel Hill: University of North Carolina Press, 1995), xi–xv. See also McCurry, *Masters of Small Worlds*, 219–224.
3. Naturally, this does not mean that white Southern households were not contested before the war, rather that this contestation took on new and urgent meaning in light of emancipation. As scholars have shown, black and white Southern women challenged the authority of masters and husbands during the antebellum years, in ways both subtle and overt. In this sense, emancipation merely gave these women further opportunity and the means with which to challenge their subordinate status. For an analysis of white women's challenges to male authority in the public and private sphere, see Elizabeth R. Varon, *We Mean to Be Counted: White Women and Politics in Antebellum Virginia* (Chapel Hill: University of North Carolina Press, 1998). For a look at both black and white women's struggles on Southern plantations, see Elizabeth Fox-Genovese, *Within the Plantation Household: Black and White Women of the Old South* (Chapel Hill: University of North Carolina Press, 1988); Laura F. Edwards, *Scarlett Doesn't Live Here Anymore: Southern Women in the Civil War Era* (Urbana: University of Illinois Press, 2004); Marli F. Weiner, *Mistresses and Slaves: Plantation Women in South Carolina, 1830–80* (Urbana: University of Illinois Press, 1997). For an analysis of slave women's experiences, see Stephanie M.H. Camp, *Closer to Freedom: Enslaved Women and Everyday Resistance in the Plantation South* (Chapel Hill: University of

North Carolina Press, 2004). For information on urban women or women on the fringes on society, see Suzanne Lebsock, *The Free Women of Petersburg: Status and Culture in a Southern Town, 1784–1860* (New York: W. W. Norton, 1984); Victoria E. Bynum, *Unruly Women: The Politics of Social and Sexual Control in the Old South* (Chapel Hill: University of North Carolina Press, 1992).

4. I sampled both appellate and chancery court cases for this chapter. The number of appellate cases was small, and I focused on a rhetorical analysis of those cases. For the county level statistics, I used all sixty circuit court cases on divorce from Franklin County, Kentucky, and Fauquier County, Virginia, between the years 1865 and 1873. Original copies of the circuit court records can be found at the Kentucky Department for Libraries and Archives, Frankfort, Kentucky, and at the Library of Virginia, accessed through the online Chancery Court Records Index. All statistics should be understood as the number of cases *of those found*, since numerous natural and man-made disasters may account for cases missing or destroyed. Technically, these divorce cases came before circuit courts "sitting in chancery." In other words, the circuit courts served, in these specific cases, as chancery, or equity courts. When I refer broadly to the courts, I use the term chancery courts. However, when referring to a specific court, I will use the name of the court, i.e. Franklin County Circuit Court, without adding "sitting in chancery."

5. Contractualism was an ideology that reflected a belief in "self-ownership, volition, and reciprocal exchange among formally equal individuals." Amy Dru Stanley, *From Bondage to Contract: Wage Labor, Marriage, and the Market in the Age of Slave Emancipation* (New York: Cambridge University Press, 1998), np, x, xii, 10, 33. In this case, "mutuality" means a sort of quasi-equality. Marriages were becoming partnerships – intellectually and socially. Nevertheless, women still had fewer legal and economic rights than men.

6. Historians have shown that the Confederate loss and the emancipation of four million slaves led to an identity crisis for many Southern men as they struggled to define their roles as household heads. White Southern women also reevaluated their positions within the household and with respect to the public sphere. Anne Firor Scott, *The Southern Lady: From Pedestal to Politics, 1830–1930* (Chicago: University of Chicago Press, 1970); George C. Rable, *Civil Wars: Women and the Crisis of Southern Nationalism* (Urbana: University of Illinois Press, 1989); LeeAnn Whites, *The Civil War as a Crisis in Gender: Augusta, Georgia, 1860–1890* (Athens: University of Georgia Press, 1995); Drew Gilpin Faust, *Mothers of Invention: Women of the Slaveholding South in the American Civil War* (Chapel Hill: University of North Carolina Press, 1996); Laura F. Edwards, *Gendered Strife and Confusion: The Political Culture of Reconstruction* (Urbana: University of Illinois Press, 1997).

7. Lowell H. Harrison, *The Civil War in Kentucky* (Lexington: University Press of Kentucky, 1975).

8. Aaron Astor, *Rebels on the Border: Civil War, Emancipation, and the Reconstruction of Kentucky and Missouri* (Baton Rouge: Louisiana State University Press, 2012), 133–144; Anne E. Marshall, *Creating a Confederate*

Kentucky: The Lost Cause and Civil War Memory in a Border State (Chapel Hill: University of North Carolina Press, 2010), 1–3, 55–62.

9. E. Merton Coulter, *The Civil War and Readjustment in Kentucky* (Chapel Hill: University of North Carolina Press, 1926), 439.

10. Faust, *Mothers of Invention*; Bardaglio, *Reconstructing the Household*; Whites, *The Civil War as a Crisis in Gender*.

11. Keith C. Barton, "'Good Cooks and Washers': Slave Hiring, Domestic Labor, and the Market in Bourbon County, Kentucky," *The Journal of American History* 84, no. 2 (September 1997): 436–460.

12. Diane Mutti Burke, *On Slavery's Border: Missouri's Small Slaveholding Households, 1815–1865* (Athens: University of Georgia Press, 2010), 9, 54–60.

13. Stephanie Cole, "Servants and Slaves in Louisville: Race, Ethnicity, and Household Labor in an Antebellum Border City," *Ohio Valley History* 11, no. 1 (Spring 2011): 3–25.

14. Astor, *Rebels on the Border*, 8. Diane Mutti Burke makes a similar argument about the effects of geography and slavery in antebellum Missouri. Burke, *On Slavery's Border*, 57–60.

15. In her pivotal work on white and black women in the slaveholding South, Elizabeth Fox-Genovese argues that although "slaveholding ladies were massively outnumbered by nonslaveholding or small-slaveholding women," this "does not undermine the power of the ideal." See Fox-Genovese, *Within the Plantation Household*, 47.

16. Anya Jabour documented these traits of companionate marriage in her study of William and Elizabeth Wirt's marriage during the early republic years in Virginia. Many of the relationship characteristics for which the Wirts strove are found in Kentucky marriages of the 1840s and 1850s. However, in many ways the end of the Revolution provided a narrow opportunity for equality in marital relationships that remained largely unfulfilled in the South in the years after the Wirts' death. While companionate marriages can certainly be found in Virginia during the late antebellum years, my research suggests they were less common than in Kentucky. Jabour, *Marriage in the Early Republic: Elizabeth and William Wirt and the Companionate Ideal* (Baltimore: Johns Hopkins University Press, 2002).

17. Jane Turner Censer has argued that many postwar Virginians sought companionate marriages. However, she argues that this depended a good bit upon age, with the youngest generation most easily adapting to emancipation and changing their marital patterns. Censer, *The Reconstruction of White Southern Womanhood, 1865–1895* (Baton Rouge: Louisiana State University Press, 2003), 32. See also Angela Boswell, *Her Act and Deed: Women's Lives in a Rural Southern County, 1837–1873* (College Station: Texas A & M University Press, 2001), 4.

18. For more information on the development of companionate marriages in the United States, see Lebsock, *The Free Women of Petersburg*, 17; Stephanie Coontz, *Marriage, a History: From Obedience to Intimacy, or How Love Conquered Marriage* (New York: Viking, 2005), 4–5; Norma Basch, *Framing American Divorce: From the Revolutionary Generation to the Victorians* (Berkeley: University of California Press, 1999); Robert L. Griswold, *Family*

and Divorce in California, 1850–1890: Victorian Illusions and Everyday Realities (Albany: State University of New York Press, 1982), 4–5; Nancy F. Cott, "Divorce and the Changing Status of Women in Eighteenth-Century Massachusetts," *William and Mary Quarterly* 33 (1976): 586–614 (see especially 593 and 613); Rebecca L. Davis, "'Not Marriage at All, but Simple Harlotry': The Companionate Marriage Controversy," *Journal of American History* 94, no. 4 (2008): 1137–1163; Brenda Stevenson, *Life in Black and White: Family and Community in the Slave South* (New York: Oxford University Press, 1996), 41–43, 47–48; Jan Lewis, *The Pursuit of Happiness: Family and Values in Jefferson's Virginia* (Cambridge: Cambridge University Press, 1983).

19. James Roark, *Masters without Slaves: Southern Planters in the Civil War and Reconstruction* (New York: Norton, 1977), 157, 203.

20. David Silkenat, *Moments of Despair: Suicide, Divorce, and Debt in Civil War Era North Carolina* (Chapel Hill: University of North Carolina Press, 2011), 2, 75, 105–106. For two analyses of the impact of Reconstruction constitutional conventions, see Victoria Bynum, "Reshaping the Bonds of Womanhood: Divorce in Reconstruction North Carolina," in *Divided Houses: Gender and the Civil War*, eds. Catharine Clinton and Nina Silber (New York: Oxford University Press, 1992), 320–333, and Suzanne Lebsock, "Radical Reconstruction and the Property Rights of Southern Women," *Journal of Southern History* 43, no. 2 (May 1977), 195–216.

21. Richard H. Chused, *Private Acts in Public Places: A Social History of Divorce in the Formative Era of American Family Law* (Philadelphia: University of Pennsylvania Press, 1994).

22. Bardaglio, *Reconstructing the Household*, 135–37. Amy Feely Morsman argues that there was a "subtle shift" from patriarchy to mutuality in postwar Virginia, but it was contingent upon the war and "especially the profound challenges that emancipation wrought." She also makes clear that this change was not without resistance on the part of planters. Additionally, I argue it happened more gradually than in Kentucky. Morsman, *The Big House after Slavery: Virginia Plantation Families and Their Postbellum Domestic Experiment* (Charlottesville: University of Virginia Press, 2010), 4–6, 8.

23. Both Anne Firor Scott and Jane Turner Censer argue that women's roles expanded in the postwar years. See Scott, *The Southern Lady* and Censer, *The Reconstruction of White Southern Womanhood*.

24. Lowell H. Harrison and James C. Klotter, *A New History of Kentucky* (Lexington: University of Kentucky Press, 1997), 187.

25. Astor, *Rebels on the Border*, 123–133. According to Astor, 57% of Kentucky's blacks served in the Army during the war, with many stationed at home. This only exacerbated postwar racial tension in Kentucky.

26. Marshall, *Creating a Confederate Kentucky*, 34.

27. Astor, *Rebels on the Border*, 122, 149–156.

28. Bardaglio, *Reconstructing the Household*, 118–120.

29. Silkenat, *Moments of Despair*, 104–111.

30. About 27% of Franklin County's population was enslaved by the eve of the war. A fifth of Kentucky's total population was enslaved in 1860. Census of the United States, 1800, 1860. See also Astor, *Rebels on the Border*, 8–13.

31. Marshall, *Creating a Confederate Kentucky*, 11–15; Ira Berlin, *Many Thousands Gone: The First Two Centuries of Slavery in North America* (Cambridge, Mass.: Harvard University Press, 1998), 7–8, 256.

32. Records of the Circuit Court of Franklin County, 1840–1873, Kentucky Department for Libraries and Archives, Frankfort, Kentucky.

33. Virginia's total slave population was a little less than one third of its total population. Census of the United States, 1860. See also Mary L. Mackall, Stevan F. Meserve, and Anne Mackall Sasscer, eds., *In the Shadow of the Enemy: The Civil War Journal of Ida Powell Dulany* (Knoxville: University of Tennessee Press, 2009).

34. Records of the Circuit Court of Fauquier County, 1850–1873, Chancery Court Records Index, Library of Virginia, Richmond, Virginia.

35. Mary Somerville Jones, *An Historical Geography of the Changing Divorce Law in the United States* (New York: Garland, 1987), 37, 40.

36. *Bailey v. Bailey*, 62 *Supreme Court of Virginia* 43 (1871); Jane Turner Censer, "'Smiling through Her Tears': Ante-Bellum Southern Women and Divorce," *American Journal of Legal History* 25 (January 1982): 24–47, 28. According to Thomas Buckley, the Virginia assembly approved only one-third of the divorce petitions it received in the antebellum era, and the "experiences of the petitioners reveal the harsh legal culture that surrounded divorce in the Old South." (In all, only about 200 divorces were granted over almost sixty years.) Thomas E. Buckley, *The Great Catastrophe of My Life: Divorce in the Old Dominion* (Chapel Hill: University of North Carolina Press, 2001), 3–4, 8–9.

37. *Bailey v. Bailey*, 62 *Supreme Court of Virginia* 43 (1871).

38. Whites, *The Civil War as a Crisis in Gender*, 222; Suzanne Lebsock, *Virginia Women: 1600–1945* (Richmond: Virginia State Library, 1987), 101. See also Morsman, *Big House after Slavery*, 4, 7–8.

39. *Craig, Mary Jane v. Craig, John* (1871), Fauquier County Circuit Court Records, Library of Virginia Online Chancery Court Index (hereafter LVA), no. 1871–024. For a discussion of Indiana as a divorce haven, see Hendrik Hartog, *Man and Wife in America: A History* (Cambridge, Mass.: Harvard University Press, 2000), 14; Nelson Manfred Blake, *The Road to Reno: A History of Divorce in the United States* (New York: Macmillan, 1962).

40. Cott, "Divorce and the Changing Status of Women in Eighteenth-Century Massachusetts," 586–614. See also Norma Basch, "Relief in the Premises: Divorce as a Woman's Remedy in New York and Indiana, 1815–1870," *Law and History Review* 8, no. 1 (Spring 1990): 1–24.

41. Hartog, *Man and Wife in America*, 70, 72–73.

42. Jones, *An Historical Geography*, 53; *Kentucky Revised Statutes, Annotated* (unknown, 1867), ch. 47, art. iii.

43. Coontz, *Marriage: A History*, 5, 8.

44. In fact, Kentucky's acceptance of mutual separation put them ahead of much of the nation. Nancy Cott calls nineteenth-century divorce an "adversarial procedure," which required that one party show the other had explicitly

broken their marital contract. Even in the postbellum years, courts frowned upon collusion. Nancy Cott, *Public Vows: A History of Marriage and the Nation* (Cambridge, Mass.: Harvard University Press, 2000), 48; *Code of Virginia*, ch. 105, sec. 6 (1873).

45. *Bailey v. Bailey*, 62 *Supreme Court of Virginia* 43 (1871).

46. *Wilson Reeves v. Elizabeth Reeves*, 3 *Kentucky Supreme Court of Appeals* 607 (1868). According to Hartog, where both parties were at fault, legal policy "declared that they became thereby 'suitable and proper companions for each other,' locked in permanent matrimony." Hartog, *Man and Wife in America*, 73.

47. Lawrence Stone, *The Family, Sex and Marriage in England, 1500 to 1800* (New York: Harper & Row, 1977); Leonore Davidoff and Catherine Hall, *Family Fortunes: Men and Women of the English Middle Class, 1780–1850* (Chicago: University of Chicago Press, 1991).

48. *Hensley, Elkanah D. v. Hensley, Orpha* (1867), Franklin County Circuit Court Records, Kentucky Department for Libraries and Archives, Frankfort, Kentucky, hereafter, cited as KDLA, no. 1042. Hensley is also spelled "Hensly" throughout the court documents.

49. *Carr, A. P. v. Carr, W. H.* (1869), Franklin County Circuit Court Records, KDLA, no. 1094.

50. *Crittenden, John J. v. Crittenden, Agnes J.* (1872), Franklin County Circuit Court Records, KDLA, no. 1162.

51. *Sayre, B. B. v. Sayre, Catherine* (1868), Franklin County Circuit Court Records, KDLA, no. 1050.

52. Respondents who did reply tried to salvage their public reputation or prevent the court from charging them with the costs of the case. For some, risking the divorce itself may not have been worth those benefits. Uncontested divorces were largely more successful than contested ones. Chused, *Private Acts in Public Places*, 8.

53. *Brent, Sarah v. Brent, Joseph* (1867), Fauquier County Circuit Court Records, LVA, no. 1867–031.

54. *Sullivan, Mary E. v. Sullivan, Arthur* (1866), Fauquier County Circuit Court Records, LVA, no. 1866–056.

55. David Silkenat has argued that the change toward legal language and clarity in North Carolina's postbellum petitions signaled a growing acceptance of divorce. Silkenat, *Moments of Despair*, 116–117.

56. Loren Schweninger, *Families in Crisis in the Old South: Divorce, Slavery, and the Law* (Chapel Hill: University of North Carolina Press, 2012), 15–16.

57. *Suddoth, Susannah E. v. Suddoth, William T.* (1866), Fauquier County Circuit Court Records, LVA, no. 1866–013.

58. *Craig, Mary Jane v. Craig, John* (1871), Fauquier County Circuit Court Records, LVA, no. 1871–024.

59. These numbers are only for those cases in which the person filing listed both a date of marriage and a date of crisis (i.e. whatever year in which their partner left them, committed adultery, or was so cruel and intemperate they were forced to flee). I did not include in the length of marriage the period *after* the crisis but *before* the filing date.

60. These data reflect the date on which a crisis occurred for which the partner either left them or decided to obtain a divorce and the date on which the actual case was filed.

61. *Sullivan, Mary E. v. Sullivan, Arthur* (1866), Fauquier County Circuit Court Records, LVA, no. 1866–056.

62. *McDonald, Ambrose v. McDonald, Lenarca* (1867), Franklin County Circuit Court Records, KDLA, no. 1043.

63. *Warren, William H. v. Warren, Cynthia E.* (1871), Franklin County Circuit Court Records, KDLA, no. 1131.

64. Laura Edwards has argued that similar rhetoric in postwar North Carolina reflected the ways in which poor white and black women "drew implicit contrasts between [themselves] and elite white women." While the language of these women in Kentucky certainly reflects a similar non-elite perspective, the usage of the terminology of freedom also introduces a new component, which could have been found in women of all social statutes. Edwards, *Gendered Strife and Confusion*, 145.

65. Schweninger, *Families in Crisis in the Old South*, 2–4, 11.

66. *Revised Statutes, Kentucky, vol. II* (1852), ch. 47, art. iii, sec. i, xi; *Code of Virginia* (1849), title 31, ch. cix, sec. 6–7, 11, 13–14). See Hartog, *Man and Wife in America*, 36, 71.

67. Schweninger, *Families in Crisis in the Old South*, 66–67; Boswell, *Her Act and Deed*, 45.

68. Hartog, *Man and Wife in America*, 85; *Cain v. McHarry*, 65 *Kentucky Supreme Court of Appeals* 263 (1867).

69. Whites, *The Civil War as a Crisis in Gender*; Faust, *Mothers of Invention*.

70. Edwards, *Gendered Strife and Confusion*, 8, 113. Discussing the ways in which wartime changes might actually have enforced old marital norms, Nancy Cott argues that "the horrors and deprivations of combat, the losses of separation, the maimings and loneliness created longings to return to prewar conventions and resume the familiar customs of home." Cott, *Public Vows*, 78.

71. *Walden, Virginia F. v. Walden, John* (1869), Fauquier County Circuit Court Records, LVA, no. 1869–037 and 1869–071.

72. *Bailey v. Bailey* (1868), Franklin County Circuit Court Records, KDLA, no. 1057; *Mack v. Mack* (1868), Franklin County Circuit Court Records, KDLA, no. 1063.

73. *Mourning v. Mourning* (1866), Franklin County Circuit Court Records, KDLA, no. 1024.

5

Axes of Empire: Race, Region, and the "Greater Reconstruction" of Federal Authority after Emancipation

Carole Emberton

As the most sacred holiday in their calendar, Easter offers Christians an opportunity to reflect upon the joyous ideas of salvation and rebirth. The events of Easter 1873, however, awakened fears of dissolution and death. As Americans read their newspapers in the following week, reports of two violent events thousands of miles apart troubled their reflections. In rural Colfax, Louisiana, white paramilitaries, members of the nascent White League movement, killed more than 100 freedpeople in an effort to unseat local Republican officeholders. The Colfax Massacre was part of a larger statewide effort by the Democratic Party to regain control of the state's political system and end Republican efforts to extend civil and political rights to the state's former slaves. That same weekend on the California-Oregon border, a small group of Modoc Indians killed Major General Edward Canby, the U.S. commander of the Pacific Northwest, and another member of his "peace council," who were attempting to entice the Modocs back onto the Klamath Reservation. The Modocs had refused previous entreaties, disrupting the process of settlement in the area with frequent skirmishes with white civilians and government officials and igniting the "Modoc War," which lasted for most of the winter and spring of 1872–1873. On the surface, these two events may seem unrelated, but in the minds of many observers at the time, they represented a disconcerting problem in the national effort to destroy slavery and reconstruct Southern society: the nation's burgeoning culture of imperialism in the West.

This essay explores the complicated reactions to the Modoc War and the Colfax Massacre, using them as a way to gauge popular understandings of the implications of emancipation and Southern Reconstruction for the nation's advancing imperial endeavors. To many nineteenth-century Americans, the Civil War and Reconstruction were part of a longer, and in some minds, darker history of territorial expansion and conquest. As critic Amy Kaplan points out, "representations of U.S. imperialism were mapped not through a West/East axis of frontier symbols and politics, but instead through a North/South axis around the issues of slavery, Reconstruction and Jim Crow segregation." In other words, western expansion and conquest of native peoples cannot be understood simply as imperatives of some frontier mentality, but rather as outgrowths of the battle over slavery, its demise, and the reconstruction of American race relations. The discourse of freedom that arose from the politics of Civil War and emancipation reshaped the meaning of the West and the importance of expansion in American political culture. In the 1860s and 1870s, the need to restrain the escalating hostilities between Indians and whites supplanted the earlier promises of unfettered liberty on the frontier. As Gregory P. Downs points out in Chapter 2 of this volume, due to "the persistent power of Whig ideological support for a strong central state, and the exigencies of war, many Republicans developed a broad vision that freedom depended upon attachment to a state that restrained everyone."[1] And as the struggles to democratize the South began to stall in the mid 1870s, it became more critical to advance the cause of federal authority west of the Mississippi. These axes of American empire converged in April 1873, as Americans pondered the violence in Oregon and Louisiana and its meaning for the nation's future. In the late nineteenth century, as Americans moved from ambivalence to acceptance at the prospect of national expansion, the intersection of race and region hastened both the retreat from Southern Reconstruction and the final conquest of indigenous people in the West. Slavery's imperial shadow loomed large over the dawn of freedom.[2]

 While many nineteenth-century Americans possessed a clear understanding of how events in the South and West informed each other, historians have been slow to reconstruct those connections. Perhaps this is because the pairing of Southern Reconstruction and western conquest disrupts the triumphal narrative that we continue to ascribe to the Civil War era. Recently, scholars have begun to build a fuller narrative that defies conventional regional and temporal boundaries. Elliott West, for instance, writes of the "greater Reconstruction," an era that he argues began with westward migration in the two decades before the Civil War and ended with the final conquest of native peoples in the two decades after.[3] In this narrative, the Civil War is no longer the culminating act in the age of emancipation but one among several in the drama of nineteenth-century American imperialistic endeavors. When viewed in context of western expansion and the conquest of indigenous people in the long nineteenth century, the contests between blacks and whites in the South over the meaning of freedom take on new, troubling implications about the transformation of American society in the late nineteenth century. The projects typically celebrated as outgrowths of freedom – the destruction of slavery and the advent of national civil rights for African Americans in the 1860s and 1870s – informed the development of imperial projects at home and abroad just as disfranchisement laws and other discriminatory legislation would in future years.[4]

The origins of the Modoc War dated to the 1850s, when hostilities erupted between white settlers moving to the northern California/southern Oregon area in the wake of the Gold Rush. During that time, internecine struggles between the indigenous peoples living the area created a familiar tripartite pitting a weak state with little formal presence in the area against white settlers and their semi-private militias.[5] In 1853, one such militia of miners massacred an unsuspecting Modoc village in retaliation for a raid against white gold prospectors near Yreka, California. As was often the case in the cycle of violence and revenge within which whites and Indians orbited, the Modocs were not the responsible party. Pitt River Indians had committed the initial raid. Unable or unwilling to differentiate between different bands of native people, the hastily formed white militia killed the first Indians they came across. According to one account, the militia knowingly murdered the Modocs simply to satiate their own blood lust.[6] The fact that Modocs were "friendly" to white settlers made no difference. Nor did it matter that the Indians they found were mostly old women and children. The militia displayed the Indian scalps to local white townspeople in Yreka, who welcomed them as heroes. Three Modocs escaped the massacre and spread the word to other villages, setting in motion a decade of violence and upheaval that cost countless lives, including the family of a young Modoc called Keintpoos. Whites would come to know him as Captain Jack.

Until his death on the scaffold for the murder of General Canby in 1873, Keintpoos and a small band of Modocs would defy the U.S. government and its attempts to place them on a reservation from a place called the Lava Beds, a remote region on the California-Oregon border near Tule Lake formed by ancient volcanoes and dotted with some 700 known caves. This rugged terrain would serve Keintpoos's band well in their battle for sovereignty and self-determination both before and after Canby's death. In 1864, the Office of Indian Affairs

signed a treaty with leaders of Modoc, Klamath, and Yahooskin peoples
that ceded some 20 million acres of land in exchange for a 2 million–acre
reservation, as well as annuity payments for the following fifteen years.[7]
Preoccupied with the Civil War in the east, the U.S. Senate failed to ratify
the treaty until 1866, resulting in a painful delay in the food and supplies. Once they finally arrived, the Indian agent on the Klamath
Reservation refused to distribute the stores fairly, a familiar refrain in
the saga of U.S.–Indian relations during the late nineteenth century.
Adding insult to injury for the Modocs, they were now forced to live in
close proximity to their enemies, the Klamaths. Unwilling to endure
further starvation and humiliation, Keintpoos led several hundred
Modocs off the reservation.

For eight years, Keintpoos defied both federal and Oregon state author-
ity. Returning briefly to the reservation only once for a few weeks in late
1869, he lived on traditional Modoc lands, despite their cession to the U.S.
While Keintpoos was willing to settle on a new reservation away from the
Klamaths, the post–Civil War migration westward saw those lands fill up
with white settlers who demanded the Indians' removal. Attempts by the
Bureau of Indian Affairs to herd Keintpoos's band back to the Klamath
Reservation ended in embarrassing failures for the United States. For
months, as few as fifty-two Modoc warriors held off several hundred U.
S. troops using the rocks, craters, and caves of the Lava Beds as a natural
defensive position. In several battles in the winter of 1872–1873, before
Canby's assassination, Modocs repulsed attempts to drive them from the
beds, killing dozens of soldiers and earning the begrudging admiration of
whites who, despite their disbelief that the recently victorious U.S. Army
could not put down a tiny band of "savages," recognized Keintpoos's
determination. A San Francisco newspaper paid homage to him with the
following verse:

> I'm Captain Jack of the Lava Beds,
> I'm 'Cock o' the walk' and chief of the reds.
> I kin 'lie the ha'r' and scalp the heads
> Of the whole United States Army.[8]

By the time Keintpoos and his men ambushed and killed General Canby,
he already had garnered a national reputation as a formidable enemy of
the United States.

Canby's assassination shook the nation. He was highest-ranking military
officer killed in the Indian Wars. (When George Armstrong Custer died
at Little Bighorn in 1876, he was a lieutenant colonel.) Canby was a

well-known Civil War veteran who drove Confederate forces out of New Mexico early in the war, oversaw the draft in New York City after the riots there in July 1863, and administered the Union occupation of Mobile, Alabama, in 1864. He had also held several key military posts in the South during the early years of Reconstruction.

Not surprisingly, Americans reacted with shock and indignation at the news of Canby's murder. They also expressed exasperation with Grant's "Peace Policy," which had promised to curtail violence between Indians and whites and make the dispossession of native lands quicker and less bloody. Upon removing Indian Affairs from the purvey of the War Department and giving its administration over to Christian missionaries, Grant had hoped to stymie not only frontier violence but also malfeasance and corruption within the department. Compassion was to replace coercion; force would turn to fealty. Through a program of Christianization and bourgeois domesticity, Indian families on reservations would learn to read and write, farm, and wear American clothing. In other words, they would be transformed into the missionaries' ideal of peaceful, productive American citizens.[9] The Modocs' violent resistance, however, cast doubt on the efficacy of such a program. Tired of the government's "half measures" toward Indians, the *New York Herald* called an end to the peace policy. "What we want with the Indians is a clear policy," the editors wrote, "and one not only simple to us, but perfectly comprehensible to them – 'Keep the peace or we shall kill you.'"[10]

As federal assaults against the Modocs intensified, Keintpoos's authority over his men began to crumble. When U.S. troops finally succeeded in killing a leading warrior named Ellen's Man in early May, Modoc unity faltered, and their resistance soon followed. Fearful that continued fighting would result in their annihilation, Keintpoos's men began to defect in the hope that their surrender would spare their loved ones. Keintpoos himself refused to capitulate, but Army scouts captured him, his wife, and their daughter on June 4, not quite two months after Canby's assassination. The Modoc War was over.

A military tribunal sentenced Keintpoos and five other Modocs to death for the murders of Canby and Thomas. Although a few reform organizations, such as the Quakers and the American Indian Aid Association, rebuked the death sentences and called for leniency for the condemned Modocs, the calls for "national vengeance" won out. President Grant pardoned two young Modoc boys whose culpability the judge advocate doubted,[11] but Keintpoos and three other warriors were hanged on October 3, 1873, at Fort Klamath. The remaining members of

Keintpoos's band – thirty-nine men, sixty-four women, and sixty children – were exiled to Indian Territory in present-day Oklahoma.

Like the Modoc War, the Colfax Massacre had deep roots in the bloody
years of national expansion in the nineteenth century. Before the gold
seekers poured into California in the 1850s, men with "Mississippi
Fever," eager to make their fortunes in the cotton industry, settled on
the Red River district of northwest Louisiana in the 1820s and 1830s.
With the aid of the federal government, the would-be cotton barons killed
or drove out what remained of the indigenous populations of the region,
replacing them with hundreds of thousands of slaves from the upper
South. But their attempt to create an independent nation for slavery failed
miserably. With their slaves freed and their fortunes ruined, white men in
Louisiana struggled to regain their power in a world they could scarcely
recognize.

The paramilitary White League represented these men's grassroots
efforts to reclaim their once-great political, if not economic, power.
Individual, localized leagues began forming sometime in 1873 in direct
response to a number of events involving federal invention in state affairs.
The first was the government's prosecution of the Ku Klux Klan in 1871–
1872 under the Enforcement Acts, which resulted in martial law in several
counties in the state. These efforts had helped secure black voting in the
1872 election despite rampant fraud and intimidation on the part of
Democrats. Democrats decried the interference and refused to acknowledge Republican victors, including the governor-elect. For a time, this
contested election resulted in rival state governments, with both parties
claiming rightful possession of the state's highest office. Eventually, the
U.S. District court, at the urging of President Grant himself, certified the
Republican candidate. Believing they had been cheated of the governor-
ship, white Democrats vowed to take back their state government at all
costs and employed local paramilitary units to terrorize black voters and
their white allies. Unlike their masked predecessors, however, members of
the White League made no attempts to hide their identities with hoods or
robes. They eschewed the mysticism surrounding the Klan and other
secret organizations. White Leaguers advertised their membership
proudly and fashioned themselves as the Minute Men of their day.[12]

The Colfax Massacre was a direct result of the contested governor's
election in 1872. Not only were there, for a time, two rival state governments, there were also rival parish officials throughout the state. Carved
out of Rapides Parish to the south in 1869 and named in honor of the
president, Grant Parish contained a slight black majority, thereby making

it a valuable Republican asset. When federal officials in New Orleans certified the election in favor of Republicans, that party's elected officials set about taking their offices in Colfax, the county seat named for Grant's first vice-president, Schuyler Colfax. The town was nothing more than several buildings erected on the site of a former cotton plantation. The courthouse had once been a barn. Its makeshift appearance, however, belied the importance that its residents placed on that building. Control of its physical structure meant control of the county's, and thus the state's, political future. In order for Democrats to take back the state from Republican control, they would need to start at the county level. But when they attempted to oust the Republican candidates from their offices, the Republican governor, who owed his authority to the president, called in a unit of the state militia, an all-black unit commanded by a former slave named William Ward. For Ward and his militiamen, Colfax's ramshackle courthouse represented the desire for political and economic independence and the hope for a better life. Losing it would be a mighty blow to those dreams and the promise of Reconstruction.

A three-day standoff ensued, with the militiamen barricading themselves inside the courthouse/barn, while whites gathered their forces from surrounding parishes and even other states. After the shooting began, many black militiamen fled into the nearby woods, where they were shot and their bodies mutilated. After two white men were shot and killed (the whites claimed that they had been ambushed while attempting to broker an armistice with the militiamen; black survivors believed the men were shot accidentally by members of their own party), whites torched the courthouse, shooting the men that attempted to flee. In the end, at least 100 black men died, their bodies left scattered throughout the town and clogging the river – a testament of the price blacks would pay for their freedom and of whites' determination to control the political future of Louisiana.[13]

The Colfax Massacre, in fact, served as a rallying event for the fledgling White League movement, which had yet to take the name at the time of the killings, giving spirit and common cause to rural whites who found the bloody display of white unity overwhelming. The spectacle of violence buoyed white morale, which had been flagging under the weight of federal oversight, by demonstrating the inability of the state government – and by extension the national government – to maintain order and protect its citizens.[14] The impotency of the federal government was further demonstrated in the days following the massacre. Like the Lava Beds, Grant Parish was similarly remote and ill suited to a quick federal response. It

took a few dozen troops three days to get there by riverboat from New
Orleans, by which time the perpetrators had dispersed back into the
wooded swamplands of Louisiana, southern Arkansas, and eastern
Texas. It took the Justice Department, the Army, and the Louisiana
state militia nearly three months to round up a total of ninety-seven
men. Of those ninety-seven, the U.S. attorney determined that the stron-
gest evidence existed against nine, whom he charged with murder and a
conspiracy to deprive freedmen of their civil rights – charges made possible by the Enforcement Acts.

While death or exile awaited Keintpoos's band for defying federal
authority, the fate of the Colfax defendants was very different. The first
of two trials ended in one acquittal and a mistrial for the other eight
defendants. Three of those eight men were found guilty in a second trial,
but the federal judge overseeing the proceedings vacated those convictions
on the grounds that the prosecution had failed to prove racial animus, and
therefore federal jurisdiction over the matter under the Enforcement Acts
and the Fourteenth Amendment was null. The federal government
appealed to the U.S. Supreme Court, which ruled that the Enforcement
Act only applied to *state* actors, not private individuals, once again
negating federal jurisdiction over the crimes committed at Colfax. White
Louisianans celebrated the judgments in these trials as vindications of
their violent assault against Reconstruction. Calling the massacre a
"wholesome lesson" to blacks that defied white authority as well as whites
that had been cowed by federal intervention in state and local affairs,
white paramilitaries set out to "redeem" the South through violence.[15] In
1874 and 1875, White Leagues proliferated across Louisiana and the rest
of the Deep South. Confident in the protection awarded them by the
Supreme Court, the White Leagues ushered in a violent counterrevolution
to "redeem" the South from bi-racial democracy.

The Modoc War and the Colfax Massacre were singular events in post-
Civil War America. In the annals of western U.S. history, the Modoc,
alongside the Nez Perce and the Chiricahua Apache, demonstrated the
power and determination of native resistance to American settler colonialism in the late nineteenth century.[16] Colfax represented a turning point
in Southern Reconstruction, when the push for black civil and political
rights succumbed to the persistent and increasingly violent assaults from
white supremacists. Yet these two seemingly disparate events, separated
by thousands of miles, also converged in the eyes of many Americans as an
opportunity to think about the broader implications of the "greater
Reconstruction" of U.S. nationalism and federal sovereignty after the

Civil War. Both events posed some troubling questions for government officials struggling for the appropriate response to violent attacks against its agents and citizens. Likewise, social reformers working on behalf of both Indians and freedpeople wondered how to manage the incorporation of racial others into the national body politic. And as they observed the growing indifference toward the plight of both freedmen and native peoples alongside the proliferation of white violence against both groups, African Americans debated their role in the nation's burgeoning culture of imperialism. In this context, the meaning of freedom for some began to resemble a new kind of slavery for others.

In the immediate aftermath of the Easter weekend violence, northeastern newspapers condemned both the Modocs and Colfax perpetrators as "savages" bent on destroying the United States. In an article entitled, "Is Civilization a Failure?," the Bangor *Daily Whig and Courier* declared, "The massacre at Colfax lacked none of the repulsive features of the Modoc savagery, while the slaughter was multiplied by the hundreds. The barbarity of the whites might well excite the wondering admiration of Capt. Jack." Reminding readers that events in Louisiana were every bit as worrisome as those in California, the paper concluded "that the 'civilization' developed under the influence of Slavery, is still capable of atrocities which Indian 'barbarians' would find it difficult to equal and impossible to exceed." In this view, the Modoc attack against General Canby and the murder of freedmen at Colfax signaled not only a failure in government policy but also a failure in society at large. The Milwaukee *Daily Sentinel* saw a Hobbesian state of affairs in the United States: "What with Modocs in Oregon and Modocs in Louisiana ... we have enough to make us believe that men are never so happy as when killing and devouring each other," the editors wrote.[17]

Similarly, readers in Massachusetts encountered dreadful comparisons between the Modocs and Louisiana White Leaguers. "We call the Modocs savages, and public opinion demands their extermination as though they were wolves or panthers," wrote the Lowell *Daily Citizen and News*. "What word, in all the catalogue of infamy, shall we give to the fiends who shot an hundred negroes in Louisiana after they had surrendered, and burned the court house in which others had taken refuge?" the paper asked. In Arkansas, another Southern state in the throes of a violent white insurgency, the Republican press advocated that "[t]he strong hand of the federal government should enclose the vile murderers and crush them, as it proposes to do to their only prototypes, the savage Modocs."[18] It is hardly surprising that Arkansas Republicans would see the Modocs and white

Southerners in the same light, but the other responses suggest that the confluence of both events momentarily emboldened public sentiment in favor of a forceful response in Louisiana just as suspicion of federal intervention in the South had been growing.

Curiously, white Louisianans allied themselves with the federal government even as they set about to subvert its authority in their own state. Put on the defensive by national outrage at the slaughter in Grant Parish, the white Democratic press in the state sought to justify the extreme violence of the White League as an unfortunate but necessary measure to sweep back the tide of disorder brought about by emancipation and Radical Reconstruction. To do so, they spoke of the federal government and the white South as "civilized nations" in a common struggle. The New Orleans *Daily Picayune* compared the black militiamen at Colfax, who they claimed killed a prominent white citizen of the parish as he tried to broker peace, to the Modocs who had killed General Canby. Both groups, they claimed, should be violently subdued and placed firmly under white control. "Now, it is, we believe, a universal law of war amongst all civilized nations," the paper declared, "that when beleaguered troops invite conference, and shoot down the ambassador or commissioner sent to meet it – they forfeit all clemency, and may be slaughtered at the will of the conqueror." White Louisianans' violent struggle for control over local and state politics clearly shaped their reading of events in the West. Despite their pleas for the return of "home rule" in the South, their project was not simply one of regional isolation; in fact, it was part of a much larger project of U.S. imperialism.

White Louisianans' attempt to ally themselves with the federal government in the cause of white supremacy was part of a complicated response among Southerners to western expansion. Since the beginning of Southern Reconstruction, white Southerners typically critiqued both federal intervention in the South and Grant's Indian policy as evidence of the government's misguided priorities, corruption, and incompetence. Native resistance in the West and freedpeople's effective grassroots political organization in the South led many critics of both the Peace Policy and Southern Reconstruction to pontificate on the "savagery" of both Indians and freedpeople. Take for instance, an editorial in a Virginia newspaper that impugned Grant for being too lenient with Indians and freedpeople. The editors wrote, "The Indians are fighting Federal troops in the West, and the niggers and scallawags [sic] are destroying the peace of society in many portions of the South. Truly, the times we live in are sadly out of joint, and don't look much like the 'peace' we hear Radicals promise."

Another Southern newspaper rebuked Grant for reining in the military in the West while declaring martial law in areas of the South.[19] "While the Indians are devastating the Western Territories, impeding travel, checking emigration and improvement, and murdering settlers," wrote the *Georgia Weekly Telegraph*, "an army of sixty thousand men is kept by the Radical Congress in the South for the purpose, sole purpose, of influencing coming elections."[20] Exaggeration of the number of soldiers aside, the *Telegraph* dismissed Grant's desire for peace as a ruse to acquire political dominance in the South. Southern critics also used the specter of Indian depredations to demean the Republican project of civil rights for blacks. Many white Southerners, therefore, understood Colfax and the ensuing Modoc War within their emerging struggle for white supremacy.

Within these anti-Reconstruction readings of westward expansion, there also emerged an anti-imperialist discourse that stood in stark contrast to white Louisianans' support for it. In an editorial entitled "The Future," the *Baltimore Gazette* warned that completion of the transcontinental railroad signaled the end of America's republican institutions. The editors feared that in order to incorporate the vast geographic and demographic diversity that the West represented it would "be compelled to organize permanently in the North and West the crushing despotism it has set up in the South." The paper imagined an explosion of "conflicting sectional interests of a violent character and on a stupendous scale," with which "Congress will be constantly meddling" but fail to reconcile. "The attempt to maintain in this country the political system under which we lived before the war will inevitably fail," the *Gazette* predicted. In other words, Southern Reconstruction entailed an important lesson for Americans eager to establish national supremacy across the continent: it would be a costly if not impossible endeavor marred by violence, coercion, and "crushing despotism." Echoing the fears of anarchy and dissolution that Amy Kaplan finds in her study of American responses to the country's imperialist entanglements later in the century, this editorial demonstrates how Southern Reconstruction and western expansion intersected in the minds of some Americans to destabilize the development of post–Civil War nationalism by calling into question both the practical and ideological implications of Manifest Destiny.

This ambivalence could manifest itself in the most curious ways. Initially, white Southerners, particularly white paramilitaries in Louisiana, deplored the comparison to Modocs. The next year, when the White League attempted an armed coup d'état of the Louisiana state government in the winter of 1875, President Grant called on General

Philip "Fighting Phil" Sheridan to restore order in New Orleans as he had done after the bloody massacre of freedpeople there in 1866. Sheridan telegrammed Grant, stating his desire to treat the White Leaguers as "banditti" and try them by military tribunal as he had with the Modocs two years earlier. When the White League intercepted this telegram and published it in the national papers, the outrage was palpable. The implied comparison between white Southerners and hostile Indians infuriated the Leaguers who saw themselves as reincarnations of Revolutionary patriots. They burned Sheridan in effigy in New Orleans, and both he and Grant received the ire of the Southern press. Eventually, the public outcry forced Grant to publicly rebuke Sheridan for the telegram. Yet at the same time in Mississippi, as White Leaguers there mounted similar campaigns against freedpeople and their white allies, one band of paramilitaries in Vicksburg called themselves "Modocs" in honor of the California Indians who had slain a U.S. general. Another example in the long history of white Euro-Americans "playing Indian," the Mississippi Modocs assumed a native identity (in name only; there is no evidence they dressed up like the Boston Tea Partiers did, for example) as a way to legitimize their use of violence and pay homage to the idea of the "noble savage" even as they hoped for his extermination.[21]

Such romanticization could make it appear that some of Grant's critics were sympathetic to the suffering of native peoples. One newspaper branded Radical Republicans as hypocrites for their "war cry" of "extermination of the Indians, while they whine like spaniels over the wrongs of the negro." Another paper claimed that Grant had violated his campaign slogan "let us have peace" with his action against the western Indian tribes.[22] Although such criticism is hardly evidence of any real humanitarian concern for Native Americans, they did reveal a troubling contradiction for Republicans who professed friendship toward both Indians and freedpeople. Not only did Republican sympathy for Indian suffering waver with the political tides, their peculiar brand of protectionism rested upon a paternalistic understanding of race relations. Just as the freedmen were expected to work diligently in Southern fields and not press their political or economic independence too hard, Native Americans were expected to relinquish their claims to their tribal homelands and either move onto reservations or assimilate into white society by assuming the mantle of bourgeois domesticity and land ownership. In either case, freed slaves and Indians would cease to be burdens to the American government. When they refused, sticks replaced carrots. Freedmen's Bureau agents routinely withheld rations from freedmen in order to entice them to work and refused to intervene when planters whipped or "turned out" uncooperative workers. While the Peace Policy, in part, responded to the escalating violence in the West and fears that natives would be driven to extinction (a similar fear whites had about freedpeople in the early years of Reconstruction), the "tender violence" of the so-called friends of the Indian nonetheless pursued a course of cultural extinction predicated on the disappearance of Indian culture. Of course, real violence – the Army – was never taken out of the picture completely, and the brutal suppression of Native American resistance was part and parcel of the government's larger civilizing mission.[23]

Although Grant's critics were no less opportunistic when it came to their professed sympathy for the nation's downtrodden peoples, the imperialist thrust underlying Republicans' Reconstruction policies circumscribed the meaning and experience of freedom in post-emancipation America. This desire to control and exploit indigenous people and their land reframes our understanding of the long freedom struggle that emerged in the decades after the Civil War. In his examination of the fate of Cherokee slaveholders and their slaves after the Civil War, Claudio Saunt demonstrates how lawmakers and reformers used the language of freedom to sever the remaining bonds of indigenous authority in Indian Territory. In what he terms "the ironic convergence between freedom and imperialism," Saunt notes how "the Reconstruction government imposed civil and political rights for blacks in the Five Tribes as part of a larger project to assert supremacy of the national state and to enlarge federal citizenship at the expense of the relationship between slaves and master, citizens and states, and Indians and indigenous governments." By requiring that Cherokee slaveholders free their slaves and grant them equal rights as members of the Cherokee Nation as conditions of the re-establishment of relations with the United States after the Civil War, the government undercut tribal sovereignty and supplanted it with the ostensibly "universal" language of citizenship rights. While loyal Indians who had sided with the Union and had owned no slaves embraced these new treaties of 1865 and 1866, others came to understand freedom as "the watchword of U.S. imperialism," and not simply because of their own racial prejudice against ex-slaves. The new treaties attached emancipation to the cession of additional tribal lands for the resettlement of other Indian groups (like Keintpoos's band of Modocs) and the consolidation of tribal government, which, as the opponents suspected, would make it easier for the United States to exploit Indian lands in the future. Thus, emancipation was part of a much larger drive to dilute indigenous authority and absorb native resources.[24]

The imperial implications of freedom extended beyond the slave-holders of the Five Tribes. The experience of Indian wars in the West in the years before and during the Civil War informed how lawmakers approached the question of Southern Reconstruction. During the heated debates in 1865–1866, Radical Republicans used Indian violence to argue for strict penalties against ex-Confederates. Radical Congressman Thaddeus Stevens used the government's repressive stance toward Native Americans as a justification for the proposed confiscation of ex-rebel property. Like Indians, Confederates had demonstrated that they, too, were a "fierce and savage people," Stevens declared, "whom we have a right to reduce to absolute submission and dependence." In fact, Stevens asserted that the Southern rebels had been more savage than Indians. Citing the atrocities of Confederate POW camps like Andersonville, Stevens admonished his colleagues that they "would do great injustice to those mild savages who owed us no allegiance, by pointing to those who perpetrated the massacre of Wyoming; or to the Comanches, or the wild Indians of the West, or the fierce tribes of the Oronoco – and yet you seize their lands and expel them from their native country." Stevens proposed no less for the secessionists and rebels, whose actions had cost far more white lives and government expense than any hostile acts by Native Americans.[25]

Although it might seem impossible for anyone to harbor more resentment for secessionists than Stevens, at least one person did, and her bitterness stemmed, in part, from the similarities she saw between slave-holders and Native Americans. Abolitionist Jane Swisshelm, who had been an outspoken critic of federal Indian Policy since the Sioux Uprising in 1862, saw both slaveholders and Indians as threats to a reconstructed American nation. Calling both groups "the scourges of this nation" who had been "pampered and pitied" by the federal government, Swisshelm advanced Stevens's call for confiscation a step further and urged a new course of action: extermination. "It is not necessary to kill all the people," she explained, "but we are rapidly exterminating Slaveholders, by taking away their power to live without labor, and we must do as much for the Indian." Swisshelm believed the Radical course to establish free labor should inform federal Indian policy, and instead of enticing natives onto reservations with food and other provisions, they should be forced to abandon their tribes, work or farm on private land, and pay taxes. "Stop the whole treaty business," Swisshelm advised. "[I]f he steals, imprison him; if he commits murder, hang him; if he loafs, let him starve." Like Radical Reconstruction, which divided the South into military districts governed by martial law, Swisshelm's solution to the Indian question also required military force, but not the half-hearted, defensive kind she observed in the West. "They go around our military like a hawk around a barnyard hen," she said of the Indians' lack of respect for the U.S. Army, "and fighting them by the rules of civilized warfare is simply a contrivance for furnishing salaries and fat contracts to officers and contractors."[26] The violence underlying both Stevens's and Swisshelm's vision of the "greater Reconstruction," and their willingness to impose it upon Native Americans, underscores the imperial vision that guided many federal policies created to bring about a more democratic South.

Where did this leave African Americans? Given their historical position as the objects of white domination, one might assume that those men and women who had so recently fought to unshackle themselves from chattel bondage might be more sensitive to ways that the federal government's imperialist designs might controvert their own claims to freedom. Some did, but the broader response from black Americans to the events of 1873 was complex, revealing the treacherous ground upon which a racially subjected people yearning to become equal citizens within a growing imperialist nation must tread. Emancipation and the subsequent civil rights legislation of Reconstruction opened up the possibility that African Americans might climb the ladder of racial hierarchy, but the hierarchy remained. Someone would be at the bottom – but who?

Nat Love found his answer. He was only fifteen years old the day in 1869 when he walked off the plantation where he had spent his life near Nashville, Tennessee, and struck out to see the world. Born into slavery, Love had come of age during the Civil War and had been free only a short time when he decided to head for Kansas because he "head heard it was something," and indeed it was. When he arrived in Dodge City, he found dance halls and saloons, gambling houses, and other establishments of ill repute that had made the frontier city notorious. Soon Love acquired a new job as a cattle herder, a set of clothes to match, and a Colt .45 pistol, the accoutrements not of a penniless freed slave but of "Deadwood Dick," the famed roper, rider, and gunslinger who would become one of the most iconic figures in the Old West mythology. Nat Love left Tennessee destitute, with little hope for independence or economic advancement, but in the West he found fame, a little fortune, and most importantly a sense of belonging, not only to the brotherhood of cowboys he so dearly loved, but

also to the nation that had held him and his fellow freedmen at arms'
length. At the age of 54, no longer a gunslinger but a respectable Pullman
porter, Love capitalized on the American fascination with the Wild West
by publishing an autobiography in which he praised the country's scenic
beauty and encouraged his readers to "See America!" and remember the
pioneer settlers, like himself, who endured countless hardships and dangers to make themselves and their nation more than they were before. "[L]
et your chests swell with pride that you are an American," Love told them,
"sprung from the same stock that men were composed of in those days."[27]

The hardships and dangers Love spoke of were not the ones he and his
family faced on the cotton plantation in Tennessee. The only story he
could tell as the former slave Nat Love was one of poverty, dependence,
and violence. However, as Deadwood Dick, he wove a tale of adventure,
independence, and rugged individualism that, as Heather Cox Richardson
points out, placated white Americans' sense of self in the late nineteenth
century.[28] Ironically, both stories were dominated by violence. In one,
freedmen like Love were usually the victims. In the other, deadly gunslin-
gers like Deadwood Dick were the perpetrators but always for a good
cause. The best cause, according to Love, was to make Indians "good";
that is, to kill them. When relating his many violent encounters with
Indians, Love often used the euphemistic language attributed to General
Phillip Sheridan, who reportedly said that the only good Indian he ever
saw was dead. Unlike Sheridan, who publicly denied he ever said those
words, Love felt no shame in dehumanizing Indians or glorifying the
violence settlers and government agents used to bring them to submission.
He apparently saw no irony either in speaking of Indians as savages when
many of his contemporaries also spoke about Southern blacks in the same
way. In Love's mind, he had overcome his degraded beginnings, had
transcended his race, and was no longer one of the savage Africans liberal
reformers fretted over and white supremacists hunted down with near
impunity. Nat Love had become American.

"For anyone concerned about the American race issue" in the late
nineteenth century, writes Nell Painter, "the parallel between white supremacy at home and imperialism abroad was obvious." But what about
imperialism at home? Before the Buffalo Soldiers rode up San Juan Hill
with Teddy Roosevelt, they rode into the American West to put down
Native-American resistance to U.S. authority. Men like Nat Love could
make a place for themselves in post-emancipation America by assuming
the mantle of "civilizer" and appeared untroubled by the part they played
in the brutal suppression of native people. Unlike Love, however, black

activists and intellectuals were acutely aware of the paradox of freedom as it emerged from the intersection of Southern Reconstruction and westward expansion, and they struggled to reconcile their hopes for ending racial violence against freedpeople with the cultural capital they gained by participating in nation-building projects like westward expansion.[29] Their responses to the Easter violence of 1873 set the tone for later engagements with U.S. imperial projects abroad in South America and Asia.[30]

One of the nation's leading black newspapers, the *Christian Recorder*, viewed both the Colfax Massacre and the planned "extermination" of the Modocs for Canby's murder as the products of white racial hatred. "It is astonishing how placid the national countenance has continued in the very presence of this bloody scene," the editors wrote in response to what appeared to be a lack of interest in yet another mass killing of freedpeople. "But how expect it, when it itself is engaged in enacting a scene of blood not altogether unlike the one in Louisiana," they continued, "engaged in killing Modoc men, and Modoc women, and Modoc children, to the end, 'that no Indian shall boast, that he or his ancestors murdered Gen. Canby.'" According to the *Recorder*, the Modoc violence was a response to years of white brutality leveled against them. While not condoning Indian aggression toward U.S. officials, the paper argued that the Modocs only "imitated, and in a small way, the mode of warfare that the Oregon whites taught them." Placing the events of Easter weekend in a broader context of violent expansionism helped the editors explain why whites seemed not to care about the Colfax murders. "When the nation in its official capacity can thus enact such heartless butchery [against the Modocs], it is altogether to be expected that Southern whites will not mince over the matter of killing a few 'niggers,'" they concluded.[31]

While the editors of the *Recorder* understood both events as a product of the quest for white supremacy, others saw the matter somewhat differently. In a eulogy for a murdered Mississippi sheriff, Bishop Haven of the Metropolitan AME Church in Washington, D.C., admonished his congregation for letting "Indian troubles" distract them from the real threat to American liberty: Southern violence against freedpeople and their white allies. "We must defend freedom of speech and freedom of ballot, or we perish from the earth," declared Haven, who called the attention given to the Modoc War and other Indian massacres a "universal national weakness" that diverted attention away from the continued killings and intimidation of Southern blacks. Haven believed that garnering sympathy for mistreatment and suffering was a zero-sum game; the more time and attention given to the West and Native Americans signaled a decrease in concern for the plight of freedpeople. And he was not wrong. The *New York Tribune* shared Haven's concern when it asked, "Is the President, on pretense of Indian troubles, removing the troops from the Southern states to the frontier, that Messrs. Wade Hampton, Forrest & Co. may have full swing of their threatened revolution?" As many Republicans had long feared, the suppression of Indian resistance in the West gave white Southerners much-needed political leverage against federal intervention in the South. The removal of troops from the South to the West no doubt eased the way for white paramilitaries to enact their armed insurrections throughout the 1870s. But both the *Tribune* and Haven's conceptualization of the South-West axis necessitated the quick and thorough suppression of indigenous people for the sake of Southern Reconstruction and civil rights. The treatment of native peoples or their sovereignty was a distraction from the *real* work of Reconstruction.[32]

Within a few months, the editors of the *Christian Recorder* began to echo Haven and the *Tribune*'s views. In a story about a Republican-Democrat coalition in Virginia, they referred to the conservative Republicans as "Modoc-Conservatives," "the Modocs," and "Modoc party," because of "their secret and underground way of working and hoodwinking the people." Like the Modocs, who they believed had ambushed General Canby at an ostensible peace conference, the Republicans (some of whom were black, according to the *Recorder*), had betrayed their constituents by allying themselves with those who sought to restrict black civil rights. These "political squirrels" had scapegoated freedpeople for personal gain.[33]

As their sympathy for the Modocs dissolved, the paper abandoned its earlier position that both Native Americans and African Americans were the objects of white racial hatred and imperial greed. Instead, the *Recorder* began to speak in the language of uplift and civilization that severed the shared history with indigenous people it recently envisioned. In a report on the outbreak of the Third Anglo-Ashanti War on Africa's Gold Coast, the *Recorder* struggled to reconcile its disapproval for British imperial violence with its equally strong disapproval for Ashanti "savagery." Calling the Ashanti "African Modocs," the paper acknowledged a continuum of colonial expansion taking place both in Africa and North America, but, at the same time, argued for a gentler hand in civilizing the dark continent, one for which African American missionaries were better suited. Like the Modoc, the "barbaric" Ashanti were guilty of gruesome atrocities, such as beheading and mutilating the bodies of British soldiers. While the paper clearly placed the Ashanti in a defensive position against British imperial greed, the editors nonetheless saw evidence of a backward people in need of Christianization. By comparing "our wars" with the Modocs and other native peoples to the British war with the Ashanti, the paper assumed the mantle of conquest even while it highlighted the ways in which both the Modocs and the Ashanti were fighting colonial domination.[34]

The *Recorder* further elucidated its position on imperialism in an article that predicted a "new era of hope" for American Indians. In it, the paper asked, "[c]ould not the African M.E. Church, or some other body of Christians make an arrangement for the removal of the Modoc Indians to the Indian territory on this side of the Rocky Mountains, and then train them in the arts of peace, open schools for the children, and preach the gospel to the adults?"[35] Foreshadowing the fate of Keintpoos's band, who were banished to Indian Territory, the *Recorder* now envisioned African Americans as potential saviors of indigenous people, a vision inspired at places such as Virginia's Hampton Institute, where, beginning in 1878, Indians sat alongside Southern blacks to learn the habits of Christian civilization. Hampton's founder, Samuel Chapman Armstrong, believed that African Americans could serve as models for Native Americans, an idea adopted by many Hampton graduates, such as Booker T. Washington, who would become the leaders of the black bourgeoisie, in part, by virtue of the authority established by their work with Indian students.[36]

Washington exemplified the black-uplift-through-Indian-uplift strategy. At Hampton, he supervised "the Wigwam," the nickname for the Indian boys' dormitory. In addition to helping his pupils "take off the blanket" and become accustomed to wearing American-style clothing and shoes, Washington kept tabs on their progress in the classroom and workshop. Like their black counterparts, male Indian students at Hampton learned a variety of skills, including farming, shoe making, blacksmithing, carpentry, printing, and tinning. Girls learned cooking, sewing, washing, and house-keeping. Writing about his work with Hampton's Indian students in a series of articles for the *Southern Workman*, Washington praised the Indian students' willingness and ability to learn the ways of civilization. They were so successful, in fact, that Washington reported that whites who had come in contact with them had changed their opinions regarding the Indians' potential for becoming civilized. Not only did the students board for the summer in Northern homes, where they impressed white families with their manners and poise, they also apprenticed with local tradesmen, who frequently remarked on their skill and work ethic. J.H. McDowell, a local mechanic who became the supervisor of Hampton's Indian Training shop, admitted that he came to the job "with no little prejudice against the race." However, after working in the shop for several months, he reported to Washington that his views were "radically changed." Although he expected to find them "indolent, indifferent, intractable, and without interest in acquiring mechanical knowledge," McDowell discovered the opposite to be true. Claiming to have found the answer to the "vexed 'Indian Question,'" McDowell's praise deeply affected Washington. "Surely if the Indian can be converted from his wrong ideas, the white man ought to be from his," Washington surmised soon after he became "Wigwam" supervisor, and McDowell's report confirmed his hope. This meant that whites could also abandon their prejudices against blacks, and by taking the lead in the field of Indian education African Americans like Washington could demonstrate blacks' progress as well. "I think the true test of civilization in any race," Washington wrote, "is shown by the desire of that race to assist those whose position is more unfortunate than theirs."[37]

By assuming the mantle of civilization, black leaders like Washington hoped to salvage some of the advancements made since emancipation. It was this reasoning that led black leaders, like Mississippi Senator Blanche Bruce, to rally behind a vision for Indian uplift and help weave it into national policy. While acknowledging that "Indian treaties have generally been made as the condition and instrument of acquiring the valuable territory" so that "the steadily growing, irrepressible white races should secure more room for their growth," Bruce accepted the reality of U.S. imperialism as inevitable. The problem, as he saw it, was that federal Indian policy had always sought to "maintain the paramount authority of the United States over Indian Territory and over Indian tribes, yet recognizing tribal independence and autonomy and local government." These contradictory aims, Bruce argued, led to confusion, mismanagement, and violence. The idea that Indian sovereignty might be preserved with the United States represented an "intangible ideal" that was "un-American." Indian liberty must be sacrificed if American authority was to be preserved. Therefore, the question for Bruce was not how to subvert the expansion of the United States but how to better care for those people who found themselves in its way. His answer was the systematic assimilation of indigenous people and the erasure of their native culture:

If the Indian is expected and required to respond to federal authority; if this people are expected to grow up into organized and well- ordered society; if they are to be civilized, in the best elements of their natures are to be developed in the exercise of their best functions, so as to produce individual character and social groups characteristic of enlightened people; if this is to be due under our system, its ultimate realization requires an adoption of a political philosophy that shall make the Indians, as an individual and as a tribe, subjects of American law and beneficiaries of American institutions, by making them first American citizens, and clothing them, as rapidly as their advancement and location will permit, with the protective and ennobling prerogatives of such citizenship.[38]

Bruce's general prescription anticipated federal Indian policy in the last two decades of the nineteenth century. Bruce advocated "the lovable and attractive side of our civilization," namely Westernized education and clothing as well as an allotment system, by which the "red-race problem" would be solved. No longer a "vagabond or fugitive," the uplifted Indian of Bruce's imagination would become "trustful and reliable."[39] These policies became federal law after passage of the Dawes Act in 1887.

The "red-race problem," as Bruce described it, was not simply a corollary to the black-race problem experienced by African Americans. Although the senator, like the editors of the *Christian Recorder* before him, acknowledged the role white imperialism played in the creation of both "problems," he saw the former as a partial solution to the latter; that is, Indian uplift and assimilation represented a civilizing mission that middle-class African Americans could participate in, thereby redeeming their own race in the eyes of whites.

In many ways, however, the suffering of indigenous people also mirrored that of American blacks, and, as such, provided black leaders with an uncomfortable glimpse into the future. Frederick Douglass pondered what the experience of Native Americans might signal for his race as Southern Reconstruction ebbed and a new era of racial segregation and disfranchisement began to flow. In an essay entitled "The Future of the Negro," published in the *North American Review*, black America's eldest statesman concluded that African Americans would not – must not – follow the path of the nation's indigenous populations. "The Hebrews in Egypt, the Moors in Spain, the Caribs in the West Indies, the Picts in Scotland, the Indians and the Chinese in our own country, show what may happen to the Negro," he explained. Like Bruce, Douglass accepted the fact of white imperialism as unavoidable and sought to make a safe place for African Americans within it through a program of uplift and assimilation. While talk of emigration to the western territories or abroad bubbled among those disgusted with the reversal of many of Reconstruction's most radical advancements, Douglass admonished black Southerners to stay put and "adjust [themselves] to American civilization" lest they "invite the fate of the Indian." Douglass explained,

The thought of setting apart a State or Territory and confining the Negro within its borders is a delusion. If the North and South could not live separately in peace, and without bloody and barbarous border wars, the white and black cannot. If the Negro could be bottled up, who could or would bottle up the irrepressible white man? What barrier has been strong enough to confine him? Plainly enough, migration is no policy for the Negro. He would invite the fate of the Indian, and be pushed away before the white man's bayonet.[40]

Douglass believed that setting themselves apart would only invite hostility and violence from whites, who would continue to see them as inferior. "The tendency of the age is unification, not isolation; not to clans and classes," he insisted. Only by demonstrating their value to American society rather than their opposition to it could African Americans secure their social and political advancement as well as their physical safety. Unlike Native Americans, who had bargained away their land and resources, allowing whites to corral them to the brink of extinction, Douglass urged black Americans to stand their ground. "Shrinking cowardice wins nothing from either meanness or magnanimity," he advised. Although "for a time the social and political privileges of the colored people may decrease," he nonetheless believed that eventually the situation would remedy itself. "[M]anly self-assertion and eternal vigilance," were the keys, according to Douglass, which apparently the Indian did not possess.[41] Struggling to be hopeful in the face of continued violence and growing legal discrimination, Douglass's juxtaposition of Native Americans and African Americans pitted the former against the latter in the march of "civilization." Freedom for African Americans would come at a cost to indigenous people.

Although imperialist culture offered different rewards for African Americans, black leaders' embrace of America's imperialist agenda reflected a larger trend in American society. That trend emerged, in part, by the convergence of South and West in the nation's political culture. By the late 1870s, recent supporters of Southern Reconstruction began to reconsider their position in the face of combined white paramilitary violence in the South and Indian resistance in the West. Unlike in 1873, however, when Republicans tended to see those paramilitaries and Modocs as a similar kind of threat to federal authority, by the end of Southern Reconstruction, Indians and freedpeople represented the real impediment to the American nation. The heady talk of freedom and individual rights, which had exemplified the hope and optimism of the early days of Reconstruction, gave way to a language of order, restraint, and civilization.

Even the most stalwart Republicans worried that there had been too much freedom. Writing in 1876, just weeks after the deaths of Custer and his men at the hands of the Sioux at Little Big Horn, editors at the *Nation* concluded that both Southern Reconstruction and the "Peace Policy" had failed for the same reason: both projects had resulted in "legalized pauperism." By giving annuities of food and clothing to Indians who agreed to go to reservations, and by administering to the impoverished condition of freedpeople through the long-defunct Freedmen's Bureau, the government had created a permanent underclass of dependent people who were "repulsive" and "a disgrace to our civilization." The failure also stemmed, according to the *Nation*, from the misguided philanthropy of missionaries and the other "riff-raff" to whom the government had entrusted the civilizing process. Echoing the complaints of Southern whites that blamed carpetbaggers, scalawags, and other political ne'er-do-wells for their violent resistance to Republican rule, the paper that had once praised the high-mindedness of Radical Reconstruction and its administrators, including President Grant, now concurred with the South's self-proclaimed Redeemers. In other words, the same mismanagement, corruption, and incompetence that had brought down the nation's financial system in 1873, as well as Radical Reconstruction, also damaged efforts to subdue western Indians and led to the shocking deaths of Custer and his men.

To right these wrongs, the *Nation* believed the United States, a relative newcomer to colonialism, should take a note from the playbook of the world's other rising imperial nation-states in order to correct these novice mistakes. "We have had this kind of work devolve on us only twice in our history – in dealing with the Indians and in dealing with the South," the editors explained, "and in both cases, where England, France, and Prussia would have used the flower of their educated youth, their most honored soldiers, and wisest lawyers and scientific men, we collected a large horde of broken-down men of all trades and callings." The magazine advised the government to take a more scientific approach to the management of its "vassals and wards." This call for a professional class of colonial managers became the hallmark of Progressive-era reform culture and the ethos of capitalist society in the twentieth century.[42]

The tangled relationship between the Civil War, emancipation, and U.S. imperialism challenges the easy and triumphant narrative of freedom and civil rights that historians typically tell about the nineteenth century. If slavery cast a long shadow over the nation, so too did freedom. White supremacist violence rolled back the tide of freedom in the South and rolled in the tide of federal authority in the West. The drive to

FIGURE 5: "Graves of Modoc Indians hanged at Fort Klamath, Oregon, for murder of Genl. Canby and Dr. Thomas of Peace Commission during Modoc War, 1872–1873."
Source: Unidentified photographer. Courtesy of the Library of Congress, Prints and Photographs Division, LC-USZ62-15540.

expand the nation, both geographically and structurally, and conquer the so-called savages who threatened this expansion, cannot be separated from the push to secure civil rights for former slaves and democratize the South. In many ways, the failure of the latter propelled the success of the former. Among its other varied and sometimes contradictory meanings, emancipation meant conquest. The dawn of freedom for enslaved African Americans signaled the dusk of sovereignty for the nation's indigenous tribes.

NOTES

1. Gregory P. Downs, Chapter 2 of this volume.
2. Amy Kaplan, *The Anarchy of Empire in the Making of U.S. Culture* (Cambridge, Mass.: Harvard University Press, 2005), 18.

3. Elliott West, *The Last Indian War: The Nez Perce Story* (New York: Oxford University Press, 2009), xx. Other studies that move the geographical focus of Reconstruction westward include Heather Cox Richardson, *West from Appomattox: The Reconstruction of America after the Civil War* (New Haven: Yale University Press, 2007); D. Michael Bottoms, *An Aristocracy of Color: Race and Reconstruction in California and the West* (Norman: University of Oklahoma Press, 2013); and Stacy L. Smith, *Freedom's Frontier: California and the Struggle over Unfree Labor, Emancipation, and Reconstruction* (Chapel Hill: University of North Carolina Press, 2013). While these works explore the dynamics of Reconstruction-era politics in western places, they generally neglect the dialectical relationship between the South and West that animated popular discourse at the time.

4. On the ways that Southern segregation informed America's colonial endeavors in the Caribbean and Pacific at the turn of the century, see C. Vann Woodward, *The Strange Career of Jim Crow* (New York: Oxford University Press, 2001 [1955]), 72; Gail Bederman, *Manliness and Civilization: A Cultural History of Gender and Race in the United States, 1880–1917* (Chicago: University of Chicago Press, 1996); Mary Renda, *Taking Haiti: Military Occupation and the Culture of U.S. Imperialism, 1915-1940* (Chapel Hill: University of North Carolina Press, 2001); Laura Briggs, *Reproducing Empire: Race, Sex, Science, and U.S. Imperialism in Puerto Rico* (Berkeley: University of California Press, 2002); and Paul Kramer, *The Blood of Government: Race, Empire, the United States and the Philippines* (Chapel Hill: University of North Carolina Press, 2006), among others.

5. General histories of the Modoc War include Jeff C. Riddle, *The Indian History of the Modoc War* (San Francisco: Marnell & Co., 1914); Keith Murray, *The Modocs and Their War* (Norman: University of Oklahoma Press, 1976 [1959]); and Arthur Quinn, *Hell with the Fire Out: A History of the Modoc War* (New York: Faber & Faber, 1997). Most recently, Boyd Cothran explores the memorialization of the Modoc War as part of the larger cultural justification for American imperialism in *Remembering the Modoc War: Redemptive Violence and the Making of American Innocence* (Chapel Hill: University of North Carolina Press, 2014).

6. Riddle, *The Indian History of the Modoc War*, 17.

7. "Treaty with the Klamath, etc., 1864," in Charles J. Kappler, ed. *Indian Affairs: Laws and Treaties*, vol. II (Washington: Government Printing Office, 1904), 865–868. See also Theodore Stern, "The Klamath Indians and the Treaty of 1864," *Oregon Historical Quarterly* 57, no. 3 (September 1956): 229–273.

8. Murray, *The Modocs and Their War*, 240.

9. On the "Peace Policy," see Robert Utley, "The Celebrated Peace Policy of General Grant," *North Dakota History* 20 (July 1953): 121–142; R. Pierce Beaver, *Church, State, and the American Indians: Two and a Half Centuries of Partnership in Missions between Protestant Churches and Government* (St. Louis, Mo.: Concordia Publishing, 1966); Robert Utley, *The Indian Frontier of the American West, 1846–1890* (Albuquerque: University of New Mexico Press, 1984); F.P. Prucha, *Documents of U.S. Indian Policy*

(Lincoln: University of Nebraska Press, 1990); H. Henrietta Stockel, *On the Bloody Road to Jesus: Christianity and the Chiricahua Apaches* (Albuquerque: University of New Mexico Press, 2004); David Sim, "The Peace Policy of Ulysses S. Grant," *American Nineteenth Century History* 9, no. 3 (September 2008): 241–268. See also Rose Stremlau, *Sustaining the Cherokee Family: Kinship and the Allotment of an Indigenous Nation* (Chapel Hill: University of North Carolina Press, 2011) and C. Joseph Genetin-Pilawa, *Crooked Paths to Allotment: The Fight over Federal Indian Policy after the Civil War* (Chapel Hill: University of North Carolina Press, 2012).

10. *New York Herald*, quoted in Memphis *Daily Appeal*, Apr. 14, 1873.
11. Murray, *The Modocs and Their War*, 295.
12. On the history of Reconstruction in Louisiana and the emergence of the White Leagues, see Joe Gray Taylor, *Louisiana Reconstructed, 1863–1877* (Baton Rouge: Louisiana State University Press, 1974).
13. Most recently, events surrounding the Colfax Massacre have been chronicled in Leanna Keith, *The Colfax Massacre: The Untold Story of Black Power, White Terror, and the Death of Reconstruction* (New York: Oxford University Press, 2008) and Charles Lane, *The Day Freedom Died: The Colfax Massacre, the Supreme Court, and the Betrayal of Reconstruction* (New York: Henry Holt, 2008).
14. I further discuss the role of the massacre in fostering white identity in *Beyond Redemption: Race, Violence, and the American South after the Civil War* (Chicago: University of Chicago Press, 2013), 188–192.
15. 43rd Congress., 2nd Sess., House Rep. 261, pt.3, "Louisiana Affairs," 771–772.
16. On the Nez Perce, see West, *The Last Indian War*. On the Chiricahua Apache, see, among others, Dan L. Thrapp, *The Conquest of Apacheria* (Norman: University of Oklahoma Press, 1967) and Edwin R. Sweeney, *From Cochise to Geronimo: The Chiricahua Apache, 1874–1886* (Norman: University of Oklahoma Press, 2010).
17. Bangor (Maine) *Daily Whig & Courier*, April 25, 1873; Milwaukee (Wisc.) *Daily Sentinel*, 20 April 1873.
18. Lowell (Mass.) *Daily Citizen and News*, April 24, 1873; Little Rock (Ark.) *Daily Republican*, April 28, 1873.
19. Staunton (Va.) *Spectator*, October 6, 1868.
20. *Georgia Weekly Telegraph*, September 18, 1868.
21. Philip Sheridan to Secretary of War Belknap, January 4, 1875. Philip H. Sheridan Papers, Library of Congress, Washington, D.C. I discuss the controversy in further detail in *Beyond Redemption*, 201–204. The account of the Mississippi Modocs is found in J. M. Gibson, *Memoirs of J. M. Gibson: Terrors of the Civil War and Reconstruction Days* (unknown, 1966). Philip Deloria explains the important historical function of white performance such as this in *Playing Indian* (New Haven: Yale University Press, 1998).
22. *Valley Virginian*, July 10, 1867; *Valley Spirit* (Pa.) March 9, 1870.
23. See Laura Wexler, *Tender Violence: Domestic Visions in an Age of U.S. Imperialism* (Chapel Hill: University of North Carolina Press, 2000).

24. Claudio Saunt, "The Paradox of Freedom: Tribal Sovereignty and Emancipation during the Reconstruction of Indian Territory," *Journal of Southern History* 70, no. 1 (February 2004): 63–94; (quotations on 71, 80).
25. *Congressional Globe*, March 19, 1867.
26. Printed in the Franklin (Pa.) *Repository*, June 12, 1867.
27. Nat Love, *The Life and Adventures of Nat Love* (New York: Arno Press, 1968), 146–147.
28. Richardson, *West from Appomattox.*
29. Nell Painter, *Standing at Armageddon: The United States, 1877–1919* (New York: Norton, 1987): 161. On the debates over U.S. imperialism among African American leaders, see Willard Gatewood, *Black Americans and the White Man's Burden, 1898–1903* (Urbana: University of Illinois Press, 1975); Kevin Gaines, *Uplifting the Race: Black Leadership, Politics, and Culture in the Twentieth Century* (Chapel Hill: University of North Carolina Press, 1996). For the twentieth century, see Penny M. Von Eschen, *Race against Empire: Black Americans and Anticolonialism, 1937–1957* (Ithaca: Cornell University Press, 1997).
30. On Buffalo Soldiers and their enthusiasm for Indian Wars, see Michelle Kuhl, "'We Have Seen the Fate of the Indian': Western Influences on African American Leadership in the Shadow of the Plains Wars," *American Nineteenth Century History* 12, no. 1 (March 2011): 25–48; 26–27.
31. *Christian Recorder*, May 1, 1873.
32. Ibid., May 23, 1873; *NY Tribune*, September 21, 1868.
33. *Christian Recorder,* September 18, 1873.
34. Ibid., November 6, 1873.
35. Ibid., October 23, 1873.
36. On Hampton Institute, see Donald F. Lindsey, *Indians at Hampton Institute, 1877–1923* (Urbana: University of Illinois Press, 1995); Robert Francis Engs, *Educating the Disfranchised and Disinherited: Samuel Chapman Armstrong and Hampton Institute, 1839–1893* (Knoxville: University of Tennessee Press, 1999); and Paulette Fairbanks Molin, "'Training the Hand, the Head, and the Heart': Indian Education at Hampton Institute," *Minnesota History* 51, no. 3 (Fall 1988): 82–98.
37. Washington's columns on Indian life at Hampton are reproduced in Louis R. Harlan, ed., *The Booker T. Washington Papers*, vol. 2 (Urbana: University of Illinois Press, 1972), 112, 94–95, 86. Washington's views on Native Americans are also discussed in Kuhl, "We Have Seen the Fate of the Indian," 35–39.
38. Blanche K. Bruce, "Speech on Indian Policy," 46th Cong., 2nd Sess., Part 3 (April 7, 1880), 2195–2196.
39. Ibid.
40. Frederick Douglass, "The Future of the Negro," *North American Review* (July 1884).
41. Ibid.
42. *Nation*, July 13, 1876.

6

Fear of Reenslavement: Black Political Mobilization in Response to the Waning of Reconstruction

Justin Behrend

In the midst of one of the most demoralizing electoral seasons in African American history, as white-line militias attacked black Republicans across the Deep South, and as the Democratic Party won numerous elections through fraud and intimidation, local black residents in Concordia Parish, Louisiana, grew increasingly apprehensive. At first glance, there seemed to be little to worry about in 1876. The parish was solidly Republican, as it had been since black enfranchisement nine years before. It was home to over thirteen thousand black people but only thirteen hundred white people, and black Republicans held nearly every local political position.[1] But even if Concordia Parish seemed relatively stable, the growing white supremacist insurgency in the surrounding parishes and counties could not be ignored. At campaign rallies, Republican speakers mentioned the merits of their party, but they also denounced, with unusual vehemence, the competing ticket. A victory for the Democrats, they warned, would not merely lead to a change in governance; it would mean, recalled Daniel Tucker, a fifty-six-year-old ex-slave farmer, that black people "would be put back into slavery."[2] On Election Day at one poll, freedpeople carried posters with images of black people being chased by white men with dogs, which was meant to indicate, according to a white planter who witnessed the scene, how "[white] southern people would treat the negro should the democratic party [sic] get into power."[3]

The possibility of reenslavement was rarely expressed openly in the Reconstruction era. African Americans were more likely to talk about, at least publicly, the progress that had been made since the abolition of slavery, as well as the present struggles to attain a fuller measure of freedom.

As William A. Link[4] and Paul Ortiz[5] explain in this volume, African Americans championed full citizenship in the United States as well as the extension of emancipation and democracy to the Caribbean and around the world. Yet as Gregory P. Downs[6] and Carole Emberton[7] point out, freedom was often dependent on proximity to federal power and subject to the vagaries of an emerging imperial state. This disconnect between claims of freedom and enforcement was one that ordinary African Americans knew all too well.

In Concordia Parish, talk of reenslavement had not surfaced among freedpeople in prior elections, and white Democrats never publicly advocated the reintroduction of slavery. And yet the memory of slavery had not receded into the distant past. Most of the black residents had been born into slavery. Former slaveholders lived within their midst, and the traumas of family separation, beatings, and other forms of abuse haunted the lives of the formerly enslaved. Indeed, the substantial efforts by freedpeople to create new churches, schools, and benevolent institutions, their struggles for better wages and to gain control over the products of their labor, and their political mobilizations that reshaped civil society in the South can be understood not merely as ends in themselves but also as an attempt to put as much distance as possible between their lives in freedom and their lives in bondage. And so while slavery loomed over the early years of emancipation, rarely was it openly acknowledged.

But reenslavement was discussed in Concordia Parish during the 1876 election, and this fact raises some important questions about freedpeople's perception of emancipation. Did ordinary freedpeople believe that reenslavement was possible? Was freedom so precarious that one election could reverse abolition? The possibility that former slaves feared reenslavement reminds us that emancipation was a process and not merely a definitive moment. Slavery's deep imprint on American culture and the lives of black people meant that it would continue to shape perceptions and reality long after the Civil War. And so we should not be surprised that some freedpeople would wonder if their legal freedom was secure and if slavery had been forever abolished.[8]

The scholarly literature on emancipation and Reconstruction has not forthrightly engaged with the possibility that freedpeople believed that slavery could return. The struggles of the postwar era have, for very good reasons, focused on forward-looking issues, namely claims of citizenship, suffrage, civil rights, land redistribution, laborers' rights, and so forth. Without a doubt, these struggles involved efforts to eradicate the culture of slavery after its legal status had been abolished. And while freedpeople often, quite rightly, feared that former Confederates and planters wanted to establish a social system with many of the hallmarks of legal bondage, the debates rarely insinuated that a return of slavery was imminent. Because abolition was accomplished through state law, military emancipation, and the Thirteenth Amendment, historians have often treated abolition as a fait accompli.[9] But did freedpeople see it that way?

Former slaves, recent scholars contend, used their memory of slavery as a touchstone to change public policies and social practices. Indeed, their new identity as "freed" men and women suggests that emancipation was definitive. In the immediate years after abolition, freedpeople made the political decision to look to the future and to frame their struggles in terms of their citizenship. What is less clear, however, is how freedpeople lived with the nightmare of slavery. How close to the surface were the memories of being chased by the slave patrol, or of being attacked by a slaveholder or other white person? Nor is it clear how freedpeople should have responded to the threat of reenslavement. Indeed, one of the more interesting aspects of this episode was their divided response to Reconstruction. One side blamed Republicans for not fully implementing a free society, while the other lamented that their freedom was insecure. Judging from the contentious Concordia Parish election of 1876, it seems that the traumatic memories of enslavement were ever present in the day-to-day lives of freedpeople, and that many considered black political power to be essential in keeping slavery in the shadows.[10]

Almost all of the residents of Concordia Parish were former slaves. In fact, ninety-three percent of the population was of African descent in 1870, making Concordia Parish the largest black majority county in the nation. Most had been forcibly transported to the parish by way of the internal slave trade to work the cotton fields for some of the wealthiest planters in the South. There they encountered some of the most fertile soil on the continent. Concordia Parish is nearly all bottomlands and bordered by rivers on three sides: the Black River to the west, the Red River to the South, and the Mississippi River to the east. As such, overflows from the rivers deposited layers of nutrient-rich silt across the seven-hundred and fifty square miles of the parish, making it one of the preeminent locations for cotton production.[11]

After the abolition of slavery, black residents' status and their influence changed considerably, even if most continued to work in the cotton fields. They were now able to choose their place of employment, with some leaving the parish while others selected plantations that offered schooling for their children.[12] After black men gained the right to vote, the electorate increased sixfold in the parish, leading to the election of Republicans in all levels of local and state government.[13] By 1876, the parish state senator, both state representatives, the sheriff, five of six justices of the peace, and five of six constables were black men.[14] And the Republican Party's twenty-four member executive committee, the parish's central partisan organizing body, was composed almost solely of black men, half of whom were laborers or farmers.[15]

The patterns of change in Concordia Parish as a result of emancipation were analogous to changes in the surrounding region, known as the Natchez District. Bisected by the Mississippi River and comprised of four Mississippi counties (Claiborne, Jefferson, Adams, and Wilkinson) and two Louisiana parishes (Tensas and Concordia), the district's most visible feature in the antebellum era was its vast cotton plantations. But during Reconstruction it earned another reputation as a stronghold of radical Republicanism. Hundreds of black men were elected to political offices in the region and a few, such as Hiram Revels and John R. Lynch, gained national renown in the halls of Congress. Moreover, these politicians, most of whom were ex-slaves, began to restructure civil society in profound ways. They modified the terms of labor and landownership, brought a measure of equality to public spaces, created public school systems, and gave voice to thousands of ordinary people's aspirations.[16]

Indeed, the changes that took place in Concordia Parish and in the Natchez District were not all that different from changes taking place throughout the South in the Reconstruction years. In the fields, black workers mobilized and gained more influence over their labor. At the local, state, and national levels, reforms initiated by Northern and Southern Republicans began to uproot the slaveocracy and put in its place political and social structures that protected the freedom of the emancipated and established a more egalitarian society. These changes, of course, were met with fierce resistance from ex-slaveholders and former Confederates. Indeed, the violent backlash from white supremacist militias testifies indirectly to the changes that mobilized freedpeople had produced. The militias, often in coordination with Democratic Party leaders, resorted to warlike violence to reverse the power that freedpeople had accumulated because other forms of coercion were unsuccessful in breaking freedpeople's sophisticated mobilization efforts.[17]

By 1876, the efforts to reconstruct the nation were at a crossroads. The violent counterrevolution was in full swing, and white-supremacist

Democrats had regained power in a number of Southern states. Republican leaders, both in Washington and in Southern state capitols, were flummoxed and dismayed by the White League insurgency but also by Northern voters, who seemed to have lost interest in protecting African American citizenship and ensuring free and fair elections. White militias had been gaining strength in Louisiana ever since the Colfax Massacre of 1873. Two years later in Mississippi, Democrats swept in to power through a concerted campaign of intimidation, electoral fraud, and violence, orchestrated by the White League. In May of 1876, just six months before the pivotal election in Concordia Parish, the murder of a local white merchant, just across the Mississippi River in Wilkinson County, precipitated a series of pitched battles between local militias. White-liner paramilitary organizations from the surrounding area poured into the county and proceeded to engage local black militias, resulting in the deaths of between thirty and fifty black men.[18] The rumblings of political terrorism were also evident in the neighboring West and East Feliciana Parishes.[19] In short, the wave of white-supremacist insurgency was lapping at the shores of Concordia Parish, threatening to unleash a torrent of violence against politically active black people and to upend the grassroots democracy that they had recently created. In addition, there was great fear that the state would flip to the Democrats and that President Grant's administration would do little to halt the violence.

And yet these fears were not so unusual, as freedpeople in other localities and in years past had faced similar threats. What was unusual was the rhetoric of reenslavement, and this rhetoric originated from the import and chaos of the 1876 election. All sides seemed to agree that the presidential contest between Rutherford B. Hayes and Samuel Tilden would be close, but few anticipated the subsequent electoral crisis that resulted from disputed returns in South Carolina, Florida, and Louisiana. With control of the executive branch up for grabs, Republicans and Democrats rushed to document the election results as they saw fit. The Republican-controlled U.S. Senate launched an investigation into the paramilitary tactics of white militias linked to the Democratic Party. Democrats in the House of Representatives countered with their own investigation into Republican fraud and intimidation. They held up examples of voter intimidation in places like Concordia Parish as equivalent in nature to the violence and fraud of the White Leagues.[20] But these claims were erroneous because no one was killed in the parish for their political beliefs, while hundreds of people in other counties and parishes were killed or assaulted for voting or identifying with the Republican Party.

Moreover, evidence of electoral fraud never surfaced in Concordia Parish. Nevertheless, the Democratic investigation had the unintended effect of documenting a local election with unusual detail. It produced three dozen affidavits from parish residents, and a total of nineteen witnesses answered questions before the House committee. These testimonies reflect a wide variety of perspectives, including white and black Democrats, fusionists, Republicans, officeholders, party agents, and ordinary voters.[21] While it may be that reenslavement rhetoric was unique to the 1876 election, it is equally possible that this rhetoric was not well recorded in other localities. Indeed, talk of a return to slavery surfaced in first-hand accounts from ordinary residents and only rarely in the documents usually associated with elections, such as newspapers and correspondence between political leaders.

While the threat of white-liner violence helps to explain why reenslavement rhetoric would surface, it was also the internal threat from political dissenters that prompted freedpeople to wonder about the permanence of their own freedom. For all of the positive changes that had emerged during Reconstruction, there were enough continuities with the past and dashed hopes for the future that a sizeable minority of Concordia Parish residents had grown frustrated with local officeholders. Black families still worked in the cotton fields (though on much improved terms), and they faced persistent poverty. Only a few were able to purchase land and those that did complained of high taxes.[22] These taxes were used primarily to fund the parish school system, yet the schools were only open for a few months a year. Teachers complained of inadequate pay, and the school buildings were often dilapidated.[23] In short, local black residents wondered if their elected officials had become ineffective, especially at a time when Republican power, nationally and regionally, was on the decline. If, as it seemed likely, Democrats were to eventually take control of the state, perhaps it was best to make some accord with Democratic Party leaders and avoid the violence that plagued so many other communities.

Building off of this grassroots discontent, a few disgruntled Republican officeholders seized the moment and formed a fusionist party. The fusionists brought together similarly disenchanted Republicans with black and white Democrats. Very few black men voted with the Democrats in the region, but an increasing number publicly identified with the party in 1876. Some believed that Democrats could bring new economic prosperity.[24] Some were chastened by Republican debacles, such as the failure of the Freedman's Savings Bank in 1874.[25] Others, such as Thomas Dorsey, a thirty-one-year-old farm laborer and the president of a black

Democratic club, hoped for specific material improvements. He told a congressional committee that Democrats had promised him that he "could lease land much cheaper; and, besides that, they talked about giving the colored people's children education."[26] As many as forty men joined Dorsey's black Democratic club, the first of its kind in the parish, in the hopes that their material prospects would also improve.[27]

While the fusionists hoped to unseat longstanding black politicians, their threat was not so much electoral as it was communal. The political community was divided. An increasing number of black men were aligning with the Democratic Party or with allies of the Democrats at precisely the same time when the Reconstruction commitment to a free and fair ballot was imperiled. It was one thing to face down white paramilitary forces. That was not unexpected. But it was altogether something else to see other former slaves and others who had once voted with the Republican Party now siding with white supremacists intent on stripping black people of their political power. It is in this context that the fears of reenslavement burst forth, and they suggest that the intended audience for these warnings were their neighbors, friends, and sometimes even spouses. It was a political campaign, in other words, over the meaning of emancipation, with one side claiming that their greatest success – the abolition of slavery – was not secure and the other side implying that Republicans had failed to extend the benefits of emancipation.

Facing a formidable external and internal challenge, local Republican leaders orchestrated a vigorous mobilization campaign that linked Democratic victory with the resurrection of slavery. The leader of the local party, David Young, who was a former runaway slave but now a state senator and minister at the leading black Baptist church, warned his audience at one political rally that "if the democrats succeeded in getting into office the colored people would be enslaved again."[28] At another rally, Young recalled the days when "hounds" and "bull-whipp[s]" were used to keep black people in bondage and admonished his constituents that those days would return "if they voted the democratic ticket."[29] These statements come from testimonies given by fusionist party leaders, who clearly had a political interest in portraying their competitors for office in a disparaging light. But ordinary black residents also reported that the reenslavement rhetoric was frequently used at Republican meetings and in everyday conversations in the days leading up to the election. Samuel Walker, a twenty-year-old black farmer, was typical of the eleven witnesses, eight of them black, who swore out affidavits asserting that the prospect of reenslavement was often discussed during the election campaign. "I have heard several colored men say previous to said election," he avowed, "that any colored man who voted the democratic ticket was voting to put himself back into slavery."[30]

While this rhetoric of reenslavement was rarely expressed during Reconstruction elections, its usage was not confined to just Concordia Parish. In similar parishes with large black majorities and Republican officeholders, both candidates for office as well as party agents warned that a Democratic victory would lead to reenslavement.[31] In Plaquemines Parish in 1876, George Williams, a thirty-two-year-old black laborer who worked in the rice fields, described a confrontation with a black Republican candidate for the state legislature. Williams, who identified himself as a Democrat, was told that he "would be put back in slavery," and when he refused to denounce the Democrats a group of black men, armed with sticks and clubs, chased him out of town.[32] Sam Robertson, a sixty-year-old black man from East Baton Rouge Parish who described his occupation as "planting," testified that a U.S. deputy marshal approached him and warned that "if colored people voted the democratic ticket they would be hunted down with negro-dogs," an allusion to the fate that befell runaway slaves.[33] Not surprisingly, noted a petition from twenty Ouachita Parish planters, "the colored voters generally were afraid to join the democratic party [sic] for fear of violence from some of their own race, and by fear of being remanded to slavery."[34]

Although the discourse of reenslavement is well documented, it is less clear how much of it was believed. Perhaps local Republican leaders and ordinary freedpeople genuinely thought that Democratic victory in 1876 would mean that black people would be put back into slavery. But it is equally plausible that the rhetoric was hyperbolic and meant to scare some into voting a straight Republican ticket. Parsing out perceptions from realities is a near impossible task in this case, but other evidence suggests that many freedpeople believed that they could be reenslaved. And they responded to this threat as one would expect – with vigorous opposition. This election was known not just for talk about returning to slavery but also for the many instances of physical intimidation and social ostracism.

We can tell that local Republican leaders treated this election differently from others because they reached out directly to black women at campaign events. It is unclear how typical it was for political speakers to address women at rallies, but no one seemed to doubt that freedwomen would be receptive to these appeals. Recalling a mass meeting on a plantation, a black constable reported that the women were counseled to "instruct their husbands to vote against" the fusionist ticket.[35] If the

men still insisted on voting with the Democrats, testified an ex-slave
landowner, "the women [were] advised to quit their husbands."[36]
William Warfield, a forty-five-year-old blacksmith, testified with veiled
outrage that prominent local leaders "told my wife to quit me."[37] The
president of a local Republican club asserted that he "heard colored women
say that if their husbands voted the democratic ticket they would quit
them."[38] Often those who testified, like Milton Ray, a forty-five-year-old
black laborer with a wife and three daughters, linked reenslavement to
female retaliation. Ray heard Republicans say that if black men voted the
fusionist ticket, "they would be remanded to slavery" and that the wives of
those men should "abandon their husbands."[39] At another mass meeting,
state Senator David Young addressed the women in the audience and
reassured those who left their husbands that "he would take care of
them" and help them "to get a divorce," according to the testimony of
multiple witnesses.[40]

Few women took up Senator Young on his offer of male protection, but
many women accepted the challenge of keeping black men – their husbands, sons, fathers, and neighbors – from voting with the Democrats.
Black farmers who voted for the Republican national ticket signed sworn
affidavits that they "often heard colored women ... say that any colored
man who voted the democratic ticket 'ought to be killed.'"[41] The night
before the 1876 election, at a Democratic club meeting of black and white
men at the Helena plantation, "several colored women came to the
room," testified the white club president, "and [they] were so discourteous
and so violent that we thought at one time we would be compelled to close
the meeting." "The wife of one of the colored men," he continued, "was
so obstreperous that she followed her husband clear to the speaker's
stand, and it was only with utmost persuasion that we could prevail
upon her not to attack her husband in the club-room."[42] James Foy's
wife ran off and left him "for two weeks" after the black justice of the
peace endorsed the Democrats.[43] "It has been so of late," concluded a
white Democratic club president, "that we cannot ride along the road
without some of the women using insulting language to us on account of
our political proclivities."[44]

While many of these accounts seem exaggerated, there is little doubt
that black women were unusually active in this campaign and that a fear
of reenslavement played a prominent role. But it was not just black
women who mobilized and pressured voters; numerous male party agents
used all manner of coercive and communal influence to stifle the fusionist
insurgency. As Election Day drew closer, those who did not embrace the

Republican ticket faced considerable social ostracism. Joe Williams, a thirty-seven-year-old black farmer, testified that black Republicans denounced black Democrats as race traitors who did not deserve "to walk alive [on] the roads of Concordia Parish."[45] In other instances, church members turned against their fellow worshippers and clerical leaders who were sympathetic toward fusionists or Democrats. The members of one church threatened to expel their minister, "and to burn his church, unless he did desist" in organizing a fusionist club, testified T. P. Jackson, one of the black fusionist leaders and the parish court clerk.[46] When Eli Johnson, a "prominent republican preacher," decided just before the election to vote against the Republican ticket, an unknown assailant targeted him for retribution by firing shots at him late one night in his front yard.[47]

If freedpeople were responding to a fear of reenslavement, the coercive actions of Republican voters in Concordia Parish become more understandable. Stepping outside the normative boundaries of election campaigning by intimidating voters and threatening violence carried substantial risks, since these actions tended to reinforce white supremacist arguments that black people did not have the proper disposition or character to be trusted with the franchise.[48] Yet facing the dissolution of their citizenship, these were risks that many black people seemed willing to accept. Joe Habit, a black farmer and landowner, complained that black Republicans threatened "to burn up my place and put me out" for voting Democrat, and that someone had killed three head of his cattle and some of his sheep.[49] At one mass meeting held on a plantation, a crowd of field-laborers, "aflourishing and aswinging sugar-knives," forced William Ridgley, a black, fusionist candidate for the state legislature, down from the speaker's platform.[50] At Black Hawk plantation, John Young, David Young's brother, along with a few associates who were armed with "pistols and sugar-knives," prevented Ridgley from addressing the gathered crowd.[51] Angry black Republicans threw bricks at Thomas Dorsey, the president of a black Democratic club, and later other men "got a club and hit me alongside the head," he testified. Dorsey's neighbors also threatened to murder "those damn democrat niggers on Morgan's place," where their club met. Dorsey was quite distressed by these verbal and physical attacks, since they were carried out at the church that he often attended and among his neighbors, whom he believed were "always good friends."[52] But friendship and neighborliness offered little respite for individuals who dared to help advance the interests of the Democratic Party during one of the most tumultuous elections in American history.

As the campaign season drew to a close, the dark warnings of slavery's imminent return and unprecedented social pressure were not having the desired effect. A sizeable number of black men still indicated that they were willing to vote with the fusionists and against the Republicans. As black men with fusionist tickets marched to the polls, one black woman standing close by began to cry because she believed that she and others would now "be sold back into slavery."[53]

But others were unwilling to watch as all the gains from emancipation were undone. One freedman justified his participation in the intimidation by declaring that "he was not going to suffer his people to vote the democratic ticket."[54] At Polls 3 and 4 in Concordia Parish, crowds of Republicans began to form when they noticed groups of black men attempting to vote the fusionist ticket.[55] The crowds soon breached the thirty-foot perimeter of the polling place that was supposed to give voters a measure of security. Dozens of people, including some with concealed weapons, surged toward the ballot box and "tore down the gallery," forcing the election commissioners to temporarily close Poll No. 3.[56] Anderson Tolliver, a black justice of the peace, carpenter, and Republican candidate for the state legislature, walked up and down the line of voters waiting at Poll No. 6 and told them that they were holding Democratic tickets. He then proceeded to take "them away and gave them Young [or Republican] tickets."[57] At another poll, freedpeople displayed posters, or "printed cuts," of "negroes chased by southern white men with dogs, pistols, &c." These visual images were, a white planter claimed, "calculated to deter colored men from voting the democratic ticket" by implying that Democrats would return black people to slavery.[58] When a white planter and the president of a Democratic club questioned the shoving and physical intimidation at the polls, local Republicans replied that "it was the only way to . . . keep the democrats from putting the whip and the stocks on them again."[59]

The aggressive actions and coercive methods of black women and men at the Concordia Parish election of 1876 were highly unusual. In the previous nine years of elections in which black men could vote, similar incidents of this kind were nonexistent in the parish. For the most part, elections took place with very little violence or coercion at the polling place. To be sure, interested parties exerted pressure and intimidated voters, but the typical culprits were white planters, not black political activists. Likewise, across the South, incidents of black Republicans threatening violence or of black women quitting their husbands for electoral reasons are difficult to find in the documentary record. The perpetrators of electoral violence were almost always white Democrats or white-supre-macist militiamen. For black women at this moment, the roving bands of armed white men who flouted the law may have brought to mind the slave patrols and the general power of white men to oppress black people. The memories of slavery – of family separation at the slave market, of sexual exploitation, and of brutal punishments – may explain why freedwomen became intensely interested in the outcome of this election and why they worked publicly to defeat the fusionist ticket.[60]

While a couple of local races were close in Concordia Parish, overall Republicans comfortably defeated the fusionists. In the race for clerk of the court, T. P. Jackson, the fusionist leader, narrowly lost to the Republican candidate by about four hundred votes, out of 2,800 cast.[61] In the statewide races, it was a different story. Eighty-seven percent of the votes cast from Concordia Parish went for the Republican candidate for governor.[62]

Nevertheless, Louisiana swung to the Democrats on the heels of an unprecedented campaign of violence and fraud orchestrated by white paramilitary forces. In East Feliciana Parish (about thirty miles from Concordia), only one Republican vote was recorded out of 2,127 regis-tered Republican voters.[63] In the wake of this divisive election, Republicans and Democrats vied for control of the state government. Groups of armed black men patrolled the state capitol in New Orleans to ensure that Stephen B. Packard, the Republican candidate who claimed the governor's office, would remain in power. Many in Packard's impro-vised protection force, reported the *New York Times*, "firmly believe that they will be returned to a condition of slavery if Packard is overthrown." One politically active black man asserted that "[i]t was only a matter of time" before Democratic political power would "lead to the slavery of the negro."[64]

The discourse of reenslavement suggests that many freedpeople harbored a deep fear that abolition could be ephemeral. Local people, who seemed to earnestly believe the warnings from Republican lead-ers, became unnerved when they saw their friends, neighbors, and husbands figuratively join hands with a Democratic Party that was committed to undoing Reconstruction. They also recognized that the administration of force had shifted from the federal government to Southern white militias, and with it their claims to freedom and equal treatment lacked effective recognition and enforcement. Undoubtedly the black residents of Concordia Parish were not the only freedpeople who felt this way, but the particularities of the 1876 election gave local people an opportunity to openly express their anxieties about the white supremacist counterrevolution in ways that black people in other places could not or would not.[65]

By way of contrast, the election of 1876 in Jefferson County, Mississippi, seemed like a place where local freedpeople would also express reenslavement anxieties. Situated right across the river from Concordia, Jefferson was demographically similar and also known as a stronghold of black Republicanism, but there was minimal internal dissent and much more of a threat from armed outsiders. White-line militias constantly harassed freedpeople throughout the campaign season and massacred at least twenty-five black men in one notorious incident. Democrats then stole the votes to ensure their victory. Local Republican leaders responded to the violence by asserting their rights as citizens to assemble in public spaces and to vote fairly and freely. They did not talk about moving backward into slavery and instead lamented that they were being prevented from moving forward as freed men and women, which seemed to be a calculated attempt to gain sympathy from Republican congressmen in Washington, D.C., who would invariably investigate the fraud and violence.[66]

The election of 1878 in Tensas Parish, just to the north of Concordia, provides another contrast. White-line militias invaded the parish from all sides and attacked black officeholders and ordinary residents, leading to the deaths of as many as seventy local freedpeople. The extensive violence, which forced many families to flee to the woods and swamps, was the key factor in hundreds, and perhaps thousands, of freedpeople deciding to leave the parish for Kansas as part of the 1879 exodus. Despite the violent terrorism, there is no indication in the documentary record that black people talked about reenslavement. Perhaps there was no need, since Democrats had taken over Louisiana's state government two years before. But it is also worth acknowledging that there was little space for such claims. Republicans made an alliance with moderately inclined white Democrats and put forward a "country people's ticket," composed of white planters and black farm laborers.[67] In this political context, reenslavement rhetoric would only address half of the electoral coalition and may well have divided the fragile alliance that bridged class and racial lines.[68]

The 1876 election in Concordia Parish suggests that the memory of slavery still had a powerful hold on black people, who had only lived in an emancipated society for a short time. They were highly reluctant to publicly discuss the traumas of slavery in normal circumstances. But when white-line militiamen roamed at the edges of their parish and when they divided over how best to preserve emancipation, the deep-seated fear that slavery could return burst forth among ordinary African Americans. These expressions ran counter to the more popular narratives of progress, such as those featured at emancipation celebrations. These forward-looking narratives told a remarkable story of liberation that freedpeople earnestly hoped would spread throughout the nation and the world. It is not surprising, then, that the regressive narratives of slavery's return did not take hold in African American discourse. Expressions of hope and of emancipation's promise should not distract us from the dark shadows of slavery that left a deep imprint on every person who survived bondage.

This election also shows the importance that freedpeople invested in electoral politics. Many thought of the vote not just as a manifestation of new rights or a means of selecting officials and voicing opinions, but also of ensuring that slavery would remain abolished. They used politics as a bulwark against the return of slavery. Finally, this episode reveals that freedpeople's premonitions were somewhat on target. Although slavery was never legally revived, white Democrats methodically rolled back many Reconstruction reforms over the next few decades and created a Jim Crow culture that was a mockery of the emancipated society freedpeople strove to create.[69]

NOTES

Portions of this essay have appeared in the following book by Justin Behrend, *Reconstructing Democracy: Grassroots Black Politics in the Deep South after the Civil War* (Athens: University of Georgia Press, 2015).

1. Census of the United States, 1880, Historical Census Browser, University of Virginia, Geospatial and Statistical Data Center, 2004, http://mapserver.lib.virginia.edu (accessed July 13, 2015).

2. Affidavit of Daniel Tucker, U.S. Senate, *Memorial of Hon. J.E. McDonald, Hon. Lewis V. Bogy, and Hon. John W. Stevenson in Relation to the Counting by the Returning Board of the Vote of the People of Louisiana for the Appointment of Presidential Electors, November 7, 1876*, 44th Cong., 2nd Sess., Senate Misc. Doc. 14, in *The Miscellaneous Documents of the Senate of the United States for the Second Session of the Forty-Fourth Congress* (Washington, D.C.: GPO, 1877), 282, (hereafter cited as *Counting by the Returning Board*; U.S. Bureau of Census, *Tenth Census of the United States: Population, 1880*.

3. Affidavit of Alexander Smart, *Counting by the Returning Board*, 284.

4. See Chapter 7.

5. See Chapter 8.

6. See Chapter 2.

7. See Chapter 5.

8. Abolition was not always permanent, as the reintroduction of slavery in Guadeloupe, eight years after the French Republic had abolished it, demonstrates. See Laurent Dubois, *A Colony of Citizens: Revolution and Slave Emancipation in the French Caribbean, 1787–1804* (Chapel Hill: University of North Carolina Press, 2004).

9. The literature on emancipation and freedpeople's struggles in the postwar era is extensive. Foundational works include Eric Foner, *Reconstruction: America's Unfinished Revolution, 1863–1877* (New York: Harper & Row, 1988); Steven Hahn, *A Nation under our Feet: Black Political Struggles in the Rural South from Slavery to the Great Migration* (Cambridge, Mass.: Belknap Press of Harvard University Press, 2003); James Oakes, *Freedom National: The Destruction of Slavery in the United States, 1861–1865* (New York: Norton, 2013).

10. For an assessment of how African Americans confronted the legacy of slavery and violence, see Kidada E. Williams, *They Left Great Marks on Me: African American Testimonies of Racial Violence from Emancipation to World War I* (New York: New York University Press, 2012). For more on the limits of citizenship, see Barbara Young Welke, *Law and the Borders of Belonging in the Long Nineteenth Century United States* (New York: Cambridge University Press, 2010).

11. Michael Wayne, *The Reshaping of Plantation Society: The Natchez District, 1860–1880* (Baton Rouge: Louisiana State University Press, 1983); Historical Census Browser. In 1870, 9,257 "colored persons" lived in Concordia Parish, which was 92.8% of the 9,977 total inhabitants.

12. Monthly Report of Schools for the Parish of Concordia, Capt. B.B. Brown, July 31, 1866, Records of the Field Offices for the State of Louisiana, m1905, Records Relating to Schools, roll 110, Records of the Bureau of Refugees, Freedmen, and Abandoned Lands, Record Group 105, National Archives, Washington, D.C.

13. On voter registration in 1867, see Joe Louis Caldwell, "A Social, Economic, and Political Study of Blacks in the Louisiana Delta, 1865–1880" (PhD. diss., Tulane University, 1988), 257.

14. "Parish of Concordia, Elected Officials," n.d., Folder 35a, October–November 7, 1875, William P. Kellogg papers, Louisiana and Lower Mississippi Valley Collections, Louisiana State University Libraries, Baton Rouge, La. Biographical information on black politicians from Concordia Parish and other parts of the Natchez District can be found in a database that I have compiled, accessible at http://go.geneseo.edu/BlackPoliticiansDB (accessed July 13, 2015), hereafter cited as BPDB.

15. *Concordia Eagle*, March 3, 1877; BPDB.

16. For more on the transformations of the Natchez District, see Justin Behrend, *Reconstructing Democracy: Grassroots Black Politics in the Deep South after the Civil War* (Athens: University of Georgia Press, 2015).

17. Foner, *Reconstruction*; Hahn, *A Nation under Our Feet*.

18. *Natchez Democrat*, May 17, May 18, May 19, May 20, May 21, 1876.

19. *New York Times*, November 14, December 1, 1876; testimonies D.A. Weber
and Emil L. Weber, U.S. Senate, *Report of the Select Committee into the
Mississippi Election of 1875*, 44th Cong., 1st Sess., 1876, Sen. Rep. 527, pp.
1543–1579; Joe Gray Taylor, *Louisiana Reconstructed, 1863–1877* (Baton
Rouge: Louisiana State University Press, 1974), 486–489.

20. U.S. House, *Select Committee on the Recent Election in the State of
Louisiana*, 44th Cong., 2nd Sess., House Report 156; *The Miscellaneous
Documents of the Senate of the United States for the Second Session of the
Forty-Fourth Congress* (Washington: GPO, 1877), 273–298.

21. By way of contrast, the testimony into the fraud, intimidation, and violence at
the 1875 election in Claiborne County, Mississippi, included only two witnesses. U.S. Senate, *Mississippi Election of 1875*, 158–220.

22. Testimony of J. Floyd King, U.S. House, *Select Committee on the Recent
Election in the State of Louisiana*, 44th Cong., 2nd Sess., House Misc. Doc.
34, p. 15, hereafter cited as *Recent Election*.

23. Testimony of David Young, U.S. Senate, *Report of the United States Senate
Committee to Inquire into Alleged Frauds and Violence in the Elections of
1878*, 45th Cong., 3rd Sess., Sen. Rep. 855, vol. 1, pp. 371–374, hereafter
cited as *Louisiana in 1878*; testimony of F.S. Shields, *Recent Election*, 192.

24. Testimony of J. Floyd King, *Recent Election*, 158; testimony of Taylor
Young, *Recent Election*, 212.

25. Affidavit of Lewis Armstrong, *Counting by the Returning Board*, 285. See
also the affidavit of Daniel Tucker, *Counting by the Returning Board*, 281.

26. Testimony of Thomas Dorsey, *Recent Election*, 168.

27. For testimony from black club members on Morgan's plantation, see
Counting by the Returning Board, 278, 279, 281, 282, 287, 288.

28. Testimony of T.P. Jackson, *Recent Election*, 227; BPDB.

29. Testimony of J. Floyd King, *Recent Election*, 157.

30. Affidavit of Samuel Walker, *Counting by the Returning Board*, 287; BPDB.
For other testimonies, see the affidavits of Milton Ray, J. C. Teniday
[Ferriday], Daniel Tucker, Alexander Smart, Stephen Armstead, Jacob
Stewart, Henry Gordon, and Alexander Williams, *Counting by the
Returning Board*, 276, 280–281, 281, 283–284, 284, 286, 287.

31. In Plaquemines, East Baton Rouge, and Ouachita Parishes, two-thirds of the
residents in each parish were listed in the 1870 census as colored persons.
Historical Census Browser.

32. Affidavit of George Williams, *Counting by the Returning Board*, 915.

33. Affidavit of Sam. Robertson, *Counting by the Returning Board*, 414–415.

34. Petition of Ouachita Parish planters, *Counting by the Returning Board*,
797–798. For other testimonies of reenslavement warnings, see *Counting
by the Returning Board*, 425–426, 792, 796–797, 803–804, 813, 914,
924–925.

35. Testimony of Robert Davis, *Recent Election*, 210.

36. Affidavit of Jos. Hubbard [Habbard], *Counting by the Returning Board*, 283.
See also *Counting by the Returning Board*, 279, 282, 284, 287, 288.

37. Affidavit of William Warfield, *Counting by the Returning Board*, 285; U.S.
Bureau of Census, *Tenth Census of the United States: Population, 1880*.

38. Affidavit of Stephen Armstead, *Counting by the Returning Board*, 284.

39. Affidavit of Milton Ray, *Counting by the Returning Board*, 276.

40. Testimony of Robert Davis, *Recent Election*, 210 (first quote); affidavit of J. C. Teniday [Ferriday], *Counting by the Returning Board*, 280 (second quote). See also the affidavits of Milton Ray and Luder [Luther] Howard, *Counting by the Returning Board*, 276, 284.

41. Affidavit of Samuel Walker, *Counting by the Returning Board*, 287. See also Stephen Armstead's affidavit, *Counting by the Returning Board*, 284.

42. Affidavit of J.C. Teniday [Ferriday], *Counting by the Returning Board*, 280.

43. Affidavit of James Foy, *Counting by the Returning Board*, 294. See also the testimony of F. S. Shields, *Recent Election*, 163; affidavit of William Scott, *Counting by the Returning Board*, 283; affidavit of J. C. Teniday [Ferriday], *Counting by the Returning Board*, 280.

44. Affidavit of J. C. Teniday [Ferriday], *Counting by the Returning Board*, 280.

45. Affidavit of Joe Williams, *Counting by the Returning Board*, 287.

46. Testimony of T. P. Jackson, *Recent Election*, 232.

47. Testimony of F. S. Shields and Eli Johnson, *Recent Election*, 193, 255.

48. For more on the parameters of voting, see Richard Franklin Bensel, *The American Ballot Box in the Mid-Nineteenth Century* (New York: Cambridge University Press, 2004). On the precariousness of black citizenship, see Rogers M. Smith, *Civic Ideals: Conflicting Visions of Citizenship in U.S. History* (New Haven: Yale University Press, 1997); Stephen Kantrowitz, *More Than Freedom: Fighting for Black Citizenship in a White Republic, 1829–1889* (New York: Penguin Press, 2012).

49. Testimony of Joe Habit, *Recent Election*, 215. For another example of threats to burn property, see the testimony of Henderson Smith, *Recent Election*, 214.

50. Testimony of William Ridgly, *Recent Election*, 221.

51. Testimony of William Ridgly, *Recent Election*, 221. For other examples of violent threats, see the testimonies of Wade R. Young, Eli Johnson, and H. E. Witherspoon, *Recent Election*, 154, 255, 273.

52. Testimony of Thomas Dorsey, *Recent Election*, 166. See also the affidavit of Thomas Dorsey, *Counting by the Returning Board*, 288.

53. Testimony of J. Floyd King, *Recent Election*, 158.

54. Quoted in the testimony of Taylor Young, *Recent Election*, 211. See also the affidavit of Wm. Hunter, L. V. Felters, T. A. Young, and Jordan Young, *Counting by the Returning Board*, 292.

55. Affidavit of T. E. Sims, Edward Hooper, M. A. Joyce, Rez R. Young, Henry Williams, and Rleas Cook, *Counting by the Returning Board*, 291; testimony of Robert Davis, *Recent Election*, 209–210; testimony of Wade R. Young, *Recent Election*, 154, 156; testimony of W. H. Nutt, *Recent Election*, 234; affidavit of C. J. Meyer, *Counting by the Returning Board*, 292; affidavit of J. Surgent Shields, George Washington, Hunter Jenkins, Robert Davis, and Beverly Brooks, *Counting by the Returning Board*, 292–293.

56. Affidavit of C. J. Meyer, *Counting by the Returning Board*, 292.

57. Testimony of Henderson Smith, *Recent Election*, 214; BPDB.

58. Affidavit of Alexander Smart, *Counting by the Returning Board*, 284.

59. Affidavit of J. C. Teniday [Ferriday], *Counting by the Returning Board*, 280–281.
60. Selective works on the sexual exploitation of female slaves, include, but are not limited to, Deborah Gray White, *Ar'n't I a Woman?: Female Slaves in the Plantation South* (New York: Norton, 1985), 78; Elizabeth Fox-Genovese, *Within the Plantation Household: Black and White Women of the Old South* (Chapel Hill: University of North Carolina Press, 1988), 190, 325–326, 374, 379–380; Thelma Jennings, "'Us Colored Women Had to Go Though a Plenty': Sexual Exploitation of African-American Slave Women," *Journal of Women's History*, 1, no. 3 (Winter 1990): 45–74; Marie Jenkins Schwartz, *Born in Bondage: Growing Up Enslaved in the Antebellum South* (Cambridge, Mass.: Harvard University Press, 2000) 172–173; Nell Irvin Painter, "Soul Murder and Slavery: Toward a Fully Loaded Cost Accounting," in *Southern History across the Color Line* (Chapel Hill: University of North Carolina Press, 2002), 15–39; Thavolia Glymph, *Out of the House of Bondage: The Transformation of the Plantation Household* (New York: Cambridge University Press, 2008), 54–55. For more on the painful memories that former slaves endured, see Carole Emberton, *Beyond Redemption: Race, Violence, and the American South after the Civil War* (Chicago: University of Chicago Press, 2013), 95–101.
61. Testimony of T.P. Jackson, *Recent Election*, 230. Jackson testified that his opponent, E. W. Wall, received 1,600 votes, while he gained 1,000 to 1,500. His best guess was about 1,200 votes.
62. Appendix, *Recent Election*. In Concordia Parish in 1876, Packard (the Republican candidate for governor) received 2,461 votes, while Nicholls (the Democratic candidate) received 366 votes, or 13%. Two years earlier in the state treasurer's race, the Republican candidate garnered 2,043 votes to the Democrat's 154 (7%).
63. *New York Times*, November 29, 1876.
64. *New York Times*, April 16, 1877.
65. The ability of Concordia Parish freedpeople to express these deep-seated fears of reenslavement suggest that they had created an emotional community, or a strong bond of affection between people sharing similar feelings. For more on emotional communities, see Barbara H. Rosenwein, "Worrying about Emotions in History," *American Historical Review*, 107, no. 3 (June 2002): 821–845.
66. U.S. Senate, *Testimony as to Denial of Elective Franchise in Mississippi at the Elections of 1875 and 1876*, 44th Cong., 2nd Sess., Misc. Doc. 45, pp. 109–115, 142–147, 156–189, 250–260, 694–700, 824–829, 895–917, 940–950.
67. William D. Rollins, *Louisiana in 1878*, vol. 1, p. 262.
68. For more on Tensas Parish in 1878, see Behrend, *Reconstructing Democracy*, 225–233.
69. Leon Litwack, *Trouble in Mind: Black Southerners in the Age of Jim Crow* (New York: Vintage, 1998); Douglas A. Blackmon, *Slavery by Another Name: The Re-Enslavement of Black Americans from the Civil War to World War II* (New York: Anchor Books, 2008).

PART THREE

REMEMBERING EMANCIPATION

7

African Americans and the Long Emancipation in New South Atlanta

William A. Link

Abraham Lincoln's Emancipation Proclamation, declared an early black historian in 1917, had "long since passed into history." Most African Americans alive knew "little of the struggles which freedom cost, and less of the men and women by whose self-sacrificing toil that freedom was achieved." The Civil War was an epochal struggle, in which African Americans "took such an active part" in their emancipation." The past was misremembered and imperfectly written. Black participants in the Civil War – freedom fighters seeking to destroy slavery – had disappeared from battlefields and victories. These "noble and heroic men and women "remained largely forgotten."[1] The Reconstruction years provided a structure of political, economic, and social equality, but emancipation did not mean equality. A Long Emancipation – essentially, a struggle over the meaning of slavery's destruction – continued to define the parameters of freedom, long after the guns fell silent. Boundaries remained untested and undefined; the absence of slavery meant the end of chattel bondage but something less than freedom. In economic, legal, and political status, vestiges of slavery survived and were transformed under white supremacy.

The contested nature of the Long Emancipation becomes apparent in memories of the Civil War, how the past was constructed, and how it became useful to delineate the present. As historians show in a variety of instances and contexts, the generations after slavery refought the war by debating the meaning of slavery and freedom. Different versions of the past connected to how the present was defined. As David Blight reminds us, a powerful narrative placing reunion over race in remembering the Civil War took hold in early twentieth-century America.[2]

A fledging town in the antebellum period, Atlanta became an important transportation, logistical, distribution, and manufacturing center of the western Confederacy. The resulting war boom drew in thousands of slaves, doubling the city's population, while its economic importance made it a target of William T. Sherman's arduous, four-month Atlanta Campaign during the summer of 1864. The city, besieged and conquered by Sherman's massive army, suffered extensive damage and destruction. Meanwhile, especially after the triumphant Atlanta Campaign, Sherman's invading force became an army of liberation, attracting scores of fleeing contrabands when it moved in its March to the Sea.[3]

Southerners, white and black, remembered Civil War and emancipation differently. Competing narratives related to the origins of what historians call the "New South." Describing a reborn region that, turning its back on its past, was industrialized, urbanized, and modernized, the New South served as a social construction rooted in an understanding of the meaning of the Civil War. This dialogue about the meaning of the Civil War and about what constituted the New South played out vividly in Atlanta's emergence as the New South's premier city.

A city that defined its past around its future, rather than the future around its past, modernizing Atlanta prided itself on having a kind of historical blank slate. The city freed itself from the constraints of the Old South as a result of the Civil War. Uniquely among southern cities, Atlanta was physically destroyed by war, first burned by fleeing Confederates in September 1864 and then torched by departing Yankees two months later. It was the only Southern city whose civilian population was expelled, an event which occurred as a result of General William T. Sherman's famous order on September 11, 1864. Months later, almost as soon as residents slowly began returning to the city, Atlanta became reborn into the Phoenix City. Like Phoenix, the mythical bird of classical antiquity, the city arose out of the flames of destruction, shedding itself of the baggage of older, more established places. Physical rebuilding certainly occurred, even before the war ended. But a psychological reconstruction also occurred, in which the city rebuilt and redefined itself.

This image of destruction and reconstruction lay at the heart of the message of New South boosters such as Henry W. Grady, editor of the *Atlanta Constitution* and a relentless promoter of the city's economic development. Grady sold Atlanta to Northern capitalists as a place clear of the debris of the past, especially slavery. Yet much of Grady's rhetoric represented not much more than empty promises; the truth was that the New South was based on assumptions of white supremacy. The New

South belied a profound conflict, mostly regarding ideas, about what the Civil War had created, what New South meant, and where the future would lead. This conflict lay rooted in different versions of the past.

This essay examines the meaning of the Long Emancipation in Atlanta, Georgia, a city that was acutely conscious of the Civil War and its role in it. While white city boosters proclaimed the arrival of the New South, black Atlanta articulated a different view, with powerful voices making the case. Even while Atlanta was the city of Henry Grady, it was also the city of W. E. B. Du Bois, Henry McNeal Turner, and many others. What these people shared was a common view of the Civil War, a version that emphasized the destruction of slavery and shared a common understanding of emancipation as a process that continued even after the guns had fallen silent.

Memories of slaves and slavery lay at the center of this contest. Grady's New South abandoned the Old South's devotion to slavery, but his construct also sought to scrub clean slavery from the past. Black Atlantans saw matters very differently. Slavery was a painful and traumatic memory, as Carole Emberton reminds us in her recent book. Memories of slavery, she writes, "paint a complicated and compelling picture of a how people, both individually and collectively, deal with trauma." In subsequent oral histories, former slaves "struggled to come to terms with slavery's myriad traumas," and they "searched for language to describe the indescribable."[4]

African American memories of slavery focused on liberation. Their remembering of the war focused on the anniversary of the Emancipation Proclamation, January 1, which in Atlanta, as elsewhere, became Emancipation Day, an event which became black Atlanta's most important holiday. Its status grew slowly, but especially so during the 1880s and 1890s. As early as 1893, Atlanta's Negro Literary and Historical Society came into existence; its main duties included organizing the annual celebration.[5] The ritual of Emancipation Day included a parade, often of black military units; a reading of the Proclamation; singing of emancipation songs; reading of freedom poems; and an annual address.[6]

Typically, at these celebrations little was said about slavery itself, except for general approval of its destruction, reflecting what one historian calls a "deep-seated ambivalence regarding the legacy of slavery."[7] Atlanta's emerging black elite, increasingly confident, expressed these views in the city's relatively hospitable surroundings. Almost exclusively the only memories that Gilded Age African Americans expressed of slavery were the rosy, romantic ones provided by whites, who often alluded to

the friendly feeling among the races and the masters' benevolence.
Emancipation Day provided a marker for the future, an annual exercise
in which black people could celebrate their accomplishments. Year One of
their history commenced with the destruction of slavery, something highlighted by the Emancipation Proclamation. To some extent, their vision of
progress adopted the language of white New South boosters, who also
disassociated themselves with the past and disowned slavery. In this sense,
the dialogue about the Civil War especially focused on what the future
would hold.[8]

Part of the purpose of the Emancipation Day festivities was to celebrate
black leadership, and these featured speakers emphasized the significance
of freedom as an ongoing process. At Atlanta's Emancipation Day celebration in January 1889, a crowd composed of black leaders from around
the state filled the Georgia House of Representatives. Black military
companies paraded into the building, while the audience heard speeches
and sang songs extolling black progress. Delivering the address was
William Henry Crogman, born free in 1841 in the West Indies, in Dutch
St. Maarten. Befriended by a visiting New England seaman, Crogman
worked eleven years aboard ships around the world. He then attended
Pierce Academy in Massachusetts, taught at the African American Claflin
College, and enrolled at Atlanta University in 1870. Graduating in its first
collegiate classes in 1876 (along with his classmate Richard Robert
Wright and four others), Crogman joined the faculty of Atlanta's Clark
College as a professor of classics. In 1903, he became Clark's president.[9]

Crogman presided over the celebration in 1889 by reading the
Proclamation, a common part of the ritual. His rhetoric bore some simi-
larity to Grady's New South ideology. Slavery represented an Old South
of "stagnation and death"; free labor fueled the New South ethos of
industry and regeneration. Slavery debauched white and black people,
Crogman declared, degrading labor and stultifying economic development. By liberating whites from the shackles of the slave-based economic
system, he declared, Emancipation Day should also be celebrated by
whites with "rejoicing and celebration." He said little else about slavery,
focusing instead on black progress. Since 1863, he said, Atlanta African
Americans had accumulated significant amounts of property, with "morality, intelligence, and education" accompanying progress.[10]

Although Crogman's rhetoric bought into New South ideology, here
the comparison with Gradyesque boosters ended. Since Lincoln's
"immortal proclamation," black Atlantans had enjoyed freedom, however imperfect – something which Crogman celebrated. Black

accomplishment had become a marvel of the age, unparalleled in history. African Americans had done so much more than white people expected. Skeptics had predicted that emancipated slaves would die out as a race; the reality was that "we are increasing fearfully and wonderfully." No matter the shape and thickness of their skulls – a sarcastic reference to the pseudo-science of phrenology – black people were "not so demented as all that." It had also been predicted that ex-slaves were incapable of learning. In reality, African Americans flocked to schools; many had become college graduates, some from Ivy League colleges.

Crogman also ridiculed white supremacy and the assumptions undergirding it. He was an inveterate opponent of racial discrimination. W. E. B. Du Bois later remembered that Crogman walked back and forth from Clark to downtown Atlanta, a round-trip distance of ten miles, rather than submit to racially segregated streetcars.[11] White supremacy, Crogman told his audience, remained a vestige of the Old South, an expression of "those who are still living in the dead past, and who feel it their duty to champion the old order of things, and to throw stumbling blocks in the path of our progress." At war with "the spirit of the age and the sermon on the mount," white supremacists contradicted the very premises of the New South ideology. Why should whites fear "negro domination" if they insisted on racial inferiority? How could so-called inferior black people succeed in dominating whites? White supremacists were inconsistent, but they blocked the general advancement of the South.[12]

In 1894, Edward Randolph Carter, pastor of Atlanta's Friendship Baptist Church, published *The Black Side*, an unusual explanation of how whites and blacks differed in their comprehension of the past, present, and future. Born enslaved in 1858 in Athens, Georgia, Carter enjoyed the sponsorship of his white master, Edward Randolph Harden, for whom he was named. Learning to read as a young slave, under Harden's patronage Carter obtained three years of schooling after the Civil War. At age eleven, he was apprenticed to a shoemaker; five years later, he taught school. Carter continued to attend white churches after the war, and had a conversion experience while listening to a sermon from the University of Georgia's chancellor, Patrick H. Hall. Called to the ministry, Carter moved to Atlanta in 1879, with fifty cents in his pocket, entering the Atlanta Baptist Seminary (later Morehouse College), where he supported his family and himself as a cobbler. In 1880, Carter became pastor of Stone Mountain Baptist Church and, two years later, was called to Friendship Baptist Church, where he remained until his death in 1944.

An avid prohibitionist, Carter led efforts to create a New Black Man in post-Reconstruction Atlanta. Early in life, he enjoyed white sponsorship. According to subsequent accounts, as a young man during the 1870s Carter became associated with Henry Grady, a fellow Athens native who had also just moved to Atlanta. What was later described as a "strong friendship" emerged; Grady found Carter a "powerful colleague in every fight for righteousness." Years later, in 1941, the white pastor of Atlanta First Baptist Church called Carter "of estimable value to us" in "leading his own people and in his attitude toward the whites."[13]

Carter was no black radical, but, despite good relationships with Atlanta whites, he articulated frustration, arguing for racial equality, self-reliance, and autonomous economic development. Hostility prevailed between the races in Atlanta, he said, as whites tried to block black economic progress. White supremacy resulted in a "feeling of unrest and everlasting perturbation, which unsettles all permanent thought and action." Even those whites inclined to helping African Americans were "clasp[ed] in fetters so binding" that they were prevented from working on an equal basis with black people. Despite having the system stacked against them, Atlanta blacks overcame obstacles, "leaped over impediments." Given an equal chance and left to their own devices, Carter said, African Americans could "accomplish what any other race has accomplished or can accomplish."[14]

Carter's view of the past in *The Black Side* differed significantly from the white version. He remembered living close enough to Atlanta during the war to hear cannon fire. In "torrents of fire, as in the days of Sodom," Atlanta's destruction served as a biblical punishment on the slaveholder state. For African Americans, Northern conquest meant freedom, a story "more of gain than loss." Sherman's shells struck the "hammer of liberty, unfastening the fetters of the accursed and inhuman institution of slavery." Black people rejoiced when they saw the Confederate flag "fall like Lucifer and trail in the dust, and in its stead the Union flag floating in the breeze." Atlanta's fall meant that a "diabolical temple of traffic in human blood had been overthrown and buried in everlasting oblivion, and the temple of the Goddess of Liberty had arisen."[15]

In Carter's version, the true history of Reconstruction remained distorted. These were years, he wrote, that were "difficult to narrate, especially when referring to the feeling which existed between the races." White supremacists portrayed Republicanism as Northern tyranny, Southern white perfidy, and black insolence; *The Black Side* saw Republican victory as a "year of jubilee." Emancipated slaves supplied the "backbone and the life-giving power of the Republican party." Ex-slaves, who only recently handled plows, saws, shovels, and picks, were now members of the Georgia state legislature. Under the capitol dome, freed slaves enjoyed "protection and security" under the Stars and Stripes.

Carter emphasized the necessity that African Americans understand their past. Every child needed to be told "of the hands which aided in the reconstruction of the government of this grand old Empire State of the South." They should be told, Carter said, "of the honors conferred upon their fathers, and the high positions to which they were chosen, notwithstanding their insufficiency in many instances." This composed a "history of the race, and is therefore worthy of repetition." Remembering also led to *The Black Side*'s consciousness of the future, Carter maintained. African Americans, "standing alone, possessing nothing," could only rely on themselves. All black people wanted was a "citizen's privilege, the rights of a tax-payer and free access to the public positions of the city."[16]

The Black Side appeared with the blessing of Henry McNeal Turner, who wrote an introduction to the book and frequently expressed an assertive view the past. Born free in Newberry, South Carolina, Turner became an African Methodist Episcopal (AME) minister in 1858, holding a pastorate when the Civil War began in Washington, D.C. Befriending anti-slavery Republicans such as Charles Sumner and Thaddeus Stevens, in May 1863 Turner helped to recruit the First District of Columbia Infantry (African Descent), becoming its regimental chaplain – the first black chaplain in the Union Army. Later known as the First Regiment of U.S. Colored Troops, the unit saw action in nine battles, including the siege of Petersburg and the capture of Wilmington and Raleigh in early 1865. The First Regiment also spent time at the Union stronghold of New Bern, in eastern North Carolina, which had become a center of black contrabands and political radicalism. During the months after Confederate surrender, Turner was assigned as a chaplain to another black regiment in Georgia, serving briefly as a Freedmen's Bureau agent.[17]

Resigning his commission, Turner became one of the key figures in the expansion of the AME from its northern urban roots to a powerful national and international denomination. At the same time, Turner became active in Reconstruction politics, becoming one of the more important architects of African American mobilization in postwar Georgia. Elected to the state constitutional convention in 1868, he also served in the state house, until the Georgia legislature, in September 1868, expelled all of its black members. Turner bitterly protested this betrayal and, in particular, how he had become a "constant target of the Democratic abuse, and venom, and white Republican jealousy."[18] Appointed the postmaster of Macon in 1869, in a newspaper campaign by anti-Reconstruction forces he was falsely charged with consorting with prostitutes and involvement in a scheme to distribute counterfeit currency, charges that forced him to move from the town. Serving a Savannah pastorate for a decade, in 1880 he returned to Atlanta as the twelfth bishop of the AME church.[19]

Turner exalted values of manhood and dignity, which he saw as essential to emancipation. As a young free black in South Carolina, a contemporary later wrote, he insisted that "no white man should scar his back with a lash."[20] As a young man, he was later described as "tiring of the hard labor and ill treatment, and with restless longings for something higher than the farmhand's fate."[21] A constant theme in his life and career was race pride and black manhood, along with a rejection of white supremacy. He "did things and said things," said a contemporary, "that probably no other man ever thought of, or having thought of, would not dare do or say."[22] Turner saw slavery, though heinous, as a stain on white society. He was a frequent commentator about emancipation, often appearing as a speaker during Emancipation Day. On January 1, 1866, he described slavery to a black audience in Augusta, Georgia, as a system by which whites prevented "all avenues of improvement and hold the Black man as he would a horse or cow." Far from civilizing slaves, the system dehumanized them and defaced "the image of God by ignorance which the black man was the representative of." This was a "crime which offended Heaven" primarily because it inhibited missionary work by keeping black people illiterate. White Christians had done nothing to Christianize the African continent, he contended, thus breaking "a trust from God." A "terrible war" became a form of divine retribution visited upon slaveholders.[23]

Turner possessed a particular faith in the power of the Fifteenth Amendment, which, in 1870, guaranteed voting rights to all citizens. The amendment was "an ensign to our citizenship," he wrote soon after its adoption, providing "impartial equity to all." The amendment, further, served as an "ascending ladder" for the dispossessed "to rise to glory and renown" and "to repel the scorching ray of wicked prejudice." Because the amendment democratized government, Turner hoped, "its symmetrical operations will constitute an axiomatic weapon, for all the oppressed nations on earth to battle with for civil liberty." The amendment was a

"National guaranty, as far as the moon, clear as the sun, and terrible as an army with banners."[24]

Turner's confidence in the ability of black people to enjoy freedom and prosperity eroded during and after Reconstruction. The white majority's expulsion of black legislators in 1868, he declared, was a gross violation of democratic principles. The legislature "turned with ruthless hands and carnivorous hearts," expelling "every man from that body whose face had not been chalked by the God of indiscrimination."[25] White men, he declared, were "not to be trusted ... They will betray you."[26] Initially skeptical about Massachusetts Republican Senator Charles Sumner's effort to enact a federal civil rights law – which Congress enacted in 1875 – Turner came to believe that it provided the most visible evidence of the remnant of federal protection for freedpeople in Reconstruction's aftermath. In 1883, the Supreme Court's decision in the *Civil Rights Cases*, which declared the law an unconstitutional exertion of congressional power, was bitterly disappointing; he described it as "that abominable decision."[27] As a result of the decision, he declared, "colored people may be turned out of hotels, cheated, abused and insulted on steamboats and railroads, without legal redress."[28]

The Supreme Court's decision, and the refusal of northern Republicans to legislate new civil rights protections, reaffirmed Turner's belief that black people would be unable to find justice in white society.[29] As early as 1868, he questioned whether emancipated slaves owed any loyalty to Georgia. "If a war was to break out to-morrow," he told the Georgia legislature in September 1868 after white members expelled black legislators, he would ask African Americans to remain neutral. "Don't fight for a country that refuses to recognize your rights as citizens."[30] Turner's denunciation of Georgia later extended to the entire nation. As both Carole Emberton[31] and Paul Ortiz[32] point out in this volume, African Americans' struggles had broadly national and international implications. During the Spanish-American War, he described imperialism as a form of racial oppression and described the American flag – which he had revered as an army chaplain during the Civil War – as a "worthless rag." Urging blacks not to enlist, he urged them to "take no oath to protect any flag that offers no protection to its sable defenders."[33]

Increasingly, Turner's views about the dismal state of freedpeople prompted him to think internationally. He thus combined a missionary zeal to expand the AME church with plans to sponsor the emigration of African Americans from the South to the Caribbean and, especially, Africa. This was a continent that possessed "inexhaustible treasures," the greatest source of natural resources in the world. God was holding these treasures, he believed, "in custody for the civilization of the Negro." God intended "for us to carry and spread enlightenment and civilization over that land."[34] Traveling to Africa four times between 1891 and 1898, he helped to broker a merger with the South African Ethiopian Church, creating an important toehold for the AME. As editor of the *Southern Recorder, Voice of Missions,* and later the *Voice of the People,* Turner sponsored expeditions, ultimately unsuccessful, to send about 500 emigrants to West Africa (most of whom eventually returned to the United States).[35]

According to an early assessment, Turner was "a peculiar mixture of peculiarities." But there can be little doubt that his life was marked by the struggle of the Civil War. He lived in "awful times of great trials and distresses," wrote early biographer Mungo Ponton, "when men's hearts were sorely tried, and the principles of adjustment of the freedman to the new state of things had not been settled." For Turner, defining and defending freedom "formed the labor of his whole life." More than most post–Civil War African American leaders, Turner showed a gritty determination, an insistence on articulating what freedom meant and how it should be defended. He had a "genius of character," wrote Ponton, and it was "by the genius of his character [that] he made his way through life."[36]

Turner was a key figure in the development of black Atlanta. He was also insistent about the importance of the past and, as a war veteran and activist, was a frequent speaker at Emancipation Day events. In January 1884, he told an audience of 4,000 that the "devil in hell would not make the distinctions against negroes that were made in this country."[37] In January 1913, two years before his death, Turner described war and emancipation in the *AME Review.* He recalled the sense of jubilation prevailing after the Emancipation Proclamation; the euphoria, he said, "has never been surpassed, if it has ever been equaled." Nor would it ever likely be again duplicated. The "very thought of being set at liberty and having no more auction blocks, no more Negro-traders, no more forced parting of man and wife, no more separation of parents and children, no more horrors of slavery," he recalled, "was so elative and heart gladdening that scores of colored people literally fell dead with joy." This was the "time of times, and a half time, nothing like it will ever be seen again in this life. Our entrance into Heaven itself will only form a counterpart."[38]

William Crogman, Edward Randolph Carter, and Henry M. Turner inhabited a cultural and political enclave in Atlanta relatively insulated from repression typical elsewhere. Although it is certainly possible to exaggerate their security, set in the context of emancipated Georgia – where terror usually prevailed – Southern urban communities provided some safety. The presence of federal troops in Atlanta during and after Reconstruction meant some protection against the racial violence sweeping through nearby Georgia counties. Another important ingredient in creating this enclave was Atlanta University, established by Northern white abolitionists of the American Missionary Association in 1869 on sixty acres located on the western side of the city. The campus was built astride surviving Confederate fortifications at Diamond Hill. "I look out upon these entrenchments," the Freedmen's Bureau's superintendent of education commented in 1869, "in wonder at the change which four short years have made." The Confederate earthworks had "defied the approach of freedom"; in their place stood "walls of brick and stone to shelter the children of the free, and endow them with the power of knowledge." "The roar of batteries," he wrote, was now "exchanged for the music of school songs and recitations."[39]

White abolitionists ran Atlanta University until the early twentieth century; the first black faculty were hired in 1895 and the first black president took office in 1929. The Northern white abolitionists, despite some failings, were remarkable people. These missionaries at Atlanta and other enclaves were committed racial egalitarians whose faith in the cause was sealed by the experience of the Civil War. Atlanta University graduates were schooled in opposition to white supremacy. During the 1870s and 1880s, Edmund Asa Ware, a New England abolitionist and a Yale graduate who served as Atlanta University's second president, regularly informed newly arriving students: "However you may be mistreated in the city or elsewhere, I want you to know that the moment you set foot on these grounds you are free men in a free country."[40] James Weldon Johnson, author and civil rights activist, described the campus during the 1890s as a "little world in itself, with ideas of social conduct and of the approach to the life distinct from those of the city within which it was situated." When students entered campus, he recalled, "they underwent as great a transition as would have resulted from being instantaneously shot from a Boston drawing room into the wilds of Borneo."[41]

A year before the establishment of Atlanta University, during the fall of 1868, the commissioner of the Freedmen's Bureau, O. O. Howard, visited Atlanta. During the Civil War, Howard had risen to the rank of major general, and, as commander of the Army of Tennessee, played a leading role in the invasion of north Georgia and the conquest of Atlanta in the spring and summer of 1864. Visiting the American Missionary

Association's Storrs School – a predecessor of what became Atlanta University – Howard addressed black parents and students. "What shall I tell the children in the North about you?" he asked the black children. A twelve-year-old boy spoke up. "Tell them, General," he said, "we're rising."[42]

The "We Are Rising" story had many apocryphal qualities, but it took on a life of its own, and the AMA frequently celebrated the tale among Northern audiences as a sort of motto of the institution. "We Are Rising" was also put to music, becoming an anthem sung by students at Atlanta University, after its founding in 1869.[43] In a sense, "We Are Rising" served as a rallying cry for black people's quest for freedom after emancipation.[44] The boy who uttered the phrase, Richard Robert Wright, later became the valedictorian of the first collegiate class at Atlanta University in 1876 in a class composed of six people. Born a slave in 1855 outside Dalton, in northern Georgia, Wright moved with his mother to Atlanta in search of schooling after the Civil War. In 1880, at age twenty-seven, Wright became the principal of the first black high school in the state, in Augusta. Serving as the founding president of Georgia State Industrial College for Colored Youth (later Savannah State), Wright was appointed in 1896 paymaster of the Army – the first time an African American occupied that position. In 1921, at the age of 67, he founded the Philadelphia Citizens and Southern Bank and Trust Company, after studying at the Wharton School at the University of Pennsylvania. His son, Richard Robert Wright, Jr., received the first PhD awarded to an African American at the University of Pennsylvania.[45]

Wright represented a new kind of emancipated ex-slave: an advocate of full racial equality. Solving the "vexing question" of race lay in awarding black people full citizenship.[46] On December 26, 1881, at the Atlanta Exposition of that year, Wright was the featured speaker at what was called "Negro Day," celebrating black accomplishments after slavery. There could be no solution to racial problems, Wright said, without "exact and untrammeled justice to all its citizens." The "spirit of universal liberty and fair-dealing," he said, "will [have] no truer worshipers than her southern votaries, white and black." Having "by his sweat and blood identified himself with every phase and fiber of American life and history, his highest ambition is to unite with the other people of our union in developing a noble manhood and a beautiful and prosperous and contented country."[47]

The "little world in itself" – the abolitionist enclave at Atlanta University – fostered a counter-narrative about the Civil War's meaning. It was no accident that Atlanta University provided an institutional base from which historian W. E. B. Du Bois began to express a scholarly version of this counter-narrative. In 1897, he joined the faculty of Atlanta University, where he remained for the next thirteen years. Educated at Fisk, Berlin, and Harvard, Du Bois later described Atlanta University as a "green oasis" in the white supremacist South. There, he said, he began his "real life work," discovering himself and his mission in life.[48] By the early 1900s, Du Bois's main mission in life was to reinterpret the meaning of race, based on a changed view of the African American past. His description of Atlanta in *Souls of Black Folk* (1903) undermined the boosterish rhetoric which characterized nearly all contemporary white accounts about the New South. Atlanta's reputation, Du Bois maintained, masked crass realities. On the one hand, it was a place consumed with money making and materialism. In the rush to create wealth, and to remember and recreate, Atlanta was dominated by people "busier and sharper, thriftier and more unscrupulous." The production of wealth had become the "mighty levers to lift this old new land; thrift and toil and saving are the highways to new hopes and new possibilities." Materialism also affected black people. It made "little difference" to Atlanta, or to the South, what black people thought or felt. They "naturally will long remain, unthought of, half forgotten."[49]

Du Bois pointed out that many African Americans actually bought into the New South message of prosperity. Along with whites such as Grady, they viewed the Civil War of epochal significance; like New South boosters, they subscribed to a doctrine of Progress. But what that meant remained fundamentally different for black people. In the era of emancipation, while white boosters saw the Civil War as a noble cause about state rights, African Americans typically insisted that the Civil War was a war of liberation. For them, the Civil War's significance turned on the fight for freedom – and middle-class African Americans were intent on establishing respectability by creating their version of the past.

Du Bois's views on the meaning the Civil War, expressed fully in his *Black Reconstruction* (1935), appeared in outline form in an address to the American Historical Association in December 1909 in New York City. Columbia historian William Dunning and his students had already begun to dominate the scholarly understanding of Reconstruction as a mistake because of the political empowerment of freed slaves. Dunning's interpretation coincided with a national reconciliation, a generation after the Civil

War, in which the North accepted white supremacy, disfranchisement, and
segregation in the Progressive Era South. With Dunning in attendance, Du
Bois challenged this orthodoxy. "There was a danger," he declared, "that
between the intense feeling of the South and the conciliatory spirit of the
North grave injustice will be done the negro American in the history of
Reconstruction." Despite the Dunningites' view that black suffrage was the
primary cause of Reconstruction's failure, these historians "must remember
that if there had not been a single freedman left in the South after the war the
problems of Reconstruction would still have been grave." The loss of
property, the war dead, and the physical destruction of agriculture and
industry were aggravated by a "quickening of hatred and discouragement –
a situation which would make it difficult under any circumstances to
reconstruct a new government and a new civilization." But Du Bois went
further, flipping the Dunningite formulation on its head. Reconstruction
had been successful, he contended, by expanding democratic participation,
providing the South's first truly public schools, and creating an array of new
social services. Black elected officials suffered from incompetence, corruption, and excess, but these had been greatly exaggerated and taken out of
their context. White politicians of varying political background were also
incompetent and corrupt generally during the Gilded Age. Opponents of
Reconstruction created "flaming and incredible stories" that distorted
reality. Once in power, anti-Reconstruction forces made

few changes in the work which these [Republican] legislatures and conventions
had done, but they largely carried out their plans, followed their suggestions, and
strengthened their institutions ... In fact, the extravagance, although great, was
not universal, and much of it was due to the extravagant spirit pervading the whole
country in a day of inflated currency and speculation. The ignorance was
deplorable but a deliberate legacy from the past, and some of the extravagance
and much of the effort was to remedy this ignorance. The incompetency was in
part real and in part emphasized by the attitude of the whites of the better class ...
Dishonesty ... has no monopoly of time or place in America.[50]

The most important challenge of Reconstruction, according to Du Bois,
was the position and status of freed slaves, which loomed "like a great
dread on the horizon." The treatment of ex-slaves was the "central
problem of Reconstruction, although by no means the only problem."
Rather than casting Reconstruction as a drama of black failure, Du Bois
portrayed it as white America's failure. Left to its own devices, the white
South would have been content to keep blacks in semi-slavery, making it
possible for them to own property and have limited political rights, while
"in most other respects the blacks would have remained in slavery." Only

a sustained federal intervention through an invigorated Freedmen's Bureau, with a program of land distribution and intensive education, could have prevented the slide back to servitude. The Civil War, though "largely fought and won [about] ... human freedom" amounted to cession of power to Southern white supremacists. Freedpeople were turned over "to the tender mercies of their impoverished and angry ex-masters." Despite the enfranchisement of black males, white Southerners, "almost to a man," remained committed to the failure of black suffrage "either by active force or passive acquiescence."[51]

Du Bois was the first African American to address the American Historical Association; until 1931, he would remain the last. His paper fell on deaf years. As his biographer writes, "the gentlemen listening to Du Bois knew that they could find no meaningful place in their tradition of inquiry," and this view of Reconstruction "virtually failed to have any impact on mainstream scholarship of the day." Before the paper appeared a few months later in the July 1910 issue of the *American Historical Review*, Du Bois had left Atlanta in order to spend nearly a quarter century working with the National Association for the Advancement of Colored People in New York City. He returned to Atlanta University in 1933, and, while there, his magisterial *Black Reconstruction* appeared in 1935. But it too was mostly ignored by professional historians until after the 1970s, when it enjoyed a revival.[52]

Du Bois remained in Atlanta for another decade, but the experience was frustrating. As one contemporary noted, he was "battering his life out against ignorance, bigotry, intolerance and slothfulness, projecting ideas nobody but he understands, and raising hopes for change which may be comprehended in a hundred years."[53] In a "postscript" which he published in 1942, a year before he left Atlanta again, he ruminated how the "world fight for democracy" occurring during the nineteenth and twentieth centuries "should have centered in the South, but there the Negro was handicapped by poverty, ignorance and crime, the legitimate children of slavery." The South maintained a system of racial control, a "vast secret system of which the Ku Klux Klan was but one phase." Elsewhere in the Western world, the labor movement became "carefully rationalized into democracy for white folk" as Europeans excluded their colonial subjects from political power and self-government.[54]

The experience of Atlanta was thus, in some respects, emblematic of a larger struggle in the modern South, waged during the Long Emancipation. This struggle flowed directly out of the physical and psychological devastation of the destruction of slavery, and it was a struggle that continued on into the twentieth century. White Atlantans promoted the city as a Phoenix, eager to receive Northern investment, with little of the heavy past and guilt of the Old South. For them, there was a convenience in that the slate was now clean, and the city was ready and open for business. But there was a deeper complexity to Atlanta and what the Civil War meant for Southerners. Certainly, African Americans carved out a different meaning which focused on the end of slavery as Year One in their history. The city became, in the era of emancipation and its aftermath, a center of a different version of the future in which African American aspiration played a crucial role.

REV. H. M. TURNER, CHAPLAIN FIRST UNITED STATES COLORED REGIMENT.

FIGURE 6: "Rev. H.M. Turner, chaplain First United States Colored Regiment, 1863."
Source: Wood engraving. Courtesy of the Library of Congress, Prints and Photographs Division, LC-USZ62-138376.

FIGURE 7: "Henry W. Grady, half-length portrait, facing left."
Source: Unidentified photographer. Courtesy of the Library of Congress, Prints and Photographs Division, LC-USZ62-93574.

NOTES

1. Mungo M. Ponton, *Life and Times of Henry M. Turner* (Atlanta: A. B. Caldwell, 1917), 37.
2. David W. Blight, *Race and Reunion: The Civil War in American Memory* (Cambridge, Mass.: Harvard University Press, 2001). See also, more recently, Caroline E. Janney, *Remembering the Civil War: Reunion and the Limits of Reconciliation* (Chapel Hill: University of North Carolina Press, 2013).

3. On Civil War–era Atlanta, see Don H. Doyle, *New Men, New Cities, New South: Atlanta, Nashville, Charleston, Mobile, 1860–1910* (Chapel Hill: University of North Carolina Press, 1990); Tera W. Hunter, *To Joy My Freedom: Southern Black Women's Lives and Labor after the Civil War* (Cambridge, Mass.: Harvard University Press, 1997); and Wendy Hamand Venet, *A Changing Wind: Commerce and Conflict in Civil War Atlanta* (New Haven: Yale University Press, 2014).

4. Carole Emberton, *Beyond Redemption: Race, Violence, and the American South after the Civil War* (Chicago: University of Chicago Press, 2013), 7, 95.

5. "The Emancipation Proclamation," *Atlanta Constitution*, January 1, 1892; "Emancipation Day," *Atlanta Constitution*, January 3, 1893; "What the Negro Is Doing," *Atlanta Constitution*, December 23, 1900; "They Celebrated Emancipation Day," *Atlanta Constitution*, January 2, 1903.

6. "To Celebrate Emancipation," *Atlanta Constitution*, December 29, 1896.

7. Mitch Kachun, *Festivals of Freedom: Memory and Meaning in African American Emancipation Celebrations, 1808–1915* (Amherst: University of Massachusetts Press, 2003), 148.

8. Blight, *Race and Reunion*, 168, 313–319. "The very remembrance of our experience is hideous," said *Christian Recorder* editor Benjamin Tanner in 1878. Ibid, 314. Fitzhugh Brundage finds that slaves collectively "did not shy away from recalling" slavery. W. Fitzhugh Brundage, *The Southern Past: A Clash of Race and Memory* (Cambridge, Mass.: Harvard University Press, 2005), 81.

9. "Emancipation Day at Atlanta," *Washington Post*, January 2, 1889; Kathleen Ann Clark, *Defining Moments: African American Commemoration and Political Culture in the South, 1863–1913* (Chapel Hill: University of North Carolina Press, 2005), 163–164.

10. "Colored Celebration," *Chicago Inter Ocean*, January 2, 1889.

11. Du Bois, "Postscript: Looking Seventy-Five Years Backward: Being the Personal Recollections of the Tower on Stone Hall," *Phylon* 3 (2nd Qtr., 1942): 238–248.

12. William Henry Crogman, "Twenty-Sixth Anniversary of the Emancipation Proclamation," address on January 1, 1889, *Talk for the Times*, 2nd edn. (Cincinnati: Jennings & Pye, 1896), 199–216.

13. "Dr. Edward Randolph Carter," *Spelman College Campus Mirror* 16 (June 1940): 2; Morehouse College Bulletin, *Morehouse Alumnus* XII (November–December 1944), 6, in Edward Randolph Carter and Andrew Jackson Lewis Collection, Box 1, Folder 3, Archives Division, Auburn Avenue Research Library on African American Culture and History, Atlanta-Fulton Public Library System. Hereinafter, cited as Carter Papers.

14. Edward R. Carter, *The Black Side: A Partial History of the Business, Religious and Educational Side of the Negro in Atlanta, Ga.* (Atlanta: n.p., 1894), 10–11; Ellis A. Fuller to Rolfe Edmondson (copied to Carter), October 22, 1941, Carter Papers, Box 3, Folder 3; Louie S. Newton, "For Sixty Years His Fruit Faileth Not," Souvenir Booklet of the Sixtieth Anniversary Celebration of the Pastorate of Dr. Edward Randolph Carter, April 19,

1942, Carter Papers, Box 1, folders 9, 10; obituary, "Dr. Edward Randolph Carter," unid. clipping, Carter Papers, Box 3, Folder 3.

15. Carter, *The Black Side*, 16–19.
16. Carter, *The Black Side*, 18.
17. Stephen Ward Angell, *Bishop Henry McNeal Turner and African-American Religion in the South* (Knoxville: University of Tennessee Press, 1992), ch. 2.
18. Quoted in M.M. Ponton, "Life of Henry McNeil Turner," ms. in Henry McNeal Turner Papers, box 1, folder 10; Manuscript Division, Moorland-Spingarn Research Center, Howard University. Hereinafter, cited as Turner Papers.
19. Angell, *Bishop Henry McNeal Turner.*
20. "Rev. Henry McNeal Turner, D.D., LL.D.," William J. Simmons, *Men of Mark: Eminent, Progressive, and Rising* (Cleveland: Geo. M. Rewell & Co., 1887), CXXI: 807.
21. "Bishop Henry Turner," *Cleveland Gazette*, October 14, 1893.
22. J.A. Jones, "Bishop H.M. Turner as a Forceful Character," *Christian Recorder*, July 8, 1915, box 1, folder 3, Turner Papers
23. "Henry McNeal Turner," Simmons, *Men of Mark*, 817.
24. "Life of Turner," box 1, folder 10, Turner Papers.
25. Turner, *The Civil and Political Status of the State of Georgia* (Atlanta: Republican member of the legislature, 1870), 4.
26. "House of Representatives," *Atlanta Constitution*, September 4, 1868.
27. "A Colored Bishop's Malediction," *New York Times*, February 14, 1886. See *Civil Rights: The Outrage of the Supreme Court of the United States upon the Black Man* (Philadelphia: AME Church, 1889).
28. "Life of Turner," box 1, folder 15, Turner Papers.
29. Edwin S. Redkey, *Black Exodus: Black Nationalist and Back-to-Africa Movements, 1890–1910* (New Haven: Yale University Press, 1969), ch. 2.
30. "House of Representatives," *Atlanta Constitution*, September 4, 1868.
31. See Chapter 5.
32. See Chapter 8.
33. Turner, *Voice of Missions*, May 1899, in Redkey, *Respect Black: The Writings and Speeches of Henry McNeal Turner* (New York: Arno Press, 1971), 185.
34. "Life of Turner," box 1, folder 10, Turner Papers.
35. James T. Campbell, *Songs of Zion: The African Methodist Episcopal Church in the United States and South Africa* (Chapel Hill: University of North Carolina Press, 1998), 80–85.
36. Ponton, *Life and Times of Henry M. Turner*, 59–60.
37. "Emancipation Day in Atlanta," *New York Times*, January 2, 1884.
38. Turner, "Reminiscences of the Proclamation of Emancipation," *AME Review*, 29 (1913): 214.
39. J. W. Alvord, *Letters from the South, Relating to the Condition of Freedmen: Addressed to Major General O. O. Howard, Commissioner Bureau R., F., and A. L. by J. W. Alvord, Gen. Sup't Education, Bureau R., F., & A. L.* (Washington, D.C.: Howard University Press, 1870).

40. George A. Towns, "Sources of the Tradition at Atlanta University," *Phylon* 3, no. 2 (2nd Qtr., 1942): 117–134.
41. James Weldon Johnson, *Along This Way: The Autobiography of James Weldon Johnson* (New York: Viking Press, 1933), 65–66.
42. Clarence A. Bacote, *The Story of Atlanta University: A Century of Service* (Atlanta: Atlanta University, 1969), 11–12.
43. J. W. Alvord, *Letters from the South. Relating to the Condition of Freedmen, Addressed to Major General O. O. Howard, Commissioner Bureau R., F., and A. L. by J. W. Alvord, Gen. Sup't Education, Bureau R., F., & A. L.* (Washington, D.C.: Howard University Press, 1870).
44. Jacqueline Jones, *Soldiers of Light and Love: Northern Teachers and Georgia Blacks, 1865–1875* (Athens: University of Georgia Press, 1980), 127.
45. Bacote, *Story of Atlanta University*, 11–12.
46. Wright, address, *American Missionary* XXXV (January 1881): 380; James D. Anderson, *The Education of Blacks in the South, 1860–1935* (Chapel Hill: University of North Carolina Press, 1988), 29–30. See also "Work of the Negroes," *Atlanta Constitution*, December 29, 1895.
47. "Negroes Congress," *Atlanta Constitution*, December 27, 1895.
48. W. E. B. Du Bois, *The Autobiography of W. E. B. Du Bois: A Soliloquy on Viewing My Life from the Last Decade of Its First Century* (New York: International Publishers, 1968), 212–213.
49. W. E. B. Du Bois, *The Souls of Black Folk: Essays and Sketches* (Chicago: A. C. McClurg, 1903), 78–79.
50. W. E. B. Du Bois, "Reconstruction and Its Benefits," *American Historical Review* 15 (July 1910): 781–799.
51. Du Bois, "Reconstruction and Its Benefits," 781, 785–786, 789.
52. David Levering Lewis, *W. E. B. Du Bois: Biography of a Race, 1868–1919* (New York: Henry Holt, 1993), 384.
53. David Levering Lewis, *Du Bois: The Fight for Equality and the American Century, 1919–1963* (New York: Henry Holt, 2000), 645.
54. W. E. B. Du Bois, "Postscript, : Looking Seventy–Five Years Backward: Being the Personal Recollections of the Tower on Stone Hall," *Phylon* 3, no. 2 (2nd Qtr., 1942): 239–240.

8

Washington, Toussaint, and Bolívar, "The Glorious Advocates of Liberty": Black Internationalism and Reimagining Emancipation

Paul Ortiz

For African Americans, the struggle against slavery did not begin and end in the United States; it was conceived of as a global conflict. From this perspective, the Haitian Revolution represented a great breakthrough in the Americas. Led by a former house slave by the name of Toussaint L'Ouverture, regiments of ex-slaves defeated colonial armies from England, Spain, and France who sought to re-impose chattel bondage on the former French colony. This was an epic story that people of the African Diaspora treasured deeply in their hearts. As African Americans understood – and as historians have reconfirmed – the Haitian Revolution was a major impetus for slavery abolition in the Americas.[1] African Americans throughout the United States commemorated the Haitian Revolution in many ways. Black newspapers regularly featured stories on the anti-slavery struggle in Haiti, and parents taught their children about the brave General L'Ouverture. Black communities named streets and neighborhoods after revolutionary heroes. Students at the Institute for Colored Youth in Philadelphia were required to learn and to recite General Jean-Jacques Dessalines's "1804 Independence Address to the Haytians."[2] *Freedom's Journal* argued in 1827 that

there are very few events on record which have produced more extraordinary men than the revolution in St. Domingo. The negro character at that eventful period, burst upon us in all the splendor of native and original greatness; and the subsequent transactions in that Island have presented the most incontestable truths that the negro is not, in general, wanting in the higher qualifications of the mind.[3]

Free African Americans in Baltimore gathered to celebrate the twenty-first anniversary of Haitian Independence in a public commemoration in

August 1825. In the fashion of early nineteenth-century commemorations, those assembled raised their glasses to offer a series of toasts in honor of the auspicious occasion. The culminating toast was: "Washington, Toussaint, and Bolivar – Unequalled in fame – the friends of mankind – the glorious advocates of Liberty."[4] In this gesture, African Americans connected the fate of their own freedom with the emancipation of their brothers and sisters in Latin America and the Caribbean. The toast promoted an understanding of the intimate connections between movements for liberty throughout the Americas. Simon Bolívar grew to become an admired figure in African American communities in part because of his June and July decrees of 1816 which freed enslaved people willing to fight on behalf of the Third Republic of Venezuela. These declarations followed Bolívar's meeting with Haitian President Alexandre Pétion, who pledged military support to *El Liberator* contingent on his ending slavery.[5]

Nearly a half century later, in 1873, hundreds of African Americans in Baltimore gathered at historic Madison Street Colored Presbyterian Church for the purpose

of adopting measures to petition the Congress of the United States to tender the powerful mediation of this great government towards ameliorating the sad condition of a half million of our brethren now held in slavery in the island of Cuba by Spain. The attendance was good, a number of those present being of the gentler sex.[6]

Samuel R. Scottron, noted black inventor and co-founder of the Cuban Anti-Slavery Committee, was the evening's keynote speaker. He reminded his audience that

they had passed through the Egyptian bondage and through the sea of blood, and having become clothed in the habiliments of freedom, knew how to sympathize with the 500,000 of their own race bowed down in Cuba. The Cuban patriots were opposing wrongs as galling as those which adduced the American patriots to rise up against the oppression of Great Britain.

Scottron's advice was that African Americans should "petition the government of the United States to extend a liberal policy to the colored race in Cuba. The 800,000 votes of the colored people here would have their weight in that direction." After Scottron concluded his speech, church deacons circulated the petition for signatures.[7]

Less than a week later Scottron joined a delegation that included Rev. Henry Highland Garnet, George T. Downing, and J. M. Langston to present petitions to President Ulysses S. Grant signed by African

Americans and allies across the country in support of the resistance movement in Cuba.[8] African Americans demanded that the U.S. government grant belligerency status to the Cuban freedom fighters and also support the abolition of slavery on the island. The Cuban solidarity movement was a national phenomenon, with organizing activities in cities including Sacramento, San Francisco, Virginia City, New Orleans, Boston, Philadelphia, New York, Washington, D.C., and many other places.[9] Estimates of the number of signatures gathered in support of the Cuban freedom fighters ranged from tens of thousands to as much as half a million.[10] "The watchword of the Cubans is Liberty and Independence," the *Christian Recorder* lectured, "and with the moral strength, which President Grant will give, they will most surely triumph. With their triumph falls the shackles of 300,000 of our kinsmen."[11] "So long as that Island [Cuba] remains under Spanish rule," the *Weekly Louisianan* argued, "slavery will continue to exist, and so long as any portion of the colored race is held in slavery on any part of God's green earth – and more especially so near our shores as Cuba – just so long will our people suffer proscription and be regarded as an inferior race."[12] Black organizers mobilized across the country to build the campaign against Spanish imperialism. The foremost African American leaders of the day, including Frederick Douglass, Bishop Henry Turner and J. Henri Burche, were among the movement's most eloquent spokespersons.

The architects of the Cuban solidarity movement expressed an internationalist conception of freedom. The centerpiece of this idea, which I call *emancipatory internationalism*, was that the destiny of democracy in the United States rested on the self-determination of workers in Latin America, the Caribbean, and Africa. Emancipatory internationalism was Pan-African because its proponents sought to build solidarity across the African Diaspora; however, advocates of this ideology supported liberation and anti-colonial struggles of people outside of the black world as well.[13] In 1912, the National Negro Independent League released a powerful statement against "color prejudice" in the United States while simultaneously praising "the native people of the Philippines for their stand for the independence of their country."[14] In the wake of the Haitian Revolution, African Americans envisioned a new kind of emancipation that transcended national borders, and they urged the opening of a global liberation front against imperialism. This project gained momentum as black organizers strengthened ties with European abolitionists and as African Americans transformed the commemoration of British West Indian Emancipation into mass public events in the 1830s.[15]

This inclusive vision of freedom flowered during Reconstruction. African Americans viewed the Thirteenth Amendment to the U.S. Constitution not as an endpoint in the battle against slavery but just the beginning. Newly enfranchised communities drew on traditions of thinking about emancipation that were rooted in the experiences African Americans had endured in bondage and in their analysis of slavery's imperial thrust. Black political theorists understood slavery as a voracious system that grew by destroying families and by waging relentless war on others. "It is idle to talk of preventing the extension or circumscribing the limits of slavery," Dr. J. McCune Smith told his audience at the Colored National Convention in 1855. "There is no foot of American Territory over which slavery is not already triumphant, and will continue triumphant, so long as there remains any foot of American Territory on which it is admitted that man can hold property in man."[16] The *Frederick Douglass Paper* explained how the nation had forced slavery across the continent: "We began by robbing the Indians, then the Texans, then the Californians, N. Mexicans, and Utahs, and then we provoked the thunders that now roll over the relics of Mexico, and send their echo from Darien to Magellan." The exasperated essayist noted, "One more Presidential term, with a Scots or Pierce at the helm, in pursuit of these platforms and this policy, and ... there will not be a spot visible where the black and bloody banner of slavery and the fugitive slave law does not wave."[17]

This is why African Americans and their white allies in the abolitionist movement conceived of slavery abolition as an anti-imperial undertaking. This idea was articulated in Benjamin Lundy's *National Enquirer* in 1836 by a writer who argued that the United States was moving toward launching a war against Mexico in order to secure an expansion of slavery into the southwest. According to the writer,

Both [President Andrew Jackson and Gen. Gaines] are mere Instruments in the hands of an extensive combination of SLAVE-HOLDERS, SLAVE-TRADERS, LAND-JOBBERS and reckless political aspirants, composed of all parties in this country, who have resolved to wrest the territory of Texas from the Mexican Republic, for the same reason that they have despoiled the southern Indians of their lands and other property, and have driven and are driving them, beyond the Mississippi.[18]

The most prescient abolitionists understood, as Carole Emberton points out in Chapter 5 of this volume, that public policies and private actions that extended American power over the continent were having deleterious effects on those who stood in the way of "progress."

In opposition to slavery's militaristic thrust, African Americans invoked emancipatory internationalism to argue on behalf of ideals of democracy and self-determination in labor, politics, and foreign policy. The core of this idea endured into the twentieth century because various forms of slavery thrived after the end of the Civil War, and African Americans observed that forced labor was an integral aspect of U.S. imperialism.[19] As slavery gave way to Jim Crow, activist intellectuals invoked emancipatory internationalism in order to level broad critiques against the exploitation of workers in the United States as well as in the Global South.

W. E. B. Du Bois's *Black Reconstruction: A History of the Part Which Black Folk Played in the Attempt to Reconstruct Democracy in America*, published in 1935, drew upon the popular wellsprings of emancipatory internationalism. The book linked the defeat of Reconstruction with the emergence of the United States as an imperial, capitalist power on the global stage.[20] *Black Reconstruction* connected the disenfranchisement of African Americans with the subjugation of "colored labour" abroad. Du Bois reveals the worldwide consequences of emancipation's retreat:

The slave went free; stood a brief moment in the sun; then moved back again toward slavery. The whole weight of America was thrown to color caste. The colored world went down before England, France, Germany, Russia, Italy and America. A new slavery arose. The upward moving of white labor was betrayed into wars for profit based on color caste. Democracy died save in the hearts of black folks.[21]

In one of the book's signature statements, Dr. Du Bois conceived of a global vision of freedom: "The emancipation of man is the emancipation of labor and the emancipation of labor is the freeing of that basic majority of workers who are yellow, brown and black."[22]

Du Bois rehearsed the central arguments of *Black Reconstruction* before a mass audience less than a decade earlier, at the 1928 national convention of the National Association for the Advancement of Colored People in Los Angeles. In his "Address to the American People," Dr. Du Bois explained that the destruction of the Black electorate ushered in an era of corruption: "Disfranchisement of the Negro in Southern States has brought about such distortion of political power in the United States," Du Bois argued, "that a small white oligarchy in the South is the dictator of the Nation."[23] To combat this state of affairs, "The American ballot must be re-established on a real basis of intelligence and character," Du Bois asserted. He continued:

Only in such way can this nation face the tremendous problems before it: the problem of free speech, an unsubsidized press and civil liberty for all people; the problem of imperialism and the emancipation of Haiti, Nicaragua, Cuba, the Philippines and Hawaii from the government of American banks; the overshadowing problem of peace among the nations and of decent and intelligent co-operation in the real advancement of the natives of Africa and Asia, together with freedom for China, India and Egypt.[24]

In joining together the problems of the "government of American banks," Jim Crow, and black freedom, Du Bois and other like-minded public intellectuals raised the bar of emancipation. These activists drew from a fountainhead of popular black anti-imperialism that thrived between the 1820s and 1920s. This potent strand of political thought helps to explain the rise of internationalist African American organizations such as the Universal Negro Improvement Association, the African Blood Brotherhood, and black left formations in the New Deal Era.[25] This capacious conception of self-determination buttressed other ideas of liberation, including black Marxism, Garveyism, anti-colonialism, and the struggle for reparations. By stressing the linkages between freedom, labor power, and national liberation, the discourse of emancipatory internationalism deepened the democratic thrust of these other belief systems and brought politics down to earth. It was an ideology that Edward W. Said would have referred to as a "traveling theory," with flexible content that changed over time, and it was deployed by individuals and groups from diverse political backgrounds. This is a key to understanding why this tendency has endured as a staple of black politics.[26]

Because emancipatory internationalism arose during a time of aggressive American expansion, however, it was not without tensions. At times, black writers offered paternalism and missionary ideals of uplift as an antidote to generations of slavery and colonialism in Africa and Latin America. Exuberance over their historic triumph over American slavery in 1865 led some African Americans to view their counterparts in the Global South as needing tutelage – not mutual support. Hence the Rev. D. W. Moore of the African Methodist Episcopal (AME) Church exulted in 1870 that "Haiti was never so accessible as now. Dominica is beseeching national union, though cognizant of the fact that national union means a Protestant faith, with its free Bibles and free schools. Cuba and Puerto Rico are walking up to a life of liberty ... missionary work in Africa will shortly be so inviting as anywhere else; made so especially by the tractable disposition of the natives."[27] In addition, black communities divided over the question of whether military intervention could contribute to national liberation. At the turn of the century, African American soldiers asked each other what they were doing serving in the Philippines, Cuba, and elsewhere in missions that appeared to be extending segregation – not freedom – to local inhabitants.[28]

African Americans who promoted emancipatory internationalism looked to the Global South when they attempted to gauge the progress of racial equality between the antebellum era and the coming of the Great Depression.[29] A few months after the end of the Civil War, the *South Carolina Leader*, a Black newspaper based in Charleston, printed a column on the prospects of abolition in Cuba as well as an editorial warning about the threat of slavery reemerging in Mexico under Emperor Maximilian's rule. What happened in Cuba and Mexico mattered dearly to black South Carolinians as they mapped out their own strategies for freedom.[30] When historians limit African American thought within a national context they often miss this global conception of politics that existed generations before Malcolm X attempted, according to Cuban writer Juana Carrasco, "the internationalization of the struggle of the Negro people in North America."[31] The remainder of this essay traces out the origins and outlines of emancipatory internationalism by exploring anti-imperialist ideas and practices in the decades before and after the U.S. Civil War.

The idea that the clash between Liberty or Death was hemispheric-wide, and that it was not the provenance of an elite group of "Founding Fathers," appears repeatedly in African American speeches, broadsides, and conventions in the nineteenth century. Those who invoked the ideals of emancipatory internationalism emphasized the role that hitherto unknown freedom fighters played in their respective abolitionist movements. Thus, William Whipper explained emancipation in the West Indies by pointing to the power of grassroots insurgencies:

How was the emancipation of the slave, and the enfranchisement of the free colored people effected there? We unhesitatingly affirm, that it was chiefly through the influence of colored men – the oppressed; by that restless discontentment that changed deeply injured slaves into insurgent runaways, by that manly bearing and living purpose, with which the free people of color contended for their rights, and which, especially in Jamaica, led the noble [Edward] Jordan and his compeers to some of the most daring and heroic acts in the annals of the race.[32]

In 1827, *Freedom's Journal* stressed the roles that peoples of African, indigenous, as well as white and mixed-race ancestry were playing in the unfolding struggle for freedom in the Americas. The writer argued that the

only hope for the survival of the republic was the genius of ordinary
people opposed to the moneyed interests:

> Who let me ask, were the Generals that commanded the armies of the Republic, in
> the days of Cromwell? From what grade of society, did France during the
> Revolution procure her Marshals, was it not from the common people? Who
> was Toussaint, Dessalines, and a number of other generals who acted so
> prominent a part of the Revolution of Hayti,–were they not domestic slaves?
> Who, in the master spirits that achieved the Revolution in Colombia and
> Mexico? What is the complexion of the common soldiery of these states? Has
> not the independence of their country from the vassalage and bondage of Old
> Spain, been accomplished by troops composed of negroes, mulattoes and
> indians?[33]

African Americans conceived of a Day of Jubilee that would not be tied
solely to nationality or constrained by borders that the United States had
militarized in order to sustain slavery in the wake of Mexican and British
abolition. "What does the past teach?" a writer asked in an 1848 issue of
The National Era, answering

> That slavery lives by expansion ... It is in this way that the acquisition of Louisiana
> and Florida has spread slavery over new regions, and established the slave power
> in State after State, at the same time that it has prevented that rapid diminution of
> the political power of slavery in the old states, which must have taken place, had
> the evil been confined to its original limits.

The National Era asked, "Why deceive ourselves? The establishment of
slavery in California, in New Mexico, or a part of it, and throughout
Texas, will invest the slave-holding class with a power, from which there
can be no escape."[34] This was a movement that conceived of the struggle
against slavery as taking place on an international stage.

   African Americans repeatedly articulated the idea that the United
States invaded other nations to cement domestic systems of racial and
economic oppression. When Mexico abolished slavery it was only a
matter of time before it faced invasion from *El Norte*. The *Colored
American* asserted in 1838 that the United States' brewing war with
Mexico was not about boundaries, national honor, or even westward
expansion. In fact, *The Colored American* asserted,

> She is trying to steal Texas from her poor neighbor Mexico, to open a new market
> for her illegitimate children. She sells her own young ones, as well as eats them. She
> used to steal men, women, and children from Africa, and her sages made a
> constitution in favor of carrying on man-stealing there – so that she could not
> stop it herself for some twenty years. She stopped it after the time was out, because
> she found it more profitable to steal and sell her own inhabitants.[35]

The *Frederick Douglass Paper* compared the Cuban Filibusterers with the men who had brought war on Mexico as the "Slaveholders, slave traders, and cold-blooded tyrants of every grade."[36] The following year, the paper published a letter from B. F. Remington, who excoriated U.S. slaveholders for their efforts to enslave the citizens of Cuba, Mexico, and South America in order to bolster their profits.[37]

CUBA MUST BE FREE: CIVIL WAR AND RECONSTRUCTION

Abolitionists who promoted emancipatory internationalism embraced a sophisticated understanding of the connections between oppression and liberation throughout the Americas. On January 14, 1862, Frederick Douglass informed an audience in National Hall, Philadelphia, that the Civil War was brought on by imperialism and appeasement of the slave power. Douglass was building on existing anti-imperial analyses of U.S. "expansionism." In one damning sentence, Douglass's narrative placed slavery and imperialism at the center of American history:

We have bought Florida, waged war with friendly Seminoles, purchased Louisiana, annexed Texas, fought Mexico, trampled on the right of petition, abridged the freedom of debate, paid ten million to Texas upon a fraudulent claim, mobbed the Abolitionists, repealed the Missouri Compromise, winked at the accursed slave trade, helped to extend slavery, given slaveholders a larger share of all the offices and honors than we claimed for ourselves, paid their postage, supported the Government, persecuted free negroes, refused to recognize Hayti and Liberia, stained our souls by repeated compromises, borne with Southern bluster, allowed our ships to be robbed of their hardy sailors, defeated a central road to the Pacific, and have descended to the meanness and degradation of negro dogs, and hunted down the panting slave escaping from his tyrant master – all to make the South love us; and yet how stands our relations?[38]

More attention needs to be paid to the ways that African Americans viewed the Civil War through a global lens. As Jane Landers noted in the conference upon which this volume is based, war and contests between great powers sometimes provided openings for the formerly enslaved to think of freedom in new ways.[39] This was certainly the case in the Civil War. African Americans cheered Mexicans who "fought with desperate bravery" against invading French troops, whom many feared would re-impose slavery and join forces with the Confederacy. When Emperor Maximilian finally imposed his will on the country, Rev. H. M. Turner urged the United States to raise an army to drive Maximilian off his "imperial throne." "I believe this government can drown Jeff. Davis and his hosts in the Red Sea, and send three hundred thousand men to Mexico to welcome Maximilian to his imperial throne, with as much canister and grape as would blow him into another region," Turner opined.[40] Rev. Turner's invasion plan was never enacted; however, small numbers of African American soldiers – including historian George Washington Williams – crossed the border to join republican forces in the struggle against the emperor.[41] As his comrades swept into Richmond in the spring of 1865, Chaplain G. H. White of the 28th United States Colored Troops stated,

Why, you need not feel at all timid in giving the truthfulness of my assertion to the four winds of the heavens, and let the angels re-echo it back to earth, that the colored soldiers of the army of the James were the first to enter the city of Richmond. I was with them, and am still with them, and am willing to stay with them until freedom is proclaimed throughout the world. Yes, we will follow this race of men in search of Liberty through the whole Island of Cuba.[42]

African Americans seized on the democratic promise of Reconstruction to spread the gospel of emancipatory internationalism. Black conventions and church meetings urged senior abolitionists to refocus their energies on fighting for emancipation in Latin America, the Caribbean, and Africa. The *Christian Recorder* argued that the work of the anti-slavery movement was far from over:

Disband the Anti-Slavery Society when Cuba, with over half a million of slaves lies at our gates! Disband the Anti-Slavery Society when Maximilian's government may be permanent, and be made slaveholding ... when Brazil still sells human flesh, and old Spain Countenances the trans-Atlantic traffic! It may be said 'These are out of the United States.' But these men– slaves, are our brothers."[43]

An African American correspondent in Salt Lake, Utah, admonished the readers of *The Elevator* over one 4th of July weekend that "While we are rejoicing over our national anniversary, let us not forget the patriotic sons of Cuba in the struggles for their national existence, from the misruling of the government of Spain; whose troops, brute-like and fiendish in disguise have perpetuated acts of brutalities and cruelties on the Cuban patriots; not for the first time have they disgraced her banner and civilization."[44]

As the Ten Years War for liberation from Spanish rule (1868–78) raged in Cuba, African Americans demanded that the United States grant belligerency status to the insurgents, thus making them eligible to receive international military assistance.[45] National efforts to build the movement for support of the Cuban struggle quickened in the wake of the election of Ulysses S. Grant in 1869. As African Americans celebrated the ratification of the Fifteenth Amendment to the U.S. Constitution, they placed the cause of Cuba center stage. Aaron L. Jackson, keynote speaker at the Fifteenth Amendment ratification celebration in Sacramento, California, swept up his listeners in the history they all had a hand in making: "I feel to-day, that it has come full and complete, to gladden the hearts of millions of my oppressed people. Then roll on, thou great power of deliverance, guided by the hand of deity, regardless of all obstacles that the puny hand of man can erect to stay thy onward progress!" Like many other African Americans, Jackson believed that emancipation in one country was not enough: "Stop not within the confines of America, but leap across the briny deep, and encircle the bleeding isle of Cuba, thence to the Brazils, where thousands of human beings are yet groaning under the cruel yoke of slavery!"[46] At the Fifteenth Amendment ratification celebration in Virginia City, Nevada, African Americans transformed sentiments in support of freedom into demands for action. The Virginia City celebrants drew up a list of resolutions that included the following statement: "RESOLVED: That our thanks are due to the Congress of the United States of America for the wise enactment, and maintaining of laws which makes all men free and equal; and that this Government, at no distant day, will extend its might and protecting arm of mercy to the struggling patriots of Cuba."[47]

The organizing assembly of the national Cuban Anti-Slavery Committee was held at the Cooper Institute in New York City on December 13, 1872. Henry Highland Garnet served as secretary of the mass meeting, and many of the most distinguished African American abolitionists were in attendance, including Charles E. Pindell, Peter Williams Ray, and Samuel R. Scottron, who chaired the meeting. The Spanish government tried to disrupt the historic meeting with paid agents who distributed leaflets titled "To the Colored Citizens of the United States," warning African Americans of "the folly of supporting the Cuban rebels." The agents were firmly rebuked by Charles E. Pindell as well as by Cuban expatriates in attendance. When Rev. Garnet rose to address the audience he was greeted with tremendous applause befitting his stature in American political life. In the antebellum era, Garnet had advocated slave rebellion and African American emigration to Mexico. During the Civil War he became a recruiter for the Union Army and barely escaped death at the hands of a New York Draft Riot mob in 1863. Rev. Garnet's prestige and knowledge of international issues made him a logical leader of the Cuban unity campaign. With great emotion, the venerable activist spoke directly to the group of Cuban exiles sitting near the front of the stage:

I see before me to-night many native Cubans, who, driven by the fierce fires of Spanish oppression, have sought and found shelter in our free land. Permit me to assure you, my exiled friends, that I know that I am justified in saying to you that this meeting, and millions of American citizens, bid you God speed in your noble cause; and in their behalf I extend to you my hand, pledging ourselves to stand united with you in your efforts for the promotion of the interests of liberty, and the universal brotherhood of man.[48]

The meeting ended with the creation of a national coordinating committee, as well as a resolution calling upon the federal government "to accord to the Cuban Patriots that favorable recognition that four years' gallant struggle for freedom justly entitles them to."[49] The headquarters of the Cuban Anti-Slavery committee were established at No. 62 Bowery and organizers immediately set about planning an educational campaign to support the petition drive. "The colored citizens of New York are doing a good thing in protesting against the conduct of Spain to Cuba," *The Christian Recorder* opined. "It is high time that liberty be brought in, even if Spain has to be kicked out."[50] Building upon preexisting networks of communication as well as the bedrock of emancipatory internationalism, the Cuban solidarity movement grew rapidly. Soon after the Cooper Institute assembly, a mass meeting was held in Boston, and resolutions were passed "calling on the American people to urge the Administration to extend all legal aid to the patriots of Cuba in their struggle for freedom."[51]

African Americans drew upon their own experiences in making the Civil War a war for freedom in order to build the Cuban solidarity movement. The emphasis on the role that the oppressed played in bringing about emancipation was reiterated. Hence *The Elevator* argued,

The Cuban struggle is not for national independence alone, although that was the original motive which induced the patriots to revolt against the power and tyranny of Spain; but finding national independence and personal slavery incompatible and incongruous ideas, and knowing that they could never achieve their object without the aid of the slaves, decreed emancipation on the same grounds that President Lincoln issued his Proclamation of Emancipation i.e., military necessity.[52]

Early the following year, African Americans in Philadelphia gathered at Mother Bethel AME Church to consider "stirring resolutions" in support of the Cuban freedom fighters. The resolutions forged by the participants spoke volumes about the ways that black people defined freedom in the Reconstruction era: "We, the colored citizens of Philadelphia, having met in mass meeting to consider the condition of Cuba ... Resolved, that [for] the oppressed of Cuba we have the warmest sympathy; for the patriots now in arms we have admiration, and for the rulers of Spain we have only indignation." The mass meeting requested, "That the old cohorts of Abolitionists, who made common cause with us in our contentions for liberty, be urged to make the same glorious common cause, with the oppressed of the Spanish dependencies." The participants urged "That President Grant be requested to reconsider his policy toward the Cuban revolutionist ... and that to ... the whole band of Spanish republicans we reach out the right hand of fellowship, and pray that as a reward for the physical freedom they would give the oppressed abroad, an ever balancing Providence may give them political liberty at home."[53]

A movement culture in support of the Cuban solidarity campaign blossomed in 1873. Movement centers emerged in Baltimore, San Francisco, Washington, D.C., southern Louisiana, and other regions where black Republicanism was strong.[54] The *New York Times* announced that "The colored citizens of Columbia will hold a mass-meeting on Thanksgiving Eve to give expression of their sympathy for the Cuban cause. Frederick Douglass will be one of the speakers."[55] Both the California State Colored Men's Convention as well as the National Civil Rights Convention, held in Washington, D.C., at the end of the year, passed strongly worded resolutions of support for the Cuban patriots.[56] Seeking to build the campaign's momentum, Rev. W. H. Hillery, keynote speaker at the fourth annual Fifteenth Amendment celebration held in Chico, California, intoned, "Cuba, after more than five years of war and rapine, shouts forth to the world – Liberty or Death."[57] Anti-Slavery Committee leaders met with Cuban insurgents in the United States to strategize; the organization also worked with white organizations that shared the same broad agenda and corresponded regularly with British anti-slavery organizations.[58]

Even as they fought the Ku Klux Klan, black political leaders in South Carolina, Florida, and Louisiana became heavily involved in the Cuban solidarity movement. South Carolina Lieutenant Governor A. G. Ranier presided over a Union League Hall meeting in Washington, D.C., called in support of the Cuban patriots. Florida's Congressman Josiah T. Walls helped lead a deliberative process that resulted in a joint resolution from the Florida State Legislature calling upon the federal government to recognize the Cuban insurgency.[59] The 1873 Convention of Colored Men in Louisiana placed the cause of the "barbarous rule of Spanish authority in Cuba" alongside the effort to end electoral fraud and anti-Black political violence in Louisiana.[60] The Louisiana Republican Party platform dedicated itself toward rebuilding their war-torn state, improving race relations, advocating a national civil-rights bill, and reminding the Republican Party, "That we sympathize with the patriotic men in Cuba who fight for liberty, and that we urge upon the national Congress the early recognition of the independence of Cuba, and hereby instruct our Representatives in Congress to use their best efforts and influence to this end."[61]

The fate of the petition campaign rested with the administration of Ulysses S. Grant. Grant had given organizers of the Cuban solidarity movement hope the previous winter when, during his message to Congress, he urged Spain to declare emancipation.[62] However, while President Grant politely received the delegation of the Cuban Anti-Slavery Society in the winter of 1873, odds were not in their favor. Secretary of State Hamilton Fish was firmly opposed to granting belligerency status to the Cuban resistance. Historian Richard H. Bradford notes that "As a businessman Fish favored the interests of Americans who had invested in sugar and slaves and perhaps stood to lose if the revolution succeeded." In addition, Bradford points to "the 'hard-money elite' of upper-class Northeasterners in both parties" who opposed Cuban belligerency rights.[63]

This rebuff did not stop African Americans from continuing to build the movement for Cuban solidarity. As the presidency of Rutherford B. Hayes loomed, the *Savannah Tribune* wrote, "CUBA. The revolution in this island, has continued eight years, and has probably cost Spain nearly a billion dollars, and over a hundred thousand lives, many of them the flower of Castilian chivalry and the gem of the Antilles is still unconquered. We hope one of the first acts of President Hayes's administration [will] be to acknowledge the belligerency of Cuba."[64] At a mass meeting held in Philadelphia the following year, Rev. Henry Highland Garnet continued to expound on the theme that the work of slavery abolitionism was incomplete. "If the veteran abolitionists of the United States had not mustered themselves out of service," Rev. Garnet argued, "I believe that there would not now have been a single slave in the Island of Cuba." "We sympathize with the patriot of Cuba," Garnet continued "not simply because they are Republicans, but because their triumph will be the destruction of slavery in that land. All Europe now frowns upon Spain, because of her attitude toward human bondage. We must take our place on the broad platform of universal human rights, and plead for the brotherhood of the entire human race." This was a cause that revived the aging abolitionist's spirits and an observer noted that "The Dr. seemed to be in excellent trim, for the speech he made reminded those who heard him, of some of his best efforts in the old Anti-slavery warfare in our own country."[65] After hearing addresses in Spanish and in English, the meeting's participants formed the American Foreign Anti-Slavery Society to address the crisis in Cuba.

A TRAGEDY THAT BEGGARED THE GREEK

The Cuban solidarity campaign launched by black anti-slavery abolitionists during Reconstruction was one of the most remarkable social movements in American history. In placing the emancipation of enslaved people and the liberation of Cuba on the same platform as the struggle for equal citizenship in the United States, African Americans created a new kind of freedom movement. The national petition campaign was an outstanding example of emancipatory internationalism in action. It built on the best traditions of anti-imperial antebellum slavery abolitionism; furthermore, it prefigured the Third World Liberation and Anti-Apartheid struggles of the twentieth century. While black organizers focused much of their energy on the question of race and slavery in Cuba, they also made it clear that they viewed the Ten Years War as a multiracial anti-colonial movement aimed at ending Spanish tyranny. In the eyes of the Cuban Anti-Slavery Committee, "white" Cuban rebels deserved support because they had abolished slavery for the same reasons that Abraham Lincoln had issued the Emancipation Proclamation in the midst of the Civil War. Finally, however, the disenfranchisement of African American voters in the final twenty-five years of the century doomed the movement.

C. L. R. James implored listeners at his 1971 Institute of the Black World lecture in Atlanta to grapple with W. E. B. Du Bois's statement that Reconstruction was "the finest effort to achieve democracy for the working millions which this world had ever seen." The defeat of Reconstruction, however, "was a tragedy that beggared the Greek; it was an upheaval of humanity like the Reformation and the French Revolution."[66] The end of Reconstruction held cataclysmic consequences for African Americans, and, as Du Bois pointed out, working-class people all over the world felt the shockwaves. The destruction of black voting rights removed the largest potential block of anti-imperial voters in the United States from the voting rolls. As Du Bois argued in *Black*

Reconstruction, the road was now wide open for the United States to lend its own terrible force to the juggernaut of white world supremacy.

This is not to say that African Americans somehow disengaged from viewing the problems of emancipation, freedom, and democracy in a context of the possibilities of global liberation; far from it. However, as a largely disenfranchised minority, African Americans lost their influence in a national political system geared to remove them from the levers of political power. Much of the momentum that could have been added to blocks of voters who were opposed to imperialism was lost for critical decades. However much charismatic individuals like Mark Twain, William James, or Robert La Follette, Sr., may have advocated for peace, there was no longer a mass base of voters to back these lofty sentiments with political muscle. African Americans recognized only too well what William Appleman Williams called the *Tragedy of American Diplomacy*, a system of expansion undertaken in the name of freedom that denied freedom to others. Black citizens were expelled from the body politic at the very moment when their voices were most desperately needed to challenge an imperial system that would soon engulf the hemisphere.[67]

JIM CROW ABROAD

Emancipatory internationalism survived into the twentieth century and helped to form the basis of a renewed black engagement with the African Diaspora and anti-colonial politics in general.[68] African American women increasingly played leading roles in this arena. Ida B. Wells Barnett, Fannie Barnett Williams, and other African American leaders convened a public meeting of mourning and protest in Chicago in the wake of Cuban revolutionary General Antonio Maceo's death at the hands of the Spanish in 1896. Five hundred attendees at Bethel AME Church drafted resolutions stating, "That the Afro-Americans of Chicago, in mass-meeting assembled, express their deep and heartfelt sympathy with Cubans in their desperate struggle to resist further merciless oppression of Spain; and be it further Revolved ... That we hereby express our willingness and readiness to render every possible assistance within our power to insure the triumph of the Cuban insurgents.[69] Three years later, the Rev. Lena Mason paid tribute to female freedom fighters in Cuba stating that, "Antonio Maceo also had more than a hundred females in his regiment– not coarse and shameless amazons, who chose the wild life for love of adventure, but mostly wives and mothers of standing and dignity. They dress in masculine attire, carried Mauser rifles, machetes, marched with men, endured all the hardships of camp and field and made as intrepid and uncomplaining soldiers as any."[70]

African American organizations continued to commemorate freedom in an internationalist spirit. The Universal Negro Improvement Association's organ, *The Negro World*, honored Simón Bolívar in 1920 and joined the people of Peru in observing the 100th anniversary of the Battle of Ayacucho, one of the final battles of the Latin American Independence wars that aided the march of emancipation. While black newspapers in the nineteenth century had promoted the memory of Ayacucho and other anti-colonial battles, the *Negro World* lamented that U.S. citizens were now ignorant of this history.[71] Celebrating the fact that Bolívar's and General José de San Martín's armies had contained a mix of "Spaniards, Scots, Irishmen, Negroes and Indians," the *Negro World* asserted: "Anglo-Saxons, who boast of tenacity and courage as if these qualities were peculiar to Nordics should read of the achievements of such men as Bolívar and San Martin. Then they might understand why their arrogant attitude has roused such resentment in the Latin American Republic[s]."[72]

African Americans used their knowledge of slavery and legal segregation to make common cause with their counterparts in Latin America, the Caribbean, and Africa. African American commentators frequently referred to "Jim Crow abroad" and warned that increasing U.S. influence and capitalist investment in Latin America, the Caribbean, and Africa would mean forced labor, disenfranchisement, and a loss of dignity.[73] The black press railed against U.S. occupations and military invasions of Haiti, the Dominican Republic, and Nicaragua throughout the 1920s. The *Washington Bee* argued that the repression of Haiti and the Dominican Republic was done "at the hands of the National City Bank group of New York City, aided and abetted by our Department of State, which in turn has been aided by our Navy Department," which the *Bee* noted was led by none other than Josephus Daniels of the Wilmington Race Riot infamy.[74]

African Americans closely watched the progress of the Nicaraguan liberation struggle against U.S. invasion forces, and many rejoiced at the successes of what they referred to as "the Indians and Negroes among the population of Northwest Nicaragua" who composed the rank and file of Augusto Sandino's rebel forces. The *Pittsburgh Courier* proudly noted that "it is assumed that the Nicaraguan patriots who are following Sandino are illiterate. Illiterate they may be, but certainly they are as surely patriots as the ragged hosts that cast their fortune with George Washington in 1776. Mention of the Negroes brings to mind the fact that in the State of *Nueva Segovia,* in Northwest Nicaragua, there are close to 10,000 Negroes, and many of them are fighting in the Army of Sandino."[75]

While the *New York Times* repeatedly referred to the Nicaraguan leader as a common criminal, a rejoinder in the *Amsterdam News* argued that:

Sandino has been called a bandit, but his words are not those of a bandit; they would have fitted the mouth of George Washington when he was fighting the British. The worst feature of the business is the curtailing of Latin American freedom of speech by American military power. In Nicaragua, the [U.S.] marines seem to be repeating their record in Haiti and the Virgin Islands. Thinkers will wish to know whether this country is to remain a republic or become an empire.[76]

"The victory of our fighting forces over the Nicaraguan rebels may have been a fine achievement for the military," the *Norfolk Journal and Guide* later lectured, "but it is nothing to reflect credit upon our country's Latin-American policy. In fact, it is rather a discredit, indeed a disgrace."[77] Echoing the antebellum critique of slaveowners and military aggression, African American newspapers now stressed the culpability of Wall Street in American imperialism.[78]

African American leaders across the political spectrum were able to connect the struggle against Jim Crow at home with battles against U.S. aggression abroad because black anti-imperialism had such deep roots. James Weldon Johnson published an exposé of Wall Street's role in the U.S. military occupation of Haiti and he lectured widely on U.S. atrocities in that nation.[79] When the national NAACP leader spoke to a Cleveland-area audience, the black press framed American war crimes in Haiti as "3,250 Lynch Murders."[80] George Schuyler's *Pittsburgh Courier*'s editorial columns railed against the exploitation of workers in Africa and Latin America. "What has happened in Liberia is precisely what has happened in Nicaragua, Haiti, Santo Domingo, Bolivia, Venezuela, Colombia, Costa Rica, Porto Rico, Honduras, Guatemala, Panama, Ecuador, and Peru, and what will some day happen in Mexico, i.e., the country is now irretrievably in the claws of the American bankers. The country is having a new day, all right, but the profits will hereafter go almost entirely to the Firestone Company and the National City Bank."[81]

African American activists created a way of understanding emancipation that transcended borders and that stressed self-determination, anti-imperialism, and solidarity between oppressed peoples. Emancipatory internationalism was forged in the century between the 1820s and 1920s. Its legacies may be found in black organizations including the Universal Negro Improvement Association, the Black Panther Party for

Self Defense, and the Rainbow Coalition – as well as the modern civil rights movement in general. In the grimmest decades of slavery, Jim Crow, and Apartheid, besieged African American communities looked to the Global South for inspiration, and tried to offer whatever support they could to overseas struggles. These bold efforts highlight the need to reorient our understanding of American political thought along a North–South axis of ideas, migrations and movements that run as deeply as the traditional East–West imaginary of Frederick Jackson Turner.[82] Shorn of the glitter of American exceptionalism, U.S. history looks much different from this vantage point. For those who embraced emancipatory internationalism, Thomas Jefferson was not the grantor of liberty who was also a slaveowner; instead, he was envisioned as the "First Imperialist."[83] U.S. history was not the story of freedom *given*, but freedom *fought for* with the blood, sweat, and tears of African Americans, Latinos, Native Americans, and others.

Black communities struggling against white supremacy invoked the names of Latin American freedom fighters including Simón Bolívar, Antonio Maceo, and Augusto Sandino as they sought to broaden the meanings of freedom beyond the confines of the United States. Character sketches of resistance leaders in the Americas drawn by Black writers were at times romanticized, but no more so than typical depictions of U.S. "founding fathers" by the nation's historians. The specific content of emancipatory internationalism changed over time. The abolitionist analysis of slaveowners, filibusters, and "land jobbers" gave way to critiques of the "Government of American Banks," Wall Street, and capitalism in the 1920s. There were certain core ideas, however, that remained firm. African Americans who embraced emancipatory internationalism never accepted the idea that the U.S. was an "isolationist" nation with a unique mission to spread democracy abroad. Emancipatory internationalists understood that their counterparts in the Global South organized their own freedom movements, and had the right to determine their own destinies – whether or not the U.S. government agreed.[84]

The robust beliefs that constitute the heart of emancipatory internationalism point the way toward a future where freedom is no longer the possession of one powerful nation to give or to take away from others. As we debate the meanings of freedom in the wake of the 150th anniversary of the Emancipation Proclamation we must incorporate the associations that African Americans have historically made between liberation at home and the right of nations and workers to be free from imperialism abroad.

FIGURE 8: "Henry Highland Garnet, noted antebellum abolitionist and leader of the Cuban Anti-Slavery Committee in the 1870s."
Source: National Portrait Gallery, Smithsonian Institution.

NOTES

I am indebted to Armin Fardis, Genesis Lara, and Sheila Payne for close readings of early drafts of this chapter. William A. Link and James J. Broomall provided invaluable editorial guidance.

1. Julius Scott, "The Common Wind: Currents of Afro-American Communication in the Era of the Haitian Revolution." (PhD diss., Duke University, Department of History, 1986); Sylvia R. Frey, *Water from the Rock: Black Resistance in a Revolutionary Age* (Princeton: Princeton University Press, 1992); David P. Geggus, ed., *The Impact of the Haitian Revolution in the Atlantic World* (Columbia: University of South Carolina Press, 2001); George Reid Andrews, *Afro-Latin America: 1800–2000* (New York: Oxford University Press, 2004); Laurent Dubois and Julius Scott, eds., *Origins of the Black Atlantic* (New York: Routledge, 2009); Michael O. West,

William G. Martin, and Fanon Che Wilkins, eds., *From Toussaint to Tupac: The Black International since the Age of Revolution* (Chapel Hill: University of North Carolina Press, 2009); Robin Blackburn, *The American Crucible: Slavery, Emancipation and Human Rights* (London: Verso, 2013); "Telling Histories: A Conversation with Laurent Dubois and Greg Grandin," *Radical History Review* 115 (Winter 2013): 11–25.

2. "Annual Examination," *Frederick Douglass' Paper*, May 6, 1859; "Hayti No. IV," *Freedom's Journal*, June 15, 1827; "The Republic of Haiti," *The Christian Recorder*, May 8, 1873; "All Signs Point," *Freeman* (Indianapolis), December 5, 1896; "Sad Bereavement," *Colored American*, July 3, 1903; "Beautiful Haiti and Its Brave Hearted People," *The Negro World*, February 21, 1925. Mitch Kachun, "Antebellum African Americans, Public Commemoration, and the Haitian Revolution: A Problem of Historical Mythmaking," in Maurice Jackson and Jacqueline Bacon, eds., *African Americans and the Haitian Revolution: Selected Essays and Historical Documents* (New York: Routledge, 2009), 93–106. African Americans named streets and districts in homage to Haiti. Hence, African Americans in Durham, North Carolina, named their community, "Hayti," which became known as the "Black Wall Street" in the twentieth century. See Leslie Brown, *Upbuilding Black Durham: Gender, Class, and Black Community Development in the Jim Crow South* (Chapel Hill: University of North Carolina Press, 2008).

3. "Toussaint L'Ouverture," *Freedom's Journal*, May 4, 1827.

4. "Haytien Independence," *The Genius of Universal Emancipation and Baltimore Courier*, September 12, 1825.

5. African American communities continued to accord a place of honor to Bolívar over the next century alongside heroes of Latin American, African, and Irish anti-colonialism, as well as European revolutionaries such as Louis Kossuth. See "William Whipper's Letters, No. II," *The Colored American*, February 20, 1841; "Gen. Antonio Maceo," *The Freeman* (Indianapolis), October 30, 1897. On the importance of the Hungarian revolutionary to abolitionists in the United States, see W. Caleb McDaniel, "'Our Country Is the World': American Abolitionists, Louis Kossuth, and Philanthropic Revolutions," *Annual Meeting of the Organization of American Historians*, March 25, 2004, 1–22. W. E. B. Du Bois, *The Negro* (1915; Philadelphia: University of Pennsylvania Press, 2001), 176, 182. For African American culture in Baltimore, see Barbara J. Fields, *Slavery and Freedom on the Middle Ground: Maryland during the Nineteenth Century* (New Haven: Yale University Press, 1985); Robert L. Hall, "Slave Resistance in Baltimore City and County, 1747–1790," *Maryland Historical Magazine* 84 (1989), 305–318; Christopher Phillips, *Freedom's Port: The African American Community of Baltimore, 1790–1860* (Urbana: University of Illinois Press, 1997).

6. "Cuban Anti-Slavery Meeting – Addresses and Resolutions," *The Sun* (Baltimore), February 14, 1873. Several meeting summaries of the Cuban Anti-Slavery Committee note the participation of women. Given the leadership role that black women played in African American communities, they undoubtedly played a major role in the national petition campaign. See

"Enthusiastic Meeting in Cooper Institute," *The New York Times,* October 25, 1877.

7. African Americans interpreted events in the Global South through selective lenses and their ideas of freedom struggles throughout the Americas were influenced by the chronic social crises they faced in the United States. As Frank Guridy notes, "The forging of diasporic linkages necessarily entails, as literary scholar Brent Edwards has shown, the messy process of translation and, inevitably, misunderstandings. Projections, mistranslations, and disagreements over meaning are embedded in all forms of Afro-diasporic interaction." Guridy, *Forging Diaspora: Afro-Cubans and African Americans in a World of Empire and Jim Crow* (Chapel Hill: University of North Carolina Press, 2010), 6–7. It may also be useful to extend Benedict Anderson's idea of "imagined community" to the African American project of creating imagined communities of struggle that transcended national borders. See Benedict Anderson, *Imagined Communities: Reflections on the Origin and Spread of Nationalism* (London: Verso, 1991).

8. "Petition to Accord Belligerent Rights to Cuba," *New York Times,* February 20, 1873; "The Spanish Republic," *The New York Times,* February 24, 1873; "Correspondence," *The Elevator* (San Francisco, Calif.), March 25, 1873.

9. "Sympathy for Cuba in Philadelphia," *The Christian Recorder,* February 13, 1873; "Local Matters," *Baltimore Sun,* February 14, 1873; "Correspondence, Sacramento," *The Elevator,* March 24, 1873; "The State Convention of Colored People," *The Elevator,* November 29, 1873; "Cuban Independence," *Weekly Louisianan,* June 13, 1874; "Civil Rights Demonstration," *Weekly Louisianan,* June 27, 1874; "Cuba," *The Savannah Tribune,* November 11, 1876; "Slavery in Cuba," *New York Times,* July 13, 1877; "Protest against Cuban Slavery," *The Christian Recorder,* November 8, 1877; "Samuel R. Scottron," *Cleveland Gazette,* June 4, 1887. Charles Vincent, *Black Legislators in Louisiana during Reconstruction* (Baton Rouge: Louisiana State University Press, 1976), 165–166. Scholars have skillfully written on connections between African American and Cuban leaders. See Lisa Brock and Digna Castañada Fuertes, *Between Race and Empire: African-Americans and Cubans before the Cuban Revolution* (Philadelphia: Temple University Press, 1998); Manning Marable, "Race and Revolution in Cuba: African American Perspectives," in Manning Marable, ed., *Dispatches from the Ebony Tower: Intellectuals Confront the African American Experience* (New York: Columbia University Press, 2000), 93–94; Penny M. Von Eschen, *Race against Empire: Black Americans and Anticolonialism, 1937–1957* (Ithaca: Cornell University Press, 1997); Gerald Horne, *Race to Revolution: The United States and Cuba during Slavery and Jim Crow* (New York: Monthly Review Press, 2014).

10. "Samuel R. Scottron, An Interesting Biographical Sketch of a Successful Member of the Race," *Cleveland Gazette,* June 4, 1887.

11. "Cuba," *The Christian Recorder,* March 20, 1869.

12. "Cuban Independence," *Weekly Louisianan,* June 13, 1874.

13. For definitions of Pan-Africanism, see St. Clair Drake, "Diaspora Studies and Pan-Africanism," in Joseph E. Harris, ed., *Global Dimensions of the African*

Diaspora (Washington, D.C.: Howard University Press, 1993), 451–514; Robin D. G. Kelley, "'But a Local Phase of a World Problem': Black History's Global Vision, 1883–1950," *Journal of American History* 86, no. 3 (December 1999), 1045–1077.

14. "Independent Political League Adopts Strong Address against US Intervention in Cuba," *The Afro-American Ledger*, July 20, 1912.

15. Jeffrey R. Kerr-Ritchie, *Rites of August First: Emancipation Day in the Black Atlantic World* (Baton Rouge: Louisiana State University Press, 2007). I discuss emancipatory internationalism more broadly in my forthcoming book, *Our Separate Struggles Are Really One: African American and Latino Histories* (Boston: Beacon Press, forthcoming). The scholarly literature on American imperialism includes William Appleman Williams, *The Tragedy of American Diplomacy* (1959; New York: Norton, 1972); Walter LaFeber, *The New Empire: An Interpretation of American Expansion, 1860–1898* (1963; Ithaca: Cornell University Press, 1998); Walter LaFeber, *Inevitable Revolutions: The United States in Central America* (New York: Norton, 1993); Gabriel Kolko, *Confronting the Third World: United States Foreign Policy, 1945–1980* (New York: Pantheon, 1988).

16. "An Address to the People of the United States," *Proceedings of the Colored National Convention* (Salem, N.J.: The National Standard, 1856), 32.

17. "Cuba," *Frederick Douglass' Paper*, October 29, 1852. See also "Southern Patriotism & Florida War," *The National Enquirer*, January 28, 1837; "Cuba and the United States," *Frederick Douglass' Paper*, September 4, 1851; "Cuba – The Reason," *Provincial Freeman*, June 3, 1854.

18. "Verge of a War with the Mexican Republic," *National Enquirer*, November 19, 1836. In 1854, the Western Anti-Slavery Society in Salem, Ohio, critiqued U.S.-based efforts to seize Cuba in order to extend American slavery: "Resolutions," *Frederick Douglass' Paper*, September 15, 1854. See also "National Rapacity," *Pennsylvania Freeman*, February 19, 1846. Historians have periodically stressed the connections between slavery and imperialism. See C. L. R. James, *Black Jacobins: Toussaint L'Ouverture and the San Domingo Revolution* (1938; repr., New York: Vintage Books, 1989); Oliver Cromwell Cox, *Caste, Class, and Race: A Study in Social Dynamics* (New York: Doubleday, 1948); Walter Johnson, *River of Dark Dreams: Slavery and Empire in the Cotton Kingdom* (Cambridge, Mass.: Harvard University Press, 2013).

19. "Haiti Humiliated," *The Washington Bee*, September 25, 1920; "Charge U.S. Imperialistic in Liberia," *The Chicago Defender*, September 8, 1928; "Darker Races Problems Hushed at Conference," *The California Eagle*, May 10, 1945; "Convicts Killed and Tortured," *The Pittsburgh Courier*, July 14, 1923; "Brutal Slavery in the United States," *The Negro World*, January 31, 1925; "Start Florida Peonage Trials This Month; Prominent Officials Involved," *The Chicago Defender*, May 2, 1925; "A New Form of Labor Peonage in Cotton Belt, *The Norfolk Journal and Guide*, November 13, 1926; "Texas Sheriff Found Guilty of Peonage," *The Pittsburgh Courier*, February 19, 1927.

20. W. E. B. DuBois, *Black Reconstruction in America, 1860–1880* (1935; repr. New York: Free Press, 1998), 706. Cedric Robinson has persuasively examined the intersections between racism and capitalism in *Black Marxism: The Making of the Black Radical Tradition* (London: Zed Press, 1983). Robinson's work is a cogent reminder that Black radical intellectuals have long studied the relationship between slavery, capitalism and racism. See T. Thomas Fortune, *Black and White: Land, Labor, and Politics in the South* (New York: Fords, Howard, and Hulbert, 1884); James, *Black Jacobins*; Eric Williams, *Capitalism and Slavery* (Chapel Hill: University of North Carolina Press, 1944); Cox, *Caste, Class and Race*. Jeffrey B. Perry, *Hubert Harrison: The Voice of Harlem Radicalism, 1883–1918* (New York: Columbia University Press, 2008); Manning Marable, *How Capitalism Underdeveloped Black America: Problems in Race, Political Economy, and Society* (1983; repr., Boston: South End Press, 2000); West, Martin, and Wilkins, eds., *From Toussaint to Tupac*.
21. W. E. B. Du Bois, *Black Reconstruction*, 30.
22. Ibid., 15–16.
23. "Political Power 'Distorted' Says Dr. Du Bois," *Plaindealer* (Topeka, Kansas), June 29, 1928.
24. "N.A.A.C.P. Publishes Text of Address," *The New York Amsterdam News*, July 18, 1928.
25. For critical analyses of these organizations and Black internationalist tendencies in general, see C. L. R. James, *A History of Pan-African Revolt* with a new introduction by Robin D. G. Kelley (1939; repr., Chicago: Charles H. Kerr, 1995); Frantz Fanon, *The Wretched of the Earth* (1961; repr., New York: Grove Press, 2005); Ula Yvette Taylor, *The Veiled Garvey: The Life and Times of Amy Jacques Garvey* (Chapel Hill: University of North Carolina Press, 2001); Michele Mitchell, *Righteous Propagation: African Americans and the Politics of Racial Destiny after Reconstruction* (Chapel Hill: University of North Carolina Press, 2004); Minkah Makalini, *In the Cause of Freedom: Radical Black Internationalism from Harlem to London, 1917–1939* (Chapel Hill: University of North Carolina Press, 2011); Christopher J. Lee, *Making a World after Empire: The Bandung Moment and Its Political Afterlives* (Athens: Ohio University Press, 2010); Fred Ho and Bill V. Mullen, eds., *Afro Asia: Revolutionary Political and Cultural Connections between African Americans and Asian Americans* (Durham: Duke University Press, 2008); Tony Martin, *Race First: The Ideological and Organizational Struggles of Marcus Garvey and the Universal Negro Improvement Association* (Dover, Mass.: Majority Press, 1986).
26. Edward W. Said, "Traveling Theory Reconsidered," in *Critical Reconstructions: The Relationship of Fiction and Life*, eds. Robert M. Polhemus and Roger B. Henkle (Stanford: Stanford University Press, 1994), 251–265.
27. "The Corresponding Secretary to the Bishop and Conference," *The Christian Recorder*, July 23, 1870. Lawrence S. Little, *Disciples of Liberty: The African Methodist Episcopal Church in the Age of Imperialism, 1884–1916* (Knoxville: University of Tennessee Press, 2000).
28. For examples of paternalism, see "What Sort Do They Want?" *The Afro-American*, August 20, 1898; "The Work of the LATH Congress," *The*

Christian Recorder, March 16, 1899; "A Glowing Tribute to the Memory and Labors of John Brown," *The Freeman* (Indianapolis), May 18, 1901; Little, *Disciples of Liberty*. For the experiences of African-American soldiers, see Willard B. Gatewood, *Black Americans and the White Man's Burden, 1898–1903* (Urbana: University of Illinois Press, 1975); Willard B. Gatewood, Jr., *"Smoked Yankees" and the Struggle for Empire: Letters from Negro Soldiers, 1898–1902* (Fayetteville: University of Arkansas Press, 1987); Claude A. Clegg, III, *The Price of Liberty: African Americans and the Making of Liberia* (Chapel Hill: University of North Carolina Press, 2004).

29. Recent scholarship on the ways that African Americans connected their freedom struggles with those of others outside of the United States includes Guridy, *Forging Diaspora*; Gaye Theresa Johnson, *Spaces of Conflict, Sounds of Solidarity: Music, Race, and Spatial Entitlement in Los Angeles* (Berkeley: University of California Press, 2013); Gordon K. Mantler, *Power to the Poor: Black-Brown Coalition and the Fight for Economic Justice, 1960–1974* (Chapel Hill: University of North Carolina Press, 2013); Max Krochmal, "Chicano Labor and Multiracial Politics in Post-World War II Texas: Two Case Studies," in Robert H. Zieger, ed., *Life and Labor in the New New South* (Gainesville: University Press of Florida , 2012), 133–177; Maria Angela Diaz, "Rising Tide of Empire: Gulf Coast Culture and Society during the Era of Expansion, 1845–1861," (PhD diss., University of Florida, 2013). See also Carey McWilliams, *Brothers under the Skin*, rev. ed. (1942; Boston: Little, Brown, 1951); Ernesto Galarza, *Farm Workers and Agri-business in California, 1947–1960* (South Bend: University of Notre Dame Press, 1977); Eduardo Galeano, *Open Veins of Latin America: Five Centuries of the Pillage of a Continent* (1973; New York: Monthly Review Press, 1997).

30. "Slavery in Cuba" and "Maximilian and Slavery," *South Carolina Leader* (Charleston), November 25, 1865.

31. *Autobiografía (The Autobiography of Malcolm X)* Prologue by Juana Carrasco. Editorial de Ciencias Sociales del Instituto Cubano del Libro (Habana, Cuba: 1974), 8. Robin D. G. Kelley has brilliantly depicted aspects of black internationalist politics in *Freedom Dreams: The Black Radical Imagination* (Boston: Beacon Press, 2003).

32. "William Whipper's Letters, No. II," *The Colored American*, February 20, 1841.

33. "Slavery," *Freedom's Journal*, November 30, 1827.

34. "Annexation of Territory," *The National Era*, February 4, 1847.

35. "Our Country," *The Colored American*, September 22, 1838.

36. "Cuba and the United States," *Frederick Douglass' Paper*, September 4, 1851.

37. "Letter from B. F. Remington," *Frederick Douglass' Paper*, February 19, 1852. "General" William Walker, a U.S. filibuster who briefly seized control of Nicaragua, wrote: "The introduction of negro-slavery into Nicaragua would furnish a supply of constant and reliable labor requisite for the cultivation of tropical products." William Walker, *The War in*

Nicaragua (New York: S. H. Goetzel, 1860), 261. See also Karl Bermann, *Under the Big Stick: Nicaragua and the United States since 1848* (Boston: South End Press, 1986); Johnson, *River of Dark Dreams*, 366–394.

38. "Speech of Frederick Douglass on the War," *Douglass Monthly*, February 1862.

39. Jane Landers, "State Emancipation, Self-Emancipation, and the Aftermaths in Spanish America," (paper presented at the conference The Shadow of Slavery: Emancipation, Memory, and the Meaning of Freedom, University of Florida, Gainesville, Florida, February 22–23, 2013).

40. "Vera Cruz," *The Christian Recorder*, May 23, 1863; "Republican Form of Government by Rev. H.M. Turner," *The Christian Recorder*, October 3, 1863.

41. Jerry Thompson, *Cortina: Defending the Mexican Name in Texas* (College Station: Texas A&M University Press, 2007), 153–154; John Hope Franklin, *George Washington Williams: A Biography* (Chicago: University of Chicago Press), 1985), 5–6; "A Mexican War, after Our Rebellion, Shall Maximilian Be Driven Out?" *Black Republican* (New Orleans), April 15, 1865.

42. "Letter from Richmond," *The Christian Recorder*, April 22, 1865.

43. "Wm. Lloyd Garrison, ESQ.," *The Christian Recorder*, February 24, 1866; "The Slavery Question," *Black Republican*, May 20, 1865.

44. "Correspondence Salt Lake, U.T.," *The Elevator*, July 4, 1873.

45. See "Our Acquisitions," *The Elevator*, January 4, 1873. Richard H. Bradford discusses the debate over granting belligerency status to the Cuban resistance in *The Virginius Affair*, foreword by Walter LaFeber (Boulder: Colorado Associated University Press, 1980). See also, Josiah Bunting, *Ulysses S. Grant* (New York: Times Books, 2004), 101–102. For an overview of the Ten Years War as well as slavery and race in Cuba, see Ada Ferrer, *Insurgent Cuba: Race, Nation, and Revolution, 1868–1898* (Chapel Hill: University of North Carolina Press, 1999); Aline Helg, *Our Rightful Share: The Afro-Cuban Struggle for Equality, 1886–1912* (Chapel Hill: University of North Carolina Press, 1995); Louis A. Perez, *Lords of the Mountain: Social Banditry and Peasant Protest in Cuba, 1878–1918* (Pittsburgh: University of Pittsburgh Press, 1989).

46. "Fifteenth Amendment Address," *The Elevator* (San Francisco), April 15, 1870. African American Fifteenth Amendment observances in California frequently incorporated solidarity messages for the Cuban struggle. For one such event held in San Francisco, see "Oration," *The Elevator*, April 5, 1873. For the fourth anniversary of the Fifteenth Amendment celebration in Chico, California, expressing support for the Cuban patriots, see "Oration," *The Elevator*, April 25, 1874.

47. "Ratification Celebration of the Colored Citizens of Virginia City, Nevada," *Territorial Enterprise*, April 8, 1870.

48. Cuban Anti-Slavery Committee, "Slavery in Cuba: A Report of the Proceedings of the Meeting Held at Cooper Institute," (New York: Powers, MacGowan A. Slipper, 1872), 16.

49. Ibid., 5.

50. "The Colored Citizens of New York," *The Christian Recorder*, December 21, 1872.

51. "Public Meetings," *The Elevator* (San Francisco), December 28, 1872; "Cuban Independence," *The Elevator*, February 15, 1873.

52. "Cuban Independence," *The Elevator*, February 15, 1873.

53. "Sympathy for Cuba in Philadelphia," *The Christian Recorder*, February 13, 1873.

54. For examples of meetings, see "Sympathy with Cuba," *The New York Times,* February 8, 1873; "Colored Men on Spanish Slavery Meeting in Washington," *The New York Times,* March 8, 1873; "The Colored Men and Cuba," *The New York Times,* March 11, 1873.

55. "The Colored People of the District of Columbia," *The New York Times,* November 19, 1873.

56. "Duty of the Colored Population," *The Elevator,* December 6, 1873; "The Civil Rights Convention," *The New York Times,* December 15, 1873.

57. "Oration," *The Elevator,* April 25, 1874.

58. "Emancipation of Cuban Slaves," *The Christian Recorder,* September 10, 1870; "Slavery in Cuba," *The New York Times,* July 13, 1877; "Samuel R. Scottron," *Cleveland Gazette,* June 4, 1887.

59. "Speech of Hon. Josiah Walls, of Florida, In the House of Representatives, January 24, 1874, On the Joint Resolution Declaring the Right of the Cuban Republic to Recognition as Belligerent," *Appendix to the Congressional Record, Congressional Record: Forty-Third Congress, First Session*, vol. II, (Washington, Government Printing Office, 1874), 27–29.

60. "The Louisiana Colored Men," *The New York Times,* November 28, 1873. Louisiana Governor P. B. S. Pinchback was also a leader of the Cuban Anti-Slavery Committee.

61. "Louisiana State Republican Resolutions and Platform," *Weekly Louisianan,* September 26, 1874. The Louisiana State Legislature also passed a joint resolution in support of the abolition of slavery in Cuba. See Vincent, *Black Legislators in Louisiana during Reconstruction,* 165–166. Vincent notes that J. Henri Burch, a leading African American legislator in the Cuban cause from Baton Rouge, was cited as "general Representative of the Republique of Cuba Abroad" by the Cuban resistance forces.

62. "Meeting of Congress, President's Message," *Weekly Louisianan,* December 7, 1872; "Petition to Accord Belligerent Rights to Cuba," The *New York Times,* February 20, 1873; "The Spanish Republic," *The New York Times,* February 24, 1873; "Correspondence," *The Elevator* (San Francisco, Calif.), March 25, 1873.

63. Bradford, *The Virginius Affair,* 14.

64. "Cuba," *The Savannah Tribune* (Georgia), November 11, 1876.

65. "Protest against Cuban Slavery," *The Christian Recorder,* November 8, 1877.

66. C. L. R. James, "The Black Jacobins and Black Reconstruction: A Comparative Analysis," public lecture published in *Small Axe,* no. 8 (September 2000), 86; Paul Ortiz, "Segregation and Black Labor before the CIO," *Against the Current,* 138 (January–February, 2009), www.solidarity-us.org/node/2035 (accessed July 19, 2015).

67. Williams, *The Tragedy of American Diplomacy.*

68. Exceptions included Key West, Florida, where, for a time, a multiracial and multilingual coalition between African American workers and veterans of the Ten Years War thrived. Antonio Maceo and Jose Marti traveled to Key West for support for the cause of *Cuba Libre* in the 1880s. See Paul Ortiz, *Emancipation Betrayed: The Hidden History of Black Organizing and White Violence in Florida from Reconstruction to the Bloody Election of 1920* (Berkeley: University of California Press, 2005), 39–40.

69. "Resolutions Adopted," *The Freeman*, January 2, 1897; "Chicago Sympathizes with Cuba," *Enterprise* (Omaha), January 1, 1897; See also "Maceo's Death Arouses Them," *Cleveland Gazette*, December 19, 1896; "Cuba's Liberty," *The Washington Bee*, December 12, 1896.

70. "Cuban Women. Some of Their Daring Acts of Bravery," *Fair Play* (Fort Scott, Kansas), March 24, 1899.

71. "Bolivar and San Martin," *The Negro World*, December 20, 1924. See, for example, "Prejudice against Color," *The Colored American*, September 5, 1840. Jorge Basadre, *El Perú Republicano: Los Fundamentos de Su Emancipación* (Sociedad Academia de Estudios Americanos, 1961). UNIA boasted hundreds of chapters throughout the Americas. James G. Spady, Samir Meghelli, Louis Jones, eds., *New Perspectives on the History of Marcus Garvey, the U.N.I.A., and the African Diaspora* (Philadelphia: Marcus Garvey Foundation Publishers, 2011).

72. "Bolivar and San Martin," *The Negro World*, December 20, 1924. See also "Sad Bereavement," [Toussaint L'Ouverture & Antonio Maceo], *Colored American*, July 11, 1903; "Song of Toussaint L'Ouverture," *The Negro World*, September 15, 1923; "Mexico's Black Lincoln," [Vicente Guerrero] *Plaindealer* (Kansas City), February 16, 1945.

73. "Should Protest Butler as Military Governor of Cuba," *The Christian Recorder*, August 11, 1898; "The Black Man in Cuba," *Plaindealer*, February 3, 1899; "The 'Color Devil' in Cuba," *The Christian Recorder*, March 2, 1899; "A Lesson to Learn," *Afro-American*, December 10, 1910; "Uprising in Cuba," *Philadelphia Tribune*, May 25, 1912; "Color Line in Cuba," *Philadelphia Tribune*, June 8, 1912.

74. "The Haitian Affliction," *The Washington Bee*, October 23, 1920.

75. "Uncle Sam's Hot Potato," *The Pittsburgh Courier*, January 14, 1928. "Nicaraguan War as Forum Topic," *The New York Amsterdam News*, January 25, 1928. General Smedley Butler, the recipient of two Congressional Medals of Honor, famously stated: "I helped purify Nicaragua for the international banking house of Brown Brothers in 1909-1912." Butler, *War Is a Racket* (1935; repr., Los Angeles: Feral House, 2003), 10. Neill Macaulay, *The Sandino Affair* (1985; repr., Micanopy, Fl.: Wacahoota Press, 1998); Thomas W. Walker, *Nicaragua: Living in the Shadow of the Eagle* (Boulder: Westview Press, 2003); Max Boot, *The Savage Wars of Peace: Small Wars and the Rise of American Power* (New York: Basic Books, 2003), 231–252.

76. "Republic or Empire?" *The New York Amsterdam News*, February 22, 1928.

77. "Our Nicaraguan War," *Norfolk Journal and Guide*, July 23, 1927.

78. See "Secretary Hughes' Little Joke," *Cleveland Gazette*, March 7, 1925; "Haitian Conditions as Described by a Native," *The Washington Bee*, June 18, 1921; "A Disgraceful Chapter," *Philadelphia Tribune*, November 6, 1920; "Haiti Bleeds Again," December 20, 1929, *Plaindealer* (Topeka, Kansas).

79. James Weldon Johnson, "The Truth about Haiti: An NAACP Investigation," *The Crisis* 5 (September 1920): 217–224; "White Hell in Black Haiti: U.S. Military Law Rules," *The Washington Bee*, September 11, 1920; "A Disgraceful Chapter," *Philadelphia Tribune*, November 6, 1920; "Whitewash for US Marines in Haiti and Santo Domingo," *Cleveland Gazette*, December 31, 1921; "More Outrages in Haiti," *The Negro World*, November 24, 1923; Mary A. Renda, *Taking Haiti: Military Occupation and the Culture of U.S. Imperialism, 1915–1940* (Chapel Hill: University of North Carolina Press, 2001).

80. "The Lynching of Haitians," *The Cleveland Gazette*, January 22, 1921.

81. "Views and Reviews," *The Pittsburgh Courier*, May 12, 1928; "New York Virgin Islanders Hold Big Mass Meeting to Protest Bad Economic Rule," *The Pittsburgh Courier*, February 23, 1924; "Annexing Another Colony," *The Pittsburgh Courier*, November 19, 1927. For the role of the National City Bank of New York in American imperialism, see Peter James Hudson, "The National City Bank of New York and Haiti, 1909–1922," *Radical History Review* 115 (Winter 2013): 91–114.

82. Historical writing with this framework includes José Martí, *Inside the Monster: Writings on the United States and American Imperialism*, Philip S. Foner, ed. (New York: Monthly Review Press, 1975); Eduardo Galeano, *Open Veins of Latin America: Five Centuries of the Pillage of a Continent* (1971; repr., New York: Monthly Review Press, 1997); Felipe Fernández-Armesto, *The Americas: A Hemispheric History* (New York: Modern Library, 2005); Sandhya Shukla and Heidi Tinsman, eds., *Imagining Our Americas: Toward a Transnational Frame* (Durham: Duke University Press, 2007).

83. "First Imperialist," *Cleveland Gazette*, October 6, 1900.

84. "More Howard University Air Programs," *The Afro-American*, November 30, 1929. See also "Mr. Hoover Says", *The Afro-American*, April 7, 1928. The continuation of these ideas throughout the twentieth century may be traced in Nikhil Pal Singh, ed., *Climbin' Jacob's Ladder: The Black Freedom Movement Writings of Jack O'Dell* (Berkeley: University of California Press, 2010); Conrad Lynn, *There Is a Fountain: The Autobiography of Conrad Lynn* (1979; repr., New York: Lawrence Hill Books, 1993); Vijay Prashad, *Everybody Was Kung Fu Fighting: Afro-Asian Connections and the Myth of Cultural Purity* (Boston: Beacon Press, 2002); Von Eschen, *Race against Empire*; Brock and Fuertes, *Between Race and Empire*.

9

Remembering the Abolitionists and the Meanings of Freedom

John Stauffer

On April 14, 1865, William Lloyd Garrison and other leading abolitionists visited Charleston, South Carolina, to celebrate the end of the war and of slavery.[1] It was their first visit to Charleston, and several noted with irony that thirty years earlier in Boston, Garrison had been dragged through the streets and almost lynched, whereas in the cradle of the Confederacy he was greeted with cheers. Following a Union flag-raising at Fort Sumter, Garrison gave a short speech at the Charleston Hotel, emphasizing the inseparability of abolition and emancipation. Referring to his recent meeting with Lincoln, Garrison said: "of one thing I feel sure, either he has become a Garrisonian Abolitionist or I have become a Lincoln Emancipationist, for I know that we blend together, like kindred drops, into one."[2]

Garrison's statement wonderfully encapsulates the *social revolution* that accompanied the war, and the role that abolitionists played in it. Everyone understood Garrison's terms. "Abolitionists" were black and white radicals who sought an immediate end to slavery *and* racial equality in theory. "Emancipationists," or "anti-slavery advocates," were liberals who sought to preserve the Union. Constituting the rank and file of the Republican Party, they, too, defined slavery as evil. But for emancipationists, the evil of slavery stemmed less from what it did to *slaves* than from what it did to the *Union*. They advocated practical, legal, and preferably gradual solutions to slavery. And, unlike the abolitionists, they opposed racial equality and were captivated by the idea of colonizing blacks in another country.[3]

But the exigencies of war had transformed Lincoln and other emancipationists into abolitionists, while Garrison and other abolitionists had become emancipationists. Preserving the Union *required* abolishing slavery, *and* vice-versa. The categories of radical versus liberal, immediatist versus gradualist, idealist versus realist, had broken down.[4]

With the war, black and white abolitionists were transformed from a tiny group of despised fanatics into respected prophets. They were considered indispensable to the war effort and the successes of Reconstruction, which brought almost unprecedented humanitarian achievements. These included the constitutional amendments that ended chattel slavery and guaranteed citizenship, equal protection under the law, and unrestricted male suffrage to blacks; the desegregation of federal post offices, courts, public transportation, and visitors' galleries in Congress; and the extraordinary rise of black literacy and black office-holders at local, state, and national levels. As David Brion Davis has noted, "few slave emancipations in history have been followed by anything equivalent to America's first civil rights legislation and the [Reconstruction] Amendments."[5]

Even Lincoln, who had resisted emancipation and championed colonization early in the war, recognized the importance of abolitionists and of blacks' role in winning the war and ending slavery. In September 1864 he said that black soldiers were the key to saving the Union; remove them "and the Union goes with" them. At the White House reception following his Second Inaugural, he publicly greeted Frederick Douglass by saying: "there is no man in these United States whose opinion I value more than yours." A month later, he told Lieutenant Daniel H. Chamberlain: "I have been only an instrument. The logic and moral power of Garrison, and the anti-slavery people of the country, and the army, have done all."[6]

As a conservative-to-moderate Republican, Lincoln was representative of other emancipationists. He not only became an abolitionist; he worked with the abolitionists to end slavery and champion some form of legal equality. Shortly before he died, he endorsed limited black suffrage and began to envision racial equality. In his April 11, 1865, address from a White House window, he noted that "it is ... unsatisfactory to some that the elective franchise is not given to the colored man. I would myself prefer that it were *now* conferred on the very intelligent, and on those who serve our cause as soldiers." John Wilkes Booth was in the crowd listening to the speech. "That is the last speech he will ever make," he told a fellow conspirator. It was this speech that convinced Booth to assassinate Lincoln and abandon his plan, supported by the Confederacy, to kidnap the president in order to negotiate favorable terms for peace. A few hours after Garrison's speech at the Charleston Hotel, Booth put a bullet through Lincoln's head for the same reason that Garrison lauded him: because Lincoln had become an abolitionist.[7]

Garrison was right: the emancipationist had become the abolitionist, and vice-versa. Indeed, from the 1840s through Reconstruction, abolitionists collaborated closely with conservative-to-liberal opponents of slavery. Together they inaugurated a social revolution, which was soon destroyed by Southern counter-revolutionaries. The Reconstruction Amendments that created legal, and in some areas social, equality for blacks could not have been possible without abolitionists collaborating with emancipationists.[8]

******

White Americans remembered the war very differently, however. In the twentieth century, in the service of sectional reconciliation, white writers and filmmakers went to great lengths to deny any merging of the abolitionist and emancipationist visions. They treated abolitionists and emancipationists as discrete, mutually exclusive categories. The abolitionists were religious zealots and political extremists (or pathetic figures), unwilling to negotiate or compromise, and dangerous, while emancipationists were shrewd, practical statesmen, always framing their hatred of slavery in larger social and political contexts.[9]

Many scholars dismiss Hollywood history film as inaccurate and thus irrelevant. But it is indispensable in shaping American historical memory, for each film reaches millions of viewers, in contrast to a few thousand readers of a scholarly history article or book. Indeed, in the twentieth century most Americans understood their history through film and television rather than books. Moreover, Hollywood films of the Civil War era have mirrored contemporaneous historiography, as Robert Rosenstone has noted. This is understandable, for filmmakers reflect the ideologies and worldviews of their own era, much as historians do. Civil War–era films "relate to the larger realm of discourse generated by" historians. Although filmmakers dispense with facts, usually in the service of image, story, or character, their message mirrors that of contemporaneous scholars. They read and are influenced by what historians write. Thus, the unsympathetic portrait of abolitionists in feature films reflects the historiography.[10]

Some scholars continue to deny or ignore the collaborations between abolitionists and emancipationists. Yet many, if not most Americans, especially in the northeast, now treat the abolitionists as heroes who helped end slavery and sought integration, as reflected in popular histories and a recent PBS documentary (though not in feature films). Several prominent scholars – Andrew Delbanco, Harry Stout, David Goldfield, and Christopher Benfey – have begun to reassess the abolitionists in light of these triumphalist narratives. They analyze them in the broader context of helping to usher in one of the bloodiest wars in history, and they recover themes from prominent white scholars of the mid-twentieth century: Abolitionists were radical idealists or religious extremists who helped usher in one of the bloodiest wars in world history. They stood totally apart from pragmatic emancipationists, who respected the messiness of democratic politics and sought legal and legislative means to end slavery. Like their predecessors, these neo-revisionists downplay the institutional power of slaveholders, the violence at the heart of slavery, and the South's suppression of civil liberties.[11]

These reassessments are important and understandable, for they emphasize the *tragic* rather than triumphalist dimension of the past, and they draw attention to the political divisiveness of our own age. But uncoupling abolitionists from emancipationists has profound effects for how we remember the Civil War era: it ignores the abolitionist founda- tions of civil rights and its integrated nature; it presents black freedom as an endpoint rather than a struggle; and it casts racial equality as a utopian dream that can never be realized.

In order to appreciate the radical revisionism involved in separating the abolitionists and emancipationists, I first sketch out the ways in which they converged and collaborated. Then I explore how and why writers and filmmakers separated them in the twentieth century, and explain how this revisionist memory of abolitionism has shaped the meanings of emancipation, freedom, and equality.

******

In an important sense, black and white abolitionists had always consid- ered themselves closely linked to emancipationists. This convergence reflected their hope that the moral foundations of abolitionism would become the law of the land. They were inspired by precedents in which moral principles had helped transform social conditions. The first genera- tion of American abolitionists had successfully and gradually abolished slavery in the Northern states, with five states granting black men unrest- ricted suffrage. The later generation of "modern," or immediatist, aboli- tionists, as they were called, celebrated this achievement and referred to the founders, especially Washington, as "practical abolitionists." Immediatists called the *gradual* and compensated emancipation of

800,000 slaves in the British West Indies one of the greatest humanitarian accomplishments in history. (The Emancipation Act included an "apprenticeship" period of twelve years, eventually reduced to four years, in which slaves worked without compensation; and Britain paid the slaves' owners a total of twenty million pounds sterling.) From the late 1830s through the Civil War, American abolitionists celebrated British emancipation as devoutly as the Declaration of Independence. Americans' celebrations of British West Indian emancipation were among the most integrated and egalitarian events in antebellum America, uniting blacks and whites, and radical and conservative opponents of slavery.[12]

Long before the Civil War, abolitionists collaborated with anti-slavery advocates in their efforts to end slavery and establish black rights. John Quincy Adams worked closely with the abolitionists Theodore Dwight Weld, Joshua Giddings, and Lewis Tappan to overturn the congressional Gag Rules that tabled all discussion of slavery and to defend the Amistad captives. Partly through this collaboration, Adams began calling himself an abolitionist.[13]

In the 1850s, abolitionists and emancipationists worked together so closely that it was sometimes difficult to distinguish them. Throughout the North they teamed up to protect fugitives and raise money to protect Kansas from slavery, and they fought together in Kansas. The fugitive slave law of 1850 transformed Northern anti-slavery sentiment. By suspending habeas corpus and requiring all citizens to hunt down suspected fugitives, it led millions of Northerners to heed higher law over slave law. It convinced Northerners that slavery was their problem too, not just the South's. It so radicalized Emerson, Thoreau, and other Transcendentalists and Unitarians that they effectively became abolitionists, even though they did not join abolition societies. And it inspired Harriet Beecher Stowe to write *Uncle Tom's Cabin* (1852), the literary phenomenon that purportedly sold more copies than any other book in the nineteenth century save the Bible. Significantly, Stowe called herself a *reluctant* abolitionist. Her novel combined anti-slavery and abolitionist principles; it endorsed both colonization and black citizenship; it thus united the abolitionist and emancipationist views.[14]

Throughout their collaborations with anti-slavery advocates, abolitionists compromised their principles. Political abolitionists in the National Liberty and Radical Abolition parties often voted Republican in their efforts to end slavery through peaceful and constitutional channels. And many Garrisonians, who considered the federal government corrupt, compromised their nonresistant principles by voting for anti-slavery candidates. Their radical rhetoric and liberal votes reflected their goal of electing Republicans and pushing the party to a more radical anti-slavery position. Although nonviolence was a founding principle among the abolitionists, they compromised their pacifist principles to help fugitives escape, defend themselves against pro-slavery men, and fight in Kansas.[15]

Abolitionists also sought, like their liberal, anti-slavery counterparts, to engage Southerners over slavery in legal, democratic settings. They encouraged Southerners to debate them at meetings and in their newspapers. They sent millions of anti-slavery petitions to Congress as another means of stimulating debate. They offered numerous proposals for compensated emancipation. And they worked with British policy-makers to use international pressure in the hopes of bringing Southerners to the bargaining table. But Southerners spurned all these attempts to stimulate democratic debate and negotiation.[16]

After the bombardment of Fort Sumter, black and white abolitionists recognized the *revolutionary* implications of working with Republican emancipationists. In late 1861, they formed the Emancipation League, which not only reunited all abolitionists for the first time since their split in 1840, but sought unity with Republicans in the hopes of pressuring the Lincoln administration to free the slaves. Abolitionists recognized that collaborating with Republicans gave them a far wider audience with which to mold public opinion and shape policy. And Republicans recognized the power of abolitionist rhetoric and morality. As Garrison said, the League offered a way to "merge ourselves, as far as we can without a compromise of principle, in the onward sweeping current of Northern [emancipation] sentiment." Although Garrison often worried about compromising his principles, he did so whenever it was expedient. The League obtained the support of the vast majority of abolition and Republican leaders.[17]

Most Garrisonians had compromised their principle of nonresistance as soon as the war came. In embracing the Union war effort they moved much closer to the position of Republicans. They recognized how easily a war against slaveowners to preserve the Union could become a war that ended slavery. Garrison defended his newfound acceptance of violent means by saying that the government, in waging war, acted "strictly in self-defense and for self-preservation." He seemed to suggest that violence in self-defense was not incompatible with pacifism. He abandoned his disunionism almost without a second thought: "when I said I would not sustain the Constitution, because it was a 'covenant with death, and an agreement with

hell,' I had no idea that I would live to see death and hell secede." Wendell
Phillips echoed these sentiments: "I was a Disunionist, sincerely, for twenty
years," he said in December 1861. "I hated the Union ... when the Union
meant making white men hypocrites and black men slaves." But with the
war, Phillips's understanding of "Union" was transformed; it now meant
the "justice" of emancipation in order to survive.[18]

Frederick Douglass rejoiced in the formation of the Emancipation
League, participated in it, and understood abolitionism as inseparable
from emancipationism. He preferred the term "abolition" to "emancipation," owing to the moral weight "abolition" carried compared to the
more legalistic and rationalistic connotation of "emancipation." In an
Emancipation League speech in early 1862, he derided the way in which
whites called emancipation "an experiment" rather than "the natural
order of human relations." Slavery was the experiment, he said, and had
proved a horrible failure. Later that year, at a 4th of July speech, he
emphasized that only "abolition" could bring national salvation: "the
only choice left to this nation is abolition or destruction."[19]

Like almost every other abolitionist and emancipationist, Douglass
considered the Emancipation Proclamation a revolutionary document
that turned the war into a "contest of civilization against barbarism"
rather than a struggle for territory, as he put it. It acquired for him "a
life and power far beyond its letter," and became another sacred text,
which restored the Declaration to its rightful place at the center of the
nation's laws. Henceforth, he said, January 1st would rank with July 4th
as the twin births of liberty.[20]

Most abolitionists *and* emancipationists also defined the war in apocalyptic terms. This eschatology "sounded its clearest note" in Julia Ward
Howe's "Battle Hymn of the Republic." First published on the cover of
Atlantic Monthly in February 1862, it became one of the most popular
wartime Union hymns (and in the twentieth century it became an unoffi-
cial American anthem). Howe's lyrics are deeply indebted to Revelation.
The first stanza comes directly from Revelation 14, in which an angel
"gathered the vine of the earth, and cast it into the great winepress of the
wrath of God." Throughout Revelation, God or his angels cast lightning
bolts and thunder into the earth, inducing an earthquake. Howe places the
narrator of her poem *within* Revelation, personalizing its phantasmagoric
imagery, and turning it into a narrative lyric:

> Mine eyes have seen the glory of the coming of the
> Lord:

> He is trampling out the vintage where the grapes of
>   wrath are stored;
> He hath loosed the fateful lightning of His terrible
>   swift sword:
> His truth is marching on.

It may seem strange that a Unitarian would know Revelation almost by heart. But Howe's intimate familiarity with it was representative, reflecting the degree to which most Americans understood the war in apocalyptic terms. Revelation offered hope for the future amid the ravages of war, for if the war was the apocalypse, then a new age of peace and harmony was not far away.[21]

Douglass elaborated on the theme of national regeneration in his speech, "The Mission of the War," which he delivered during the winter of 1863–1864. In response to the rise of Copperheads denouncing the war as an "abolition war," he turned the allegation into an ethical imperative with a "platform of principles": "no war but an Abolition war; no peace but an Abolition peace; liberty for all, chains for none; the black man a soldier in war, a laborer in peace; a voter at the South as well as at the North; America his permanent home, and all Americans his fellow-countrymen." It was a revolutionary vision of racial equality that antici- ⅄ pated Radical Republicans' aims for Reconstruction, as David Blight has noted. It was also a rich encapsulation of what the war meant to him and countless other Republicans. If Northerners acted righteously, the tribulation – the horrible amount of suffering and death – would yield a new age of national regeneration.[22]

******

Efforts to uncouple the moral imperative of abolitionism from legal emancipation, and thus halt the social revolution, also began during the war. A new emancipation journal, the *Continental Monthly*, was launched in early 1862 and continued almost until the end of the war. Its chief aim was to sever the union between "abolition" and "emancipation." The journal coined the American term "emancipationist" to express its opposition to abolitionists' humanitarianism. Inspired by Hinton Rowan Helper, the Southern racist who opposed slavery solely because it degraded poor whites, the *Monthly* emphasized in its first issue that emancipation should be simply "for the sake of the Union and the white man." For thirty years abolitionists had appealed to Americans' sense of humanity in their efforts to free the slaves, but without success. "Now let us try some other expedient. Let us regard [the slave] not as a man and a brother, but as a 'miserable nigger,' if you please, and a nuisance. But whatever he be, if the effect of owning such creatures is to make the owner an intolerable fellow, seditious and insolent, it becomes pretty clear that such ownership should be put an end to."[23]

The *Continental Monthly* was not the only voice threatening the social revolution that could yield national regeneration. Early in the war, Lincoln expressed horror over the idea of a social revolution – which was precisely what abolitionists wanted – and defined emancipation solely as a war measure. In his annual message to Congress in 1861, he said that in considering what policies to use to suppress the rebellion, he was "anxious and careful" that the conflict "shall not degenerate into a violent and remorseless revolutionary struggle." A year later, in his December 1862 message to Congress, he downplayed the humanitarianism of the Emancipation Proclamation and instead emphasized its utilitarian nature. "In *giving* freedom to the *slave*, we *assure* freedom to the *free* – honorable alike in what we give, and what we preserve." And of course he framed the Proclamation solely as a war measure.[24]

Some abolitionists also characterized emancipation as a war measure and downplayed its morality in the hopes of gaining wider support. In November 1861 Charles Sumner privately told fellow abolitionist John Jay, the grandson of the first chief justice, that emancipation should be presented "strictly as a measure of military necessity ... rather than on the grounds of philanthropy." Sumner and other abolitionists empathized with slaves and sought emancipation for humanitarian reasons; but they pitched their message in ways that would reach the broadest possible audience.[25]

The *Continental Monthly* and these other powerful voices point to an ideological fissure in the North that escalated in the last two years of the war. Abolitionists increasingly heard reports of soldiers and civilians who felt no concern for blacks and became "emancipationists" solely out of self-interest. Their opposition to slavery stemmed chiefly from a desire to vanquish the Confederacy and preserve the Union rather than from an "intelligent moral conviction," as Douglass said in February 1863. And that worried him: "A man that hates slavery only for what it does to the white man stands ready to embrace it the moment its injuries are confined to the black man." Such expressions of racism were festering sores in the wartime North, threatening any hope of national regeneration that made blacks equal citizens.[26]

Douglass and other abolitionists were right to worry that the North would abandon emancipation in all but name once blacks ceased being a military necessity. Blacks remained a military necessity during the early years of Reconstruction. This was partly because Northerners recognized Reconstruction as the continuation of war (a smaller-scale paramilitary war). More significantly, they knew that black citizenship and suffrage would greatly bolster the power of the Republican Party, which dominated Northern politics. But by 1874, four years after the Fifteenth Amendment was ratified and two years before the end of Reconstruction, citizens of Boston called for a federal withdrawal from the South. The Republican Party had "outgrown" the ideas of Douglass, Garrison, and Phillips, according to the *New York Times*. It no longer needed the abolitionists. The black Bostonian William Wells Brown summed up the sentiment by saying: "There is a feeling all over this country that the negro has got as much as he ought to have."[27]

******

From the end of Reconstruction to the end of the nineteenth century, Northerners recognized abolitionists' rich collaborations with their more conservative emancipationists. They treated abolitionists as heroes who had played crucial roles in ending slavery, winning the war, and amending the Constitution to guarantee equality before the law for blacks and whites. The magisterial, multi-volume histories by Massachusetts Senator Henry Wilson and Hermann Von Holst, who helped establish history as a discipline in American colleges and became the first chair of the History Department at the University of Chicago, emphasized the collaborations between abolitionists and emancipationists. These works were highly respected.[28] The first four volumes of James Ford Rhodes's popular *History of the United States from the Compromise of 1850* (1892–99) similarly emphasized these collaborations. In his portrayals of slavery, the Confederacy, and Reconstruction, Rhodes contributed to national reconciliation between the North and South. But at the same time, he acknowledged the intimate connections between the abolitionists and the Republican Party; and he drew attention to abolitionists' impact "in rousing the Northern conscience and laying the foundations of a triumphant Republican Party."[29]

Charles Sumner, the abolitionist senator from Massachusetts, was so revered in the North that his fellow congressmen passed a diluted version of his Civil Rights bill in 1875, a year after he died, "mainly as a gesture to his departed spirit." *Harper's Weekly*, perhaps the most popular Northern newspaper, devoted two full issues to Sumner's death and funeral, and declared that his death "more deeply touched the heart of

the American people" than any other event since Lincoln's assassination.
Biographers and literary men also wrote effusively about the abolitionists.
In 1903 Henry James portrayed Sumner as an exemplary "statesman and
patriot" and called his epistles "irresistible."[30]

The twentieth century, however, was unkind to the abolitionists. As
Peter Novick has summarized, the century's opening coincided with "the
racist downgrading of the Negro" by white historians, coupled with their
"need for reconciliation of the sections, and the desire to strike a posture
of impartiality, fairness, detachment, and objectivity." As a result, white
historians became "harshly critical of the abolitionists" and called them
"irresponsible agitators." More generally, white writers and filmmakers
went to great lengths to *uncouple* the links between abolitionists and
emancipationists. Abolitionists became religious zealots, dangerous and
often insane extremists who helped cause an apocalyptic war; or they were
pathetic figures because war was inevitable. Emancipationists, on the
other hand, were shrewd, balanced, practical statesmen, always framing
their hatred of slavery in larger social and political contexts.[31]

In stark contrast to this Radical Reconstruction of abolitionists
by white writers, *black* writers throughout the twentieth century, from
George Washington Williams and W. E. B. Du Bois, to John Hope
Franklin, Benjamin Quarles, Nathan Huggins, Waldo Martin, and
James Horton, were consistently charitable toward the abolitionists.
They recognized that the convergence of abolitionists and emancipation-
ists reflected a social revolution. These black writers resemble British,
French, and Brazilian writers, who have long remembered *their* abolition-
ists as heroes, working closely with political leaders to end slavery.[32]

By 1900, few Southern whites longed for a return to chattel slavery,
even though "slavery provided a metaphor that explained and justified
race relations," according to John David Smith. Jim-Crow segregation
and lynching solved the "problem" of slavery – treating persons as legal
property – while reestablishing de facto black unfreedom. Most whites,
North and South, were horrified by the idea of racial equality. Scientific
justifications of racism replaced religious beliefs asserting that all
humans were "of one blood" and equal before God. The rise of racism
fueled the uncoupling of abolitionists from emancipationists and the
concomitant demonization of the abolitionists and elevation of
emancipationists.[33]

The image of Lincoln at his centennial both reflected and profoundly
shaped the degree to which whites had uncoupled abolitionists and
emancipationists. In 1909, Robert E. Lee remained the great *Southern*

hero, but Lincoln became the *national* hero. According to the Southern historian J. G. de Roulhac Hamilton, the New South now admired Lincoln for his Southern birth and blood, his democracy, and even for his nationalism, since it no longer threatened the South. "All of us are now Unionists," he declared. Lincoln was the redeemer president because he redeemed the nation, not because he redeemed blacks. As a national hero, he became a prophet of white supremacy, without any trace of abolitionism in him.[34]

The most influential proponents of this nationalist Lincoln were three Southerners who moved North after Reconstruction: Woodrow Wilson, the Princeton historian and first Southern president since Andrew Johnson; Thomas Dixon, author of the best-selling Civil War novels *Leopard's Spots* and *The Clansman*; and D. W. Griffith, who wrote and directed *The Birth of a Nation* (1915), which was viewed by 200 million people between 1915 and 1946 and became among the most influential films in the twentieth century. Dixon studied history at Johns Hopkins with Wilson before becoming a Baptist minister and then a historical novelist. Griffith based *Birth of a Nation* on Dixon's *The Clansman* and on Wilson's *History of the American People* (1902), from which he quotes in the film to support historical authenticity.[35]

Politicians loved *Birth of a Nation* and became boosters. Griffith screened it at the White House for Woodrow Wilson and quoted the president as saying that his film "teaches history by lightning." Dixon, who also attended the screening, embellished Wilson's purported praise, and quoted him as saying that *Birth* was like "writing history with lightning ... My only regret is that it is all too true." The film was also shown to 500 political dignitaries including Chief Justice Edward White and members of the Supreme Court, Congress, and the Diplomatic Corps. Although blacks and white radicals protested and boycotted the film throughout the North, not one congressman opposed its historical message.[36]

As part of their vision of national reconciliation, Wilson, Dixon, and Griffith all expressed their love for Lincoln. Wilson considered him the ideal American. Dixon worshipped him, noting that his own advocacy of white supremacy and colonization had been inspired by Lincoln. Griffith, too, loved Lincoln, as reflected by his portrayal of him (played by Joseph Henabery) in *Birth of a Nation*.[37]

Lincoln's appearances in *Birth* are brief but significant. After Fort Sumter, he signs the call for 75,000 troops, then begins to cry, wipes his eyes with a handkerchief, and clasps his hands in prayer. He reappears

near the end of the war to sign a pardon for Ben Cameron (Henry
Walthall), the rebel son of Mrs. Cameron (Josephine Crowell) of South
Carolina: "Mr. Lincoln has given your life back to me," Mrs. Cameron
tells Ben. Lincoln's pardon enables Ben Cameron and his family to found
the Klan that redeems the nation. After Appomattox, four title cards
underscore Lincoln's policy of clemency toward Confederates. "I shall
deal with them as though they had never been away," he declares. As a
result, "the South under Lincoln's fostering hand goes to work to rebuild
itself." For a brief period, "a healing time of peace was at hand" in the
South. When the Camerons learn of Lincoln's assassination they are
devastated: "Our best friend is gone," Dr. Cameron (Spottiswoode
Aitken) wails. "What is to become of us now!"[38]

The film's final reference to Lincoln highlights his significance to the
nation. His assassination opens the way for Austin Stoneman (Ralph
Lewis), the Radical Republican based on Thaddeus Stevens, to become
"the greatest power in America." A political and military race war ensues
in the South. Near the end of the film some South Carolinians seek refuge
from a black mob organized by Stoneman and his mulatto protégé Silas
Lynch (George Seigmann). Two Union veterans who have remained in the
South invite the Southerners into their log cabin, which looks exactly like
the house where Lincoln was purportedly born. As the Southerners enter,
a title card announces: "The former enemies of North and South are
united again in common defense of their Aryan birthright." Lincoln in
memory, here depicted by his log cabin, symbolizes national rebirth.[39]

The brief epilogue elaborates on the theme of national rebirth and
white reconciliation by emphasizing peace. It begins with a title card:
"Dare we dream of a golden day when the bestial War shall rule no
more. But instead – the gentle Prince in the Hall of Brotherly Love in the
City of Peace." Then there is a dreamscape counterposing the muscular
god of war on a horse, wielding his sword and surrounded by dead bodies
and people pleading with him, with a scene of Christ, "the prince of
peace," his arms outstretched as he looks out onto a heavenly city of
whites smiling and promenading in the street. The image of Christ recalls
the Christ-like Lincoln, who had emphasized charity toward all and
malice toward none. The final title card repeats a famous quote by
Daniel Webster, which Lincoln's legacy fulfills: "Liberty and union, one
and inseparable, now and forever!"[40]

Griffith wanted *Birth of a Nation* to be understood as an anti-war film.
It was released five months after World War I had begun in Europe, at a
time when most Americans vehemently opposed the war. In promoting his

film, he repeatedly said that it offered "the greatest indictment against war that any man could devise." He defended his dreamscape epilogue, which was the only part of the film white critics considered flawed, by calling it "one of the most realistic sermons against the horrors of war that could be preached." And he warned that the Great War, like the Civil War, would not bring peace: "Peace after war is not real peace. Hatred, malice and bitterness, direct results of the long four years' struggle, were apparent in the relations of the North and South for twenty years after the actual cessation of hostilities."[41]

In *Birth of a Nation*, abolitionists are the enemies of peace and the chief cause of the malice and bitterness following Appomattox. Throughout this three-hour epic, Lincoln, the peaceable emancipationist, stands worlds apart from the demonic abolitionists, as represented by Stoneman; Lydia Brown (Mary Alden), Stoneman's mulatto housekeeper and apparent lover; Silas Lynch, who briefly becomes lieutenant governor of South Carolina; and Charles Sumner (Sam De Grasse). These black and white abolitionists "blight the nation" and threaten Lincoln's vision of national redemption.[42]

Importantly, *Birth of a Nation* identifies the cause of the war and suggests a way to prevent it. It opens with two announcements and two scenes, all in quick succession. The first announcement foreshadows the epilogue; it is an anti-war message: "If in this work we have conveyed to the mind the ravages of war to the end that war may be held in abhorrence, this effort will not have been in vain." The second announcement identifies the cause of the war: "the bringing of the African to America planted the first seed of disunion." War is horrible, and slavery and blacks caused it.[43]

The first two scenes suggest an antidote to the horrors of the Civil War. In the first scene, a minister prays over manacled slaves awaiting auction; presumably he is Christianizing them, thereby "civilizing" them. The second scene depicts an abolitionist meeting. Against the back wall and in the center of the frame is a large oval portrait of George Washington, who seems to be looking into the camera. In front of Washington stands a white abolitionist, also facing the camera, speaking to a white audience. At his left are two well-dressed black men, sitting apart from the rest of the whites in the room. A young slave boy is then led up the aisle toward the speaker and Washington. Although the slave is in the foreground, he appears to be standing at the feet of the abolitionist speaker, and far below Washington. A collection plate is passed around, presumably to purchase the boy's freedom. These abolitionists are in fact emancipationists, who offer a peaceful solution to slavery and war: gradual emancipation with compensation to masters, coupled with assimilation of blacks into white society without threatening white supremacy. As Casey King has argued, these abolitionists are cast "not as hotheaded radicals, but as members of an orderly society." The black boy, and a black future, are "at the white man's feet." In the meetinghouse, as in the country, order is possible and war preventable "provided everyone knows his or her place."[44]

Sumner and, especially, Stoneman prevent this peaceful alternative to war, however. During "the gathering storm," Sumner, the "leader of the Senate," confers with Stoneman, "the master of Congress." Together they threaten "the power of the sovereign states," as title cards state. As a result, the South vows to secede "if the North carries the election." Lincoln's election provokes the South to secede, but Lincoln is not to blame. Abolitionist leaders have hijacked the North and repudiated the balance of power between state and national sovereignty.[45]

Birth of a Nation helped establish an important foundation in the twentieth century that cast abolitionists as villains, enemies of the "good" emancipationists. This filmic uncoupling *mirrored* contemporaneous historiography. It echoed the portrayal of abolitionists in the existing scholarship, from Wilson's *History of the American People* (1902) and J. W. Burgess's *Reconstruction and the Constitution* (1902), to William Dunning's two books, *Essays on the Civil War and Reconstruction* (1897) and *Reconstruction, Political and Economic, 1865–1877* (1907).[46]

******

In *Santa Fe Trail* (1940), another blockbuster, abolitionists are even more demonic than in *Birth of a Nation*. The film focuses on John Brown (Raymond Massey) and his men in Bleeding Kansas, and it culminates with Brown's raid on Harpers Ferry. Brown is a totalitarian leader bent on "breaking up the Union." Kansas Territory bleeds solely because of him and his fellow abolitionists; the rest of the settlers, mostly Southerners, are peaceful. Cyrus Holliday (Henry O'Neill), who is building the Santa Fe Railroad, summarizes the conflict: "One side is for slavery. Most Kansas people are from the South. The other side is abolitionists, led by John Brown and sons. They have made Kansas a boiling pot of rebellion and massacre." Religion is "the crutch on which Brown's fanaticism walks." As his men encircle him, he prays for power and glory: "The Lord is a man of war; and thy right hand [Brown] shall become glorious through power. Thy right hand, O God, shall dash in pieces thy enemy."[47]

Brown stands apart from every other character in his inhumanity. He never smiles or laughs, and with his three-piece suit, wide-brimmed hat, and long beard he looks like a depraved, Old Testament figure. (The historical Brown did not grow a beard until 1859.) He is a man with whom it is impossible to sympathize.

Even blacks disapprove of Brown. None fight with him at Harpers Ferry, and instead prefer Southern soil to Northern. After two fugitives are "liberated" from Brown's regime in Kansas, one says, "I came to Kansas cuz of John Brown. But if this is freedom, I don't want any of it. I want to go back to the South." The other agrees: "Yes! I want to get back to Texas and stay there til kingdom come."

The villainy of Brown and the abolitionists stands in stark contrast to Southerners, who articulate a peaceful means for ending slavery and are allied with pragmatic, emancipationist Northerners. This alliance is reflected by the friendship of J. E. B. Stuart (Errol Flynn) and George Custer (Ronald Reagan). Early in the film, Custer sympathizes with Brown's principled opposition to slavery: "there's a purpose behind [Brown's] madness," he tells Stuart, "one that can't easily be dismissed." Stuart disagrees: "It isn't our job to decide who's right and who's wrong about slavery, any more than it is John Brown's." Custer acknowledges his error and apologizes.

The union of emancipationist Southerners and Northerners is further captured by Stuart's courtship of Kit Carson Holliday (Olivia de Havilland), the anti-slavery Northern daughter of Cyrus Holliday. "Can't the slaves be freed before it's too late?" she asks Stuart. Slavery "will be stopped," he replies, "when we hang John Brown. Then the South can settle [its] own problem without loss of pride, of being forced into it by a bunch of fanatics." Both Custer and Stuart vie for Holliday's hand; Stuart wins and marries her, suggesting that the relations between North and South are naturally affectionate.

In this story, Southerners, especially Stuart and Robert E. Lee (Moroni Olsen), are the wise, pragmatic heroes. Lee has few lines but is described as "brilliant." Stuart, his best soldier, elaborates on how Southerners, if left alone, will peacefully end slavery themselves. "The people of Virginia have considered a resolution to abolish slavery for a long time. They sense it's a moral wrong, and the rest of the South will follow Virginia's example. All they ask is time."

Lee provides the central message of the film. After Brown is hanged, he says: "So perish all such enemies of the Union, such foes of the human race." His words end the film and encapsulate its moral: abolitionists like

Brown are totalitarians, and they need to be silenced. But Brown's words have *not* been silenced, as the film notes. At Brown's hanging, Holliday recalls an Indian prophetess who had earlier portended Civil War. She cries, but not because of Brown: "I see something else up there" on the gallows with Brown; "something much more terrible than just one man." John Brown, the film suggests, is a crucial catalyst of Civil War. In a brief epilogue, Holliday marries Stuart; but their intersectional union is meant to be ironic in the face of impending Civil War.[48]

Much like *Birth of a Nation*, *Santa Fe Trail* echoed the contemporaneous historiography. The film borrows heavily from Robert Penn Warren's influential biography, *John Brown: The Making of a Martyr* (1929). In both stories, Brown is a major catalyst of Civil War and resembles Milton's Satan: a figure so demonic, so psychologically complex in justifying his means, that he is fascinating, even captivating. The film borrows Warren's quote of Jason Brown, who calls his father's murders at Pottawatomie "an uncalled for, wicked act." And it borrows Warren's ending. The last line of Warren's biography is a quote from John T. L. Preston, who witnesses Brown's hanging and then declares: "So perish all such enemies of Virginia! All such enemies of the Union! All such foes of the human race!" *Santa Fe Trail* has Lee utter Preston's maxim.[49]

Santa Fe Trail also owes something to Avery Craven's 1932 biography of the secessionist Edmund Ruffin and his short but immensely influential book, *The Repressible Conflict* (1939). Craven's work, together with Warren's biography, helped inaugurate a historiographical shift in which leading scholars systematically began blaming John Brown and the abolitionists for inciting Southerners to secede and sparking Civil War. This interpretation is a *leitmotif* of Warren's biography. He describes in detail how Brown successfully turned himself into a martyr with his words and actions at Harpers Ferry. His martyrdom "was all so thin that it should not have deceived a child, but it deceived a generation." Leading Northerners, from Emerson and Lydia Maria Child to Garrison, Wendell Phillips, and Henry Ward Beecher, became "able demagogues" as they celebrated Brown's martyrdom, thus elevating the influence of "demagogues in the South." As a result,

the attack on the Ferry made many sincere Unionists in the South reconsider their position. If such a thing was not only condoned but applauded in the North, if the press and pulpit talked about the gallows and the cross, these men had to admit their error and say with considerable regret that the Union they had worked for could not be saved.

Warren's biography would be cited by Allan Nevins and other leading Civil War historians. C. Vann Woodward drew heavily on it for his own influential 1952 essay on Brown and the abolitionists. With minor shifts in emphasis, historians for decades would accuse Brown and the abolitionists of being crucial catalysts of a Civil War that was "repressible."[50]

Indeed, from the 1930s through the 1970s, a "potent, pro-Southern bias" dominated American history and literature scholarship, according to Hugh Tulloch. White writers followed Warren and *Santa Fe Trail* in characterizing abolitionists as demagogues or as Communist or Nazi totalitarians. Vann Woodward referred to Brown and his supporters as "fellow travelers." Warren, in *The Legacy of the Civil War* (1961), argued that the abolitionists longed "for the 'total solution,' to purge in violence" existing social tensions. "Their love of man meant the hatred of men." By contrast, the Confederate Constitution "implied that slavery itself was an evil." And Frank Owsley, in his 1940 presidential address to the Southern Historical Association, singled out leading abolitionists when he said, "as far as I have been able to ascertain, neither Dr. Goebbels nor Stalin's propaganda agents have as yet been able to plumb the depths of vulgarity and obscenity reached and maintained by Wendell Phillips, Charles Sumner, Stephen Foster, and other abolitionists of note." These were among the most influential scholars of American history and literature in the twentieth century. Their perspective was clear: respectable politicians and anti-slavery advocates kept their distance from vulgar abolitionists. Never did the twain meet.[51]

******

By the end of the 1960s, owing to the successes of the civil rights movement, many historians began treating the abolitionists with sympathy, but they still referred to them as uncompromising zealots, who stood totally apart from emancipationists. As Tulloch noted, New Left historians now characterized *society* as mad, and abolitionists as sane in their "dedicated opposition" to it. But despite this rehabilitation, abolitionists remained uncoupled from emancipationists.[52]

One sees this uncoupling especially in both college and high-school textbooks which began to dominate survey courses in the humanities in the 1970s. In their highly acclaimed (and still indispensable) 1973 primary source reader, the Yale team of Robert Penn Warren, Cleanth Brooks, and R.W.B. Lewis emphasized that abolitionism was *not* the same thing as emancipationism. Jefferson, Melville, Lincoln, and Robert E. Lee were emancipationists, but they were *not* abolitionists. For an emancipationist, the problem of slavery, no matter how important, was to be treated in a general context ... But for an abolitionist the problem of slavery was paramount, central, burning, and immediate. The context did not matter.

In most U.S. history college textbooks, abolitionists are *still* described as "uncompromising" extremists, unwilling to collaborate with moderates and conservatives, while emancipationists are cast as balanced, practical, and heroic.[53]

Hollywood, too, has continued to uncouple abolitionists and emancipationists. It should be emphasized that abolitionists have rarely been portrayed in film, but when they do appear, they remain villainous. In many respects, Steven Spielberg's *Amistad* (1997) and *Lincoln* (2012) echo themes from Griffith's *Birth of a Nation*. All three films went to great lengths to establish historical authenticity, and each one contrasts "good" emancipationists (or anti-slavery politicians) from "evil" abolitionists.[54]

Amistad casts John Quincy Adams (Anthony Hopkins) and Roger Baldwin (Matthew McConaughey) as shrewd politicians and brilliant legal minds, in contrast to the pathetic white abolitionists, notably Lewis Tappan (Stellan Skarsgård). It thus ignores or downplays Adams's and Baldwin's collaboration with the abolitionists. It is disdainful of principled action, as reflected by an exchange between Baldwin, Tappan, and Theodore Joadson (Morgan Freeman), the first sympathetically rendered black abolitionist in film. Baldwin summarizes the case for the captives by telling Tappan: "Ignore everything but the preeminent issue at hand – the wrongful transfer of stolen goods."[55]

Tappan responds haughtily: "This war must be waged on the battlefield of righteousness."

"But Christ lost," Baldwin counters, and then turns to Joadson. "At least you want to win, don't you?"

"Yes," Joadson says, nodding his head. The exchange belittles white abolitionists, their alliances with blacks, and the religious and civil rights foundations of abolitionism. It also turns black abolitionists into secular, liberal politicians rather than radicals.[56]

In disparaging Tappan and casting Joadson as a secular, pragmatic figure, the film mirrors the contemporaneous historiography. *Amistad* relied heavily on Howard Jones's *Mutiny on the Amistad* (1987) (Jones served as a consultant), and Jones's portrait of Tappan stemmed from

Bertram Wyatt-Brown's unflattering 1969 biography. Although Jones is more sympathetic toward Tappan and other abolitionists than Wyatt-Brown, both historians call Tappan "an uncompromising moralist" who "did not want balance." The secular characterization of Joadson similarly echoes the historiography Jones used, which contrasts the religious zealotry of white abolitionists with the comparatively secular black abolitionists and foregrounds racial tensions between the two groups.[57]

In Spielberg's *Lincoln* (2012), the parallels with *Birth of a Nation* are much more subtle. Spielberg follows the long tradition of uncoupling shrewd, pragmatic political actors like Lincoln from despicable abolitionists. But in *Lincoln*, far more than in *Birth*, Thaddeus Stevens (played by Tommy Lee Jones) champions racial equality less from spiritual or ethical principles than from self-interest – political power coupled with his love for his housekeeper Lydia, made explicit in a scene with them in bed together. After refusing to embrace racial equality during the congressional debate over the Thirteenth Amendment, he becomes a hero. Charles Sumner (John Hutton) reprimands Stevens for his backsliding and becomes a despicable idealist, a characterization that parallels the portrait of Sumner in David Donald's prize-winning biography.[58]

The message of *Lincoln*, much like that of *Amistad*, is that principled action is a liability rather than an asset. Both films totally ignore the successes of black citizenship and equal protection under the law, and the ongoing warfare during Reconstruction. They thus ignore (perhaps in their desire to reach a broad audience) the specter of a social revolu- ⅄
tion that for a while would bring racial equality.

✳✳✳✳✳✳

In the past twenty years, some progressive writers, while lauding black militancy, have cast white abolitionists as incurably racist, devoted to free- ⅄
dom but not equality. They thus downplay or ignore the integrated communities and the foundations of civil rights that the abolitionists established. Most recently, Stephen Kantrowitz, in his otherwise superb new book on Boston abolitionists, inexplicably refuses to apply the label to blacks. Why? Because he says the term "abolitionist" implies a desire only for freedom and does not encompass blacks' larger vision of equality and citizenship. But virtually every one of his black characters defined *themselves* as abolitionists. As I have already noted, Frederick Douglass invoked an "abolition war" and "abolition peace" as ethical imperatives. For him

THE

ATLANTIC MONTHLY.

A MAGAZINE OF LITERATURE, ART, AND POLITICS.

VOL. IX.—FEBRUARY, 1862.—NO. LII.

BATTLE HYMN OF THE REPUBLIC.

MINE eyes have seen the glory of the coming of the Lord :
He is trampling out the vintage where the grapes of wrath are stored ;
He hath loosed the fateful lightning of His terrible swift sword :
    His truth is marching on.

I have seen Him in the watch-fires of a hundred circling camps ;
They have builded Him an altar in the evening dews and damps ;
I can read His righteous sentence by the dim and flaring lamps :
    His day is marching on.

I have read a fiery gospel writ in burnished rows of steel :
" As ye deal with my contemners, so with you my grace shall deal ;
Let the Hero, born of woman, crush the serpent with his heel,
    Since God is marching on."

He has sounded forth the trumpet that shall never call retreat ;
He is sifting out the hearts of men before His judgment-seat :
Oh, be swift, my soul, to answer Him ! be jubilant, my feet !
    Our God is marching on.

In the beauty of the lilies Christ was born across the sea,
With a glory in his bosom that transfigures you and me :
As he died to make men holy, let us die to make men free,
    While God is marching on.

FIGURE 9: *"Battle Hymn of the Republic* on the cover of *The Atlantic Monthly,*
February, 1862."
Source: The Atlantic Monthly, *Vol. IX, No. 52, February 1862, cover. Collection
of John Stauffer.*

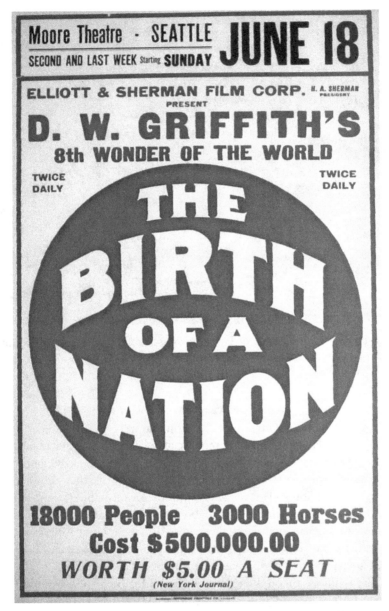

FIGURE 10: *"The Birth of a Nation movie poster, 1915."*
Elliott & Sherman Film Corp. Present D.W. Griffith's 8th Wonder of the World:
The Birth of a Nation.
Source: Riverside Printing Co., Milwaukee, 1915, color print (poster). Library of Congress (Public Domain).

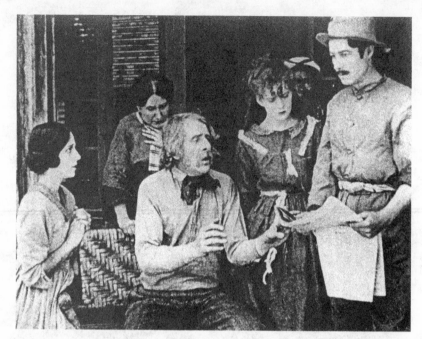

FIGURE 11: After learning of Lincoln's assassination, Dr. Cameron exclaims, "Our best friend is gone. What is to become of us now!"
Source: D.W. Griffith, The Birth of a Nation, *1915, film still. Collection of John Stauffer.*

and other blacks, abolitionism was a revolutionary vision of racial equality and the foundation of civil rights – a term that he sometimes used.[59]

By downplaying or ignoring interracial collaborations and friendships, some progressive scholars thus cast white abolitionists as emancipationists who sought only freedom, not equality. In other words, they continued to *uncouple* abolitionists from emancipationists, an uncoupling based on race. The failure to acknowledge the collaboration and friendship between black and white radicals highlights the degree to which white Americans, for more than one hundred years, have either been despairing of, or horrified by, a social revolution that upends segregation.[60]

The ongoing uncoupling of abolitionists from emancipationists also suggests that before integration can occur, Americans first need to *remember* abolitionists as the founders of civil rights, intimately aligned with emancipationists. Filmmakers' and writers' failures to do so points not only to their despair or horror at the idea of a social revolution; it highlights their inability to understand revolution as a *continuous interaction* between people at the margins and those in the

FIGURE 12: *"Santa Fe Trail* movie poster, 1940."
Source: Santa Fe Trail, *color print (poster), 1940. Collection of John Stauffer.*

FIGURE 13: Ronald Reagan and Errol Flynn in *Santa Fe Trail*, 1940. *Source*: Santa Fe Trail, *1940, film still. Corbis.*

seats of power, between radicals and moderates. And finally, the ongoing uncoupling of abolitionists and emancipationists presents black freedom not as a constant struggle, as Justin Behrend[61] and Carole Emberton[62] emphasize in their essays, but as an endpoint. Reconstruction then becomes a failure rather than an extraordinary though brief success. And racial equality is understood as a temporary phenomenon that was, and is, doomed to fail.

NOTES

1. Congress had passed the Thirteenth Amendment in January 1865, and by April 1865 nearly three-quarters of the states had ratified it. See "Banquet in Charleston," *The Liberator*, May 12, 1865; and especially Michael Vorenberg, *Final Freedom: The Civil War, the Abolition of Slavery, and the Thirteenth Amendment* (Cambridge, UK: Cambridge University Press, 2001), ch. 6.

2. "Banquet in Charleston," *The Liberator*, May 12, 1865. See also Thomas E. Schneider, *Lincoln's Defense of Politics: The Public Man and His Opponents in the Slavery Crisis* (Columbia: University of Missouri Press, 2006), 105.

3. On the distinctions between anti-slavery advocates and abolitionists, see David Brion Davis, "The Emergence of Immediatism in British and American Antislavery Thought," *From Homicide to Slavery* (New York: Oxford University Press, 1986), 238–257; John Stauffer, "Fighting the Devil with His Own Fire," in Andrew Delbanco, with Stauffer, Manisha Sinha, Darryl Pinckney, and Wilfred McClay, *The Abolitionist Imagination* (Cambridge, Mass.: Harvard University Press, 2012), 57–80. "Emancipationist" was coined in 1862 by the *Continental Monthly*. See *Continental Monthly* 1 (January–February 1862): 97–98, 113–14; James M. McPherson, *The Struggle for Equality: Abolitionists and the Negro in the Civil War and Reconstruction* (1964; reprint, Princeton: Princeton University Press, 1992), 90–93.

4. John Stauffer, *GIANTS: The Parallel Lives of Frederick Douglass and Abraham Lincoln* (New York: Twelve, 2008); James Oakes, *The Radical and the Republican: Frederick Douglass, Abraham Lincoln, and the Triumph of Antislavery Politics* (New York: Norton, 2007).

5. Edward J. Blum, *Reforging the White Republic: Race, Religion, and American Nationalism, 1865–1898* (Baton Rouge: Louisiana State University Press, 2005), 5; David Brion Davis, *The Problem of Slavery in the Age of Emancipation* (New York: Alfred A. Knopf, 2014), 332; David Brion Davis, *Inhuman Bondage: The Rise and Fall of Slavery in the New World* (New York: Oxford University Press, 2006), 328; McPherson, *Struggle for Equality*, 81–90, 99–133, 229–232, 341–366, 417–432; McPherson, "Abolitionists and the Civil Rights Act of 1875," *The Journal of American History* 52, no. 3 (December 1965): 493–510; Vorenberg, *Final Freedom*, chs. 3–7; Garrett Epps, *Democracy Reborn: The Fourteenth Amendment and the Fight for Equal Rights in Post-Civil War America* (New York: Henry Holt, 2006), chs. 6–11; Philip Dray, *Capitol Men: The Epic Story of Reconstruction through the Lives of the First Black Congressmen* (Boston: Mariner Books, 2010); Eric Foner, *Freedom's Lawmakers: A Directory of Black Officeholders during Reconstruction* (Baton Rouge: Louisiana State University Press, 1996); Foner, *Reconstruction: America's Unfinished Revolution, 1863–1877* (New York: Harper & Row, 1988), chs. 1–2, 6–10.

On the significance and legacy of the Reconstruction Amendments, see also Akhil Reed Amar, *The Bill of Rights: Creation and Reconstruction* (New Haven: Yale University Press, 1998), Part II; and Amar, *America's Constitution: A Biography* (New York: Random House, 2006), ch. 10.

6. Roy P. Basler, ed., *The Collected Works of Abraham Lincoln* cited as here-
   after CWAL, vol. 8 (New Brunswick, N.J.: Rutgers University Press, 1953), 2;
   Frederick Douglass, *Life and Times of Frederick Douglass* (1892; reprint,
   New York: Collier Books, 1962), 366; Daniel H. Chamberlain, quoted from
   New York Tribune, November 4, 1883, in *William Lloyd Garrison, 1805–
   1879: The Story of His Life, Told by His Children*, vol. 4 (New York: The
   Century Co., 1889), 132n. Chamberlain said he quoted Lincoln "in exact
   substance, and very nearly in words." For corroboration of Lincoln's state-
   ment to Douglass at the reception following the Second Inaugural, see
   Memorial of Sarah Pugh: A Tribute of Respect from Her Cousins
   (Philadelphia: J.B. Lippincott & Co., 1888), 107.

7. CWAL, vol. 8, 403; William A. Tidwell, *Come Retribution: The Confederate
   Secret Service and the Assassination of Lincoln* (Jackson: University Press of
   Mississippi, 1988), 408, 421; John Rhodehamel and Louise Taper, eds.,
   "Right or Wrong, God Judge Me": The Writings of John Wilkes Booth
   (Urbana: University of Illinois Press, 1997), 154; Henry Louis Gates, Jr.,
   "Abraham Lincoln on Race and Slavery," *Lincoln on Race and Slavery*
   (Princeton: Princeton University Press, 2009), xxv; David Herbert Donald,
   Lincoln (New York: Simon & Schuster, 1995), 585–588.

8. James Oakes, *Freedom National: The Destruction of Slavery in the United
   States, 1861–1865* (New York: Norton, 2013), xix–xxi, 284, 450–451,
   489–492; McPherson, *Struggle for Equality*, 81–90, 99–133, 229–232,
   341–366, 417–432; McPherson, "Abolitionists and the Civil Rights Act,"
   493–510; Vorenberg, *Final Freedom*, chs. 3–7; Epps, *Democracy Reborn*,
   chs. 6–11; Foner, *Reconstruction*, chs. 1–2, 6–10.
   On distinctions between legal and social equality in Reconstruction, see Kate Masur,
   *An Example for All the Land: Emancipation and the Struggle over Equality in
   Washington, D.C.* (Chapel Hill: University of North Carolina Press, 2010), 9–11.

9. See, for example, Hugh Tulloch, *The Debate on the American Civil War Era*
   (Manchester: Manchester University Press, 1999), ch. 3. Although Tulloch
   does not distinguish between abolitionists and emancipationists in his historiography, it's clear that the two categories are separate.

10. Robert A. Rosenstone, "Does a Filmic Writing of History Exist?" *History
    and Theory* 41 (December 2002): 134–144, quotation from 137;
    Rosenstone, *History on Film/Film on History* (New York: Pearson, 2012);
    Rosenstone, ed., *Revisioning History: Film and the Construction of a New
    Past* (Princeton: Princeton University Press, 1995). Richard Slotkin,
    *Gunfighter Nation: The Myth of the Frontier in Twentieth-Century
    America* (New York: Atheneum, 1992), 1–28; Richard Slotkin, "Prologue
    to a Study of Myth and Genre in American Movies," *Prospects* 9 (1984);
    Casey King, "Abolitionists in American Cinema: From Birth of a Nation to
    Amistad," in Timothy Patrick McCarthy and John Stauffer, eds., *Prophets
    of Protest: Reconsidering the History of American Abolitionism* (New
    York: The New Press, 2006), ch. 15; Linda Williams, *Playing the Race
    Card: Melodramas of Black and White from Uncle Tom to O. J. Simpson*
    (Princeton: Princeton University Press, 2001).

11. Delbanco, *Abolitionist Imagination*, 1–56, 153–164; Harry S. Stout, *Upon the Altar of the Nation: A Moral History of the Civil War* (New York: Penguin Books, 2006); David Goldfield, *America Aflame: How the Civil War Created a Nation* (New York: Bloomsbury Press, 2011); Christopher Benfey, "Terrorist or Martyr," *The New York Review of Books*, March 7, 2013; Christopher Benfey, "Introduction," in Allen Tate, *Collected Poems, 1919–1976* (New York: Farrar Straus Giroux, 2007), xiii–xix. Although much more subtle, Sean Wilentz echoes C. Vann Woodward by characterizing the abolitionists as "fellow travelers." See Wilentz, *The Rise of American Democracy: Jefferson to Lincoln* (New York: Norton, 2005), 650. See also Yael A. Sternhell, "Revisionism Reinvented? The Antiwar Turn in Civil War Scholarship," *The Journal of the Civil War Era* 3 (June 2013): 239–256.

12. Davis, *The Problem of Slavery in the Age of Emancipation*, ch. 9; Julie Roy Jeffrey, "'No Occurrence in Human History Is More Deserving of Commemoration than This': Abolitionist Celebrations of Freedom," *Prophets of Protest*, 256–267.

13. William Lee Miller, *Arguing about Slavery: John Quincy Adams and the Great Battle in the United States Congress* (New York: Vintage Press, 1998); Henry Wilson, *History of the Rise and Fall of the Slave Power*, vol. 2 (Boston: Houghton Mifflin, 1884), 161–163.

14. Davis, *Problem of Slavery in the Age of Emancipation*, ch. 9; Allan Nevins, *Ordeal of the Union, vol. 1: Fruits of Manifest Destiny, 1847–1852* (1947; reprint, New York: Collier Books, 1992), 380–386; Robert M. Cover, *Justice Accused: Antislavery and the Judicial Process* (New Haven: Yale University Press, 1975), 175–191; Stanley W. Campbell, *The Slave Catchers: Enforcement of the Fugitive Slave Law, 1850–1860* (1968; reprint, New York: Norton, 1972), 124–130, 199–207; Albert J. Von Frank, *The Trials of Anthony Burns: Freedom and Slavery in Emerson's Boston* (Cambridge, Mass.: Harvard University Press, 1998); David S. Reynolds, *Mightier than the Sword: Uncle Tom's Cabin and the Battle for America* (New York: Norton, 2011), ch. 4; Joan D. Hedrick, *Harriet Beecher Stowe: A Life* (New York: Oxford University Press, 1994), 208–271.

15. Charles Stearns, "The Civil War in Kansas," *Liberator*, January 4, 1856; Henry Mayer, *All on Fire: William Lloyd Garrison and the Abolition of Slavery* (New York: St. Martin's Press, 1998), ch. 20, esp. 474–477; Richard H. Sewell, *Ballots for Freedom: Antislavery Politics in the United States, 1837–1860* (New York: Oxford University Press, 1976), 287; Philip S. Foner, ed., *Life and Writings of Frederick Douglass*, vol. 2 (New York: International Publishers, 1950), 396–401; Stauffer, *GIANTS*, 153; W. Caleb McDaniel, *The Problem of Democracy in the Age of Slavery: Garrisonian Abolitionists and Transatlantic Reform* (Baton Rouge: Louisiana State University Press, 2013), chs. 8–9.

16. James Brewer Stewart, *Holy Warriors: The Abolitionists and American Slavery*, rvd. edn. (New York: Hill & Wang, 1996), chs. 2–7; Stewart, *Abolitionist Politics and the Coming of the Civil War* (Amherst: University of Massachusetts Press, 2008), 3–35, 203–226; Davis, *Inhuman Bondage*,

250–267; John Stauffer, *The Black Hearts of Men: Radical Abolitionists and the Transformation of Race* (Cambridge, Mass.: Harvard University Press, 2002), 134–144; Bruce Laurie, *Beyond Garrison: Antislavery and Social Reform* (New York: Cambridge University Press, 2005); Miller, *Arguing about Slavery*; Betty L. Fladeland, "Compensated Emancipation: A Rejected Alternative," *Journal of Southern History* 42, no. 4 (May 1976): 169–186.

17. Garrison to Henry Cheever, Sept. 9, 1861, in Walter M. Merrill, ed., *Letters of William Lloyd Garrison, vol. 5: Let the Oppressed Go Free, 1861–1867* (Cambridge, Mass.: Harvard University Press, 1979), 35–36; Matthew Furrow, "Samuel Gridley Howe, the Black Population of Canada West, and Racial Ideology of the 'Blueprint for Radical Reconstruction,'" *Journal of American History*, 97, no. 2 (September 2010): 344–370. On the Emancipation League, see McPherson, *Struggle for Equality*, 75–79, 178–181, 279–281. On Garrison's willingness to compromise principle for reasons of expediency, see William H. Pease and Jane H. Pease, "Antislavery Ambivalence: Immediatism, Expediency, Race," *American Quarterly* 17, no. 4 (Winter 1965): 682–695; Aileen S. Kraditor, *Means and Ends in American Abolitionism: Garrison and His Critics on Strategy and Tactics, 1834–1850* (1967; reprint, Chicago: Ivan R. Dee, Inc., 1989).

18. "Garrison's Speech in New York," *The Liberator*, January 24, 1862, quoted in Walter M. Merrill, ed., *The Letters of William Lloyd Garrison*, 59; Garrison, *The Abolitionists, and Their Relation to the War: A lecture delivered at the Cooper Institute, New York, January 4, 1862* (New York: Pulpit and Rostrum, number 26, 1862), 46; Wendell Phillips, "The War for the Union," December 1861, in *Speeches, Lectures, and Letters* (Boston: Lee and Shepard, 1870), 440; McPherson, *Struggle for Equality*, 99–100.

19. Frederick Douglass, "The Mission of the War," in John W. Blassingame and John R. McKivigan, eds., *The Frederick Douglass Papers*, ser. 1, vols. 3–4 (New Haven, Conn.: Yale University Press, 1985–1991), cited as hereafter TFDP, 1:3, 496–497, 505. Douglass and Garrison both lectured for the Emancipation League, reuniting after a fourteen-year rift during which Garrison had refused to attend any abolition meeting where Douglass was present.

20. Douglass, "The Proclamation and a Negro Army," TFDP, 1:3, 435–445, 549–569, quotations from 437, 551, 552, 563–564; Douglass, *Life and Times of Frederick Douglass*, 354–355 (quoted). See also Stauffer, GIANTS, 242–246; David Brion Davis, "The Emancipation Moment," in Gabor S. Boritt, ed., *Lincoln, The War President: The Gettysburg Lectures* (New York: Oxford University Press, 1992), 63–88.

21. John Stauffer and Benjamin Soskis, *The Battle Hymn of the Republic: A Biography of the Song That Marches On* (New York: Oxford University Press, 2013), 83–84; Ernest Lee Tuveson, *Redeemer Nation: The Idea of America's Millennial Role* (Chicago: University of Chicago Press, 1968), 187–214; James H. Moorhead, *American Apocalypse: Yankee Protestants and the Civil War, 1860–1869* (New Haven: Yale University Press, 1978), 79–81. When Lincoln heard the hymn sung at the U.S. Capitol in 1864, tears

welled in his eyes after the final chorus. "Sing it again!" he yelled, and then said: "Take it all in all, the song and the singing, that was the best I ever heard." See Stauffer and Soskis, *The Battle Hymn*, 93–94; Bristol, *Life of Chaplain McCabe*, 198–200; 202,George Stuart to Abraham Lincoln, June 18, 1864, in Abraham Lincoln Papers, Library of Congress: http://memory. loc.gov/ammem/alhtml/malhome.html (accessed July 8, 2015).

22. TFDP, 1: 4, 3–24, quotations from 11, 24; David W. Blight, *Frederick Douglass' Civil War: Keeping Faith in Jubilee* (Baton Rouge: Louisiana State University Press, 1989), 175–176.

23. *Continental Monthly* 1 (January–February 1862): 97–98, 113–114; McPherson, *Struggle for Equality*, 90–93. On Hinton Rowan Helper, see George M. Fredrickson, "Antislavery Racist: Hinton Rowan Helper," in *The Arrogance of Race: Historical Perspectives on Slavery, Racism, and Social Inequality* (Middletown, Conn.: Wesleyan University Press, 1988), 28–53; William Freehling, *The Road to Disunion, vol. 2: Secessionists Triumphant, 1854–1861* (New York: Oxford University Press, 2007), 236–268. According to the Oxford English Dictionary, "emancipationist" was used as early as 1822 in England by Robert Southey in reference to the advocates of Catholic emancipation from English law.

24. CWAL 5, 48–49, 537. Emphasis in the original.

25. Sumner, quoted in Edward L. Pierce, *Memoir and Letters of Charles Sumner*, vol. 4 (Boston: Roberts Brothers, 1893), 49; McPherson, *Struggle for Equality*, 90–91.

26. TFDP, 1: 3, 560–561; McPherson, *Struggle for Equality*, 92–93.

27. TFDP, 1: 3, 560–561; Blum, *Reforging the White Republic*, 126; Philip A. Klinkner with Rogers M. Smith, *The Unsteady March: The Rise and Decline of Racial Equality in America* (Chicago: University of Chicago Press, 1999), 73, 85, quotation from William Wells Brown on 85; William Gillette, *Retreat from Reconstruction, 1869–1879* (Baton Rouge: Louisiana State University Press, 1979) 256–258; McPherson, *Struggle for Equality*, 81–90, 92–93, 99–133, 229–232, 341–366, 417–432; McPherson, "Abolitionists and the Civil Rights Act of 1875," *The Journal of American History* 52, no. 3 (December 1965): 493–510; Epps, *Democracy Reborn*, chs. 6–11; Dray, *Capitol Men*; Foner, *Reconstruction*, chs. 1–2, 6–10; Goldfield, *America Aflame*, 501.

28. Henry Wilson, *History of the Rise and Fall of the Slave Power in America*, 3 vols. (Boston: James R. Osgood and Company, 1872–77); Hermann von Holst, *The Constitutional and Political History of the United States*, 8 vols. (Chicago: Callaghan and Company, 1876–1892), esp. vols. 7–8; John L. Myers, "The Writing of *History of the Rise and Fall of the Slave Power in America*," *Civil War History* 31, no. 2 (June 1985): 144–162; Peter Novick, *That Noble Dream: The "Objectivity Question" and the American Historical Profession* (Cambridge: Cambridge University Press, 1988), 25; Thomas L. Haskell, "Objectivity Is Not Neutrality: Rhetoric vs. Practice in Peter Novick's *That Noble Dream*," *History and Theory* 29, no. 2 (May 1990): 129–157, 137, n13; Eric F. Goldman, "Hermann Eduard von Holst: Plumed Knight of American Historiography," *The Mississippi Valley Historical Review* 23:4 (March 1937): 511–532; Eric F. Goldman,

"Importing a Historian: Von Holst and American Universities," *The Mississippi Valley Historical Review* 27, no. 2 (September 1940): 267–274.
29. James Ford Rhodes, *History of the United States from the Compromise of 1850*, 8 vols. (New York: Macmillan, 1892–1919), esp. vol. 1, chs. 1, 3, 5; vol. 2, ch. 7; Tulloch, *Debate*, 74 (quoted); David W. Blight, *Race and Reunion: The Civil War in American Memory* (Cambridge, Mass.: Harvard University Press, 2001), 231–237, 357–359.
30. James M. McPherson, *The Abolitionist Legacy: From Reconstruction to the NAACP* (Princeton: Princeton University Press, 1975), 14 (quoted); McPherson, "Abolitionists and the Civil Rights Act of 1875," *The Journal of American History* 52, no. 3 (December 1965): 493–510, 506; "Charles Sumner," *Harper's Weekly*, April 4, 1874, Front Page (quoted); *Harper's Weekly*, June 20, 1874; Henry James, *William Wetmore Story and His Friends: From Letters, Diaries, and Recollections*, 2 vols. (Boston: Houghton, Mifflin & Co., 1903), vol. 1, 30–31, 234, vol. 2, 31; Stauffer, "Fighting the Devil with His Own Fire," 64.
The first full biography of Sumner, exhaustive in scope and magisterial in style, remains the best. See Pierce, *Memoir and Letters of Charles Sumner*. On nineteenth-century memories of the abolitionists, see also Tulloch, *Debate*, 71–74; Blight, *Race and Reunion*, 231–237; Julie Roy Jeffrey, *Abolitionists Remember: Antislavery Autobiographies and the Unfinished Work of Emancipation* (Chapel Hill: University of North Carolina Press, 2008).
31. Novick, *That Noble Dream*, 76–77; Tulloch, *Debate*, ch. 3.
32. George W. Williams, *History of the Negro Race in America, 1619–1880* (New York: G. P. Putnam's Sons, 1883), chs. 9–21; W. E. B. Du Bois, *John Brown* (Philadelphia: G.W. Jacobs, 1909); Du Bois, *The Gift of Black Folk: The Negroes in the Making of America* (Boston: Stratford Co., 1924); Du Bois, *Black Reconstruction: An Essay toward a History of the Part Which Black Folk Played in the Attempt to Reconstruct Democracy in America, 1860–1880* (New York: Russell & Russell, 1935); John Hope Franklin, *From Slavery to Freedom: A History of American Negroes* (1947; repr., New York: Knopf, 1971), 242–270; Benjamin Quarles, *The Negro in the Civil War* (1953; reprint, New York: Da Capo, 1989); Benjamin Quarles, *Black Abolitionists* (New York: Oxford University Press, 1969); Nathan Huggins, *Black Odyssey: The Afro-American Ordeal in Slavery* (New York: Pantheon Books, 1977); Waldo E. Martin, Jr., *The Mind of Frederick Douglass* (Chapel Hill: University of North Carolina Press, 1984); James Oliver Horton and Lois E. Horton, *Black Bostonians: Family Life and Community Struggle in the Antebellum North* (1979; reprint, New York: Holmes & Meier, 1999), chs. 7–9; Horton and Horton, *In Hope of Liberty: Culture, Community and Protest among Northern Free Blacks, 1700–1860* (New York: Oxford University Press, 1997), chs. 9–10. On British abolitionists, see the synthesis by Adam Hochschild, *Bury the Chains: Prophets and Rebels in the Fight to Free an Empire's Slaves* (Boston: Houghton Mifflin, 2005). On French abolitionists, see Lawrence C. Jennings, *French Anti-Slavery: The Movement for the Abolition of Slavery in France, 1802–1848* (Cambridge: Cambridge

University Press, 2000); and Seymour Drescher, *Abolition: A History of Slavery and Antislavery* (New York: Cambridge University Press, 2009).

33. John David Smith, *An Old Creed for the New South: Proslavery Ideology and Historiography, 1865–1918* (1985; reprint, Carbondale: Southern Illinois University Press, 2008), 5 (quoted), ch. 8; Blight, *Race and Reunion*, 338–397.
    U. B. Phillips's preface to the first edition of *American Negro Slavery* (1918) brilliantly captures how Southern redemption represented a metaphor of slavery but without the problem of slaves as property. Phillips describes a segregated Army camp in the South and the great "harmony" between blacks and whites "evinced by the very tone of the camp." He concludes his observation by noting that "a generation of freedom has wrought less transformation in the bulk of the blacks than might casually be supposed." This continuity solves the dilemma that "slaves were both persons and property, and as chattels they were investments." U. B. Phillips, *American Negro Slavery* (1918; reprint, Baton Rouge: Louisiana State University Press, 1994), xxiii, xxiv, xxv.

34. J. G. de Roulhac Hamilton, "Lincoln and the South," *The Sewanee Review* 17, no. 2 (April 1909): 129–138; Merrill D. Peterson, *Lincoln in American Memory* (New York: Oxford University Press, 1994), 190–195, quotation from 191.

35. Conrad Pitcher, "D. W. Griffith's Controversial Film, 'The Birth of a Nation,'" *OAH Magazine of History* 13, no. 3 (Spring 1999): 50–55; Michael Rogin, "The Sword Became a Flashing Vision": D. W. Griffith's *The Birth of a Nation*," in Robert Lang, ed., *The Birth of a Nation: D.W. Griffith, Director* (New Brunswick: Rutgers University Press, 1994), 250–253; Arthur Lennig, "Myth and Fact: The Reception of 'The Birth of a Nation,'" *Film History* 16, no. 2 (2004): 117–141.
    On my reading of *Birth of a Nation*, I have also been inspired by interpretations in Peterson, *Lincoln in American Memory*, 167–170; Linda Williams, *Playing the Race Card: Melodramas of Black and White from Uncle Tom to O. J. Simpson* (Princeton: Princeton University Press, 2001); Thomas Cripps, *Slow Fade to Black: The Negro in American Film, 1900–1942* (New York: Oxford University Press, 1993); Richard Slotkin, *Gunfighter Nation: The Myth of the Frontier in Twentieth-Century America* (New York: Atheneum, 1992); Robert Sklar, *Movie-Made America: A Cultural History of American Movies* (New York: Vintage Books, 1994); Casey King, "Abolitionists in American Cinema: From Birth of a Nation to Amistad," *Prophets of Protest*, ch. 15; Rosenstone, *Revisioning History*. Woodrow Wilson's influence on the film was significant. Griffith originally titled it *The Clansman*, after Dixon's novel, but after the preview Dixon suggested renaming it *The Birth of a Nation*, the new title reflecting Wilson's thesis in *History of the American People* that before the war the United States had been "a collection of states," "jangling, discordant, antagonistic," and only after the war "did it become a united nation." The film was copyrighted as *The Birth of a Nation; or The Clansman*. See Lennig, "Reception of 'Birth of a Nation,'" 119–120; Woodrow Wilson, *History of the American People, vol. V: Reunion and Nationalization* (New York: Harper & Bros., 1902), 128–131.

36. Lennig, "Reception of 'Birth of a Nation,'" 120–122; Rogin, in Lang, ed., *Birth of a Nation*, 251. Griffith's film reflected Wilson's own interpretation of the "birth" of the nation in his *History of the American People*. The source of Wilson's purported tribute originated from an interview with Griffith in the

New York American on February 28, 1915. See Lennig, "Reception of 'Birth of a Nation,'" 122.

37. Thomas Dixon, *The Clansman* (New York, 1905), 47; Peterson, *Lincoln in American Memory*, 169. Dixon read General Benjamin Butler's memoir, in which Butler remembered a conversation with Lincoln near the end of the war, and described Lincoln as wondering about the feasibility of colonization. In Dixon's *A Southerner: A Romance with the Real Lincoln* (1913), he writes into his historical novel that near the end of the war Lincoln and Butler planned to colonize blacks. John Hay, Lincoln's former secretary, biographer, and secretary of state, endorsed the historical authenticity of *The Clansman*.
38. Lang, ed., *Birth of a Nation*, 82, 87, 93. Lang's script includes the title cards.
39. Lang, ed., *Birth of a Nation*, 93, 134. The log cabin in the film appears to have been modeled on the photograph of the house in which Lincoln was born, published in *McClure's Magazine*, December 1895; see Peterson, *Lincoln in American Memory*, 178.
40. Lang, ed., *Birth of a Nation*, 155–156; Peterson, *Lincoln in American Memory*, 170. Webster's quote first appears after Appomattox. It is repeated with emphasis (underlined) as the final title card.
41. Griffith, quoted in Lennig, "Reception of 'Birth of a Nation,'" 118–119.
42. Lang, ed., *Birth of a Nation*, 51.
43. Ibid. 44 (emphasis in the original).
44. King, "Abolitionists in American Cinema," 273.
45. Lang, ed., *Birth of a Nation*, 49–50.
46. Rosenstone, "Does a Filmic Writing of History Exist?" 137; King, "Abolitionists in American Cinema," 268–270; Lang, ed., *Birth of a Nation*, 93. For the contemporaneous historiography, see Tulloch, *Debate*, 114–117, 126, 212–236; Wilson, *History of the American People*, vol. 5 (1902); J. W. Burgess, *Reconstruction and the Constitution, 1866-1876* (1902); William Dunning, *Reconstruction, Political and Economic, 1865–1877* (1907); and Dunning, *Essays on the Civil War and Reconstruction and Related Topics* (1897).
47. In this and subsequent paragraphs, all quotes are my transcriptions from the film.
The quote, "crutch on which … walks" is from Robert Penn Warren, *John Brown: The Making of a Martyr* (1929; reprint Nashville: J. S. Sanders & Company, 1993), 434. The only article that discusses *Santa Fe Trail* in depth, which was not helpful, is Robert E. Morsberger, "Slavery and the Santa Fe Trail; or, John Brown on Hollywood's Sour Apple Tree," *American Studies* 18, no. 2 (Fall 1977): 87–98.
48. After Stuart, Custer, and other soldiers run Brown out of Kansas, an Indian fortune teller prophesies to Holliday, who translates to the soldiers: "one day," she says, you soldiers will "all be famous men, great in battle but bitter enemies." When asked "who's going to start the fight," she says, "the fight is already started. Somewhere in the East a man is lighting a torch." The plot then immediately cuts to Boston, where Brown meets with abolitionists. "Is your wish to destroy the Union?" they ask. "Yes," says Brown. "The devil with the Union. We've got to fight sometime. It might as well be now."

49. Warren, *John Brown*, 168, 439. On John Brown historiography, see Stephen B. Oates, "John Brown and His Judges: A Critique of the Historical Literature," *Civil War History* 17, no. 1 (March 1971): 5–24.

50. Warren, *John Brown*, 391, 414, 418. Avery Craven, *Edmund Ruffin, Southerner: A Study in Secession* (New York: D. Appleton and Company, 1932), esp. chs. 8–9; Craven, *The Repressible Conflict, 1830–1861* (Baton Rouge: Louisiana State University Press, 1939); C. Vann Woodward, "Introduction," in Warren, *John Brown*, xi–xvii; Woodward, "John Brown's Private War" (1952), reprinted in *The Burden of Southern History*, 3rd edn. (Baton Rouge: Louisiana State University Press, 1993), 41–68; Tulloch, *Debate*, 80–83.

51. Tulloch, *Debate*, 10; C. Vann Woodward, "John Brown's Private War," 51; Robert Penn Warren, *The Legacy of the Civil War* (1961; repr., Lincoln: University of Nebraska Press, 1998), 22–23, 88; Frank L. Owsley, "The Fundamental Cause of the Civil War: Egocentric Sectionalism," *The Journal of Southern History* 7 (February 1941): 3–18, 16. See also Oakes, *Freedom National*, xv–xvii.

52. Tulloch, *Debate*, 89–100, quotation from 93; Merton L. Dillon, "The Abolitionists: A Decade of Historiography, 1959–1969," *The Journal of Southern History* 35 (November 1969): 500–522.

53. Cleanth Brooks, R. W. B. Lewis, Robert Penn Warren, *American Literature: The Makers and the Making*, vol. 1 (New York: St. Martin's Press, 1973), 335; James A. Henretta et al., *America: A Concise History*, 3rd edn., vol. 1 (Boston: Bedford/St. Martin's, 2006), 368.

54. King, "Abolitionists in American Cinema," 268–271.

55. Ibid., 291–293. The quotes are my transcriptions of the film.

56. King, "Abolitionists in American Cinema," 291–293.

57. Howard Jones, *Mutiny on the Amistad: The Saga of a Slave Revolt and Its Impact on American Abolition, Law, and Diplomacy* (New York: Oxford University Press, 1987), 38–39, 227, quotation from 39; Bertram Wyatt-Brown, *Lewis Tappan and the Evangelical War against Slavery* (Cleveland: Case Western Reserve University Press, 1969); Gerald Sorin, *Abolitionism: A New Perspective* (New York: Praeger, 1972); Merton L. Dillon, *The Abolitionists: The Growth of a Dissenting Minority* (DeKalb: Northern Illinois University Press, 1974); Lawrence J. Friedman, *Gregarious Saints: Self and Community in American Abolitionism, 1830–1870* (New York: Cambridge University Press, 1982). On Jones as a consultant to the film, see the review by Bertram Wyatt-Brown, who calls the film "compelling," "brilliant," "sophisticated, and moving"; "Spielberg has translated a highly complex legal tangle into a film of remarkable intensity." Wyatt-Brown, "*Amistad*," *Journal of American History* 85, no. 3 (December 1998): 1174–1175, quotation from 1174.

58. Stevens's enemies and most biographers have asserted that he had a sexual relationship with his housekeeper, Lydia Hamilton Smith. Smith was probably a "confidante," but there is no evidence that she was his mistress. The most sustained allegation of a sexual relationship is by Fawn Brodie. In her biography she accuses Stevens of acting little different from slaveowners who

kept concubines. Her evidence of a sexual liaison is based on the following: Smith worked for Stevens for twenty years and lived in his house; he bequeathed her money after his death ($500/year or $5,000 in a lump sum) and deeded her property; he insisted on being buried in an interracial cemetery; and he commissioned a portrait of her. The first two assertions were common arrangements between trusted housekeepers and employers in the nineteenth century. It is also understandable that Stevens, a bachelor, would commission a portrait of his confidante. And most abolitionists insisted on being buried in interracial cemeteries. Stevens and Smith were buried in different cemeteries – Smith in the cemetery of St. Mary's Catholic Church in Lancaster, Pennsylvania, where she had long been a member, and Stevens in Shreiner's Protestant Cemetery.

The most compelling evidence, which no one has pursued, of intense spiritual, emotional, and possible sexual intimacy is that, just before Stevens died, he received the Roman Catholic rite of baptism, possibly at the request of Smith, a Catholic. Perhaps Smith wanted to be buried beside Stevens, and so had him baptized in her faith. Stevens was probably unaware "of what was going on." See Hans L. Trefousse, *Thaddeus Stevens: Nineteenth-Century Egalitarian* (Chapel Hill: University of North Carolina Press, 1997), 69–70, 240 (quoted); Fawn M. Brodie, *Thaddeus Stevens, Scourge of the South* (New York: W. W. Norton, 1959), 17, 20, 52–53, 86–93. On Donald's unflattering portrait of Sumner, see David Herbert Donald, *Charles Sumner* (New York: Da Capo Press, 1996), an unabridged republication of Donald's two-volume biography of Sumner published in 1960 and 1970.

59. Stephen Kantrowitz, *More Than Freedom: Fighting for Black Citizenship in a White Republic, 1829–1889* (New York: Penguin Press, 2012), 4; TFDP, 1: 4, 11, 24; Blight, *Frederick Douglass' Civil War*, 175–178. Joseph Yanielli's prize-winning essay cites other recent uncharitable assessments of white abolitionists; Yanielli, "George Thompson among the Africans: Empathy, Authority, and Insanity in the Age of Abolition," *The Journal of American History* 96 (March 2010): 979–1000.

David Walker is the only major figure in Kantrowitz's book who does not define himself as an abolitionist. This is because he bridged the gradualist and immediatist movements, indeed helped to launch the immediatist, or modern abolitionist, movement that embraced racial equality and integration. As I note elsewhere, "In essence, the liberal abolitionists of the early Republic became the colonizationists and 'liberal' anti-slavery advocates of the antebellum era." Stauffer, "Fighting the Devil with His Own Fire," 74.

60. Of course segregation still plagues society – more so in the North than in the South since 1990, according to scholars who analyze the reverse migration of blacks returning to the South. See Isabel Wilkerson, *The Warmth of Other Suns: The Epic Story of America's Great Migration* (New York: Random House, 2010), 527–538; William H. Frey, "The New Great Migration: Black Americans' Return to the South, 1965–2000," *The Brookings Institution: The Living Cities Census Series* (May 2004): 1–17; Gavin Wright, "Urban Entrepreneurship in the Post-Civil War South," Meeting of the Economic History Association, New Haven, CT, September 13, 2008; Roderick J. Harrison, "The Great Migration, South," *The New Crisis* 108, no. 4 (July/August 2001): www.questia.com/magazine/1P3-77463404/the-great-migration-south (accessed July 17, 2015); Cliff Hocker, "Black Migration in

Reverse: Americans Are Leaving Major Cities for Opportunities in the South," *Black Enterprise* (May 2005): www.blackenterprise.com/mag/black-migration-in-reverse (accessed July 27, 2015); John Stauffer, "The Great Northern Migration," *The Wall Street Journal*, March 26, 2010: www.wsj.com/articles/SB10001424052748703467004575463852823978496 (accessed July 17, 2015).
61. See Chapter 6.
62. See Chapter 5.

Epilogue: Emancipation and the Nation

Laura F. Edwards

Historians once treated African Americans as passive recipients of freedom, which came definitively, although piecemeal, through federal policies, starting with the Emancipation Proclamation and leading inevitably to the Thirteenth, Fourteenth, and Fifteenth Amendments. Those assumptions still linger in the historiography, despite our best efforts to eliminate them. Historians, for instance, still refer to the collapse of slavery or the extension of rights, phrasing that obscures not just the efforts of African Americans to claim freedom, but also the conflicts involved in securing it and making it meaningful. Still, such references give us pause now, precisely because they lag so far behind current conceptual paradigms, which characterize emancipation as a process and emphasize the importance of African Americans in that dynamic.[1] The essays in *Rethinking Emancipation: Legacies of Slavery and the Quest for Black Freedom* build on those insights, treating the Emancipation Proclamation as one among many points in a much longer journey about what America would be without slavery.

That journey was a long one, because slavery's influence was so pervasive. The essays in *Rethinking Emancipation* show how pervasive it was, tracing the implications beyond African Americans, the South, and race relations in that region to people, places, and issues that, on the surface, might appear only loosely connected to slavery, if at all. On this broad canvas, the essays also challenge the meaning so often given to emancipation in the historiography. In these essays, emancipation is less about specific acts – such as the Emancipation Proclamation or the Thirteenth Amendment, or even the efforts of individual African Americans to flee slavery – and more a way of exploring the challenges and conflicts of remaking American life without slavery. Such an approach emphasizes emancipation's multiple meanings, which ranged from narrow conceptions that entailed nothing more than the elimination of slavery to expansive notions of racial equality. It also breaks the concept of emancipation apart, making it possible to see it as a process that unfolded at many levels: in individual lives as well as in the nation's social, economic, political, and legal structures. Some of the essays explore emancipation in terms of structural changes with wide-reaching effects. Others characterize it as a deeply personal experience, one navigated by individuals: the African Americans who fled from slavery, the Union troops who dealt with those refugees, and the white Southerners who refused to accept the end of slavery. Collectively, the essays show that these two aspects of emancipation, while distinct, existed in dynamic tension — a dynamic that ultimately remade the nation.

The structural aspects of emancipation loom large in many of the essays in *Rethinking Emancipation*, which suggest that removing slavery from the nation's governing structures proved far more difficult than simply proclaiming it gone. More than that, ending slavery and realizing freedom were not things that individuals could achieve on their own. Both required the backing of law and the willingness of government to enforce it. That point is most clear in Gregory P. Downs's chapter,[2] which highlights the extent and importance of the U.S. military's occupation of the South. As Downs argues, compliance with the laws mandating emancipation and the recognition of African Americans' civil and political rights depended on the U.S. military's presence and willingness to enforce the laws. The significance of government authority, particularly federal authority as embodied by the military, runs through other chapters as well, although the implications are not always as clear cut as they are in Downs's analysis. As William A. Blair argues, the U.S. military used its authority to disfranchise those men thought to be loyal to the Confederacy, thus throwing key races in 1863 and 1864 to the Republicans and altering the course of federal Reconstruction policies by making passage of the Thirteenth Amendment, abolishing slavery, possible. At first glance, the power of the state seems distant from Yael A. Sternhell's chapter,[3] which characterizes emancipation as "first and foremost a complex lived experience, a daily reality that took multiple, shifting, and often contradictory forms." But both the Confederate and U.S. governments still played decisive roles in the background, as the forces that shape the terrain on which individuals acted. The U.S. military upended the South's social structure and sent Southerners in different directions, looking to remake their lives. While the Confederacy positioned enslaved African Americans and white Confederates very differently, both ended up fleeing exploitation sanctioned by the Confederacy's legal order: African Americans deserted slavery, and white Confederates deserted from the Army. The collapse of the Confederacy order, which made flight possible, also made it dangerous and uncertain.

Carole Emberton and Justin Behrend pick up the story later, in the Reconstruction era. Linking federal policies in the South to imperial expansion in the West, Emberton argues in Chapter 5 that "projects typically celebrated as outgrowths of freedom" – the end of slavery and federal protection for Americans' civil and political rights – fueled a national vision that left no room for different cultures within the geographic boundaries of the United States. Freedom for African Americans resulted in the destruction of Native Americans' freedom. Ultimately, the results were ambiguous for African Americans as well. Even as the rhetoric of freedom drove imperial expansion in the West, the federal government's actual commitment to freedom faltered in the South. It is no wonder, as Justin Behrend shows in Chapter 6, that African Americans in Louisiana linked Republican defeat to reenslavement in the 1876 election. Freedom was fragile without the strong backing of the state.

These essays bring the authority of the state – represented through the federal government's laws and officials in both the United States and the Confederacy – into the process of emancipation. The emphasis is on the complicated and unpredictable dynamics of the state's authority on the ground. As such, the essays shift the historiographical perspective in significant ways. Political and social historians generally have placed individuals at the center of their narratives of the Civil War: political historians have focused on the ideas and intent of the lawmakers who formulated, passed, and interpreted the nation's laws, while social historians have highlighted the actions of ordinary Americans, particularly African Americans, in shaping the major changes of the era, including the destruction of slavery. The chapters in *Rethinking Emancipation*, however, turn our attention to the structures of power that shaped the terrain on which individuals worked – terrain defined by the power of the state. The state presented constraints as well as possibilities for all those who tried to harness it. Its backing was essential to the realization of emancipation and, in a larger sense, of freedom, but the state was never a neutral player. Nor was its power ever controlled completely by any particular group, even the government officials charged with enforcing it. Instead, the state – and the body of laws that defined it – shaped the meaning of freedom in unintended, unforeseen ways.

This approach to the state also suggests new elements to the very policies – namely the Emancipation Proclamation and the Thirteenth Amendment – that historians once identified with emancipation and that receive less attention in *Rethinking Emancipation*. It is understandable that these policies do not occupy center stage in a volume that challenges the notion that emancipation was achieved through a specific act, or a particular government policy, at a given moment in time. The one exception is Yael A. Sternhell's chapter,[4] which deals directly with the efforts of African Americans to seize freedom in the years before either the Emancipation Proclamation or the Thirteenth Amendment. Echoing the direction of recent literature, she argues that African Americans' rejection of slavery and their movement toward Union lines altered the terms of debate about abolition: through their actions, African Americans made slavery and the condition of slaves less "an abstraction" and more about "fully-volitional human beings resolved to decide their own fate." Yet, as Sternhell's chapter and the others in this volume suggest, the dynamic between individual conceptions of emancipation and the state's policies led in unpredictable directions. So it is worth pausing to consider how both the Emancipation Proclamation and the Thirteenth Amendment fit within the volume's approach to emancipation – an approach that characterizes it as a dynamic, highly contingent process that involved both individuals and the state.

The chapters in *Rethinking American Emancipation* raise an important question: Why do we assume that there was a straight line between *individual* efforts to end slavery or to achieve freedom and the *legal* abolition of slavery? That assumption runs through much of the existing historiography. Yet the legal abolition of slavery required structural change in the nation's laws, which made the leap from individual claims to legal abolition much less certain than the historiography suggests. As Frederick Douglass put it, the challenge was finding a way of "translating antislavery sentiment into antislavery action," given the limits of the existing legal system.[5] Individual slaves, for instance, could obtain freedom without changing a legal order that sanctioned slavery. Nor was emancipation solely a matter of mobilizing the political will of the nation's lawmakers. To be sure, the politics of emancipation were formidable, involving a delicate balance among seemingly irreconcilable concerns: the differing views on slavery, federal power, and the nation's war goals as well as the immediate needs of military commanders in the field. But the nation's political leaders could do nothing until they confronted a legal structure that gave the federal government very little power over the legal status of individuals. In fact, the only way that the nation's law-makers could end slavery throughout the entire United States was to change the U.S. Constitution in ways that ultimately affected all Americans. That the U.S. Constitution was amended also underscores the complicated process of legal change, particularly the importance of enslaved African Americans, whose refusal to act as slaves not only made it impossible for federal officials to ignore slavery, but also forced them to confront the place of slavery within the nation's legal order.[6]

When the first enslaved people abandoned their plantations at the start of the war, they set that process in motion. Military officers were the first to have to deal with the issue. The iconic story of General Benjamin Butler's experience at Fortress Monroe captures essential elements of the dynamic and the intractability of the legal issues. In May 1861, three enslaved men "delivered themselves up" to Butler's picket guards. What to do? The Fugitive Slave Act mandated that all runaways be returned, and Abraham Lincoln still insisted that nothing would be done to interfere with slavery in the states where it already existed, despite the outbreak of war. Current law and Republican policy statements, however, did not anticipate the situation that Butler faced: three African American men who sought shelter with U.S. troops because they did not want to work for the Confederate commander to whom they were enslaved. Butler saw an opportunity. He needed labor, and so he put the men to work there. Shall the Confederates, Butler asked rhetorically, "be allowed the use of this property against the United States, and we not be allowed its use in aid of the United States?" Then he put the issue in legal terms, defining the African Americans as "contraband": property seized as a consequence of war. And, finally, he asked his superiors for instruction, who found "much to praise ... and nothing to condemn " in Butler's handing of the matter.[7]

Butler looked to the law to justify his actions, because the law provided authority that his orders alone could not. He could not turn to federal law, which allowed for slavery in states where it already existed. Nor could he hope for a different interpretation of existing law, given Lincoln's position on slavery. Butler found a way out of the conundrum by invoking inter-national law, which allowed for the seizure and use of enemy property and therefore – theoretically – slaves. If slaves were appropriated as contra-band, then Butler and other military commanders could act without contradicting federal policy that forbid interference in slavery. Yet the principle of "contraband of war" was meant to apply only to property seized from neutral parties who were shipping war materiel to the enemy. There were no neutral parties at Fortress Monroe, unless African Africans were defined as both the neutral parties and the war materiel. Butler knew he was applying the concept of "contraband" loosely, but he believed it was the only way to resolve the dilemma posed by enslaved people who were seeking refuge at Fortress Monroe. "The truth is," Butler wrote of the contraband argument in his 1892 memoir, "as a lawyer I was never very proud of it, but as an executive officer I was very much comforted with it as a means of doing my duty."[8]

It did not take long for the actions of enslaved African Americans to upset the legal fiction of contraband. "Since I wrote my last dispatch," Butler informed Scott three days after the initial letter about the three refugees, "the question in regard to slave property is becoming one of very serious magnitude." Enslaved men were being forced to work on Confederate fortifications, and there were rumors that enslaved women and children would be shipped out of the area. Families with children were now asking for shelter at Fortress Monroe, which made it impossible for Butler to continue to maintain that he was holding the slaves as contraband of war, claiming their labor as property confiscated from the enemy. So Butler recognized the refugees for what they were: families, not property. As he explained, "I have therefore determined to employ, as I can do very profitably, the able-bodied persons in the party, issuing proper food for the support of all, and charging against their services the expense of care and sustenance of the non-laborers, keeping a strict and accurate account as well of the services as of the expenditure having the worth of the services and the cost of the expenditure determined by a board of Survey hereafter to be detailed."[9]

Butler knew that he was on increasingly shaky legal ground. So he justified his actions in strategic terms. If the African Americans in his charge were still enslaved, he informed General-in-Chief Scott, they would be worth somewhere in the neighborhood of sixty thousand dollars, which represented a significant loss for the Confederacy. Without their labor, moreover, Confederate forces could not have constructed fortifications as quickly as they had. But Butler could not hide the fact that his handling of the situation involved more than considerations about the strategic value of slavery in the war effort. That was clear in the questions that he posed to General-in-Chief Scott: "As a political question and a question of humanity can I receive the services of a Father and a Mother and not take the children? Of the humanitarian aspect I have no doubt. Of the political one I have no right to judge." As Butler saw it, mothers, fathers, and children could not actually be dealt with as either slaves or contraband, despite what the law said.[10]

The African Americans who sought shelter at Fortress Monroe were shaping Butler's decisions. Butler did not support slavery. But neither was he an abolitionist – at least, not at the outset of the Civil War. In 1860, he was a Democrat, sympathetic to states' rights, who had voted for Stephen A. Douglas, not Abraham Lincoln. Previously, when in command in Maryland, he assured that state's governor that he would not interfere in slavery and even offered to put down any "servile insurrections" there. The Civil War gave African Americans the opportunity to change Butler's mind, by exploiting the fundamental legal contradiction of slavery: people were not the same as other forms of inanimate property, which made it extremely difficult to apply property law to them.[11] It was because African Americans were human beings with feelings, desires, and the capacity for rational decision making that they kept coming to Union lines. Butler and other military commanders found it impossible to ignore their actions, if only because laws premised on the assumption that people could be governed in the same way as inanimate property tended to fall apart in practice.[12]

African Americans' actions ultimately forced questions about their status out of the military's hands and into those of the nation's lawmakers. When Congress finally took up the issue, late in 1861, they ran into the same problem that military commanders had: it was difficult to deal with the situation of individual African Americans without dealing with the place of slavery in the American legal system and, ultimately, confronting larger constitutional questions about the basic structure of law and governance in the nation. To say that federal policy inched toward emancipation one small step at a time, as so much of the literature in social and political history does, is to misconstrue the depth and breadth of the legal issues involved and difficulties of eradicating slavery from the nation's legal structure. That scholarship often focuses on the moral and ethical dimensions of the problem, charting lawmakers' course in grappling with their own feelings about slavery and their efforts to persuade others to act, assuming that abolition could be accomplished once the tide of opinion turned. But the law made it difficult for even the most principled official to use federal power to end slavery – and federal power was the only way to eradicate slavery everywhere in the nation.

Federal policy reflects those legal constraints as clearly as it did federal officials' convictions about abolition. Legislation first focused on areas where the federal government did have clear jurisdiction: the District of Columbia, the territories, and conquered parts of the Confederacy.[13] Policies also tended to rely on war powers. The Emancipation Proclamation, for instance, defined abolition as necessary to the war and, thus, limited. It offered freedom to some individuals and it had distinct limits. It applied only to enslaved people within the Confederacy, and they had to leave for areas occupied by federal forces to take advantage of emancipation, because the Confederacy did not recognize U.S. authority. Even then, huge swaths of the Confederacy that were occupied by Union troops, including the entire state of Tennessee, were excluded. Emancipation, in these terms, was not the same thing as the legal end of slavery, which still lingered in the nation's laws at both the federal and state levels.[14]

In some ways, the Emancipation Proclamation did nothing more than legitimize what enslaved African Americans had been doing since 1861. But, in so doing, it escalated the terms of the conflict, moving beyond the battlefield to make war on the Confederacy's social order. It also solidified the status of enslaved African Americans who escaped to Union lines. But the Emancipation Proclamation did not legally abolish slavery. It did what other federal legislation did, acknowledging the freedom of certain individuals, while leaving the institution of slavery legally in place. The limitations of the Emancipation Proclamation and of federal policy reflect divisions among lawmakers and white Americans: there was as yet no consensus on the future of slavery in the United States. But those same limitations also underscore the power of escaped slaves' actions, which forced both federal lawmakers and white Americans to confront an issue many wished to avoid.[15]

Slavery would remain legal in the United States until the ratification of the Thirteenth Amendment, after the end of the war. Despite all the legal efforts to dismantle slavery during the war, it was impossible to eliminate it without a constitutional amendment. Even so, the dynamics culminating in passage of the Thirteenth Amendment were, simultaneously, definitive and ambiguous. They were definitive in the sense that the growing popular consensus for an amendment underscored how much had changed as a result of the Civil War. Yet ambiguities remained. When the amendment moved from Congress to the states, it was subjected to considerable debate, particularly in the states of the old Northwest, which had the most racially restrictive laws. Iowa, for instance, did not approve the amendment until 1866, after it had been ratified by two-thirds of the

states. The approval process also ran into difficulties in other states where
the Democratic Party had a significant presence, including New York and
New Jersey. The states of the former Confederacy were all but required to
pass it as part of President Andrew Johnson's Reconstruction plan. Even
then, political leaders in those states debated the amendment as if they still
had choice in the matter.[16]

The difficulties of ratification reflected larger divisions over the meaning of the Thirteenth Amendment and the difficulties of abolishing slavery
more generally. Republican leaders who supported abolition and racial
equality saw it as a means to both ends. For them, the abolition of slavery
meant full civil and political equality of African Americans. Some
Republicans also envisioned civil and political rights as a set of principles
under the purview of the federal government, not the states, and that
extended universally to all people – or, at least, all adult men – within
the nation. That interpretation did not sit well with Democrats and
moderate Republicans who supported abolition but not equality for
African Americans or a national vision of rights. Many Republicans
supported an expansive federal role in the South on a temporary basis,
to address the immediate crisis, but flatly opposed the idea of extending
federal jurisdiction permanently over civil and political rights through the
entire United States.[17]

In this sense, passage of the Thirteenth Amendment ended slavery
only to expose the extent of slavery's influence in the social order as well
as the nation's laws. In fact, slavery was so entwined with the nation's
governing structures that it was impossible to legally abolish slavery
without addressing a whole host of questions about the status of all
Americans. The chapters in *Rethinking Emancipation* expose the implications and reveal how difficult slavery was to eradicate from the
nation's social order and governing structures. Without the strong-
handed tactics of the military in the 1863 elections, as William A. Blair
shows,[18] the Thirteenth Amendment might never have passed. Without
the presence of the military, as Gregory P. Downs argues,[19] African
Americans might never have been able to take advantage of the freedoms
promised in federal legislation. The situation was still so tenuous in the
1870s that, according to Justin Behrend,[20] African Americans feared reenslavement. Their fears had foundation, as indicated by Yael A.
Sternhell's discussion of the violence experienced by slavery's refugees[21]
and Carole Emberton's analysis of the Colfax Massacre in Louisiana.[22]

Slavery's place in the governing structures of the nation meant that
abolition alone would not eliminate its influence. Those difficulties were

already apparent during the Civil War. Wartime enactments established the freedom of African Americans who found their way to Union lines in a very limited sense. African Americans were no longer enslaved. But the policies that released them from slavery said very little about what else freedom entailed. The omission was intentional, because questions relating to the legal status and rights of individuals lay with states and localities. Those who escaped slavery thus found themselves in a legal netherworld. Occupied areas were controlled by the federal government and governed by martial law, which held out the promise of more equitable treatment than state or local courts that had kept African Americans enslaved. But these venues were ill equipped to handle the legal problems of formerly enslaved people, because such matters had traditionally been within the jurisdiction of states and localities, not the federal government or the military.[23]

Slavery's influence was profound in those jurisdictions. It was present even in states that had abolished the institution. All free states placed definite legal limits on the rights of all free African Americans to varying degrees. The enactment of racially restrictive legislation followed hard on the heels of abolition in the North, reflecting an enduring connection between racism and abolition. Many white Americans who opposed slavery still believed that African Americans were inferior to whites and incapable of exercising civil or political rights responsibly. Given those racist presumptions, it followed that legal restrictions were necessary to police free blacks and to protect the larger public. By 1860, free blacks could vote in only six states – Maine, Massachusetts, New Hampshire, Rhode Island, Vermont, and New York, which had substantial property requirements for free blacks that did not apply to whites. Legal limits extended to free blacks' civil rights and included restrictions on their ability to testify in court, enter contracts, hold property, and congregate. States in the Old Northwest – Illinois, Indiana, Iowa, Ohio, Michigan, and Wisconsin – enacted particularly draconian measures. Some denied free blacks entry altogether. Local ordinances and custom further limited free blacks, segregating them in the least desirable locations, forcing them into the most menial jobs, and policing their behavior in a host of other ways.

Racial inequality followed black troops into the military during the Civil War. It was not until June 1864 that Congress passed legislation equalizing pay for black soldiers. The racism that fueled reduced pay also resulted in deplorable conditions in the field. The commander of a North Carolina regiment was outraged to find that his troops had been ordered to prepare camp for white regiments. He put the issue bluntly: "It IS a draw-back that they are regarded as, and called 'd – d Niggers' by so-called 'gentlemen' in uniform of U.S. Officers, but when they are set to menial work doing for white regiments what those Regiments are entitled to do for themselves, it simply throws them back where they were before and reduces them to the position of slaves again."[24]

The rights of refugees also varied widely, depending on the military commander. In December 1862, a committee of "chaplains and surgeons" from Helena, Arkansas, complained of conditions all too common throughout occupied areas of the Confederacy. "The Contrabands within our lines," they wrote to the Commander of the Department of Missouri, "are experiencing hardships oppression & neglect the removal of which calls loudly for the intervention of authority." That situation had allowed soldiers in the U.S. military to rob refugees, rape the women and attack the men who tried to intervene, and refuse to pay them for their work. "For the sake of humanity, for the sake of christianity, for the good name of our army, for the honor of our country," they begged, "cannot something be done to prevent this oppression & to stop its demoralizing influences upon the Soldiers themselves?"[25]

Military policies, moreover, often circumscribed the range of possibilities for refugees. The system of compulsory labor was particularly important. Military officials considered such a coercive system consistent with free labor in the sense that former slaves entered into contractual agreements and were compensated for their labor. The logic reflected fundamental assumptions about the individual rights of wage workers within a free labor system more generally: freedom was not measured in terms of either the circumstances that brought a person into a labor contract or the terms of that contract, but in the ability to contract. Advocates of free labor, moreover, expected force in establishing such a system: people unused to it would have to be coerced into labor contracts and subjected to harsh contractual terms, until they understood its dynamics and accepted its benefits. Racism tended to narrow this vision still further. Many free labor proponents in the Union believed that former slaves might eventually internalize the values that made reliable, manual workers, if instructed properly and carefully. But until then, they needed to be kept in line – by whatever means necessary. In fact, some doubted that former slaves would ever learn and saw legal coercion as an essential, permanent component of freedom. Such policies blurred the line between wage labor and slavery, particularly when commanders held workers' wages until the end of the contract or applied them to payment for supplies instead of paying them directly. Complaints about compulsory service, with little or no pay, streamed into the War Department from sympathetic white observers as well as the African Americans forced to labor.[26]

Only the federal government could address the patchwork of state and local laws that placed African Americans into a different legal status than white Americans. And before the federal government could act, the nation's lawmakers had to alter the balance of power to give it more authority over the legal status of individuals. The Thirteenth Amendment established the precedent by reaching over the states to create direct legal ties between the federal government and the people on the key issue of slavery: the federal government protected the people's rights insofar as it prohibited states from keeping people enslaved. In so doing, the amendment extended the federal government's authority over all states in the Union, not just those in the former Confederacy. The Fourteenth and Fifteenth Amendments, along with related legislation, built on that edifice, extending the federal government's purview to questions involving the civil and political rights of all Americans. In the late nineteenth and twentieth centuries, the Fourteenth Amendment drew the federal government into a wide range of issues involving the rights of women, laborers, corporations, dissidents, and those accused of crimes. At the same time, the results also made emancipation a deeply personal issue for many Americans.

Other essays in the volume explore those elements of slavery's end that reached into individual lives of African Americans – and other Americans as well. In law, the relation between husband and wife established a relationship of dependency analogous to that between master and slave. As women's rights activists argued, emancipation and federal protection of African American men's civil and political rights also challenged the subordinate status of women. They failed to include women within the Reconstruction Amendments. But, as Allison Fredette shows in Chapter 4, the implications of emancipation for women were complicated and, ultimately, dependent on place. White Kentuckians, Fredette argues, uncoupled race and gender, enacting harsh laws that limited all African Americans, while also giving women greater leeway within marriage and more freedom to exit marriage. By contrast, Virginians held tightly to a vision of marriage that kept women dependent on their husbands and continued to tie racial and gender inequality together. As Paul Ortiz argues in Chapter 8, abolitionists always connected the end of slavery in the United States to the status of workers more generally. It was an

international vision, which considered economic issues as central to freedom and which linked the status of African Americans to working people
regardless of race. It is a point that echoes Yael Sternhell's analysis, which
connects the plight of ordinary Confederate soldiers to that of African
Americans, in the sense that both endured the Confederacy's exploitative
policies. Their circumstances were radically different, as were their political allegiances. However, in the internationalist perspective that Ortiz
provides, their differences did not completely erase their commonalities.

   Ultimately, the limits of the Reconstruction Amendments left much of
the work of defining the meaning of emancipation to ordinary Americans,
particularly African Americans in the South. The Fourteenth Amendment
and related legislation (the various Civil Rights Acts) gave the federal
government supervisory authority over states' handling of rights. Some
Congressional Republicans argued for a more direct role for the federal
government in the form of national standards that would allow federal
jurisdiction over the rights of all citizens, regardless of where they lived.
That position, however, collided with a commitment to maintain states'
traditional authority in this area. As a result, the Fourteenth Amendment
placed restrictions on states, prohibiting them from making or enforcing
"any law which shall abridge the privileges or immunities of citizens of the
United States," or depriving any person "of life, liberty, or property,
without due process of law." Then it gave the federal government the
power to enforce their provisions. But the Fourteenth Amendment itself
did not give the federal government the power to define or grant rights in
state jurisdictions – although the federal Bill of Rights, of course, still
applied to federal cases. Later Civil Rights Acts extended federal authority
in ways that brought it into state law more actively, by giving federal
officials enhanced discretion over the ways that states interpreted and
applied rights by strengthening its enforcement powers. However, given
the political opposition and the limited resources of federal enforcement
agencies, that authority was never fully utilized.[27]

   That situation meant that African Americans had to define emancipation for themselves. They began building a new relationship to the governing system as soon as they could, as existing scholarship as well as the
chapters in *Rethinking American Emancipation* show. During and immediately after the Civil War, when state and local courts were either non-
existent or hostile, African Americans sought out venues at the federal
level, such as military courts or, later, the Freedmen's Bureau courts. As
the nature of their claims suggest, African Americans expected the federal
government to address the same kinds of issues that would have fallen to

local courts and that had been handled within the framework of maintaining the peace: interpersonal conflicts, often involving violence and including domestic issues, as well as matters involving broader questions of social justice, such as the treatment of refugees, payment of wages, and reunification of families. The various courts under federal jurisdiction, which lacked an established body of law to handle this diverse array of claims, struggled to keep up. But African Americans persisted, in a manner that legal historians refer to as forum shopping – that is, seeking out a responsive and, hopefully, supportive legal forum. When Southern states reconstituted their governments under the Reconstruction and federal venues closed down, African Americans moved back to local and state courts. As they saw it, it was the responsibility of government – at all levels – to protect the peace of the social order, one in which they could now participate actively in ways they had not been able to before.[28]

Their efforts were often met with violence, and African Americans ultimately lost the battle to realize full civil and political rights. They nonetheless tried to keep that vision alive, as both William A. Link's[29] and John Stauffer's[30] fine chapters show. According to Link, white and black Atlantans linked the city's future to very different versions of slavery's history. White boosters sold the city "to Northern capitalists as a place clear of the debris of the past, especially slavery." It was a vision that denied the power of the past so as to obscure the link between white supremacy and slavery. Black Atlantans also cut the link between past and present, but they did so by linking slavery's end to the promise of civil and political equality – promises that remained powerful, but unfulfilled, and that also extended the process of emancipation well into the twentieth century. Stauffer extends that process further into the twentieth century, arguing that historians have not only exaggerated the difference between emancipationists (who supported the Union, gradual emancipation, and racial inequality) and abolitionists (who supported the legal eradication of slavery and racial equality), but also understated abolitionists' commitment to racial equality. The results marginalize the importance of radical abolitionists to policy changes of the period, resulting in historical narratives that tend to make emancipation and federal recognition of African Americans' civil and political rights seem inevitable, when they were actually radical, contested, and hard-fought goals that required courage and strength to achieve.

In all the chapters in *Rethinking Emancipation*, African Americans' efforts to define the meaning of emancipation are inseparable from a

FIGURE 14: "Contrabands escaping."
*Source: Edward Forbes, Courtesy of the Library of Congress, Prints and
Photographs Division, LC-DIG-ppmsca-20701.*

much wider array of issues – issues that involve all Americans and the
future of the nation. The legal abolition of slavery was part of a
process through which people who had been enslaved claimed and
defined freedom. But to see emancipation only in those terms is to
miss the importance of slavery and its emancipation in the governing
structures of the nation. That wider perspective neither marginalizes
nor diminishes African Americans' struggles to seize freedom and to
make it meaningful in their own lives. To the contrary, it highlights
the importance of African Americans' claims to freedom, showing
how they challenged the nation's basic governing structures and ultimately helped remake them in ways that spilled over to other people
and other issues – often in unpredictable ways. As this volume shows,
the process of emancipation is the story of America.

NOTES

1. Martha S. Jones, "History and Commemoration: The Emancipation
   Proclamation at 150," *The Journal of the Civil War Era* 3, no. 4
   (December 2013): 452–457, makes this point directly. It is also closely
   associated with the work of the Freedmen and Southern Society Project,

which has done so much to make the wartime records relating to slavery and African Americans available. See Ira Berlin et al., eds., *Freedom: A Documentary History of Emancipation, 1861–1867*, ser 2: *The Black Military Experience* (New York: Vintage, 1982); ser. 1, vol. 1: *The Destruction of Slavery* (New York: Vintage, 1985); ser. 1, vol. 3: *The Wartime Genesis of Free Labor: The Lower South* (New York: Vintage, 1990); ser. 1, vol. 2: *The Wartime Genesis of Free Labor: The Upper South* (New York: Vintage, 1993); Steven Hahn et al., *Freedom: A Documentary History of Emancipation, 1861–1867, Series 3, vol. 1: Land and Labor, 1865* (Chapel Hill: University of North Carolina Press, 2008). For more recent work, see Thavolia Glymph, *Out of the House of Bondage: The Transformation of the Plantation Household* (New York: Cambridge University Press, 2008); Steven Hahn, *A Nation under Our Feet: Black Political Struggles in the Rural South from Slavery to the Great Migration* (Cambridge, Mass.: Belknap Press of Harvard University Press, 2003); Stephanie McCurry, *Confederate Reckoning: Power and Politics in the Civil War South* (Cambridge, Mass.: Harvard University Press, 2010); Bruce Levine, *The Fall of the House of Dixie: The Civil War and the Social Revolution That Transformed the South* (New York: Random House, 2013). But the larger point – that African Americans played a central role in destroying slavery – was first made by African American historians in the early twentieth century: W.E.B. Du Bois, *Black Reconstruction: An Essay toward a History of the Part Which Black Folk Played in the Attempt to Reconstruct Democracy in America, 1860–1880* (New York: Russell & Russell, 1935); Benjamin Quarles, *The Negro in the Civil War* (Boston: Little, Brown, 1953).

2. See Chapter 2.
3. See Chapter 1.
4. See Chapter 1.
5. Quoted in Eric Foner, *The Fiery Trial: Abraham Lincoln and American Slavery* (New York, 2010), 72–73.
6. Laura F. Edwards, *A Legal History of the Civil War and Reconstruction: A Nation of Rights* (New York: Cambridge University Press, January 2015), particularly chapter 3. The book argues that the Civil War and Reconstruction not only extended the reach of the U.S. federal government, but also altered the terms of its relationship to the American people by connecting to them through a highly individualized notion of rights. For a similar argument, see Stephen Sawyer and William J. Novak, "Emancipation and the Creation of Modern Liberal States in America and France," *The Journal of the Civil War Era* 3, no.4 (December 2013): 467–500.
7. Commander of the Department of Virginia to the General-in-Chief of the Army, May 27, 1861, available at the Freedmen and Southern Society Project, www.history.umd.edu/Freedmen/Butler.html (accessed January 18, 2013).
8. Quoted Kate Masur, "'A Rare Phenomenon of Philological Vegetation': The Word 'Contraband' and the Meanings of Emancipation in the United States," *Journal of American History* 93, no. 4 (March 2007): 1050–1084 (quotation

on 1054); Edwards, *A Legal History of the Civil War and Reconstruction*, chapter 3.

9. Commander of the Department of Virginia to the General-in-Chief of the Army. Edwards, *A Legal History of the Civil War and Reconstruction*, chapter 3.

10. Commander of the Department of Virginia to the General-in-Chief of the Army. Edwards, *A Legal History of the Civil War and Reconstruction*, chapter 3.

11. Butler's change reflects the point Yael A. Sternhell makes in the opening of her chapter. It also echoes Chandra Manning's argument, in *What This Cruel War Was Over: Soldiers, Slavery, and the Civil War* (New York: Knopf, 2007), that many white soldiers in the U.S. Army ended up opposing slavery because of their experiences in the war. Edwards, *A Legal History of the Civil War and Reconstruction*, chapter 3.

12. Edwards, *A Legal History of the Civil War and Reconstruction*, chapter 3.

13. See, for instance, An Act for the Release of Certain Persons Held to Service of Labor in the District of Columbia, 12 U.S. Statutes at Large 376 (1862); Law Enacting Emancipation in the Federal Territories, 12 U.S. Statutes at Large 432 (1862). Edwards, *A Legal History of the Civil War and Reconstruction*, chapter 3.

14. The Emancipation Proclamation: January 1, 1863, available at the Avalon Project, http://avalon.law.yale.edu/19th_century/emancipa.asp (accessed August 20, 2014). Also see The Preliminary Emancipation Proclamation, available at the Freedmen and Southern Society Project, www.history.umd.edu/Freedmen/prelep.htm (accessed August 20, 2014). Edwards, *A Legal History of the Civil War and Reconstruction*, chapter 3.

15. The Emancipation Proclamation: January 1, 1863, available at the Avalon Project, http://avalon.law.yale.edu/19th_century/emancipa.asp (accessed August 20, 2014). Also see The Preliminary Emancipation Proclamation, available at the Freedmen and Southern Society Project, www.history.umd.edu/Freedmen/prelep.htm (accessed August 20, 2014).

16. Michael Vorenberg, *Final Freedom: The Civil War, the Abolition of Slavery, and the Thirteenth Amendment* (New York: Cambridge University Press, 2001), particularly 221–250. Edwards, *A Legal History of the Civil War and Reconstruction*, chapter 3.

17. Edwards, *A Legal History of the Civil War and Reconstruction*, chapter 4.

18. See Chapter 3.

19. See Chapter 2.

20. See Chapter 6.

21. See Chapter 1.

22. See Chapter 5.

23. Edwards, *A Legal History of the Civil War and Reconstruction*, chapter 3.

24. Commander of a North Carolina Regiment to Commander of a Black Brigade, September 13, 1863, available at the Freedmen and Southern Society Project, www.history.umd.edu/Freedmen/Beecher.html (accessed August 20, 2014). Edwards, *A Legal History of the Civil War and Reconstruction*, chapter 3.

25. Committee of Chaplains and Surgeons to the Commander of the Department of Missouri, December 29, 1862, Freedmen and Southern Society Project, www.history.umd.edu/Freedmen/Sawyer.html (accessed August 20, 2014). Edwards, *A Legal History of the Civil War and Reconstruction*, chapter 3.
26. Louis S. Gerteis, *From Contraband to Freedman: Federal Policy toward Southern Blacks, 1861–1865* (Westport, Conn.: Greenwood Press, 1973); Thomas C. Holt, "'An Empire over the Mind': Emancipation, Race, and Ideology in the British West Indies and the American South," in J. Morgan Kousser and James McPherson, eds., *Region, Race, and Reconstruction: Essays in Honor of C. Vann Woodward* (New York: Oxford University Press, 1982), 283–331. Edwards, *A Legal History of the Civil War and Reconstruction*, chapter 3.
27. Edwards, *A Legal History of the Civil War and Reconstruction*, particularly chapter 4; Edwards, "Reconstruction and the History of Governance," in Gregory P. Downs and Kate Masur, eds., *The World the Civil War Made* (Chapel Hill: University of North Carolina Press, forthcoming 2015).
28. Edwards, "Reconstruction and the History of Governance"; Laura F. Edwards, "Status without Rights: African Americans and the Tangled History of Law and Governance in the Nineteenth-Century U.S. South," *American Historical Review* 112, no. 2 (April 2007): 365–393. For scholarship that emphasizes African Americans' involvement in the legal system throughout the nineteenth century, see Ariela J. Gross, *Double Character: Slavery and Mastery in the Antebellum Southern Courtroom* (Princeton: Princeton University Press, 2000); Dylan C. Penningroth, *The Claims of Kinfolk: African American Property and Community in the Nineteenth-Century South* (Chapel Hill: University of North Carolina Press, 2003).
29. See Chapter 7.
30. See Chapter 9.

Index